AI-Driven Cybersecurity Insurance:

Innovations in Risk, Governance, and Digital Resilience

Moatsum Alawida
Abu Dhabi University, UAE

Ammar Almomani
Al-Balqa Applied University, Jordan

Mohammad Alauthman
University of Petra, Jordan

IGI Global
Scientific Publishing
Publishing Tomorrow's Research Today

Vice President of Editorial	Melissa Wagner
Director of Acquisitions	Mikaela Felty
Director of Book Development	Jocelynn Hessler
Production Manager	Mike Brehm
Cover Design	Jose Rosado

Published in the United States of America by
IGI Global Scientific Publishing
701 East Chocolate Avenue
Hershey, PA, 17033, USA
Tel: 717-533-8845
Fax: 717-533-7115
Website: https://www.igi-global.com E-mail: cust@igi-global.com

Library of Congress Cataloging-in-Publication Data

LCCN: 2025027509 (CIP Data Pending)
ISBN13: 979-8-3693-7743-7
Isbn13Softcover: 979-8-3693-7744-4
EISBN13: 979-8-3693-7745-1
British Cataloguing in Publication Data
A Cataloguing in Publication record for this book is available from the British Library.

Table of Contents

Detailed Table of Contents

As cyber threats become more complex and unpredictable, traditional cyber insurance methods struggle to keep pace. This chapter explores autonomous cyber underwriting agents that use reinforcement learning and multi-agent systems to dynamically assess, price, and manage digital risk. It outlines the limitations of static risk models and introduces adaptive, data-driven approaches powered by AI. Key concepts include real-time risk scoring, portfolio optimization, and system architectures that support scalability, security, and compliance. Rather than replacing human underwriters, these agents augment decision-making, enabling faster, smarter, and more resilient cyber risk management.

Quantum computing poses significant risks to cybersecurity by threatening the integrity of widely used cryptographic systems like RSA, ECC, and DH. This chapter examines the urgency of rethinking traditional cyber insurance risk models in response to these quantum-enabled threats. It introduces a quantum-aware risk modeling approach that incorporates factors such as PQC migration readiness and dynamic premium adjustments. The chapter also explores how insurers can embed quantum resilience into policies through cryptographic agility requirements and third-party risk assessments. Regulatory initiatives, particularly NIST's PQC standardization, are discussed for their role in guiding industry preparedness. Simulated breach scenarios highlight potential challenges in underwriting and claim resolution in a post-quantum era. This chapter offers a forward-looking roadmap for building a resilient, adaptive cyber insurance ecosystem prepared for the quantum future.

AI-Driven Benchmarking and Standards in Cybersecurity Insurance explores the integration of artificial intelligence (AI) technologies in enhancing the risk assessment, compliance, and underwriting processes of cybersecurity insurance. With the rapid escalation of cyber threats, traditional methods of assessing and insuring against cybersecurity risks have become increasingly inadequate. This chapter examines how AI, particularly through machine learning and natural language processing, can automate and refine the benchmarking of cybersecurity practices against established global standards such as ISO/IEC 27001, the NIST Cybersecurity Framework, and GDPR. AI-driven tools enable real-time risk analysis, adaptive benchmarking, and continuous compliance monitoring, ensuring that insurance policies accurately reflect an organization's current cybersecurity posture. The chapter also delves into how AI can facilitate cross-industry benchmarking, enabling insurers to evaluate an organization's cybersecurity maturity in relation to its peers and adjust premiums accordingly.

Cybersecurity insurance is a vital risk mitigation tool as cyber threats grow in complexity. However, the absence of standardized evaluation metrics and benchmarking frameworks creates challenges in assessing cybersecurity risks and determining policy premiums. Artificial Intelligence (AI) is transforming this field by enabling data-driven risk assessment, automated underwriting, and predictive analytics. This chapter examines AI's role in establishing benchmarking methodologies and driving standardization in cybersecurity insurance. It explores how AI models utilize historical data, threat intelligence, and real-time monitoring to assess cyber risk, automate compliance checks, detect fraud, and enable adaptive

Preface

CHAPTER OVERVIEW

The escalating frequency, complexity, and impact of cyberattacks have transformed cybersecurity from a technical concern into a central pillar of risk governance for governments, industries, and institutions. In this rapidly evolving digital landscape, traditional cyber insurance models—often reactive, rigid, and ill-equipped for the dynamism of cyber threats—are being challenged to evolve. Artificial Intelligence (AI) emerges as a transformative force in this evolution, offering unprecedented capabilities in risk prediction, fraud detection, underwriting automation, policy customization, and digital governance.

This edited volume, *AI-Driven Cybersecurity Insurance: Innovations in Risk, Governance, and Digital Resilience*, brings together researchers and practitioners from across disciplines to explore how AI is reshaping the future of cyber insurance. From post-quantum risk modeling to autonomous underwriting agents and AI-driven governance benchmarks, the chapters reflect both the urgency and the innovation driving this domain forward. The book emphasizes not only technical advancement but also the critical need for responsible deployment — balancing automation with human oversight, predictive accuracy with privacy, and agility with accountability.

The following chapter overview provides a roadmap to the themes and contributions presented across ten thought-provoking chapters:

Chapter 1: AI-Enabled Predictive Analytics in Cybersecurity Insurance

Wael Hadi et al. introduce the foundational shift from reactive loss recovery to proactive risk prevention. This chapter explores how machine learning transforms underwriting by forecasting breach probabilities and suggesting real-time mitigation strategies. The authors also highlight challenges in bias, data governance, and integration into legacy systems — underscoring the need for human-AI collaboration in achieving digital resilience.

Chapter 2: Autonomous Cyber Underwriting Agents

Salam Al-E'mari and colleagues delve into the emergence of intelligent underwriting agents powered by reinforcement learning and multi-agent systems. These agents enable adaptive, real-time risk scoring and portfolio optimization. The chapter argues for a hybrid model where human expertise is amplified — not replaced — by AI-driven decision-making.

Chapter 3: Quantum-Aware Risk Modeling

In anticipation of a post-quantum future, the same authors present a compelling framework for quantum-aware risk modeling. This chapter explores the vulnerabilities posed by quantum computing to current cryptographic standards and offers strategies for integrating cryptographic agility into insurance policies. A forward-looking contribution that prepares insurers for the next technological inflection point.

Chapter 4: AI-Driven Benchmarking and Standards in Cybersecurity Insurance

Muhammad Usman Tariq examines how AI technologies such as natural language processing and machine learning can enhance compliance and standardization in the insurance sector. The chapter offers insights into real-time benchmarking against global cybersecurity standards, enabling more accurate premium modeling and continuous compliance tracking.

Chapter 5: Leveraging AI to Establish Cybersecurity Insurance Benchmarks and Guidelines

Nabeel Alassaf and collaborators expand on the benchmarking theme, emphasizing AI's role in creating transparent, data-driven frameworks for risk assessment and policy pricing. This chapter tackles core challenges in standardization, fraud detection, and ethical use of data, offering practical solutions for AI integration in regulatory and compliance contexts.

Chapter 6: Emerging Trends and Innovations Using Generative AI

Bhupinder Singh et al. explore how generative AI is revolutionizing fraud detection and policy customization. The chapter introduces hyper-personalized insurance solutions driven by dynamic risk modeling, while also addressing the potential and pitfalls of using synthetic data in real-time threat environments.

Chapter 7: Fraud Detection and Mitigation in Cybersecurity Insurance

Continuing the focus on fraud, Muhammad Usman Tariq investigates AI's application in detecting anomalies and fraudulent claims with high accuracy. This chapter details best practices for integrating AI with traditional workflows, highlighting the delicate balance between automation and human judgment.

Chapter 8: Decrypting the Shadows — Forensics and Investigation of Ransomware Attacks

Shashank Dave and co-authors bring a forensic lens to the discussion, detailing how investigators use advanced tools to analyze ransomware attacks. The chapter provides a comprehensive overview of methodologies—ranging from memory dumps to blockchain analysis—that support both legal action and insurance claims processing.

Chapter 9: Supply Chain & Third-Party Risk Transfer

Mohammad Al Khaldy and his team examine risk transfer strategies across interconnected vendor ecosystems. Addressing the unique vulnerabilities in digital supply chains, this chapter proposes new models such as parametric triggers and continuous risk assessment protocols to improve multi-tier coverage and resilience.

Chapter 10: The Role of AI in Developing a Corporate Governance Index

Hamza Naim and colleagues offer a broader application of AI by proposing an AI-enabled Corporate Governance Index (CGI). This chapter situates cybersecurity within the larger framework of corporate governance, advocating for regional customization of indices to reflect diverse market conditions. It highlights both the potential and the limitations of AI in capturing qualitative governance metrics.

Together, these chapters capture the transformative potential of AI in redefining the future of cybersecurity insurance. By integrating advanced analytics, autonomous systems, quantum readiness, and governance frameworks, this volume offers a roadmap for stakeholders — insurers, regulators, technologists, and academics — committed to building a more resilient and intelligent digital risk ecosystem.

We hope this collection inspires further research, cross-sector collaboration, and responsible innovation in this critical domain.

Moatsum Alawida
Abu Dhabi University, UAE

Ammar Almomani
Al-Balqa Applied University, Jordan

Mohammad Alauthman
University of Petra, Jordan

Chapter 1
AI-Enabled Predictive Analytics in Cybersecurity Insurance Optimising Risk Transfer and Digital Resilience

Wael Hadi
https://orcid.org/0000-0002-7575-9287
Department of Information Security, University of Petra, Amman, Jordan

Ahmad Al-Qerem
https://orcid.org/0000-0003-2187-6194
Computer Science Department, Faculty of Information Technology, Zarqa University, Jordan

Ala Hamarsheh
https://orcid.org/0000-0002-4736-7331
Computer Science, Faculty of Information Technology, Arab American University, Jenin, Palestine

Amjad Aldweesh
https://orcid.org/0000-0001-9358-1323
College of Computing and Information Technology, Shaqra University, Saudi Arabia

Saad Alateef
https://orcid.org/0009-0002-3219-0833
School of Computing Science, Newcastle University, Newcastle Upon Tyne, UK

DOI: 10.4018/979-8-3373-5545-0.ch001

ABSTRACT

Artificial intelligence and advanced analytics are transforming cyber-insurance from retrospective loss recovery to proactive risk prevention. Machine-learning engines digest threat-intel feeds, network telemetry, and external attack-surface data to forecast breach probability, size, and knock-on costs, enabling underwriters to price coverage precisely, recommend pre-loss controls, and dispatch just-in-time mitigation when anomalies appear—cutting claim frequency and severity. But algorithms alone cannot carry the market. Insurers must manage bias, privacy, volatile data quality, and fast-moving threat landscapes. Governance that enforces model validation, continuous monitoring, and clear explanations—combined with tight integration into legacy policy-administration and incident-response workflows—turns predictions into usable action. As attacks grow in scale and sophistication, AI-driven prediction is fast becoming a core capability that helps carriers, clients, and society convert data-driven foresight into economic value and digital resilience.

1. INTRODUCTION

Health insurance market has struggled to keep up with new challenges represented by increasing costs, ageing populations, and widespread prevalence of diseases that are chronic and require constant care, which overwhelms the traditional model and necessitates better patient outcomes. Majority of the countries spend as much as 7-18 percent of their GDP on healthcare but find it hard to produce corresponding population health outcomes (Sahni et al., 2023). This financial stress and urgency have put forward a great need of new and creative ideas on how the quality of care provided to the patients can be raised and at the same time spending their money is lessened.

Two recent emerging technologies, artificial intelligence (AI) and predictive analytics, appear in a position to accomplish both goals since they allow insurance organizations to move beyond reacting to cost control to proactive health improvement. In contrast to the more narrowly defined traditional approach to insurance, i.e., claims management and risk pooling, predictive analytics facilitated by AI drivers enable insurance companies to predict health risks, pre-empt negative outcomes, and better mobilize resources in the most mutually beneficial ways toward patients and payers (Dixon et al., 2024).

The potential that AI may bring to healthcare insurance relates to processing extremely large amounts of data such as electronic health records, claims histories, demographic data, lifestyle data, and time-sensitive health tracking data to create insights that can be used to inform action regarding population and individual risks to health. Such discoveries allow the development of specific interventions to curtail the progression of the disease, hospital readmissions, streamline treatment processes, and minimize the issue of unnecessary health system visits (Hossain et al., 2024).

The latest issues prove such massive outcomes in the implementation of AI in healthcare insurance settings. According to Dixon et al. (2024), AI models are able to anticipate the progression of diseases, identify and prioritize patients at risk, as well as customize the interventions, resulting in less emergency hospitalization and better health outcomes. The extensive analysis indicated tangible advantages such as 25 per cent decreasing in operational cost and 15-20 per cent reduction in admission rates of institutions, which implement the AI-powered predictive analytics.

Business Case The business case of predictive analytics enabled by AI is deeper than direct cost savings, and encompasses foundational care delivery and patient satisfaction gains. According to the projection made by Sahni et al. (2023), the extensive application of AI has the potential to lead to the decrease in healthcare spending by 5-10 percent without compromising the quality and can save hundreds of billions of dollars per year as it will improve the health outcomes of citizens by providing more timely, suitable, and personalized interventions of care.

Nevertheless, introduction of AI-based predictive analytics to healthcare insurance may also have such challenges as algorithmic bias, data privacy and regulatory compliance issues, and the necessity the organizational change to facilitate data-based decision making. To achieve success it must be systematic in the use of technology, stakeholders and constancy of quality improvement both the technical and human factors should be addressed.

The given chapter offers the in-depth study of the predictive analytics in healthcare insurance with AI, testing the effect of these mechanisms on patient outcomes, cost-effectiveness of limitations, and the existing literature and implementation frameworks in their concerns as well as the real-life case studies. We visit the ways in which those technologies are reinventing insurance work and discuss the risks and opportunities in terms of further advancement.

2. LITERATURE REVIEW AND THEORETICAL FRAMEWORK

2.1 Evolution of Predictive Analytics in Healthcare Insurance

The use of predictive analytics in healthcare insurance has changed a lot since the mere use of actuarial indicators on the population to more complex machine learning systems with a capability of handling complex, multidimensional data. The initial applications were concerned mostly with the simple task of risk assessment and fraud detection based on rule-based systems and statistical models (Alkhelb & Alshagrawi, 2025).

The advent of big data analytics and machine learning opened the way to more subtle use in predictive modeling, care management and population health optimization. The evolution described by Mehta and Pandit (2018) was identified as something with tremendous potential in enhancing quality of care and reducing waste and error, which means that the cost of care will also decrease owing to the insights made with data that has never been possible at scale.

2.2 Theoretical Foundations of AI-Enabled Predictive Analytics

The theoretical foundation for AI-enabled predictive analytics in healthcare insurance rests on several interconnected principles:

Predictive Risk Modeling Theory: Traditional insurance relies on retrospective analysis of population-level risks. AI enables prospective, individual-level risk prediction that can anticipate health events before they occur, enabling preventive interventions that improve outcomes while reducing costs (Rao et al., 2024).

Systems Theory and Care Coordination: Healthcare outcomes result from complex interactions between clinical, behavioral, social, and environmental factors. AI systems can model these interactions to identify intervention points that optimize overall system performance rather than addressing isolated factors.

Value-Based Care Economics: The shift toward value-based payment models aligns financial incentives with health outcomes. AI-enabled predictive analytics support this transition by enabling accurate outcome prediction and intervention targeting that improves both clinical and economic performance.

Information Processing Theory: Healthcare decision-making involves processing vast amounts of complex information under time constraints. AI systems can augment human cognitive capabilities by identifying patterns, generating recommendations, and providing decision support that improves both efficiency and effectiveness.

2.3 Current State of Research and Evidence

Recent literature reveals increasing evidence of AI in its effects on patient results and cost effectiveness in a healthcare insurance setting. The comprehensive narrative review of Dixon et al. (2024) showed that AI-based predictive analytics helps to make disease prediction, prioritization of risks, and the process of tailoring interventions to them proactive, resulting in measurable outcomes of both clinical and financial improvements.

As Hossain et al. (2024) evidence offered via a systematic review, the use of AI has the potential to reduce operational expenses by around 25 percent and lower the rates of readmission by 15-20 percent. These results indicate that AI-powered predictive analytics have a potential to solve the trade-off between cost and quality that has historically been difficult to manage as a more efficient and effective delivery of care will then be possible.

Nonetheless, implementation gaps pose a major challenge too within the area. The study by Obermeyer et al. (2019) indicated the possibility of bias in the algorithms used in predictive analytics systems that hamper the equity and effectiveness of the models because more precise models with a positive effect on patient outcomes can be developed that improve the overall predictive analytics-informed healthcare delivery across patient populations.

Figure 1. AI-enabled predictive analytics framework for dual optimization

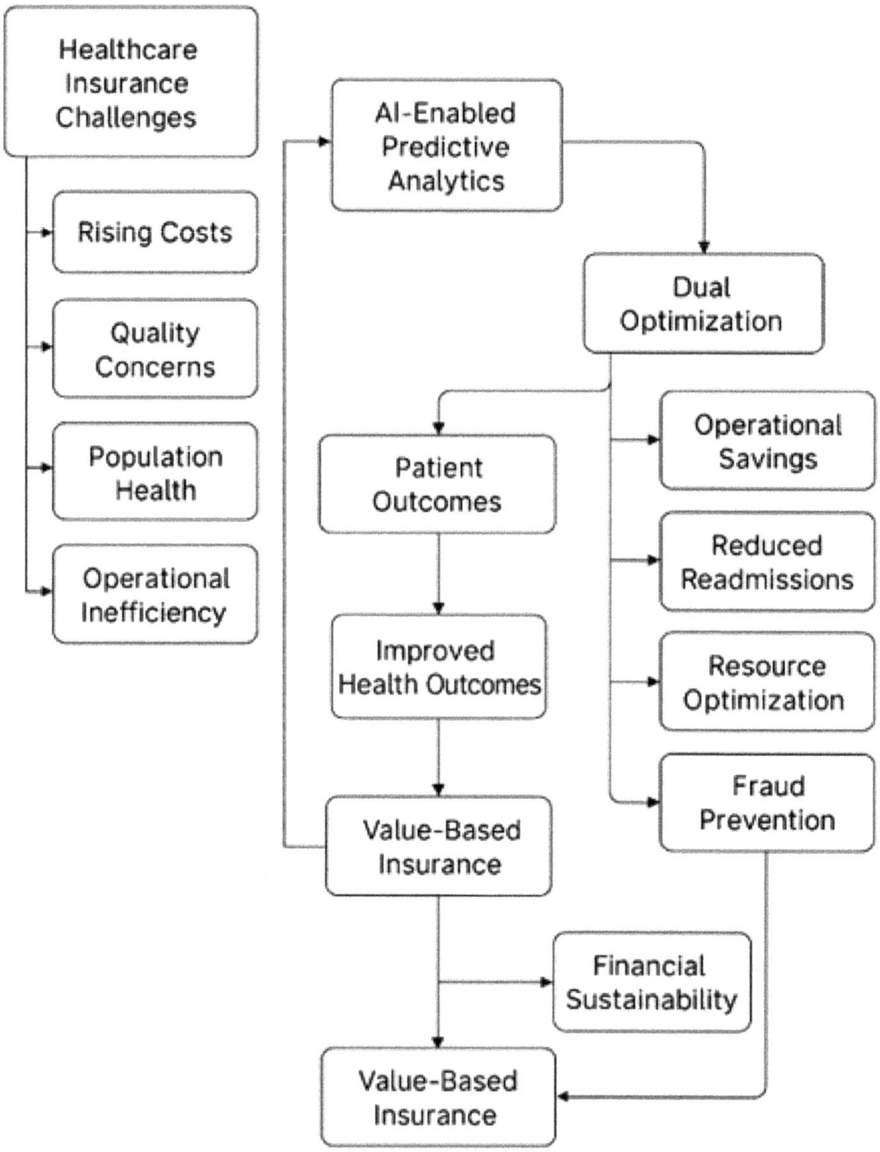

3. AI-ENABLED PREDICTIVE ANALYTICS TECHNOLOGIES

3.1 Machine Learning Algorithms and Applications

Predictive analytics in healthcare insurance use an array of machine learning algorithms that are optimised in functioning and used according to the differing prediction tasks and data types. According to Rao et al. (2024), the authors compared several methods such as regression models, decision trees, and ensemble methods to forecast healthcare costs, which revealed that pinnacle ensemble techniques, such as CatBoost regression, outperformed other techniques with R 2 -approximately 0.85 in regard to total treatment-cost predictions.

The decision regarding the algorithm to apply is determined by use cases, data properties and interpretability needs. Although deep learning models can produce better results on predictive accuracy of complex pattern recognition problems, tree-based models tend to be more suitable in clinical decision support archetypes where it is imperative to be able to understand why there were predictions made as hospitals need to adopt and trust the predictions offered in order to succeed in such instances.

In choosing suitable algorithms to use in the application of healthcare insurance, the differences in performance of different types of data must also be taken into concern. Hadi (2010) evaluated the Naive Bayes classification algorithm and Support Vector Machine classification model with respect to text values and the performance varied enormously according to the characteristics of the data. These results call attention to the significance of the choice of the algorithm due to the certain characteristics of the data when conducting predictive modeling in risk assignment factors in the healthcare setting.

Table 1. Machine learning algorithms in healthcare insurance predictive analytics

Algorithm Type	Primary Applications	Accuracy Range	Interpretability	Implementation Complexity	Key Advantages
Linear Regression	Cost prediction, risk scoring	70-80%	High	Low	Simple, transparent, fast
Decision Trees	Risk stratification, rule generation	75-85%	High	Medium	Interpretable rules, handles missing data
Random Forest	Multi-factor prediction, feature importance	80-90%	Medium	Medium	Robust, handles overfitting
Gradient Boosting	Complex pattern recognition	85-95%	Medium	High	High accuracy, feature interactions

continued on following page

Table 1. Continued

Algorithm Type	Primary Applications	Accuracy Range	Interpretability	Implementation Complexity	Key Advantages
Neural Networks	Image analysis, NLP, complex patterns	85-95%	Low	High	Flexible, handles unstructured data
Support Vector Machines	Classification, anomaly detection	80-90%	Low	Medium	Effective with high-dimensional data

3.2 Data Sources and Integration

Successful application of predictive analytics needs multiple sources of information to be used to form the complete picture on patient health risks and care demands. The AI systems of the present ages are able to analyze both types of data structured data in the form of electronic health records and claims, as well as unstructured data in the form of clinical notes, imaging studies, and patient-generated health data.

The productivity of healthcare prediction models strongly depends on the nature and richness of their training data. Alauthman et al. (2023) discussed the generation of tabular data to achieve better results in disease classification diagnosis thus showing the existence of synthetic data to raise the level of model performance when handling with small datasets. Their strategy can bring a significant contribution to understanding by healthcare insurance companies unable to work with large volumes of data to construct predictive models of rare diseases or new health trends.

As shown in the study by Park and Han (2018), the use of large claim and clinical data allows recognizing high-risk patients in whom individual care management measures of care can be used. Their framework demonstrated that a complete data integration results in predicting risks more accurately and efficiently targeting intervention.

3.3 Real-Time Analytics and Continuous Learning

Real-time healthcare analytics systems enhance the functioning of advanced pattern recognition capabilities in a great way. Randhawa et al (2024) tested the applicability of Diagonal Evasion Generative Adversarial Networks developed with deep reinforcement learning in identifying the anomalous patterns in the data that are difficult to discern. They can use their methodology to monitor in a more dynamic way that would adapt to new patterns- and that is especially valuable when seeking to recognize new threats to health or exceptional patterns of utilizing insurance coverage controls information.

As the authors explained (Mangharamani and Agarwal, 2025), self-learning AI tools constantly evolve depending on emerging information and results and can provide more accurate forecasts and effective treatment, with time. In comparison, these systems are a massive development compared to the static models that need revisions after a certain period.

The capabilities of natural language processing (NLP) allow AI systems to make useful insights out of inaccessible and unstructured clinical notes, communications with patients, and data on social determinants, which could otherwise not be used to make any inferences about them. Such a feature largely improves the completeness and precision of risk forecasting models.

3.4 Natural Language Processing and Unstructured Data

Natural language processing (NLP) capabilities enable AI systems to extract valuable insights from unstructured clinical notes, patient communications, and social determinants data that would otherwise be inaccessible for analysis. This capability significantly enhances the comprehensiveness and accuracy of risk prediction models.

4. IMPACT ON PATIENT OUTCOMES

4.1 Early Disease Detection and Prevention

Predictive analytics with the help of AI are proficient in picking up the faintest trends within health data that can lead to future health risks as opposed to acute conditions that can necessitate the cost-intensive interventions. Early screening means a chance to control the disease development and enhance the prospective prognosis.

According to Oliver Wyman Health (2020), the presently available AI options are able to identify such abnormalities as heart failure upon hearing a single heartbeat with extraordinary precision. With such early detection abilities, the interventions have the capability to stave off the escalation of the condition to costly acute episodes with the additional benefit of earlier and less invasive treatment that improves the lifestyle of the patient.

High preciseness in the early detecting systems is possible to achieve with the help of advanced anomaly detection methods. Alauthman et al. (2020) came up with an effective methodology that uses reinforcement learning to identify abnormal patterns that are not expected to be in complex systems. These methods fruitfully applied to healthcare data can detect some unobvious clues to developing health issues before they can turn into acute events. On the same note, Randhawa et al. (2018) proposed an anomaly-based detection scheme of distributed attacks in cloud environments it is possible to suggest an adaptation of the described methodology to detect unusual trends in the health data of patients that may reveal early development or risk factors that need to be prophylactically addressed.

Table 2. AI-enabled early detection applications and outcomes

Condition Category	Detection Method	Early Detection Accuracy	Intervention Success Rate	Outcome Improvement	Cost Avoidance
Cardiovascular Disease	ECG pattern analysis, risk factor modeling	85-92%	70-80%	30% reduction in cardiac events	$15,000-25,000 per case
Diabetes	Glucose patterns, lifestyle factors	80-88%	75-85%	25% improvement in HbA1c control	$5,000-8,000 per patient/year
Mental Health	Behavioral indicators, communication patterns	75-85%	60-75%	40% reduction in crisis episodes	$10,000-20,000 per episode
Cancer	Imaging analysis, biomarker patterns	90-95%	80-90%	20% improvement in 5-year survival	$50,000-100,000 per case
Chronic Kidney Disease	Laboratory trends, comorbidity analysis	82-90%	70-80%	35% slower progression rate	$20,000-40,000 per patient
Respiratory Conditions	Environmental data, symptom tracking	78-85%	65-75%	30% reduction in exacerbations	$8,000-15,000 per episode

4.2 Personalized Treatment Optimization

AI systems will be able to utilize the specifics of an individual patient, the reaction to treatment and outcomes to streamline the choice of treatment and dosages to be more effective and have fewer side effects. This customization results in enhanced clinical outcomes and patient satisfaction as well as possible cost savings by enhancing efficiency of treatment procedures.

Topol (2019) highlighted the ability of AI to change delivery of reactive sick-care to proactive health-care with persistent risk-assessment and individualized intervention programs. Such an approach appreciates that the best cures differ widely among people due to genetic, behavioral, and environmental causes.

4.3 Chronic Disease Management

Most medical expenses are due to chronic diseases and are major areas of AI-powered positive change in outcome and cost savings. AI technologies will be able to track indicators of chronic illnesses in real-time and offer individual solutions to change the treatment, lifestyle, and organize care.

The study conducted by Bardhan et al. (2020) based on the experience of patients with congestive heart failure proves the effectiveness of AI-based chronic disease management. Their model of predicting who is at risk of readmission at 30days was shown to be better than the conventional methods, thus allowing them to intervene on the at-risk patients and the readmission rate decreased, as did the patient outcomes.

4.4 Care Coordination and Communication

Care coordination can receive incremental improvement by virtue of the fact that AI systems can fill gaps in care, communicate between providers, and ensure proper follow-up care is provided to patients. This synchronization is of special importance in the case of patients who have many chronic conditions and visit more than one provider on the same day.

Figure 2. AI-driven patient outcome optimization process

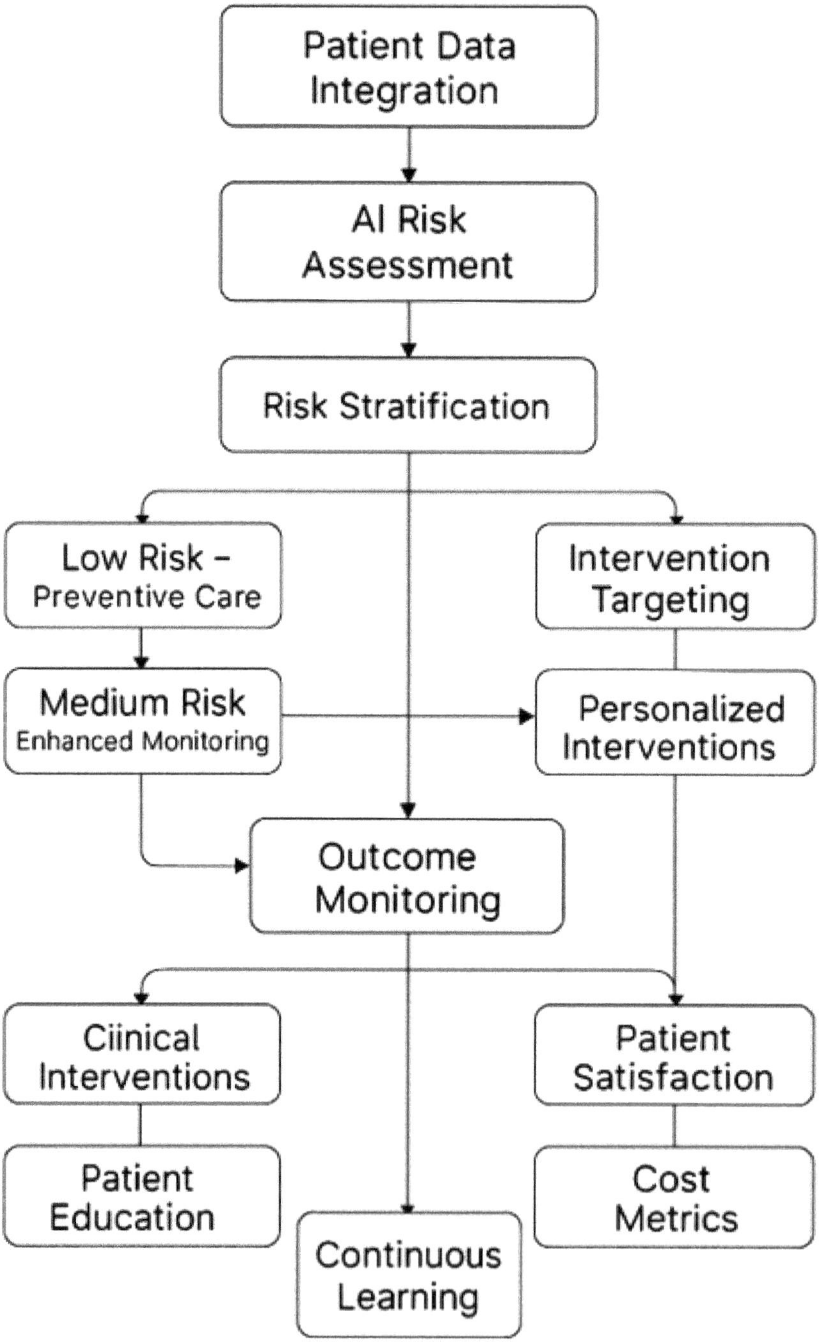

5. COST EFFICIENCY BENEFITS

5.1 Operational Cost Reductions

Predictive analytics powered by AI can create significant reductions in operations costs through automation of mundane tasks, optimized resources and elimination in the administrative inefficiencies. This saving enables the organizations to shift funds to patient care and quality optimization efforts.

The group by Hossain et al. (2024) traced the following statements: AI adoption helps to cut operational expenses by approaching ~25 percent and lower readmission rates by 15 to 20 percent. These operational savings are as a result of efficient claims processing procedures, automation of the risk evaluation procedure, efficient care management procedures, and less human oversight criteria.

Table 3. Operational cost reduction areas through AI implementation

Cost Category	Traditional Annual Cost (Large Insurer)	AI-Optimized Cost	Reduction Percentage	Annual Savings	Primary AI Applications
Claims Processing	$500 million	$250 million	50%	$250 million	Automated adjudication, fraud detection
Medical Management	$300 million	$180 million	40%	$120 million	Risk stratification, care protocols
Customer Service	$150 million	$75 million	50%	$75 million	Chatbots, automated responses
Underwriting	$100 million	$40 million	60%	$60 million	Automated risk assessment
Provider Management	$80 million	$56 million	30%	$24 million	Network optimization, quality monitoring
Quality Assurance	$70 million	$42 million	40%	$28 million	Automated auditing, pattern detection

5.2 Clinical Cost Reductions

AI also provides significant levels of clinical cost savings besides operation efficiencies due to overall enhanced care delivery, prevention of unnecessary procedures, and the avoidance of expensive complications. The savings may go beyond the operational savings; they are also sustainable since better population health is achieved as a result of these savings.

According to the forecast made by Sahni et al. (2023), the comprehensive implementation of AI-based solutions is likely to decrease healthcare expenditures by 5-10 percent due to the optimal guidance of treatment choices, avoided unneeded procedures, and disease diagnosis at an earlier stage, thus avoiding costly complications. A saving in services holds up over time because of more healthy long term health effects of better care provided at the cost of the same amount of service.

5.3 Readmission Reduction and Prevention

There is a major cause of costs and measure of quality in healthcare in hospital readmissions. Prediction models based on AI can tell the patients who are most likely to be readmission, as well as allow conducting specific interventions with the resultant decrease in the readmission rates and costs thereof.

Bardhan et al. (2020) showed that predictive analytics used to minimize the number of hospital readmissions of high-danger patients may produce sizable fundsavings accompanied by enhanced patient outcomes. The congestive heart failure model helped them to provide specific focuses after the discharge that greatly lowered the 30-day readmission rates.

5.4 Fraud Detection and Prevention

AI systems are quite good at spotting patterns that represent fraudulent or inappropriate billing, and therefore can be more effective in preventing the fraud, and the investigation cost is lowered. Expert pattern recognition will be able to discern subtle signs of fraud, signs which a human reviewer would find hard or next to impossible to discern without fail.

High-technology machine learning methods help to detect health care malpractices. Alkasassbeh et al. (2019) compared performance of various machine learning algorithms as intrusion detection systems across alleviating algorithms on determining the anomalous behavior in complex systems and reported that there were major variances in performances of the various algorithms. Their methodology of comparative analysis offers a good advice in the selection of the best algorithms to use in design of the fraud detection systems in processing healthcare claims. According to their research ensemble methods tend to perform better than single-algorithms in detecting more subtle changes in the patterns of transactions.

Table 4. Clinical cost reduction mechanisms and impact

Mechanism	Description	Average Cost Reduction	Implementation Timeline	ROI Period	Sustainability Factors
Preventive Interventions	Early identification and treatment of risk factors	30-40% per prevented episode	6-12 months	12-18 months	Continuous monitoring, protocol updates
Readmission Prevention	Targeted post-discharge care management	15-25% readmission cost reduction	3-6 months	6-12 months	Care coordination, patient engagement
Appropriate Utilization	Reducing unnecessary procedures and tests	20-30% utilization cost reduction	12-18 months	18-24 months	Provider education, decision support
Medication Optimization	Personalized therapy selection and monitoring	15-20% pharmacy cost reduction	6-12 months	12-18 months	Clinical integration, adherence monitoring
Emergency Prevention	Proactive care to prevent acute episodes	25-35% emergency cost reduction	12-24 months	24-36 months	Risk model accuracy, intervention effectiveness
Care Coordination	Reducing duplication and improving efficiency	10-20% coordination cost reduction	6-18 months	12-24 months	System integration, provider adoption

6. IMPLEMENTATION FRAMEWORK AND BEST PRACTICES

6.1 Strategic Planning and Organizational Readiness

Effective adoption of predictive analytics using AI demands a thorough strategic planning that should consider issues relating to organizational preparedness, alignment of the stakeholders and change management concerns. Organisations need to evaluate their existing strengths, fill enough gap and come up with road maps on how to adopt technology systematically.

Clear statement of business objectives, measures of business success and outcome should start the implementation process. Whether a leadership team, cross-functional team made up or influence leaders, commitment and formation of cross-functional team is needed to address the technical, operational and cultural changes necessary to adopt AI successfully.

6.2 Data Infrastructure and Governance

The strong data infrastructure can be taken as the key to successful AI implementation. Organizations should have data governance structures that help to safeguard data quality, data security and protect data privacy as well as adhere to various regulatory policies as the organization tries to integrate and process data in order to perform higher levels of analytics works.

Mathauer and Oranje (2024) supported the role of governance models that include risks and allow innovations as well. In such a conclusion, they declared that practical governance should weigh the advantages of audit technology-driven efficiency against the protection of justice, privacy, and equal access to cover.

When the AI systems in the healthcare insurance settings are implemented, they necessitate extensive systems of risk management especially in cases where cloud-based healthcare insurance systems are implemented. The study by Alhawari et al. (2017) was focused on risk management in relation to cloud computing and presented an implementation of data that can be of great use to healthcare insurers moving sensitive analytics to cloud environments. Their study stresses the importance of a systematic risk evaluation before use because it can significantly mitigate risks and help achieve the scalability potential of cloud infrastructure in the context of the analysis of extensive amounts of healthcare data.

Table 5. Implementation framework components and requirements

Framework Component	Key Elements	Success Criteria	Common Challenges	Mitigation Strategies
Data Infrastructure	Integration platforms, storage systems, security protocols	99.9% uptime, real-time processing	Legacy system integration	Phased migration, API development
Analytics Platform	ML models, deployment systems, monitoring tools	Model accuracy >85%, low latency	Model complexity, scalability	Cloud infrastructure, automated pipelines
Governance Framework	Policies, procedures, oversight committees	Regulatory compliance, audit success	Resource allocation, expertise gaps	Training programs, external partnerships
Change Management	Training, communication, process redesign	User adoption >80%, satisfaction scores	Resistance to change, skill gaps	Comprehensive training, change champions
Performance Monitoring	KPIs, dashboards, reporting systems	Real-time visibility, trend analysis	Data silos, metric alignment	Integrated reporting, standardized metrics
Continuous Improvement	Feedback loops, model updates, optimization	Performance improvement trends	Complacency, resource constraints	Regular reviews, innovation culture

6.3 Technology Architecture and Integration

Deployment of AI involves complex technology architecture that should be capable of integrating data, deploying models, and processing information in real-time and smoothly integrating them with the other business systems. The nature of the architecture needs to be scalable, secure and be able to support, continuous learning and model improvement.

Multipurpose cloud-based platforms are useful, as they typically offer flexibility and scalability needed in cases of AI implementations, but they minimize infrastructure expenditure and the complications that may arise. Nevertheless, data sovereignty, security demands, and integration issues ought to be keenly regarded as the organization chooses the technology platform.

6.4 Quality Assurance and Model Validation

To make the AI systems accurate, reliable and safe, there needs to be rigour quality assurance and model validation processes. Such processes need to cover technical validation of model performance and clinical validation of outcomes and safety.

It is necessary to perform model monitoring and update regularly in order to sustain performance with time as data distribution changes and new data appear. Organizations need to develop a protocol of retraining, validation and deployment of the models that will constitute continuous improvement and system stability at the same time.

Figure 3. AI implementation timeline and milestones

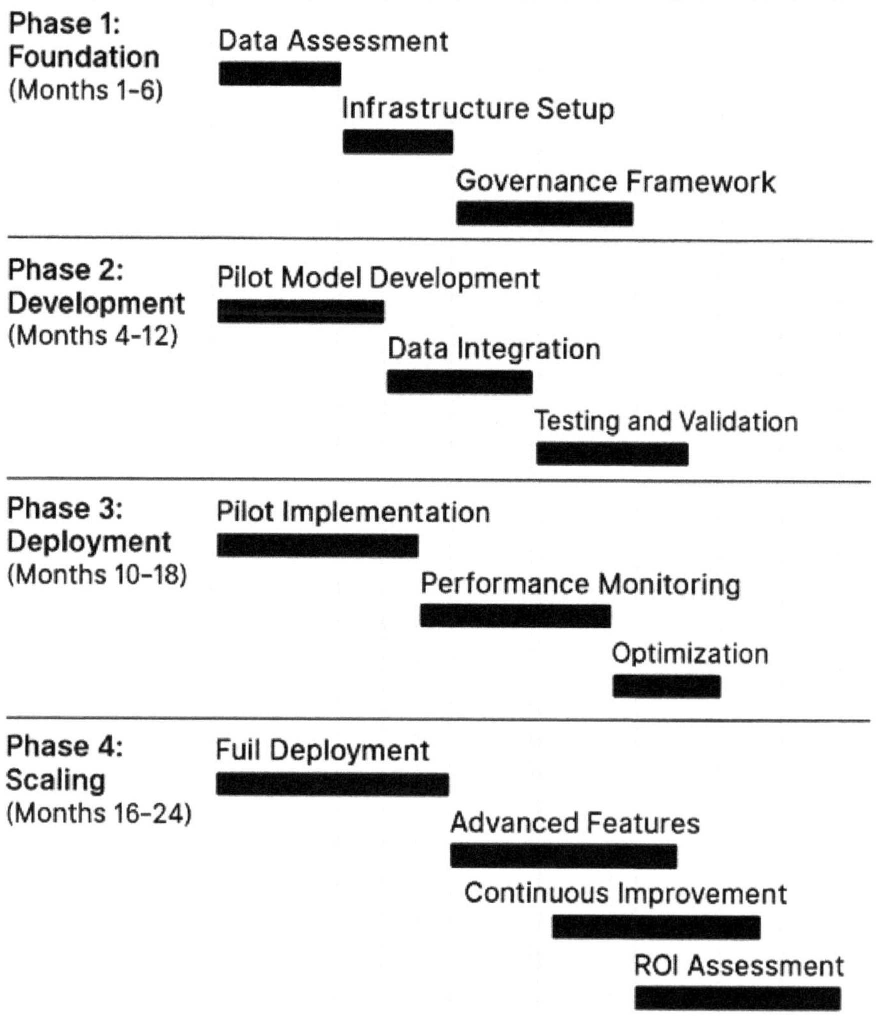

7. CHALLENGES AND LIMITATIONS

7.1 Algorithmic Bias and Fairness

One of the most prominent risks of applying AI in predictive analytics is overcoming algorithmic bias capable of creating or reinforcing the current health disparities. The experience of Obermeyer et al. (2019) with highly popular healthcare algorithms being potentially discriminatory against specific groups due to a mismatch between the optimization objective and the equity objective, deserves to be known as a landmark demonstration.

They found that algorithms that considered cost as the objective instead of medical need consistently lowered the likelihood of identifying Black patients as candidates of care management programs even though they had the same degree of ill health. Such discovery indicates dire need of attentive algorithm design and constant monitoring so they can produce equal and just results.

7.2 Data Privacy and Security Concerns

Healthcare data is considered one of the most sensitive personal data, and the highest level of privacy protection is needed together with security. To do this, AI systems should be compliant with such regulations as HIPAA, GDPR, and other jurisdiction-specific requirements and should facilitate the sharing and processing of data required to manage predictive analytics effectively.

This all gets worse when AI systems get access to data spanning the connected health monitoring devices. Alauthman et al. (2024) explored cryptographic protocols which are developed in relation to Internet of Things (IoT) security applications with a focus on lightweight protocols as well as implementation factors (protective measures) applied to transfer sensitive information. Their model is especially applicable to healthcare insurers who engage the use of predictive analytics systems that combine data retrieved by wearable devices and remote monitoring equipment. Moreover, Alsmadi, D et al. (2023) investigated the impact of the COVID-19 pandemic on cybersecurity behaviours and awareness to inform healthcare organizations who quickly introduced remote analytics support but had insufficient security evaluation at the beginning of the global health crisis.

The issue is especially sharp when it comes to the AI systems which need vast amounts of data to train and potentially consist of integrating various sources of data. Individual privacy should be maintained by organizations through privacy-preserving methods (such as differential privacy, federated learning, and secure multi-party computation) that will allow useful AI uses without jeopardizing privacy.

7.3 Model Interpretability and Trust

The decision-making associated with healthcare must be transparent and explainable, especially in cases where AI suggestions influence patient care preferences or care coverage. The opacity of most complex AI models, as the so-called black boxes, might introduce adoption and trust limitations to healthcare professionals and patients.

Orji and Ukwandu (2024) underlined the role of explainable AI in healthcare insurance cost forecasting by stating that interpretable predictive models help improve knowledge about drivers behind the cost and decision factors. This interpretability is important in developing trust and proper utilization of AI recommendations.

7.4 Integration and Interoperability Challenges

Healthcare organizations tend to move with many legacy systems that may not be easy to incorporate and integrate with the contemporary AI platform. Ensuring smooth flow of data and system interoperability needs high technological skills, and possibly, it might require heavy investments on infrastructures.

Table 6. Key implementation challenges and mitigation strategies

Challenge Category	Specific Issues	Potential Impact	Mitigation Strategies	Success Indicators	Timeline
Technical Complexity	Data integration, system scalability, model deployment	Implementation delays, cost overruns	Phased approach, cloud platforms, expert consultation	System performance metrics, deployment milestones	12-24 months
Algorithmic Bias	Discrimination, unfair outcomes, equity concerns	Legal liability, reputation damage	Diverse datasets, bias testing, fairness constraints	Equity metrics, audit results	Ongoing
Data Privacy	Regulatory compliance, security breaches, consent management	Legal violations, trust erosion	Privacy-preserving technologies, robust security protocols	Compliance audit results, security incident rates	Continuous
Change Management	User resistance, skill gaps, process disruption	Low adoption, poor outcomes	Comprehensive training, change champions, gradual rollout	Adoption rates, user satisfaction scores	6-18 months
Financial Investment	High upfront costs, uncertain ROI, resource constraints	Budget overruns, project cancellation	Business case development, phased investment, ROI tracking	Financial metrics, cost-benefit analysis	24-36 months
Regulatory Compliance	Evolving regulations, audit requirements, liability concerns	Legal penalties, operational restrictions	Proactive compliance, legal consultation, documentation	Regulatory approval, audit success	Ongoing

8. CASE STUDIES AND REAL-WORLD APPLICATIONS

8.1 Successful Predictive Analytics Implementations

A number of healthcare insurance companies have already managed to introduce AI-enabled predictive analytics which has an evident effect on patient outcomes and cost effectiveness. Such case studies can bring in good insights regarding implementation methods, the factors associated with success, and lessons learned.

In their article, Park and Han (2018) describe a successful experience of using predictive analytics in finding high-risk patients with the need of cost-effective care regime. Their structure utilized massive claims and clinical data sets to identify patients that would require some sort of patient intervention like case management or prevention. The outcomes were depicted by an increase in efficiency in care delivery, measurement of which involved more timely interventions resulting in less number of emergency visits and readmissions.

8.2 Chronic Disease Management Success Stories

Bardhan et al. (2020) presented an elaborate case study of how predictive analytics is implemented in reducing hospital readmission by the congestive heart failure patients. They did better than conventional methods to predict 30-day readmission, which allowed addressing high-risk patients with specialized measures.

The introduction as part of a collaboration between a hospital and an insurance provider proved to have a tremendous clinical and cost-related performance. Post-discharge intercessions that focused on readmission significantly decreased readmission levels, which also led to better patient health along with tremendous cost savings on part of the insurance firm.

8.3 Lessons Learned from Early Adopters

Early adopters of AI-enabled predictive analytics have identified several critical success factors:

- **Leadership Commitment**: Executive support and resource allocation are essential for overcoming implementation challenges and sustaining long-term success.
- **Cross-Functional Collaboration**: Successful implementations require collaboration between clinical, technical, and business teams to ensure that AI systems address real-world needs and integrate effectively with existing workflows.

- **Pilot Testing**: Starting with limited pilot programs allows organizations to learn and refine approaches before full-scale deployment.
- **Continuous Monitoring**: Ongoing performance monitoring and model refinement are essential for maintaining effectiveness and addressing emerging challenges.

9. ECONOMIC IMPACT AND RETURN ON INVESTMENT

9.1 Comprehensive Cost-Benefit Analysis

AI-Powered predictive analytics have economic implications that address more than the reduction of direct expenses through better health outcomes, optimization of operations, and competitive benefits. The overall cost-benefit comparison should include costs of implementation, change of operation, training facilities and both immediate and long term gain.

Costs prediction plays a pivotal role in operations of healthcare insurance and models should ensure that they offer predictability (accuracy) alone and at the same time should be interpretable. The study by Al-Smadi et al. (2023) provided evidence that Shapley interpretable machine learning models can also be effectively applied to make accurate predictions related to software defects, and it is plausible to adopt this mechanism to predict healthcare costs that align with the idea of maximum transparency in the processes associated with cost determinants. Their methodology can allow insurance analysts to know what is behind the costs in order to predict what or why they are developing the costs and this is important in the development of precise intervention strategies.

Sahni et al. (2023) performed economic modeling of the macro-level effect of AI on healthcare costs and projected substantial effects of widescale use of AI on healthcare costs; the modeling could result in a 5-10% savings in healthcare costs without a decrease in quality. Such savings are achieved by means of simplified administrative procedures, rationalized treatment decisions, and early diagnosis of the disease avoiding costly complications.

9.2 Return on Investment Timelines

The ROI of organizations that have deployed AI-enable predictive analytics is usually achieved within 12-36 months depending on the scale of implementation and intended use cases. Automation and improved efficiencies translate into operational savings in a shorter period as compared to clinical savings in improved health.

Health improvements have a compound characteristic whereby clinical benefits that are deposited over the years due to continued better care and prevention enables maintenance of better health system and along with lowered health care expenses.

9.3 Value Creation Across Stakeholders

AI-enabled predictive analytics create value for multiple stakeholders through different mechanisms:

For Patients: Improved health outcomes, earlier detection and treatment of health issues, more personalized care, and potentially lower out-of-pocket costs through preventive care emphasis.
For Insurance Organizations: Reduced claims costs, improved risk selection, enhanced operational efficiency, better customer satisfaction, and competitive differentiation in the marketplace.
For Healthcare Providers: More engaged patients, better care coordination, reduced administrative burden, and improved clinical decision support.
For Society: More efficient healthcare resource utilization, improved population health outcomes, and reduced overall healthcare cost burden.

10. FUTURE DIRECTIONS AND EMERGING TRENDS

10.1 Advanced Analytics and Emerging Technologies

Further improvements in machine learning methods, computer capabilities, and availability of information will probably influence the future of AI-supported predictive analytics in healthcare insurance. Advanced neural networks, quantum computing, and edge computing are emerging as new technologies, making them better able to conduct more sophisticated analysis and process in real-time.

Hypothetically, Oliver Wyman Health (2020) thought that AI algorithms would eventually be able to determine conditions with near perfect accuracy based on very few data input, and thus could monitor contiguously and intervene as soon as the system has detected any threats to the health. This will turn insurance into health optimization as opposed to a reactive coverage.

One of the biggest healthcare predictive analytics problems is a scarcity of training data when it comes to a rare illness or a new trend in health behaviours. Alauthman et al. (2024) conducted research on this shortcoming through improvement of the performance of classification of small medical datasets through Generative Adversarial Networks (GANs). Their methodology shows that synthetic data can generate improved models on conditions that have very few previous data; hence of interest to insurers that want to determine rare but high cost health events.

10.2 Integration with Precision Medicine

With the AI-powered insurance analytics, specific healthcare actions can be instigated, and risk assessment will be even more accurate due to the combination of genetic, environmental, and lifestyle factors and precision medicine. This will facilitate personalized healthcare strategies that are indeed individualistic and consider individual biological and behavioral peculiarities.

10.3 Real-Time Health Monitoring and Intervention

The enhanced wearable technology, IoT sensors, and m-health apps will deliver a steady flow of health data that can be used to determine the risk in real-time and create opportunities to intervene immediately. This will facilitate prevention orientated insurance models that will keep people healthy rather than causally curing them with illnesses.

10.4 Ecosystem Integration and Interoperability

The AI systems of the future are likely to be based upon a healthcare ecosystem where data is shared and coordinated seamlessly across different providers, payers and technology platforms. This will allow increased detailed and efficient predictive analytics and fewer administrative complexities.

11. REGULATORY AND ETHICAL CONSIDERATIONS

11.1 Evolving Regulatory Landscape

The regulatory environment for AI in healthcare insurance continues to evolve as policymakers seek to balance innovation benefits with consumer protection requirements. Regulatory frameworks must address algorithm transparency, bias prevention, data privacy, and fair access to coverage while enabling beneficial AI applications.

Mathauer and Oranje (2024) emphasized the need for proactive regulatory engagement to address biases and privacy issues while safeguarding fairness and universal coverage goals. They noted that regulatory oversight must evolve to address AI-specific challenges while supporting innovation that improves healthcare delivery and cost efficiency.

11.2 Ethical AI Development and Deployment

Ethical considerations in AI-enabled predictive analytics include fairness, transparency, accountability, and respect for individual autonomy. Organizations must establish ethical frameworks that guide AI development and deployment while ensuring that systems serve the best interests of patients and society.

Key ethical principles include:

- **Beneficence**: AI systems should promote patient welfare and improve health outcomes
- **Non-maleficence**: Systems should avoid harm and unintended negative consequences
- **Justice**: Benefits and risks should be fairly distributed across all populations
- **Autonomy**: Patients should maintain control over their health decisions and data

11.3 Stakeholder Engagement and Public Trust

Building and maintaining public trust in AI-enabled healthcare insurance requires ongoing stakeholder engagement, transparent communication about AI capabilities and limitations, and demonstrated commitment to ethical principles and patient welfare.

Organizations must engage with patients, providers, regulators, and community organizations to ensure that AI implementations reflect diverse perspectives and address legitimate concerns about privacy, fairness, and accountability.

12. CYBERSECURITY INSURANCE: AI-POWERED RISK PREDICTION AND DIGITAL RESILIENCE

12.1 The Evolving Cyber-Risk Landscape

AI is a double-edged sword for cyber insurers: attackers use large-language-model phishing kits and automated vulnerability discovery, while carriers deploy the same technologies to measure exposure and blunt losses. Global premiums reached roughly US $14 billion in 2024 and are projected to double by 2027, yet more than half of underwriters still expect cyber-risk severity to "grow greatly" this year.

12.2 Data Sources and Predictive Models

Where health-insurance models ingest EHRs and claims, cyber models draw on:

- High-frequency network and endpoint telemetry (SIEM, EDR)
- External attack-surface scans (e.g., Shodan-style exposure scores)
- Real-time threat-intelligence feeds (CVE exploit chatter, ransomware leak sites)
- Company-specific hygiene signals (MFA coverage, patch latency, backup resilience)

Gradient-boosted ensembles and graph neural networks convert these inputs into breach-likelihood and loss-severity scores that refresh daily, enabling continuous underwriting rather than annual point-in-time assessments.

12.3 AI-Driven Underwriting and Pricing

Hard-market conditions have eased: average U.S. cyber-rates fell 5–7% in late 2024 and Q1 2025 as underwriters used AI scores to segment risks with "responsive" controls and reward them with broader limits. Dynamic pricing engines now pair loss-cost curves with simulated attack scenarios to offer usage-based or parametric cover that adjusts as exposure changes.

12.4 Real-Time Risk Mitigation, Claims and Incident Response

Leading carriers embed AI agents on insured networks that watch for anomaly clusters (e.g., lateral-movement patterns) and trigger pre-approved containment playbooks—often before the policyholder submits a claim. Coalition's 2025 data show overall claims frequency down 7%, with average losses about US $115 k, illustrating how proactive monitoring curbs both frequency and severity even as email-based attacks persist.

12.5 Governance, Regulation and Public-Private Support

Model governance mirrors healthcare's algorithm-audit requirements but must also align with cyber-security frameworks such as NIST CSF 2.0 and Europe's NIS-2/DORA mandates. Insurers are pressing for government backstops to handle "uninsurable" systemic events (e.g., a cloud-provider outage crippling global payments), similar to terrorism or flood pools.

12.6 Challenges and Future Directions

- **Correlation risk:** AI reveals hidden supply-chain dependencies that can concentrate losses across portfolios.
- **Adversarial adaptation:** Attackers may probe underwriting models, forcing continuous red-team testing.
- **Equitable access:** Small firms without mature controls risk exclusion or high deductibles, raising questions of digital divide.
- **Next horizon:** Combining generative AI with causal inference could forecast not just breach probability but the *marginal loss-reduction* of a specific control, enabling insurers to sell "embedded security credits" alongside coverage. munichre.com

13. CONCLUSION

The trend of AI-powered predictive analytics in healthcare insurance is a revolutionary process that, at the same time, streamlines patient outcomes and achieves high cost-saving rates. According to empirical evidence, there are notable benefits, which include massive cost savings in operations, reduced readmission, better quality of care due to early intervention and increased efficiency of resource allocation.

Patient outcomes and cost-efficiency dual optimization helps to solve a longstanding problem in healthcare delivery, in which the conventional methods often required making trade-offs between quality and cost. AI-enabled systems create evidence that the best health outcomes and financial sustainability can be achieved simultaneously due to data-based insights, predictive intervention, and individually tailored care solutions.

To succeed, systematic considerations of the technical infrastructure, organizational preparation, stakeholder involvement, and ethical issues are required. Such challenges as the bias in the algorithms, data privacy issues, complexity in integrations, and change management needs should be overcome simultaneously with guaranteeing the welfare of the patients and regulatory adherence.

The economic value is not only job and cost savings but also core changes in the efficiency of healthcare delivery and population health outcomes. There is evidence that 25 percent of operational costs and 1520 percent of readmission rates can be reduced, which means that AI-enabled predictive analytics can create significant value to all stakeholders and enable more sustainable healthcare financing models.

Further development of technology is set to expand the potential and use of predictive analytics enabled by AI. Whereas integrations with precision medicine, real-time monitoring, and interoperability between the ecosystem will allow even more complex and efficient methods of health optimization and cost-control.

However, to achieve the potential of these technologies, it is necessary to pay continuous attention to ethical aspects, regulatory adherence, and equal distribution of gains. In the end, there will be a success not only in the enhancement of financial performance but also in the real changes in population health outcomes and equitable access to high-quality healthcare by all individuals in society.

That transformation that the AI-enabled predictive analytics promises is not just about technological progress; it is the paradigm shift toward preventive, personalized, and value-based healthcare where financial incentives are aligned with health outcomes. Organizations which can effectively deploy such capabilities whilst managing related challenges will be in a good position to succeed in a changing healthcare environment that requires not only high quality patient care but also financial sustainability.

With the growing healthcare expenses worldwide and the ever-growing demand on quality, predictive analytics with AI as an enabling technology can become a key competency in the effort to develop sustainable insurance models that act as a vehicle to meet individual and societal health agendas. The combination of better patient outcomes and reduction in cost effectiveness provides a way forward to more equitable, effective, and financially sustainable healthcare systems that will benefit all stakeholders.

REFERENCES

Al-Smadi, Y., Eshtay, M., Al-Qerem, A., Nashwan, S., Ouda, O., & Abd El-Aziz, A. A. (2023). Reliable prediction of software defects using Shapley interpretable machine-learning models. *Egyptian Informatics Journal, 24*(3), 100386. DOI: 10.1016/j.eij.2023.05.011

Alauthman, M., Al-Qerem, A., Sowan, B., Alsarhan, A., Eshtay, M., Aldweesh, A., & Aslam, N. (2023). Enhancing small medical-dataset classification performance using GAN. *Informatics (MDPI), 10*(1), 28. DOI: 10.3390/informatics10010028

Alauthman, M., Aldweesh, A., Al-Qerem, A., Aburub, F., Al-Smadi, Y., Abaker, A. M., Alzubi, O. R., & Alzubi, B. (2023). Tabular data generation to improve classification of liver-disease diagnosis. *Applied Sciences (Basel, Switzerland), 13*(4), 2678. DOI: 10.3390/app13042678

Alauthman, M., Aldweesh, A., Al-Qerem, A., Al Maqousi, A. Y., & Almomani, A. (2024). Cryptographic protocols for Internet of Things (IoT) security: Lightweight schemes and practical deployment. In Innovations in Modern Cryptography (pp. 431–448). DOI: 10.4018/979-8-3693-5330-1.ch018

Alauthman, M., Aslam, N., Al-Kasassbeh, M., Khan, S., Al-Qerem, A., & Raymond Choo, K.-K. (2020). An efficient reinforcement-learning-based botnet detection approach. *Journal of Network and Computer Applications, 150*, 102479. DOI: 10.1016/j.jnca.2019.102479

Alhawari, S., Al Jarrah, M. A., & Hadi, W. (2017). Implementing risk-management processes into a cloud-computing environment. *International Journal of Web Portals, 9*(1), 1–12. DOI: 10.4018/IJWP.2017010101

Alkhelb, A. A., & Alshagrawi, S. (2025). Role of artificial intelligence in healthcare insurance: Systematic literature review. Exploration of Digital Health Technologies, 3, Article 101145. https://doi.org/10.37349/edht.2025.101145

Alsmadi, D., Maqousi, A., & Abuhussein, T. (2024). Engaging in cybersecurity proactive behavior: Awareness in COVID-19 age. *Kybernetes, 53*(1), 451–466. DOI: 10.1108/K-08-2022-1104

Bardhan, I., Oh, J., & Zheng, Z. (2020). Predictive analytics for reducing hospital readmissions of high-risk patients. *Information Systems Research, 31*(3), 855–875.

Dixon, D., Sattar, H., Moros, N., Kesireddy, S. R., Ahsan, H., Lakkimsetti, M., & Hassan, M. J. (2024). Unveiling the influence of AI predictive analytics on patient outcomes: A comprehensive narrative review. *Cureus, 16*(5), e59954. DOI: 10.7759/cureus.59954 PMID: 38854327

Hadi, W. M., Salam, M., & Al-Widian, J. A. (2010, June). Performance of NB and SVM classifiers in Islamic Arabic data. In Proceedings of the 1st International Conference on Intelligent Semantic Web-Services and Applications (ISWSA) (pp. 14:1–14:6). ACM. https://doi.org/10.1145/1874590.1874604

Hossain, S., Ahmed, A., Khadka, U., Sarkar, S., & Khan, N. (2024). AI-driven predictive analytics, healthcare outcomes, cost reduction, machine learning, patient monitoring. *Advanced International Journal of Multidisciplinary Research*, *2*(5), 1–20.

Mangharamani, R., & Agarwal, R. (2025). AI-driven predictive risk modeling in health insurance: Optimizing coverage and cost efficiency with self-learning systems. *International Journal of Progressive Research in Engineering Management and Science, 5*(3), 1 420–1 430.

Mathauer, I., & Oranje, M. (2024). Machine learning in health financing: Benefits, risks and regulatory needs. *Bulletin of the World Health Organization*, *102*(3), 216–224. DOI: 10.2471/BLT.23.290333 PMID: 38420574

Mehta, N., & Pandit, A. (2018). Concurrence of big data analytics and healthcare: A systematic review. *International Journal of Medical Informatics*, *114*, 57–65. DOI: 10.1016/j.ijmedinf.2018.03.013 PMID: 29673604

Obermeyer, Z., Powers, B., Vogeli, C., & Mullainathan, S. (2019). Dissecting racial bias in an algorithm used to manage the health of populations. *Science*, *366*(6464), 447–453. DOI: 10.1126/science.aax2342 PMID: 31649194

Oliver Wyman Health. (2020). AI will enable personalized, proactive, and smarter care []. Oliver Wyman.]. *The Innovation Journal*, *4*, •••.

Orji, U., & Ukwandu, E. (2024). Machine learning for an explainable cost prediction of medical insurance. *Machine Learning with Applications*, *15*, 100516. DOI: 10.1016/j.mlwa.2023.100516

Park, S., & Han, J. (2018). Using predictive analytics to identify high-risk patients for cost-effective care management. *Journal of Medical Systems*, *42*(12), 233.

Randhawa, R. H., Aslam, N., Alauthman, M., Khalid, M., & Rafiq, H. (2024). Deep reinforcement learning-based Evasion Generative Adversarial Network for botnet detection. *Future Generation Computer Systems*, *150*, 294–302. DOI: 10.1016/j.future.2023.09.011

Rao, A. R., Jain, R., Singh, M., & Garg, R. (2024). Predictive interpretable analytics models for forecasting healthcare costs using open healthcare data. *Healthcare Analytics*, *6*, 100351. DOI: 10.1016/j.health.2024.100351

Sahni, N., Stein, G., Zemmel, R., & Cutler, D. M. (2023). The potential impact of artificial intelligence on healthcare spending (NBER Working Paper No. 30866). National Bureau of Economic Research.

Topol, E. J. (2019). High-performance medicine: The convergence of human and artificial intelligence. *Nature Medicine*, *25*(1), 44–56. DOI: 10.1038/s41591-018-0300-7 PMID: 30617339

Chapter 2
Autonomous Cyber Underwriting Agents Reinventing Risk Evaluation Through Reinforcement Learning and Multi-Agent Systems

Salam Al E'mari
https://orcid.org/0000-0002-2134-4158
University of Petra, Jordan

Yousef Sanjalawe
https://orcid.org/0000-0002-4442-1865
University of Jordan, Jordan

Fadi Fataftah
https://orcid.org/0000-0002-3299-0972
University Canada West, Canada

ABSTRACT

As cyber threats become more complex and unpredictable, traditional cyber insurance methods struggle to keep pace. This chapter explores autonomous cyber underwriting agents that use reinforcement learning and multi-agent systems to dynamically assess, price, and manage digital risk. It outlines the limitations of static risk models and introduces adaptive, data-driven approaches powered by AI. Key concepts include real-time risk scoring, portfolio optimization, and system architectures that support

DOI: 10.4018/979-8-3373-5545-0.ch002

scalability, security, and compliance. Rather than replacing human underwriters, these agents augment decision-making, enabling faster, smarter, and more resilient cyber risk management.

INTRODUCTION

In today's hyper-connected world, organizations increasingly rely on digital infrastructure for daily operations, customer engagement, and strategic growth. While this digital transformation fuels innovation and efficiency, it simultaneously exposes organizations to an expanding array of cyber threats, ransomware attacks, data breaches, supply chain vulnerabilities, and insider threats, to name just a few. Against this backdrop, cyber insurance has emerged as a critical financial tool to transfer and manage the risk of digital exposure. However, underwriting such policies is a formidable challenge (Arbore, 2025).

Cyber underwriting, the process of evaluating the potential risk of a digital incident and determining appropriate coverage terms, has traditionally relied on static assessments, historical claims data, and manual reviews of an organization's cybersecurity posture (Tsohou et al., 2023). This worked to an extent when the cyber threat landscape was relatively stable and attacks were less frequent. But the modern reality is far more dynamic: threat actors adapt rapidly, technologies evolve overnight, and digital ecosystems grow in complexity with cloud adoption, IoT integration, and remote work models.

In such a fluid environment, conventional risk evaluation methods are not just slow, they're often outdated by the time an assessment is complete. Worse, many insurers face a significant data asymmetry: while attackers operate with increasingly sophisticated tools and real-time intelligence, insurers struggle to keep pace, often relying on fragmented, static risk indicators. The result? Underwriting decisions that either underestimate risk, leading to unsustainable losses, or overestimate it, pushing premiums too high and reducing market competitiveness. Cyber underwriting is, therefore, at a crossroads. The need for smarter, faster, and more adaptive decision-making is urgent. And this is where artificial intelligence, particularly reinforcement learning and multi-agent systems, offers a promising path forward (Bergese, 2021).

The Shift Toward Autonomy in Risk Assessment

As cyber risks become more complex and multidimensional, the underwriting process must evolve from being reactive and rule-based to proactive and intelligence-driven. This shift calls for systems that can not only analyze large volumes of data in real time but also learn and adapt as new threats emerge. In short, the industry needs underwriting agents that think, learn, and act, autonomously (Kolhar, 2025).

These agents represent a new generation of AI-enabled systems designed to assess risk dynamically, based on real-time data feeds, behavioral analysis, and adaptive learning. Drawing from reinforcement learning, these agents are capable of making decisions by interacting with their environment, optimizing for long-term outcomes rather than short-term heuristics. In practice, this means they can adjust their risk evaluation models as they observe new types of attacks, client behaviors, or changes in regulatory standards (Landoll, 2021).

But risk assessment is rarely a solo activity. The underwriting process involves many moving parts, data validation, threat intelligence interpretation, policy negotiation, portfolio balancing, and compliance checks. That's where Multi-Agent Systems (MAS) become invaluable. In a MAS framework, multiple autonomous agents collaborate, each with specialized roles. Some may focus on scanning real-time threat landscapes, others on pricing optimization or anomaly detection. These agents communicate, negotiate, and adapt as a collective, allowing the underwriting system to remain flexible, distributed, and resilient in the face of uncertainty (Maldonado et al., 2024).

The implications of this technological shift are profound. Autonomous underwriting agents can reduce decision latency, uncover hidden risk correlations, and respond to emerging threats faster than any human underwriter possibly could. More importantly, they promise to bring scalability to an insurance function that is increasingly stretched thin by the volume and velocity of cyber risk data. Of course, autonomy in underwriting is not without its challenges, ethical, legal, and technical. But the direction is clear: the future of cyber risk evaluation lies not in spreadsheets or static checklists, but in intelligent, learning agents capable of evolving in tandem with the threats they're designed to insure against (Jansen, Nguyen & Shams, 2025).

This chapter explores how reinforcement learning and multi-agent systems can power the next generation of cyber underwriting, transforming risk assessment from a static process into a living, learning, and adaptive ecosystem.

Foundations of Cyber Underwriting

Cyber underwriting, as a discipline, is still relatively young. Compared to more established areas of insurance like property, health, or auto, where decades of actuarial data guide underwriting decisions, cyber insurance has emerged within just the past two decades—and matured even more recently. Initially, underwriting cyber risk followed a cautious, conservative model. Insurers leaned heavily on checklists, self-reported questionnaires, and broad industry averages to make sense of an organization's exposure to digital threats. Risk was often assessed in terms of technical posture: presence of firewalls, use of antivirus software, frequency of security audits, and compliance with standards like ISO 27001 or NIST (Beuchelt, 2025).

This approach, while a reasonable starting point, came with significant shortcomings. For one, many risk assessment frameworks relied on static inputs, snapshots of security measures at a specific point in time. But cybersecurity is inherently dynamic; an organization considered "secure" last month may become vulnerable today due to a new software vulnerability, employee turnover, or a subtle misconfiguration in its cloud infrastructure (Alquwayzani, Aldossri & Frikha, 2024).

Moreover, traditional underwriting failed to fully capture behavioral and contextual factors. For instance, two companies in the same sector with similar technology stacks might have vastly different cyber risk profiles depending on their internal culture, employee training programs, third-party vendors, and incident response capabilities. These nuances are difficult to quantify using standardized forms and fixed models (Falco & Rosenbach, 2022).

Claims data, the bedrock of actuarial science, has also been lacking in the cyber domain. Many organizations underreport breaches, and when incidents are disclosed, the data is often incomplete, delayed, or legally restricted. This scarcity makes it difficult for underwriters to predict future risk based on historical patterns, a challenge that is compounded by the constantly evolving nature of cyber threats (Sun, 2024).

Finally, the traditional model struggles with scalability. As demand for cyber insurance grows across industries and geographies, underwriters face mounting pressure to process more applications in less time. Manual evaluations simply don't scale to meet the demand, and shortcuts in assessment introduce even more risk into insurers' portfolios (Chowdhary, 2025).

Evolving Threat Landscapes in Cybersecurity Insurance

The digital threat landscape has changed dramatically in recent years, both in scope and sophistication. Cybercriminals are no longer lone actors operating in isolation. Many are now part of well-funded, organized groups, some with ties to state actors. Ransomware-as-a-service, phishing kits, and exploit marketplaces have lowered the barrier to entry, enabling even relatively unskilled attackers to carry out devastating attacks (Stoddart, 2022). This industrialization of cybercrime has significant implications for cyber insurers. Attacks are no longer isolated or random, they are strategic, scalable, and often targeted based on insurers' own coverage data. For example, there have been cases where threat actors specifically targeted organizations known to hold cyber policies, assuming they'd be more likely to pay ransom (Dambra, Bilge & Balzarotti, 2020).

In parallel, the surface area for attack is expanding rapidly. Cloud migration, remote workforces, BYOD (Bring Your Own Device) policies, and growing reliance on third-party vendors all contribute to a more porous digital perimeter. Each new integration or software dependency adds another layer of complexity and potential vulnerability; factors that traditional underwriting methods struggle to evaluate holistically (Rah, 2023).

Regulatory and legal developments further complicate the landscape. Laws such as the GDPR, CCPA, and the evolving global regulatory patchwork have raised the stakes for data breaches, introducing steep fines and reputational costs. This makes understanding and predicting liability in cyber insurance even more critical, and more difficult (Agboola, 2025). What's becoming clear is that cyber risk is no longer a technical problem alone; it's a systemic business risk that cuts across organizational boundaries. It requires an underwriting approach that can grasp context, adapt to change, and make decisions at machine speed (Hubbard, 2020).

In this shifting landscape, traditional risk evaluation methods are simply not agile enough. The industry needs models that can evolve in real time, interpret a complex web of signals, and collaborate across systems and domains. This is the impetus for a new underwriting paradigm, one built on reinforcement learning, data-driven intelligence, and autonomous agents capable of operating within decentralized, multi-agent ecosystems.

AUTONOMOUS AGENTS IN RISK EVALUATION

Autonomous underwriting agents represent a fundamental shift in how cyber risk is assessed, priced, and managed. Unlike traditional software tools or decision-support systems that operate based on predefined rules or human input, autonomous agents are designed to function independently. They perceive their environment, make decisions based on internal logic or learned behaviors, and continuously adapt their strategies to improve outcomes over time (Singireddy et al, 2024).

In the context of cyber underwriting, an autonomous agent is a software-based entity capable of performing tasks typically associated with human underwriters, but at scale, in real-time, and with a level of consistency and responsiveness that exceeds human capabilities. These agents can gather and analyze diverse data sources—network telemetry, threat intelligence feeds, compliance records, behavioral logs, and even geopolitical signals. Based on this information, they evaluate a client's cyber risk posture, recommend coverage limits and premiums, and, in some cases, negotiate terms or suggest mitigative measures (Rao, Harrison & Mulloth,

2020). Several core characteristics distinguish autonomous underwriting agents from conventional AI tools (Apergis, 2024):

1. Reactivity: These agents continuously monitor the environment and respond to changes, such as a new vulnerability being exploited in the wild or a client adding a third-party integration, without requiring human intervention.
2. Proactivity: Beyond reaction, they can anticipate future scenarios using predictive modeling, identifying latent risks before they manifest.
3. Learning Capability: Powered by reinforcement learning and similar techniques, autonomous agents improve over time. They learn from previous underwriting decisions, claims outcomes, and shifts in the cyber threat landscape to refine their models.
4. Goal Orientation: Each agent operates with defined objectives, such as maximizing underwriting accuracy, minimizing claim ratios, or balancing portfolio risk, which guide their decision-making in complex, often uncertain environments.
5. Autonomy and Collaboration: While capable of independent operation, these agents are often deployed in multi-agent ecosystems, where they collaborate, compete, or coordinate with other agents to optimize global outcomes.

This architecture enables insurers to move away from rigid workflows and static evaluation models toward a more fluid, intelligence-driven underwriting process.

Benefits of Autonomy in High-Frequency Decision-Making Environments

Cyber risk doesn't operate on a quarterly cycle, it evolves by the hour, sometimes by the minute. Zero-day exploits, nation-state attacks, and viral malware campaigns can reshape the risk profile of entire industries overnight. In this high-frequency environment, autonomous agents bring a distinct set of advantages that make them indispensable (Bompos, 2020).

1. Speed and Scalability: Autonomous agents can evaluate hundreds or thousands of clients simultaneously, executing risk assessments at machine speed. This scalability is critical as cyber insurance demand rises across sectors, and as insurers aim to penetrate Small and Medium-Sized Enterprise (SME) markets, where margins are thin and manual underwriting is cost-prohibitive (Adriko & Nurse, 2024).
2. Consistency and Objectivity: Human underwriters bring valuable intuition and expertise, but also inconsistency. Decisions may vary based on experience level, risk appetite, or cognitive bias. Autonomous agents, in contrast, apply uniform

criteria and continuously optimize their models based on data-driven feedback loops, ensuring a high degree of consistency across evaluations.

3. Responsiveness to Real-Time Data: Unlike traditional systems, which rely on periodic updates or static reports, autonomous agents are designed to ingest and act on live data streams. This means risk models can shift immediately in response to indicators like a ransomware campaign targeting a specific sector, or a sudden surge in phishing activity against a cloud service provider.
4. Adaptive Risk Pricing: Reinforcement learning allows agents to not only evaluate risk but also dynamically adjust pricing strategies. For example, an agent might increase premiums for a client who delays patching critical vulnerabilities or offer discounts to those adopting advanced threat detection systems. This adaptive pricing can incentivize better security behavior and align coverage with real-world risk exposure.
5. Operational Efficiency: By automating repetitive or data-intensive tasks—such as scanning security configurations, validating questionnaire responses, or cross-referencing threat intelligence, autonomous agents' free human underwriters to focus on strategic oversight, complex accounts, and portfolio management.

In short, autonomy brings more than just automation, it introduces a fundamentally new operating model for cyber insurance, one built around continuous learning, situational awareness, and strategic foresight. As cyber threats grow more volatile and insurance markets more competitive, the ability to make accurate, fast, and scalable underwriting decisions is not just a competitive advantage, it's a survival requirement.

Reinforcement Learning in Cyber Underwriting

Reinforcement Learning is a subset of machine learning where an agent learns to make decisions by interacting with its environment. Unlike supervised learning, where models learn from labeled data, or unsupervised learning, which focuses on pattern discovery, RL is grounded in the concept of trial and error. An RL agent takes actions in an environment, receives feedback in the form of rewards or penalties, and adjusts its strategy to maximize cumulative reward over time (Morales & Escalant, 2022).

At its core, RL mimics how humans and animals learn: by exploring different paths, assessing outcomes, and gradually shaping behavior through feedback. It's particularly powerful in situations where (Neftci, 2019):

- The environment is complex or uncertain
- Decisions need to be made sequentially

- And outcomes may be delayed or non-linear

This makes RL especially well-suited to the field of cyber underwriting. Underwriting decisions are rarely one-off calculations, they're part of a larger system where the impact of today's pricing or coverage choice may not be evident until a claim is filed months later, or until systemic risks emerge from patterns in a portfolio (Redman, 2014).

In the context of cyber underwriting, RL agents can operate in environments where they continuously learn from underwriting outcomes, client behaviors, security changes, and evolving cyber threats. As data accumulates, these agents refine their decision-making policies, becoming more adept at identifying high-risk clients, pricing premiums accurately, and adapting to new forms of cyber exposure.

USE CASES OF RL IN RISK MODELING AND BEHAVIOR ADAPTATION

RL's value in cyber underwriting emerges most clearly when it is applied to dynamic, feedback-rich environments, which cyber risk evaluation certainly is.

1. Adaptive Risk Scoring: Traditional risk scoring models often rely on fixed metrics or human judgment. An RL agent, however, can learn to adjust risk scores over time as it observes correlations between certain digital behaviors (e.g., patching frequency, use of outdated software, third-party integrations) and eventual incident outcomes. This allows for scoring models that evolve with the threat landscape, rather than becoming stale or outdated (Beckley, 2025).
2. Pricing Optimization: RL can be used to optimize premium pricing strategies by simulating the long-term impact of pricing decisions across a portfolio. For instance, an RL agent might learn that offering lower premiums to clients with strong proactive security controls results in fewer claims, while penalizing clients who delay vulnerability remediation improves risk-adjusted profitability (Srinivasagopalan, 2024).
3. Portfolio Balancing: Insurers must maintain a healthy mix of low, medium, and high-risk clients to prevent concentration risk. RL agents can learn to recommend underwriting decisions that balance individual client profitability with the broader objective of portfolio diversification, adjusting their behavior as new data comes in (Correia, 2023).
4. Behavioral Incentivization: An advanced use of RL involves modeling how clients respond to different incentives. For example, an RL agent might learn that offering reduced premiums to clients who install endpoint detection systems

leads to a measurable reduction in breach probability. Over time, the agent refines these "carrots" to subtly shape client behavior, aligning it with both security and financial objectives (Sivamayil et al., 2023).

Reward Functions Aligned with Insurance Objectives

The effectiveness of an RL agent hinges on the quality of its reward function, the signal that tells the agent whether a particular action led to a desirable outcome. In cyber underwriting, designing a reward function involves balancing multiple, often competing goals. It's not just about reducing claim frequency, but also ensuring profitable pricing, encouraging better cybersecurity behavior, and managing aggregate risk across the portfolio (Sarin et al., 2024).

Examples of tailored reward signals in cyber underwriting might include:

- Claim-Free Periods: Rewarding agents for underwriting decisions that result in fewer or smaller claims over time.
- Profitability Margins: Reinforcing actions that improve loss ratios and maximize premium-to-payout efficiency.
- Security Improvements: Incentivizing the selection of clients whose risk profiles improve after onboarding due to security investments or training.
- Client Retention: Balancing strict risk management with pricing strategies that avoid churn among low-risk clients.

A well-calibrated reward function enables the agent to learn subtle trade-offs, such as when it's better to accept a moderately risky client at a high premium versus rejecting them outright. It also helps avoid short-sighted strategies, such as focusing only on immediate profitability at the cost of long-term risk exposure (Cornell & Damodaran, 2020).

Ultimately, reinforcement learning equips cyber insurers with agents that don't just automate tasks, they learn from experience, adapt intelligently, and make underwriting decisions that are both data-driven and strategically aligned with organizational goals.

MULTI-AGENT SYSTEMS (MAS) FOR COLLABORATIVE INTELLIGENCE

As cyber risks become more intricate and interconnected, the limitations of single-agent decision-making become increasingly apparent. This is where multi-agent systems (MAS) step in, offering a scalable, intelligent, and collaborative approach to solving complex problems like cyber underwriting. In a MAS, multiple autonomous agents operate within a shared environment, each with specific tasks, knowledge, and goals. These agents can collaborate, compete, or operate in parallel, contributing to a more holistic and responsive underwriting system (Bi, 2023).

In cyber underwriting, a MAS architecture might include different types of agents working together across the lifecycle of risk analysis (Kanavas, 2023):

- Data Collection Agents mine internal systems and external feeds for relevant cyber intelligence (e.g., new vulnerabilities, breach reports, threat actor behavior).
- Risk Assessment Agents evaluate a client's digital footprint and security practices to produce a contextualized risk score.
- Pricing Agents model loss potential and recommend premiums based on predicted exposure and portfolio balancing goals.
- Compliance Agents monitor regulatory requirements, ensuring policy terms are aligned with local and international standards.
- Monitoring Agents continuously scan the client's environment post-onboarding, flagging behavior or configuration changes that may impact underwriting assumptions.

Rather than relying on a monolithic AI model, MAS allows insurers to build modular, specialized intelligence that reflects the inherently distributed nature of cyber risk itself. This architecture mirrors the real-world dynamics of cyber ecosystems, where different domains (technical, legal, financial) must be evaluated in tandem, often in real-time.

Agent Communication, Negotiation, and Coordination

The true power of a multi-agent system lies not just in the capabilities of individual agents, but in how they communicate, negotiate, and coordinate to achieve shared objectives. In underwriting, this means agents must exchange information about risk models, resolve potential conflicts in assessments, and align decisions to serve the insurer's broader strategic interests (Gheysari & Tehrani, 2022).

For instance, if a Risk Assessment Agent flags a new client as borderline high-risk due to outdated software, a Pricing Agent may propose a premium increase. However, a Portfolio Management Agent might intervene, noting that the insurer already has heavy exposure in that sector, suggesting a more conservative approach. These kinds of negotiations, done automatically and rapidly, help MAS deliver nuanced, balanced underwriting decisions that reflect complex trade-offs (Hadijah, A. S., & Karmila, 2024).

Agent communication in MAS can take various forms, including:

- Direct Messaging: Where agents exchange information through defined protocols (e.g., contract net protocols or publish/subscribe systems).
- Shared Knowledge Bases: Where agents contribute to and draw from a common repository of data or decisions.
- Blackboard Systems: Where agents post observations and wait for others to respond or take action.

Coordination strategies depend on the system's objectives. Some MAS setups prioritize cooperation (maximizing collective intelligence), while others use competitive dynamics (e.g., multiple Pricing Agents proposing optimal bids) to discover better solutions.

These interactions aren't just technical abstractions, they're critical to achieving underwriting decisions that are fast, fair, and risk-informed. Effective MAS communication reduces redundancy, resolves ambiguity, and ensures that each underwriting outcome reflects the best available data and analysis.

Decentralized vs. Centralized MAS in Underwriting

A key design decision in building MAS for cyber underwriting lies in choosing between centralized and decentralized architectures. In centralized MAS, a supervisory agent or system coordinates the actions of all other agents. This can make coordination easier, ensure global consistency, and facilitate portfolio-level oversight. For example, a central Portfolio Agent might oversee all underwriting decisions to avoid sector concentration or risk correlation across policies. However, centralization can become a bottleneck—especially when speed and scalability are critical. It also creates a single point of failure, which is undesirable in security-sensitive environments (Singireddy et al., 2024).

In contrast, decentralized MAS architectures allow agents to operate more autonomously, making local decisions based on local information and peer-to-peer communication. This approach is more scalable and resilient, especially when dealing with high-frequency underwriting tasks across diverse markets or geographies. Decentralized systems also allow for more dynamic adaptation, agents can evolve independently, learn from their specific contexts, and develop specialized expertise without waiting for top-down updates. That said, decentralization requires sophisticated trust, coordination, and conflict-resolution mechanisms. In underwriting, this might include ensuring that local pricing agents don't violate global portfolio constraints or that risk assessments maintain consistency across different markets (Dorri, Kanhere & Jurdak, 2018).

In practice, many advanced MAS architectures adopt a hybrid approach, using decentralized agents for tactical decision-making while reserving centralized oversight for strategic functions like compliance, profitability tracking, or systemic risk management.

By leveraging MAS, cyber underwriting systems gain more than just automation, they gain a form of collective intelligence. It's an architecture designed for a world where risk is fluid, data is abundant, and decision-making must be both distributed and intelligent. When implemented well, MAS transforms cyber underwriting from a linear workflow into a living ecosystem, responsive, adaptive, and aligned with the pace of digital change.

SYSTEM ARCHITECTURE FOR AUTONOMOUS CYBER UNDERWRITING

The integration of reinforcement learning and MAS in cyber underwriting isn't just a conceptual leap, it's a practical engineering challenge. It involves weaving together AI models, communication protocols, data infrastructures, and domain knowledge into a unified ecosystem that can deliver real-time, reliable, and explainable underwriting decisions (Bibri., Huang & Krogstie, 2024). Figure 1 illustrates the overall architecture of an autonomous underwriting system, highlighting the flow of data from external sources into specialized agents and their interaction with external insurance functions.

Figure 1. Architecture of an autonomous cyber underwriting system integrating multi-agent and RL components.

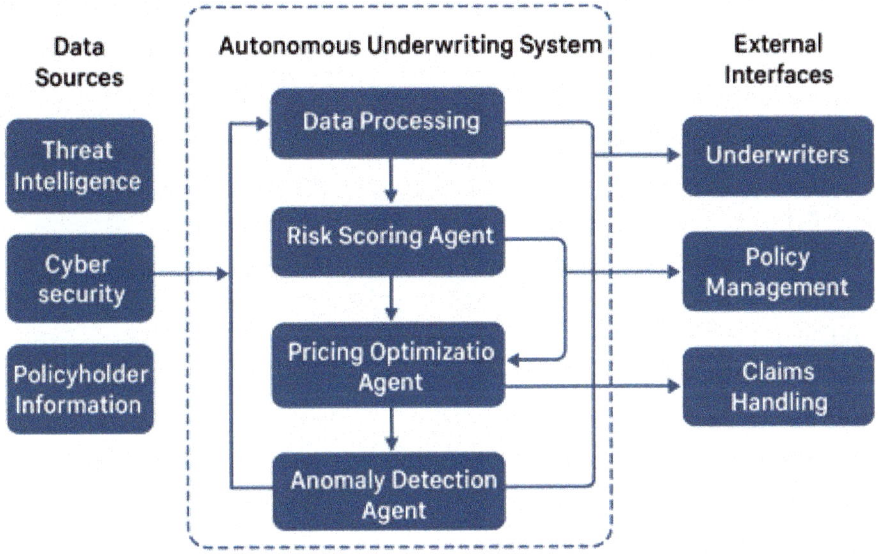

At the heart of such systems lies a modular architecture where different agents, each potentially powered by RL, handle discrete components of the underwriting process. For example (Apergis, 2024):

- A Risk Assessment Agent, trained via RL, evaluates dynamic threat indicators and adapts its scoring criteria based on historical claims and evolving threat vectors.
- A Pricing Agent optimizes premiums through simulated portfolio performance, balancing risk and revenue using long-term reward strategies.
- A Compliance Agent ensures underwriting proposals align with regulations, adapting to new laws or standards across jurisdictions.

These agents operate within a multi-agent framework, communicating through structured protocols and decision layers. RL models are embedded within agents where learning from experience is crucial, such as optimizing decisions based on delayed feedback or exploring trade-offs between conflicting underwriting goals.

To deploy such systems in the real world, integration with existing insurance platforms, policy management systems, claims databases, customer interfaces, is essential. APIs, microservices, and modular containerization (e.g., with Kubernetes or

Docker) support interoperability and continuous deployment, making the system not only intelligent but also operationally viable.

Data Pipelines, Feedback Loops, and Human Oversight

Autonomous cyber underwriting systems depend heavily on real-time, high-quality data. Designing robust data pipelines is critical to ensure agents have the information they need to learn, reason, and act. These pipelines typically ingest data from (Dickerson & Worthen, 2024):

- Internal systems (historical claims, policy performance, client portfolios)
- External feeds (threat intelligence, vulnerability databases, regulatory updates)
- Client-specific telemetry (endpoint logs, network activity, security assessments)

Once ingested, this data is pre-processed, labeled, and stored in feature-rich formats accessible to both human analysts and autonomous agents. Key to this pipeline is a feedback loop mechanism: outcomes of underwriting decisions (e.g., claims filed, breaches avoided, client retention) are cycled back into the system to update models and retrain RL agents (Goyal et al., 2022).

This closed-loop learning allows the underwriting system to continuously improve, adjusting not only its predictions but also its strategic behavior in light of long-term results. Despite automation, human oversight remains essential. Human experts are positioned as supervisors, interpreters, and auditors. Their responsibilities include:

- Reviewing decisions in high-risk or novel scenarios
- Intervening when agent outputs fall outside predefined thresholds
- Validating model assumptions and tuning reward structures
- Ensuring transparency and accountability for regulatory purposes

This human-in-the-loop design ensures that autonomy doesn't come at the cost of control, ethics, or explainability, especially important in regulated environments like insurance. Figure 2 depicts the data pipeline architecture that supports autonomous underwriting agents, highlighting the sequential flow from data collection to feedback-driven model refinement.

Figure 2. Data pipeline for autonomous cyber underwriting agents.

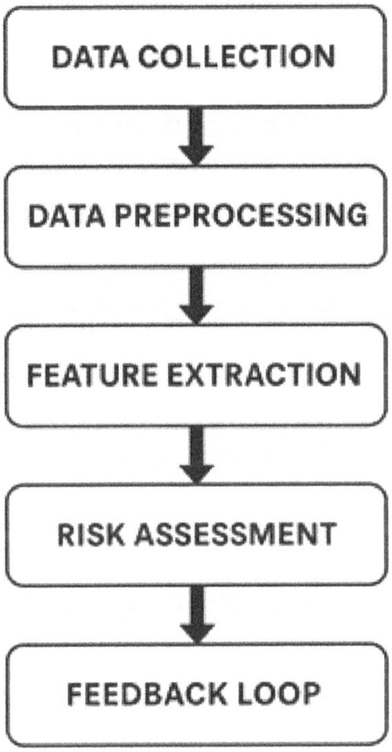

Scalability, Security, and Compliance Considerations

For autonomous cyber underwriting to succeed at scale, its architecture must be designed with scalability, security, and compliance in mind. *Scalability* requires distributed processing capabilities. As the number of clients grows, so too does the volume of data, the complexity of models, and the frequency of decisions. Systems must support horizontal scaling, both in data handling (e.g., through distributed databases or data lakes) and in agent execution (e.g., through container orchestration and parallel computing environments) (Hu et al., 2014).

Security is especially critical given the sensitive nature of cyber insurance data. The system must implement:

- End-to-end encryption for data in transit and at rest
- Role-based access controls and audit logs
- Isolation of learning environments to prevent adversarial manipulation
- Defensive mechanisms against model poisoning or inference attacks

Moreover, agents themselves must be secure, resilient to tampering and capable of functioning reliably even under degraded conditions or partial data loss.

Compliance is non-negotiable. The system must adhere to data protection laws (e.g., GDPR, CCPA), insurance regulations, and AI governance principles. This includes maintaining explainability for automated decisions, enabling user opt-outs, and ensuring fairness and non-discrimination in model outcomes. To support compliance, many architectures embed *explainable AI (XAI)* modules, which track how underwriting decisions were made and provide human-readable justifications. Auditability is built into each layer, from data logging to decision recording, ensuring traceability for both internal governance and external regulators.

Ethical, Legal, and Regulatory Challenges in Autonomous Underwriting

While autonomous cyber underwriting agents offer significant potential for improving speed, accuracy, and scalability, their deployment introduces critical ethical, legal, and regulatory considerations. As AI systems increasingly influence high-stakes decisions such as risk evaluation, coverage eligibility, and premium pricing, the question of accountability and fairness becomes paramount. One of the foremost challenges lies in the explainability of decisions made by reinforcement learning agents. These models are often considered "black boxes," making it difficult for insurers to justify outcomes to customers, regulators, or even internal auditors. This opacity can lead to distrust, particularly when coverage is denied or premiums are unusually high. Embedding explainable AI (XAI) mechanisms within the underwriting pipeline can help by generating human-readable justifications that align with regulatory expectations such as those stipulated under the GDPR or the upcoming EU AI Act.

Additionally, bias and discrimination in data-driven models pose legal risks. Historical claims data may contain implicit biases based on industry, region, or company size. If not properly mitigated, AI agents could perpetuate or even exacerbate these inequities, unintentionally disadvantaging certain clients. Fairness-aware machine learning techniques and bias audits are thus necessary to ensure equitable underwriting practices.

From a regulatory standpoint, compliance with data protection laws is mandatory. Underwriting agents must operate under stringent data governance frameworks, ensuring secure data handling, consent management, and auditability. Moreover, autonomous systems must include human-in-the-loop mechanisms to allow expert oversight—particularly in novel or high-risk cases—maintaining a level of human accountability that regulators often demand.

Finally, there are open questions around legal liability. If an autonomous agent makes a flawed decision leading to financial loss, who is responsible: the developer, the insurer, or the AI system itself? These questions are actively being debated in legal and policy circles, and insurers should anticipate regulatory frameworks that define specific obligations for AI-powered systems. Addressing these challenges is essential not only for regulatory compliance but also for building public trust in autonomous underwriting solutions. Ethical design, legal foresight, and transparent operations must be treated as foundational components—not afterthoughts—of next-generation cyber insurance platforms.

CONCLUSION

The cyber insurance landscape is evolving rapidly, pushed forward by the increasing scale, sophistication, and unpredictability of digital threats. Traditional underwriting models, grounded in static assessments and historical data, are no longer equipped to keep pace with this dynamic environment. Insurers today must go beyond manual reviews and checkbox questionnaires, they need systems that can think, adapt, and learn as fast as the risks themselves change.

Autonomous cyber underwriting agents represent a significant leap forward. By combining reinforcement learning with the collaborative power of multi-agent systems, insurers can create intelligent, distributed ecosystems capable of real-time risk evaluation, adaptive pricing, and proactive portfolio management. These agents do more than automate, they actively interpret complex signals, negotiate trade-offs, and optimize decisions based on long-term strategic goals.

As this chapter has explored, the foundation of such systems lies in their architecture: data pipelines that fuel continuous learning, feedback loops that close the gap between decision and outcome, and robust mechanisms for oversight, transparency, and compliance. While challenges remain, particularly around explainability, security, and regulatory alignment, the direction is clear. Cyber underwriting is on the brink of a transformation, and AI-driven autonomy is at the heart of it.

But this transformation is not about replacing human underwriters—it's about augmenting them. The future will be defined by hybrid intelligence, where human expertise and machine precision work hand in hand. Underwriters will shift from manual assessors to strategic supervisors, guiding autonomous systems, interpreting edge cases, and shaping the ethical frameworks within which machines operate.

Ultimately, this is more than a technological upgrade, it's a reimagining of how we understand, evaluate, and manage digital risk. And in a world where cyber threats grow more pervasive by the day, this shift isn't just necessary, it's inevitable.

REFERENCES

Adriko, R., & Nurse, J. R. (2024). Cybersecurity, cyber insurance and small-to-medium-sized enterprises: A systematic Review. *Information and Computer Security*, *32*(5), 691–710. DOI: 10.1108/ICS-01-2024-0025

Agboola, D. (2025). The Evolving Landscape of Data Privacy: How Regulations are Shaping the Digital World. *Available at SSRN* 5187183. DOI: 10.2139/ssrn.5187183

Alquwayzani, A., Aldossri, R., & Frikha, M. (2024). Prominent Security Vulnerabilities in Cloud Computing. *International Journal of Advanced Computer Science and Applications*, *15*(2). Advance online publication. DOI: 10.14569/IJACSA.2024.0150281

Apergis, A. (2024). The role of cognitive assistants in medical insurance underwriting.

Arbore, A. (2025). *Market strategies in a hyper-connected world*. EGEA spa.

Beckley, J. (2025). Advanced risk assessment techniques: Merging data-driven analytics with expert insights to navigate uncertain decision-making processes. *Int J Res Publ Rev*, *6*(3), 1454–1471. DOI: 10.55248/gengpi.6.0325.1148

Bergese, F. (2021). *Bond Risk Assessment from Fundamental Analysis to Portfolio Optimization* (Doctoral dissertation, Politecnico di Torino).

Beuchelt, G. (2025). Information Technology Security Management. In *Computer and Information Security Handbook* (pp. 475–508). Morgan Kaufmann. DOI: 10.1016/B978-0-443-13223-0.00027-8

Bi, M. (2023). *Distributed decision-making in disrupted industrial environments using a multi-agent framework* (Doctoral dissertation).

Bibri, S. E., Huang, J., & Krogstie, J. (2024). Artificial intelligence of things for synergizing smarter eco-city brain, metabolism, and platform: Pioneering data-driven environmental governance. *Sustainable Cities and Society*, *108*, 105516. DOI: 10.1016/j.scs.2024.105516

Bompos, K. (2020). *Development time of Zero-Day cyber exploits in support of offensive cyber operations* (Doctoral dissertation, Monterey, CA; Naval Postgraduate School).

Chowdhary, M. A. M. (2025). *Financial Network Infrastructure: Scalability*. Security and Optimization.

Cornell, B., & Damodaran, A. (2020). *Valuing ESG: Doing good or sounding good?* NYU Stern School of Business.

Correia, H. C. (2023). *Investment policy statement for individual investors: medium-low risk aversion client multi-asset balanced portfolio* (Master's thesis, Universidade de Lisboa (Portugal)).

Dambra, S., Bilge, L., & Balzarotti, D. (2020, May). SoK: Cyber insurance–technical challenges and a system security roadmap. In *2020 IEEE Symposium on Security and Privacy (SP)* (pp. 1367-1383). IEEE. DOI: 10.1109/SP40000.2020.00019

Dickerson, P., & Worthen, J. (2024, May). Optimizing Pipeline Systems for Greater Precision, Efficiency & Safety Using Emerging Technologies. In *PSIG Annual Meeting* (pp. PSIG-2426). PSIG.

Dorri, A., Kanhere, S. S., & Jurdak, R. (2018). Multi-agent systems: A survey. *IEEE Access : Practical Innovations, Open Solutions*, *6*, 28573–28593. DOI: 10.1109/ACCESS.2018.2831228

Falco, G. J., & Rosenbach, E. (2022). *Confronting cyber risk: An embedded endurance strategy for cybersecurity*. Oxford University Press. DOI: 10.1093/oso/9780197526545.001.0001

Gheysari, M., & Tehrani, M. S. S. (2022). The Role of Multi-Agent Systems in IoT. In *Multi Agent Systems: Technologies and Applications towards Human-Centered* (pp. 87–114). Springer Nature Singapore. DOI: 10.1007/978-981-19-0493-6_5

Goyal, A., Friesen, A., Banino, A., Weber, T., Ke, N. R., Badia, A. P., & Guez, A.. "Retrieval-augmented reinforcement learning." In *International Conference on Machine Learning*, pp. 7740-7765. PMLR, 2022.

Hadijah, A. S., & Karmila, K. (2024). Evaluating the Role, Costs, and Benefits of Insurance and Hedging in Financing Decisions. *Advances in Economics & Financial Studies*, *2*(2), 88–101. DOI: 10.60079/aefs.v2i2.313

Hu, H., Wen, Y., Chua, T. S., & Li, X. (2014). Toward scalable systems for big data analytics: A technology tutorial. *IEEE Access : Practical Innovations, Open Solutions*, *2*, 652–687. DOI: 10.1109/ACCESS.2014.2332453

Hubbard, D. W. (2020). *The failure of risk management: Why it's broken and how to fix it*. John Wiley & Sons. DOI: 10.1002/9781119521914

Jansen, M., Nguyen, H. Q., & Shams, A. (2025). Rise of the machines: The impact of automated underwriting. *Management Science*, *71*(2), 955–975. DOI: 10.1287/mnsc.2024.4986

Kanavas, A. (2023). *Cyberinsurance as a risk management tool* (Master's thesis, Πανεπιστήμιο Πειραιώς).

Kolhar, A. (2025). Future Trends and Innovation in Machine Intelligence for Cyber Risk Management. In *Machine Intelligence Applications in Cyber-Risk Management* (pp. 415–438). IGI Global Scientific Publishing.

Landoll, D. (2021). *The security risk assessment handbook: A complete guide for performing security risk assessments*. CRC press. DOI: 10.1201/9781003090441

Maldonado, D., Cruz, E., Torres, J. A., Cruz, P. J., & Benitez, S. D. P. G. (2024). Multi-agent Systems: A survey about its components, framework and workflow. *IEEE Access : Practical Innovations, Open Solutions, 12*, 80950–80975. DOI: 10.1109/ACCESS.2024.3409051

Morales, E. F., & Escalante, H. J. (2022). A brief introduction to supervised, unsupervised, and reinforcement learning. In *Biosignal processing and classification using computational learning and intelligence* (pp. 111–129). Academic Press. DOI: 10.1016/B978-0-12-820125-1.00017-8

Neftci, E. O., & Averbeck, B. B. (2019). Reinforcement learning in artificial and biological systems. *Nature Machine Intelligence, 1*(3), 133–143. DOI: 10.1038/s42256-019-0025-4

Rah, A. (2023). *Device Management in the Security of "Bring Your Own Device" (BYOD) for the Post-pandemic, Remote Workplace*. University of Fairfax.

Rao, B., Harrison, A. J., & Mulloth, B. (2020). Defense technological innovation: Issues and challenges in an era of converging technologies.

Redman, J. C. A. (2014). *The diwaniyya: guestroom sociability and bureaucratic brokerage in Kuwait*. The University of Utah.

Sarin, S., Singh, S. K., Kumar, S., Goyal, S., Gupta, B. B., Alhalabi, W., & Arya, V. (2024). Unleashing the Power of Multi-Agent Reinforcement Learning for Algorithmic Trading in the Digital Financial Frontier and Enterprise Information Systems. *Computers, Materials & Continua, 80*(2), 3123–3138. DOI: 10.32604/cmc.2024.051599

Singireddy, S., Adusupalli, B., Pamisetty, A., Mashetty, S., & Kaulwar, P. K. (2024). Redefining Financial Risk Strategies: The Integration of Smart Automation, Secure Access Systems, and Predictive Intelligence in Insurance, Lending, and Asset Management. *Journal of Artificial Intelligence and Big Data Disciplines, 1*(1), 109–124. DOI: 10.70179/k86dcv60

Singireddy, S., Adusupalli, B., Pamisetty, A., Mashetty, S., & Kaulwar, P. K. (2024). Redefining Financial Risk Strategies: The Integration of Smart Automation, Secure Access Systems, and Predictive Intelligence in Insurance, Lending, and Asset Management. *Journal of Artificial Intelligence and Big Data Disciplines*, *1*(1), 109–124. DOI: 10.70179/k86dcv60

Sivamayil, K., Rajasekar, E., Aljafari, B., Nikolovski, S., Vairavasundaram, S., & Vairavasundaram, I. (2023). A systematic study on reinforcement learning based applications. *Energies*, *16*(3), 1512. DOI: 10.3390/en16031512

Srinivasagopalan, L. N. (2024). Reinforcement Learning For Optimizing Healthcare Insurance Premium Pricing.

Stoddart, K. (2022). Non and sub-state actors: cybercrime, terrorism, and hackers. In *Cyberwarfare: threats to critical infrastructure* (pp. 351–399). Springer International Publishing. DOI: 10.1007/978-3-030-97299-8_6

Sun, M. M. (2024). Comprehensive statistical modeling of cyber risks and analysis of data breaches with applications in cyber insurance.

Tsohou, A., Diamantopoulou, V., Gritzalis, S., & Lambrinoudakis, C. (2023). Cyber insurance: State of the art, trends and future directions. *International Journal of Information Security*, *22*(3), 737–748. DOI: 10.1007/s10207-023-00660-8 PMID: 36684688

Chapter 3
Quantum-Aware Risk Modeling Preparing Cyber Insurance for the Post-Quantum Era

Salam Al E'mari
https://orcid.org/0000-0002-2134-4158
University of Petra, Jordan

Yousef Sanjalawe
https://orcid.org/0000-0002-4442-1865
University of Jordan, Jordan

Fadi Fataftah
https://orcid.org/0000-0002-3299-0972
University Canada West, Canada

ABSTRACT

Quantum computing poses significant risks to cybersecurity by threatening the integrity of widely used cryptographic systems like RSA, ECC, and DH. This chapter examines the urgency of rethinking traditional cyber insurance risk models in response to these quantum-enabled threats. It introduces a quantum-aware risk modeling approach that incorporates factors such as PQC migration readiness and dynamic premium adjustments. The chapter also explores how insurers can embed quantum resilience into policies through cryptographic agility requirements and third-party risk assessments. Regulatory initiatives, particularly NIST's PQC standardization, are discussed for their role in guiding industry preparedness. Simulated breach scenarios highlight potential challenges in underwriting and claim resolution in

DOI: 10.4018/979-8-3373-5545-0.ch003

a post-quantum era. This chapter offers a forward-looking roadmap for building a resilient, adaptive cyber insurance ecosystem prepared for the quantum future.

1. INTRODUCTION

Over the past decade, quantum computing has moved from theoretical possibility to an emerging technological reality. Once confined to the imaginations of physicists and science fiction authors, quantum systems are now being built by major tech companies, research institutions, and governments around the world. At the heart of this transformation is the promise of solving certain computational problems far beyond the capability of classical computers. Tasks such as factoring large integers, simulating quantum phenomena, and optimizing complex systems may soon be executed in minutes, what would have taken conventional machines millennia (Ofoegbu & LAGUO, 2023).

This quantum leap, however, brings not only opportunities but profound risks. One of the most pressing concerns is the vulnerability of modern cryptographic systems. Much of today's digital infrastructure, including online banking, secure communications, and digital signatures, relies on cryptographic algorithms like RSA, ECC, and DH, which are theoretically susceptible to quantum algorithms such as Shor's. Once a sufficiently powerful quantum computer becomes available, these encryption methods could be rendered obsolete, exposing data to retrospective decryption and widespread breaches. In essence, the arrival of quantum computing may not just introduce new threats but unravel decades of cybersecurity foundations (Dalal et al., 2024).

In response to the escalating frequency and complexity of cyberattacks, cyber insurance has emerged as a crucial instrument in risk management. Organizations, from small businesses to global enterprises, rely on cyber insurance policies to mitigate financial losses stemming from data breaches, ransomware attacks, business interruptions, and legal liabilities. Over time, insurers have developed increasingly sophisticated models to assess risk, calculate premiums, and structure coverage terms based on a mix of historical data, threat intelligence, and sector-specific risk profiles (Kanavas, 2023).

Yet, the cyber insurance industry faces a difficult truth: it is largely reactive by design. Policies are constructed on the assumption that risk can be understood and priced through past behavior. But quantum computing represents a paradigm shift. It introduces a class of risks that are not only novel but currently unquantifiable. Unlike conventional cyber threats, the quantum threat does not evolve gradually, it may arrive abruptly, triggered by a technological breakthrough. Worse still, malicious actors may already be harvesting encrypted data today in anticipation of future quantum decryption capabilities, a threat model commonly referred to as "harvest now, decrypt later," (Lindsay, 2020).

These quantum-specific risks pose significant challenges for existing cyber insurance frameworks. How does one underwrite a risk that cannot yet be observed? How can insurers verify a client's preparedness against quantum threats when the benchmarks for readiness are still being defined? The tools and assumptions used to model cyber risk in the classical computing era must now be critically reassessed (Aslam, 2025).

This chapter sets out to explore how the cyber insurance sector can adapt to the quantum era, with a focus on rethinking risk modeling in light of emerging quantum threats. It seeks to provide a conceptual and practical framework for integrating quantum-awareness into the underwriting process, policy development, and long-term strategic planning of insurers. The chapter begins by mapping the quantum threat landscape, offering a clear explanation of how quantum computing undermines current cryptographic standards and what timelines are projected for such developments. It then turns to an overview of existing cyber insurance practices, identifying areas of fragility and potential misalignment with quantum-era risks.

Next, we introduce a proposed risk modeling framework that incorporates quantum-specific factors, such as cryptographic agility, migration to post-quantum standards, and exposure to long-term data compromise. We also examine the regulatory and compliance landscape, highlighting how insurers can align their practices with evolving standards and government initiatives. To ground these discussions in real-world implications, the chapter includes case studies and scenario analyses that simulate the impact of a quantum breakthrough on insured organizations. Finally, we reflect on the research and policy gaps that must be addressed to build a resilient cyber insurance ecosystem capable of withstanding the transformative impact of quantum computing.

Through this exploration, we aim to equip readers with the tools and insights necessary to navigate the uncertain, but rapidly approaching, post-quantum future.

2. THE QUANTUM THREAT LANDSCAPE

As organizations race to strengthen their digital defenses, one looming challenge has begun to reshape the cybersecurity conversation: the impending obsolescence of widely-used encryption methods. Today's public-key cryptographic systems, such as RSA, Elliptic Curve Cryptography (ECC), and Diffie–Hellman (DH), are foundational to everything from secure web browsing to digital signatures and blockchain technologies. These algorithms are built on mathematical problems that are currently hard to solve with classical computers. However, in the quantum era, this foundation is no longer secure (Shreedevi et al., 2024).

The field of Post-Quantum Cryptography (PQC) has emerged as a proactive response to this looming threat. PQC refers to cryptographic algorithms that are believed to be secure against both classical and quantum attacks. Yet designing, analyzing, and standardizing these algorithms is an immense challenge. Unlike traditional cryptographic methods, PQC often requires more computational resources, larger key sizes, and different assumptions about threat models. Moreover, transitioning from current cryptographic infrastructure to quantum-resistant alternatives is not as simple as swapping out code. It requires system-wide migrations, updates to protocols, retraining of personnel, and careful consideration of backward compatibility, all while maintaining operational integrity (Geremew, Amare, & Mohammad, 2024).

What complicates matters further is the uncertainty surrounding the quantum threat itself. While post-quantum cryptographic standards are being developed, led notably by the U.S. National Institute of Standards and Technology (NIST), their adoption and global implementation are still in early stages. Many organizations are unsure when or how to begin transitioning, and insurers, in turn, are left guessing at how to evaluate a company's quantum readiness. The gap between awareness and action poses a serious risk as adversaries prepare to exploit vulnerabilities that most systems are not yet equipped to address (Alagic et al., 2022).

Quantum Algorithms and Vulnerabilities (e.g., Shor's and Grover's)

To understand why current encryption methods are at risk, one must grasp the capabilities of certain quantum algorithms. The most well-known of these is Shor's algorithm, developed in the mid-1990s. It allows a sufficiently powerful quantum computer to efficiently factor large integers, a task that underpins the security of RSA, and compute discrete logarithms, which undermines ECC and DH. With Shor's algorithm, quantum computers could theoretically decrypt data encrypted today, once they reach adequate scale (Tom et al., 2023).

While practical quantum computers capable of running Shor's algorithm on real-world cryptographic keys do not yet exist, the theoretical implications are so profound that governments and industries are already reacting. In the context of cyber insurance, Shor's algorithm represents a potential systemic risk: a single breakthrough could simultaneously invalidate the confidentiality guarantees of millions of systems (Singh & Sakk, 2024).

Another important algorithm is Grover's algorithm, which provides a quadratic speedup for brute-force search problems. In cryptographic terms, this means that symmetric key algorithms, such as AES, would see their effective key strength halved.

While AES-256 would still be secure under Grover's algorithm, AES-128 would become significantly more vulnerable. The implication is that symmetric encryption remains relatively safe, if appropriately upgraded, but must still be evaluated and managed with the quantum threat in mind (Gorine & Suhaib, 2024).

Together, these algorithms illustrate the asymmetric threat posed by quantum computing: a well-prepared adversary needs only one breakthrough, while defenders must anticipate, prepare for, and mitigate a broad spectrum of quantum-driven risks.

Timeline and Readiness for Quantum Advancements

The question on everyone's mind is: *When will quantum computers pose a real, operational threat to cybersecurity?* The answer remains uncertain, but the timelines are tightening. Estimates vary, with some experts suggesting we could see cryptographically relevant quantum computers within 10 to 20 years, while others argue that the breakthroughs could come sooner.

Governments are taking the risk seriously. The U.S. National Security Agency (NSA) has already issued guidance to migrate to quantum-resistant algorithms by the end of the decade. NIST, meanwhile, is finalizing its first suite of standardized PQC algorithms, and industry leaders are beginning to test hybrid solutions that incorporate both classical and quantum-resistant schemes. Despite this progress, many organizations remain in a reactive mode, waiting for clear mandates or confirmed threats before taking decisive action (Holland, 2024).

This delay could prove costly. The threat is not just future decryption but "harvest now, decrypt later" attacks, in which encrypted data is stolen today with the expectation that it can be broken once quantum capabilities mature. For insurers, this introduces a unique challenge: policies must account for data that may appear secure at the time of underwriting but could be compromised years later. As illustrated in Figure 1, the projected timeline of quantum computing threat maturity highlights critical milestones—from qubit thresholds that jeopardize classical encryption to regulatory and industry responses—underscoring the urgency for timely cryptographic readiness and migration strategies.

Figure 1. Projected timeline of quantum computing threat maturity and cryptographic readiness

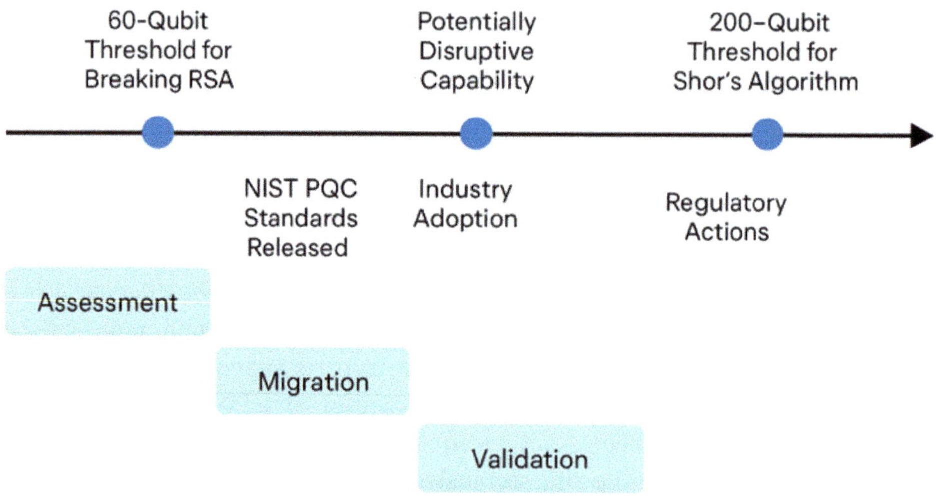

In short, the quantum threat landscape is not hypothetical—it is unfolding. While the exact timeline remains fluid, the risk is tangible enough that insurers, technologists, and policymakers must begin planning now (Marrow, 2025). Quantum-aware risk modeling, which anticipates these technological shifts, will be essential for maintaining trust, resilience, and financial stability in the cybersecurity ecosystem of tomorrow.

3. CYBER INSURANCE IN THE DIGITAL AGE

Cyber insurance has emerged as an essential pillar of risk management in an increasingly digital world. As organizations grow more dependent on digital infrastructure and interconnected services, the threat landscape has expanded accordingly. From data breaches and ransomware attacks to business email compromise and supply chain vulnerabilities, cyber incidents are no longer rare events, they are routine and often costly (Malempati et al., 2023).

At its core, cyber insurance is designed to mitigate the financial impact of such events. Policies typically cover a range of costs, including incident response, legal fees, data recovery, public relations efforts, business interruption losses, and even regulatory fines in certain jurisdictions. For many companies, cyber insurance serves not only as a financial safety net but also as a signal of risk maturity and operational resilience (George, 2025).

The models that support cyber insurance policies are grounded in traditional actuarial principles, but with key differences. Unlike auto or life insurance, where long-standing statistical models and clearly defined parameters exist, cyber risk is dynamic and often poorly understood. The lack of standardized metrics, combined with the evolving nature of cyber threats, makes it difficult to predict loss frequency and severity with high confidence (Insua et al., 2020). Consequently, insurers must rely on a mixture of threat intelligence, incident history, and proprietary risk scoring systems to set premiums and determine coverage.

Risk Assessment in Classical Security Environments

In classical (non-quantum) environments, cyber insurers have developed relatively stable frameworks for evaluating organizational risk. These assessments often begin with evaluating a client's cyber hygiene, that is, the effectiveness of basic cybersecurity practices such as firewalls, endpoint protection, regular patching, employee training, and access control policies. Industry-specific threats, prior incident history, and the complexity of IT infrastructure are also factored in (Segate & Daly, 2024).

Some insurers partner with cybersecurity firms to conduct technical assessments, vulnerability scans, or penetration tests before issuing a policy. Others leverage cyber risk scores provided by third-party platforms, which evaluate publicly visible indicators such as exposed services, expired certificates, or leaked credentials (Keskin et al., 2021).

At the heart of these models lies the assumption that risk can be understood through past behavior and current posture. That is, a company with no recent incidents, strong internal policies, and up-to-date technology is generally considered a lower risk. Additionally, classical models often treat cyber incidents as isolated or organization-specific events. While systemic risks, such as widespread ransomware campaigns, are acknowledged, they are not always priced into premiums comprehensively (Mehrizi et al., 2022).

This model has worked relatively well for the classical era of cyber threats. It allows insurers to differentiate between clients, encourage better security practices, and offer competitive pricing. However, it assumes that the tools used to protect data today will remain effective tomorrow, an assumption that quantum computing directly challenges.

Current Underwriting Practices and Limitations

Despite ongoing refinements, cyber insurance underwriting remains an inexact science. The unpredictable nature of cyberattacks, the absence of long-term historical data, and the interconnectedness of digital ecosystems all conspire to make accurate risk modeling extremely difficult. Insurers are often forced to balance between offering broad coverage that appeals to clients and limiting their own exposure to catastrophic loss (Tsohou et al., 2023).

One of the key limitations of current underwriting practices is the lag between technological change and policy adjustment. As new attack vectors emerge, it can take years before underwriting guidelines evolve to reflect the associated risks. For example, while ransomware is now a major driver of claims, it took several high-profile incidents before insurers recalibrated their pricing and exclusions accordingly (Akkor & Ozyukse, 2020).

Furthermore, many cyber insurance policies do not explicitly address emerging risks such as quantum computing. This omission is not due to a lack of concern but rather a lack of clarity. Underwriters struggle to define how quantum-related risks would materialize, how they could be measured, and whether such risks are already latent in existing exposures (such as encrypted data that could later be decrypted). There is also a systemic risk challenge. If a cryptographically relevant quantum computer were developed, the impact would not be confined to a handful of clients, it could affect vast portions of the digital economy simultaneously. In such a scenario, insurers could face aggregate losses far exceeding what current models anticipate (Canetti et al., 2020).

Ultimately, while cyber insurance has evolved to keep pace with many digital threats, it remains tethered to a risk modeling approach rooted in classical assumptions. As we move closer to the post-quantum era, it is increasingly clear that this model must evolve, rapidly and thoughtfully, to account for the unprecedented risks that lie ahead.

4. IMPLICATIONS OF QUANTUM COMPUTING ON CYBER RISK

The most immediate and profound impact of quantum computing on cybersecurity lies in its ability to break the cryptographic systems that currently secure global digital infrastructure. Public-key cryptography, such as RSA, ECC, and DH, underpins nearly every aspect of secure communication, from online banking and digital certificates to Virtual Private Networks (VPNs) and blockchain protocols. When quantum computing reaches a critical level of maturity, it will render these encryption methods vulnerable, effectively stripping away the core defenses of countless systems overnight (Hammad, Saleh & Alomari, 2024).

This vulnerability isn't confined to individual organizations; it's systemic. Because cryptographic protocols are universally embedded in modern IT architectures, a sufficiently powerful quantum computer could expose massive volumes of sensitive data across sectors and geographies simultaneously. The result would not resemble a typical cyberattack with localized effects, it would be a widespread cryptographic collapse with ripple effects on national security, financial markets, healthcare, energy infrastructure, and beyond (Lehto, 2022).

For cyber insurers, this scenario poses an existential risk. If many insured entities suffer simultaneous losses due to quantum-enabled breaches, claims could easily overwhelm current capital reserves. Unlike traditional cyber threats, where exposure is generally distributed across time and space, the quantum threat is a *one-to-many* risk, potentially impacting millions of systems with a single advancement in computing power. Existing actuarial models, which rely on probabilistic independence between insureds, are not equipped to handle such a systemic shock (Sodiya et al., 2024).

Long-Term Liability and Data Harvesting Risk

One of the most insidious threats introduced by quantum computing is "harvest now, decrypt later" strategies. In this model, adversaries steal encrypted data today, not with the intent to use it immediately, but with the knowledge that it may be decrypted in the future when quantum computers become powerful enough. This practice is especially dangerous when the stolen data has long-term value: government secrets, intellectual property, medical records, or sensitive communications (Kubecka, 2024).

This delayed threat introduces new complexity into both cybersecurity planning and insurance underwriting. How should a risk be valued if the damage will not manifest for a decade or more? How can insurers measure liability for breaches that occurred under "secure" encryption but later lead to exposure through quantum decryption? (Tiwo et al., 2025).

Moreover, this temporal dimension blurs the line between incident occurrence and impact realization, a crucial distinction in most cyber insurance policies. Today's coverage models are designed around the idea of a well-defined breach timeline. However, in the post-quantum context, damages may be discovered years after the initial compromise, potentially creating extended liability trails that span multiple policy periods (Argetsinger, 2024).

This also challenges legal frameworks and regulatory compliance. Organizations may believe they are following best practices today, only to discover years later that their encrypted archives were compromised in a way that affects customer privacy, intellectual property ownership, or compliance with regulations like GDPR or HIPAA (AllahRakha, 2024). The resulting claims may be difficult to attribute or fairly adjudicate, especially in the absence of clear quantum risk clauses in insurance contracts.

Impact on Confidentiality, Integrity, and Availability (CIA Triad)

Quantum computing has the potential to disrupt all three pillars of the CIA triad: Confidentiality, Integrity, and Availability, the foundational goals of any cybersecurity strategy (Sutradhar et al., 2025).

- *Confidentiality* is the most directly threatened. As mentioned, public-key cryptographic systems currently protect data confidentiality across digital channels and storage. If these protections are broken by quantum computers, private communications, sensitive databases, and encrypted archives could all become accessible to unauthorized parties.
- *Integrity* is also at risk, particularly when digital signatures, used to verify software updates, documents, and transactions, are rendered forgeable. If attackers can use quantum techniques to mimic legitimate entities or forge trusted certificates, they could manipulate data and systems with little to no detection. This could lead to fraudulent transactions, tampering with critical infrastructure, or the deployment of malicious updates under the guise of trusted software vendors.
- *Availability*, though less directly tied to quantum attacks, is not immune. As systems are forced to undergo large-scale cryptographic migrations or react to unexpected vulnerabilities, there is a risk of downtime, service disruption, or denial of service. Furthermore, a widespread panic following a credible quantum breakthrough could lead to system overloads, as organizations scramble to resecure their networks in real time.

In sum, quantum computing doesn't merely threaten cybersecurity, it challenges the assumptions that underlie how we measure, manage, and insure cyber risk. The industry must not only prepare for new attack vectors but also rethink what resilience, liability, and trust look like in the post-quantum age.

Types of Quantum Threats: Real-Time vs. Deferred Risk

Quantum threats fall into two distinct categories, each with different implications for cybersecurity and insurance modeling:

Harvest Now, Decrypt Later (HNDL): In this deferred risk model, adversaries collect encrypted data today in anticipation of future quantum decryption capabilities. The threat is insidious because it implies that secure-looking data may already be compromised, with breaches only revealed years after the initial exfiltration. This poses long-term liability and extended breach timelines for insurers.

Real-Time Quantum Exploitation: These are immediate, live attacks using operational quantum computers that can break cryptographic protocols in real-time. While such systems have not yet materialized, their eventual emergence could allow instant compromise of secure channels, credentials, and systems.

Understanding both threat types is crucial for insurers. Deferred threats like HNDL call for policy clauses addressing retroactive claims and long-term liability. Real-time threats demand real-time cryptographic agility and insurer-led client auditing.

5. QUANTUM-AWARE RISK MODELING FRAMEWORK

Traditional cyber risk models have long relied on indicators like industry sector, historical breach frequency, data sensitivity, and cybersecurity posture to assess and price risk. However, these parameters were not designed with quantum computing in mind. As we approach a new computational era, insurers and risk analysts must begin to adapt their models to account for quantum-specific factors. This means introducing quantum-adapted risk parameters that reflect an organization's exposure to quantum threats and their preparedness for a post-quantum world (Wilkens & Moorhouse, 2023). Figure 2 illustrates the core components of a quantum-aware cyber insurance risk model, highlighting how quantum-specific inputs such as cryptographic asset inventory and PQC migration status are processed into risk outputs like classification, premium adjustment, and policy customization.

Figure 2. Quantum-aware risk modeling framework.

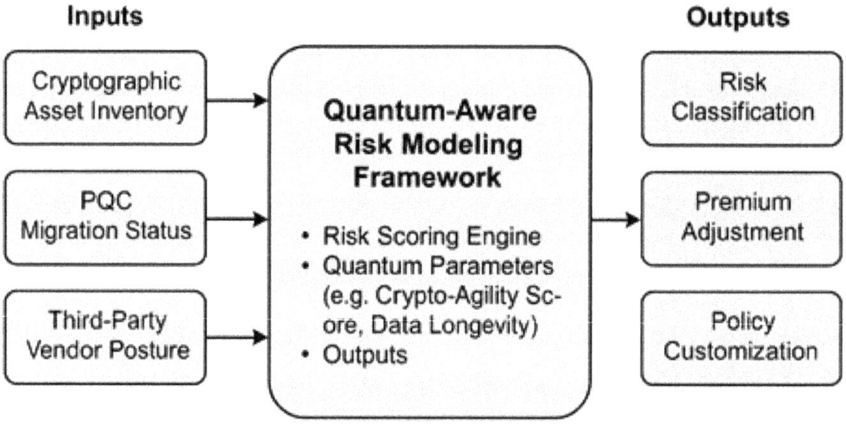

Such parameters could include the proportion of digital assets currently secured by vulnerable cryptographic standards, the presence of long-lived sensitive data (which may be valuable even years from now), and the extent to which a business depends on third-party services that may not be quantum-ready. Organizations that rely heavily on legacy infrastructure or proprietary encryption systems may be at significantly greater risk than those proactively adopting post-quantum standards or cryptographic agility (Alsalman, 2023).

Another important factor is data longevity. Not all information is equal in its sensitivity over time. Customer credit card numbers may lose value within months, but classified research, patient health records, or national security data can remain sensitive for decades. The longer the data must remain secure, the more serious the quantum risk becomes (Zornetta, 2024).

By embedding these types of quantum-aware attributes into underwriting questionnaires, risk scoring tools, and actuarial models, insurers can begin to differentiate between clients that are passively exposed and those actively mitigating quantum vulnerabilities.

Modeling Risk for PQC (Post-Quantum Cryptography) Migration

One of the key mitigation strategies for the quantum threat is migrating from vulnerable encryption methods to Post-Quantum Cryptographic (PQC) standards. However, this transition is complex, resource-intensive, and often slow. For insurers, it's critical to model not just whether an organization *plans* to migrate, but how effectively and systematically it is managing the transition (Hasan et al., 2024).

A robust risk model should therefore assess the maturity of PQC migration efforts across several dimensions: inventorying cryptographic assets, prioritizing migration based on data sensitivity and system criticality, and deploying quantum-safe alternatives in a phased and controlled manner. This process, often referred to as "crypto-agility", requires that an organization be able to quickly adapt to cryptographic changes without rewriting entire systems or disrupting operations (Alnahawi et al., 2023).

Risk models might also account for whether a client has integrated NIST-recommended PQC algorithms into their security roadmap, whether internal security teams are trained in quantum risk, and whether third-party vendors are being held to post-quantum compliance standards. The presence of hybrid cryptographic implementations, using both classical and quantum-safe encryption in tandem, could be viewed as a sign of proactive risk management.

These insights allow insurers to better gauge both the *likelihood* of future exposure and the *resilience* of an organization if a quantum-enabled attack were to occur. Moreover, they help insurers offer tailored guidance to clients on how to improve their posture and potentially reduce premiums.

Dynamic Premium Pricing Based on Quantum Threat Levels

One of the more innovative opportunities in quantum-aware insurance is the development of dynamic premium models that adjust based on the evolving quantum threat landscape. Unlike traditional cyber risks, which may follow observable patterns and historical trends, quantum risk is driven by rapid scientific advancement and breakthrough research. This makes it a moving target—uncertain, yet potentially catastrophic (Boretti, 2024).

To respond to this volatility, insurers could implement models that link premium pricing to real-time indicators of quantum risk. For example, premiums could adjust based on public benchmarks of quantum computing progress, such as the number of qubits achieved in stable systems, announcements of practical quantum error correction, or breakthroughs in algorithm optimization. Risk indices published by governments or academic institutions could also feed into actuarial models, triggering premium adjustments or alerts to policyholders (Nguyen, 2025).

In addition, organizations that demonstrate continued investment in quantum-safe infrastructure and compliance with emerging standards could benefit from quantum-readiness discounts—incentivizing proactive security behavior in much the same way that multi-factor authentication or regular penetration testing is rewarded today (Awotidebe, 2025).

Ultimately, dynamic premium pricing reflects a more adaptive, real-time approach to risk management. It acknowledges that quantum risk is not static, and that both threat levels and defensive capabilities will evolve over time. By integrating this mindset into pricing and policy design, insurers can better align incentives, drive awareness, and promote resilience in an uncertain technological future.

6. INTEGRATING POST-QUANTUM RESILIENCE INTO INSURANCE POLICIES

As the quantum threat becomes more credible and time-sensitive, cyber insurance must evolve from being a financial safety net into a tool that actively encourages proactive risk mitigation. One of the most direct and effective ways to drive this evolution is by embedding post-quantum resilience directly into policy language. By defining clear expectations, incentivizing best practices, and penalizing negligence, insurers can help shape a security-conscious market that is better prepared for a post-quantum future.

Clauses for Quantum-Safe Infrastructure

Traditionally, cyber insurance policies have included language around data protection, incident response, and regulatory compliance. However, they rarely make reference to the underlying cryptographic infrastructure, let alone its resilience against future threats. As the post-quantum era approaches, it becomes essential for insurers to address this gap by introducing explicit clauses related to quantum-safe infrastructure (Baanstra, 2024).

Such clauses may require policyholders to conduct a formal inventory of cryptographic assets, identify systems that rely on vulnerable algorithms like RSA or ECC, and present a roadmap for migration to post-quantum alternatives. Policy language could mandate that, within a defined timeframe, critical systems be upgraded to include quantum-resistant encryption methods, particularly for sensitive data or long-term archives (Ramakrishna & Shaik, 2024).

Additionally, insurers could offer tiered coverage or pricing models based on the extent of an organization's quantum resilience. For example, a company that has deployed hybrid cryptographic solutions, incorporating both classical and PQC algorithms, might receive enhanced coverage terms or lower premiums. These clauses do more than just transfer risk; they actively promote better cybersecurity practices by aligning financial incentives with technological preparedness (Pallaria, 2023).

Mandating Cryptographic Agility in Contracts

One of the most important capabilities organizations will need in the quantum era is cryptographic agility, the ability to switch between cryptographic algorithms without overhauling entire systems. Agility ensures that once a viable post-quantum algorithm is approved or a specific quantum threat is identified, systems can be rapidly reconfigured to adapt (Aydeger et al., 2024).

Unfortunately, many legacy systems lack this flexibility. Hard-coded algorithms, proprietary implementations, and patchwork infrastructures make the transition to new cryptographic standards slow, expensive, and risky. Recognizing this, insurers can begin to mandate cryptographic agility as a contractual requirement (Pasek, 2023).

This could include requiring that all new applications and services deployed by a policyholder are built with modular cryptographic frameworks, allowing for algorithm replacement without full-system rewrites. Insurers might also demand that clients conduct regular crypto-inventories, test their ability to implement new standards, or integrate automatic key rotation mechanisms that can accommodate larger PQC key sizes and complexities (Park et al, 2021).

By including such mandates in policy language, insurers create a feedback loop that encourages organizations to build future-proof systems. This not only reduces individual exposure but also contributes to broader systemic resilience, an increasingly critical consideration in a globally connected digital economy.

Third-Party Vendor and Supply Chain Considerations

Quantum resilience isn't just about an organization's internal systems. In today's interconnected world, third-party vendors and supply chains are often deeply integrated into business operations, sometimes with privileged access to core systems or sensitive data. This means that a weak link in the supply chain can introduce quantum-era vulnerabilities, even if the primary organization has robust defenses (Akhai & Kumar, 2024).

To account for this, insurance policies must begin to extend quantum readiness requirements to third-party relationships. This could take the form of due diligence expectations, requiring organizations to assess the quantum resilience of key suppliers, cloud providers, and partners. Policyholders may also be required to incorporate quantum-safe requirements into vendor contracts, ensuring that external services adhere to the same cryptographic standards and migration timelines (Näther et al., 2024).

Some insurers may go further, offering endorsements or policy extensions specifically for third-party quantum risk, covering incidents where a breach or data leak originates in a non-compliant vendor. To qualify, clients might need to demonstrate robust vendor management frameworks, regular third-party assessments, and clear contractual obligations tied to post-quantum security benchmarks.

Incorporating third-party considerations into quantum-aware insurance policies reinforces the idea that cybersecurity, and quantum resilience in particular, is not an isolated concern, but a collective responsibility. Organizations that take the lead in securing their digital ecosystems end-to-end will be better positioned to meet insurer expectations, respond to future threats, and maintain trust with stakeholders.

7. REGULATORY AND COMPLIANCE LANDSCAPE

As quantum computing edges closer to real-world impact, the urgency to establish regulatory guidance and standards for post-quantum security is growing. Governments, international organizations, and standard-setting bodies are beginning to take proactive steps to ensure that both public and private sectors are prepared for the disruptive changes quantum technology will bring. For cyber insurers and their clients, understanding and aligning with these developments is not just a matter of compliance, it's a strategic imperative.

Global Initiatives on Quantum Readiness (e.g., NIST PQC Standardization)

One of the most significant global efforts in quantum preparedness is the NIST Post-Quantum Cryptography (PQC) Standardization Project. Launched in 2016 by the U.S. National Institute of Standards and Technology, this multi-year initiative aims to identify and standardize cryptographic algorithms that are secure against both classical and quantum attacks. After several rounds of public competition and rigorous vetting, NIST announced in 2022 a set of finalist algorithms, with final standards expected to be published by 2024–2025 (Alagic et al., 2025).

These upcoming standards are expected to become the foundation for post-quantum cryptography in both government and industry settings. For insurers, the emergence of NIST-approved algorithms offers a clearer benchmark for assessing a client's quantum readiness. Policies can begin referencing these standards directly, setting expectations for the types of cryptographic protocols that qualify as "quantum-safe" or "PQC-compliant" (Baseri, Chouhan & Hafid, 2024)

Other nations and regions are also taking action. The European Union's ENISA (European Union Agency for Cybersecurity) has published guidance on quantum threats and migration strategies. In China, quantum research is deeply integrated into national cybersecurity policy. Collectively, these efforts signal that quantum preparedness is transitioning from a research topic to a policy priority, a trend that insurers must factor into their risk models and underwriting processes (Grabowska, 2022).

Policy Implications for Insurers and Clients

As governments and regulators begin to formalize post-quantum expectations, both insurers and insureds will face new policy implications. For insurers, this means updating coverage language, exclusions, and risk assessments to reflect quantum vulnerabilities. Underwriting standards may begin to require documentation of a client's cryptographic roadmap, evidence of migration to PQC algorithms, or formal risk disclosures related to long-lived data and legacy systems.

Clients, in turn, will be expected to demonstrate active compliance with emerging quantum readiness standards. This includes identifying cryptographic dependencies across their IT environments, implementing crypto-agility, and participating in industry-specific working groups or compliance initiatives. Failure to do so could result in higher premiums, limited coverage, or in some cases, denial of claims related to preventable cryptographic failures (Boto et al., 2023).

Moreover, mandates that organizations implement appropriate security measures for personal data. If quantum decryption renders once-secure data exposed, and no efforts were made to mitigate that risk, organizations could face regulatory penalties in addition to financial and reputational damage. Insurers will need to assess how such legal exposures impact claim liability and how to structure policies to cover, or exclude, quantum-related regulatory penalties (Balarabe, 2025).

Alignment with Cybersecurity Frameworks (NIST, ISO, etc.)

To bridge the gap between regulation, practice, and insurance, existing cybersecurity frameworks will play a crucial role. Frameworks like the NIST Cybersecurity Framework (CSF) and ISO/IEC 27001 already provide structured approaches to risk assessment, data protection, and system security. These frameworks are likely to evolve to include quantum-resilience guidelines, and forward-looking insurers can begin aligning their policy requirements with these updates (Koza, 2022).

For example, future iterations of the NIST CSF may include new categories related to cryptographic agility, PQC implementation, and quantum threat modeling. ISO/IEC 19790, which outlines requirements for cryptographic modules, is already being reviewed for alignment with quantum-safe practices. When these frameworks are updated, insurers can reference them directly in policy clauses, compliance checklists, and premium calculations (Shamo, 2024).

Furthermore, alignment with such frameworks creates a common language among insurers, clients, auditors, and regulators. It streamlines the process of evaluating quantum risk and ensures that policyholders understand what is expected of them in concrete terms. This clarity benefits all parties, insurers gain more reliable risk data, and organizations gain actionable paths to compliance and coverage (Singhal, Goyal & Singhal, 2024).

In summary, the regulatory and compliance landscape surrounding quantum computing is rapidly maturing. Staying ahead of these developments will be essential for insurers and clients alike. As the line between "prepared" and "exposed" becomes clearer, those who align with emerging standards will be better protected, both operationally and contractually, against the seismic shifts that quantum computing will bring.

8. CASE STUDIES AND INDUSTRY PERSPECTIVES

As the theoretical risks of quantum computing begin to gain practical relevance, the industry is seeking real-world insight into how these threats might manifest, and how the cyber insurance sector should respond. While no quantum-enabled breach has yet occurred in the wild, simulated scenarios, industry surveys, and historical parallels offer valuable foresight. By examining plausible attack simulations, insurer preparedness, and lessons from past cryptographic shifts, stakeholders can better anticipate the road ahead and make informed decisions about managing quantum-era risks.

Simulated Quantum Breach Scenario and Insurance Response

Imagine a scenario in which a quantum-enabled adversary successfully uses Shor's algorithm to break RSA encryption, decrypting private communications between a multinational corporation and its legal counsel. Though the breach is not immediately discovered, the adversary quietly extracts sensitive information, trade secrets, intellectual property agreements, and merger discussions, and leaks them strategically months later to disrupt a major acquisition.

The organization files a cyber-insurance claim, citing data theft, reputational damage, and loss of competitive advantage. However, the policy in place had no explicit exclusions or inclusions for quantum-related incidents. The investigation reveals that the data was stolen years earlier, encrypted under RSA, and stored in long-term archives. The insurer now faces a difficult dilemma: Is this a covered event if the breach technically occurred under what were then "industry-standard" protections? Does retroactive decryption qualify as a new breach or a continuation of a past event?

This simulated scenario illustrates how quantum capabilities could blur the definitions and timelines that traditional cyber insurance policies rely on. Without updated language and risk modeling that includes quantum-specific variables, such as data longevity, encryption types, and decryption timing, both clients and insurers may find themselves in legal and operational grey zones.

Insurer Readiness Levels and Risk Forecasting

Across the industry, readiness for quantum threats remains uneven. While a few leading insurers have begun integrating quantum risk discussions into their underwriting practices, many remain in the exploratory phase. According to recent industry reports, only a minority of insurers currently require or even ask about cryptographic agility or post-quantum readiness in their cyber risk assessments.

The challenge lies partly in the difficulty of forecasting. Quantum computing does not follow the predictable trajectory of conventional cybersecurity threats, which evolve based on observed attacker behavior. Instead, it hinges on research breakthroughs, hardware innovation, and theoretical milestones, many of which are difficult to track, let alone quantify in an actuarial sense.

Some insurers have started experimenting with scenario-based risk forecasting, working with quantum researchers and cybersecurity firms to model potential points of failure. These exercises simulate not just the impact of a quantum breach, but the operational disruption, regulatory fallout, and correlated losses that could ripple through insured networks.

However, the lack of standardized quantum risk metrics continues to limit the sophistication of these forecasts. Without a widely accepted framework for measuring an organization's quantum vulnerability or preparedness, insurers are left to rely on qualitative assessments and client self-reporting, neither of which provide the granularity needed for precision underwriting.

Lessons from Historical Crypto-Breaking Transitions

History, though not an exact guide, offers useful parallels. Consider the retirement of the MD5 and SHA-1 hashing algorithms, or the gradual phase-out of SSL in favor of TLS. These transitions weren't sparked by quantum threats, but by improved computational techniques and increasing evidence of exploitable weaknesses. In many cases, the industry was slow to react, leading to avoidable breaches and expensive retrofits.

The most significant lesson is that early warning doesn't always lead to early action. Cryptographic systems are often deeply embedded, and upgrading them is costly, disruptive, and fraught with backward-compatibility issues. Organizations tend to delay migration until forced, either by a breach or a regulatory deadline.

Cyber insurers, during those periods of transition, struggled to define liability when clients failed to adopt updated standards quickly enough. The same dynamic is likely to play out in the post-quantum transition. Unless insurance policies clearly define expectations for post-quantum readiness, and unless industry regulators enforce migration timelines, organizations may once again defer critical upgrades until it is too late.

From these lessons, insurers can derive a clear imperative: encourage proactive behavior, reward early adoption of post-quantum measures, and build flexibility into policy structures to accommodate emerging standards. Waiting for the quantum moment to arrive may leave both insurers and clients dangerously exposed.

10. CONCLUSION

As quantum computing continues to evolve, its implications for cybersecurity and, by extension, cyber insurance are becoming increasingly urgent. This chapter has outlined the pressing need for quantum-aware risk modeling, emphasizing that traditional assessment frameworks are ill-equipped to handle the systemic, long-term, and unpredictable nature of quantum-enabled threats. Public-key cryptography, once the bedrock of digital trust, now represents a potential point of failure at a global scale, requiring a fundamental shift in how risk is quantified, mitigated, and insured.

To meet this challenge, cyber insurers must embrace a strategic transformation. This includes integrating quantum-specific parameters into underwriting models, incentivizing cryptographic agility, and aligning policies with emerging standards such as those from NIST and ISO. Insurers will also need to engage more deeply with clients, regulators, and technology providers to develop dynamic pricing models and clear contractual language that accounts for evolving quantum threats. The development of simulated breach scenarios and case studies can further support preparedness and help bridge the gap between theory and practice.

Looking ahead, the path to a quantum-resilient insurance future will not be linear or simple. It will require ongoing collaboration, adaptability, and a willingness to confront uncertainty head-on. However, the opportunity is significant: insurers that lead the charge in quantum readiness will not only protect their portfolios from emerging risks but also position themselves as trusted partners in a new era of digital security.

In the end, building resilience is not just about anticipating quantum breakthroughs—it's about reshaping the entire insurance ecosystem to be flexible, forward-thinking, and equipped to safeguard the next generation of cyber infrastructure.

REFERENCES

Akhai, S., & Kumar, V. (2024). Quantum resilience and distributed trust: The promise of blockchain and quantum computing in defense. In *Sustainable Security Practices Using Blockchain, Quantum and Post-Quantum Technologies for Real Time Applications* (pp. 125–153). Springer Nature Singapore. DOI: 10.1007/978-981-97-0088-2_7

Akkor, D. G., & Ozyukse, S. (2020). The effects of new technologies on the insurance sector: A proposition for underwriting qualifications for the future. *Eurasian Journal of Business and Management*, *8*(1), 36–50. DOI: 10.15604/ejbm.2020.08.01.004

Alagic, G., Alagic, G., Apon, D., Cooper, D., Dang, Q., Dang, T., ... & Smith-Tone, D. (2022). Status report on the third round of the NIST post-quantum cryptography standardization process.

Alagic, G., Bros, M., Ciadoux, P., Cooper, D., Dang, Q., Dang, T., & Waller, N. (2025). *Status report on the fourth round of the nist post-quantum cryptography standardization process*. National Institute of Standards and Technology. DOI: 10.6028/NIST.IR.8545

AllahRakha, N. (2024). Cybersecurity Regulations for Protection and Safeguarding Digital Assets (Data) in Today's Worlds. *Lex Scientia Law Review, 8*(1).

Alnahawi, N., Schmitt, N., Wiesmaier, A., Heinemann, A., & Grasmeyer, T. (2023). On the state of crypto-agility. *Cryptology ePrint Archive*.

Alsalman, A. I. S. (2023). Accelerating Quantum Computing Readiness: Risk Management and Strategies for Sectors. *Journal of Quantum Information Science*, *13*(2), 33–44. DOI: 10.4236/jqis.2023.132003

Argetsinger, C. R. (2024). The Promise and Peril of Quantum Computing and Its Implications for Cyber Insurance. *Journal of Emerging Issues in Litigation/Winter*, *4*(1), 65-73.

Aslam, A. (2025). *Quantum Computing Threats to Cryptography: A Comprehensive Analysis of Vulnerabilities*. Countermeasures, and Future-Proofing Strategies.

Awotidebe, M. (2025). The Race to Quantum-Resilient Infrastructure: National and Global Strategies for Cybersecurity Readiness.

Aydeger, A., Zeydan, E., Yadav, A. K., Hemachandra, K. T., & Liyanage, M. (2024). Towards a quantum-resilient future: Strategies for transitioning to post-quantum cryptography. In *2024 15th International Conference on Network of the Future (NoF)* (pp. 195-203). IEEE.

Baanstra, C. A. (2024). Scenarios and Interventions for the Dutch Energy Market: Preparing to be Quantum-Safe.

Balarabe, K. (2025). Quantum Computing and the Law: Navigating the Legal Implications of a Quantum Leap. *European Journal of Risk Regulation, 16*(2), 1–20. DOI: 10.1017/err.2025.8

Baseri, Y., Chouhan, V., & Hafid, A. (2024). Navigating quantum security risks in networked environments: A comprehensive study of quantum-safe network protocols. *Computers & Security, 142*, 103883. DOI: 10.1016/j.cose.2024.103883

Boretti, A. (2024). Technical, economic, and societal risks in the progress of artificial intelligence driven quantum technologies. *Discover Artificial Intelligence, 4*(1), 67. DOI: 10.1007/s44163-024-00171-y

Boto, K., Amos, G., Moran, J., Robbins, J., & Welden-Iley, J. (2023). The Rise of Fintech: Liability and Insurance. In *The Global Insurance Market and Change* (pp. 246–285). Informa Law from Routledge. DOI: 10.4324/9781003319054-10

Canetti, R., Kalai, Y. T., Lysyanskaya, A., Rivest, R. L., Shamir, A., Shen, E., ... & Weitzner, D. J. (2020). Privacy-preserving automated exposure notification. *IACR Cryptol. ePrint Arch.*

Dalal, Y. M., Supreeth, S., Amuthabala, K., Satheesha, T. Y., Asha, P. N., & Somanath, S. (2024, September). Optimizing Security: A Comparative Analysis of RSA, ECC, and DH Algorithms. In *2024 IEEE North Karnataka Subsection Flagship International Conference (NKCon)* (pp. 1-6). IEEE. DOI: 10.1109/NKCon62728.2024.10775183

George, A. S. (2025). The Critical Role of Cybersecurity Insurance in an Era of Exponential Threats: A Review of Emerging Risk Realities and Policy Safeguards for Enterprise Resilience. *Partners Universal International Research Journal, 4*(1), 1–23.

Geremew, A., & Mohammad, A. (2024). Preparing critical infrastructure for post-quantum cryptography: Strategies for transitioning ahead of cryptanalytically relevant quantum computing. *International Journal of Engineering Science and Technology, 6*(4), 338–365. DOI: 10.46328/ijonest.240

Gorine, A., & Suhaib, M. (2024). Exploring AES Encryption Implementation Through Quantum. *Computing Techniques.*

Grabowska, M. (2022). Legal, Political and Organizational Aspects of Cybersecurity in the European Union. *Online Journal Modelling the New Europe*, (38), 106–132. DOI: 10.24193/OJMNE.2022.38.05

Hammad, A., Saleh, H., & Alomari, M. (2024). Advancements in Cybersecurity: Novel Approaches to Protecting Against Emerging Threats and Vulnerabilities. *CyberSystem Journal, 1*(1), 9–23. DOI: 10.57238/r15e5074

Hasan, K. F., Simpson, L., Baee, M. A. R., Islam, C., Rahman, Z., Armstrong, W., Gauravaram, P., & McKague, M. (2024). A framework for migrating to post-quantum cryptography: Security dependency analysis and case studies. *IEEE Access : Practical Innovations, Open Solutions, 12*, 23427–23450. DOI: 10.1109/ACCESS.2024.3360412

Holland, H. (2024). Quantum Computing and US Cybersecurity: A Case Study of the Breaking of RSA and Plan for Cryptographic Algorithm Transition.

Insua, D. R., Baylon, C., & Vila, J. (Eds.). (2020). *Security Risk Models for Cyber Insurance*. CRC Press. DOI: 10.1201/9780429329487

Kanavas, A. (2023). *Cyberinsurance as a risk management tool* (Master's thesis, Πανεπιστήμιο Πειραιώς).

Keskin, O. F., Caramancion, K. M., Tatar, I., Raza, O., & Tatar, U. (2021). Cyber third-party risk management: A comparison of non-intrusive risk scoring reports. *Electronics (Basel), 10*(10), 1168. DOI: 10.3390/electronics10101168

Koza, E. (2022). Semantic analysis of ISO/IEC 27000 standard series and NIST cybersecurity framework to outline differences and consistencies in the context of operational and strategic information security. *Med. Eng. Themes, 2*, 26–39.

Kubecka, C. (2024). Secrets From the Future: Hacking in a Post-Quantum Cryptography World: Implications for Cyber Security and National Defense.

Lehto, M. (2022). Cyber-attacks against critical infrastructure. In *Cyber security: Critical infrastructure protection* (pp. 3–42). Springer International Publishing. DOI: 10.1007/978-3-030-91293-2_1

Lindsay, J. R. (2020). Surviving the quantum cryptocalypse. *Strategic Studies Quarterly, 14*(2), 49–73.

Malempati, M., Pandiri, L., Paleti, S., & Singireddy, J. (2023). Transforming Financial And Insurance Ecosystems Through Intelligent Automation, Secure Digital Infrastructure, And Advanced Risk Management Strategies. *Jeevani, Transforming Financial And Insurance Ecosystems Through Intelligent Automation, Secure Digital Infrastructure, And Advanced Risk Management Strategies* (2023).

Marrow, A. A. (2025). *Quantum Computing: Evaluating the Threat Landscape and Risk Management Strategies* (Doctoral dissertation, Capitol Technology University).

Mehrizi, M. H. R., Nicolini, D., & Modol, J. R. (2022). How do organizations learn from information system incidents? A synthesis of the past, present, and future. *Management Information Systems Quarterly, 46*(1), 531–590. DOI: 10.25300/MISQ/2022/14305

Näther, C., Herzinger, D., Gazdag, S. L., Steghöfer, J. P., Daum, S., & Loebenberger, D. (2024). Migrating Software Systems Towards Post-Quantum Cryptography–A Systematic Literature Review. *IEEE Access : Practical Innovations, Open Solutions, 12*, 132107–132126. DOI: 10.1109/ACCESS.2024.3450306

Nguyen, P. N. (2025). Quantum technology: A financial risk assessment. *Digital Finance*, •••, 1–40.

Ofoegbu, W. C., & LAGUO, L. G. (2023). Simulation: A tool for system design and analysis. *GPH-International Journal of Social Science and Humanities Research, 6*(11), 98-111.

Pallaria, A. (2023). Risk-mitigation techniques: from (re-) insurance to alternative risk transfer.

Park, J. Y., Moon, Y. H., Lee, W., Kim, S. H., & Sakurai, K. (2021). A survey of polynomial multiplication with RSA-ECC coprocessors and implementations of NIST PQC Round3 KEM algorithms in Exynos2100. *IEEE Access : Practical Innovations, Open Solutions, 10*, 2546–2563. DOI: 10.1109/ACCESS.2021.3138807

Pasek, A., Lin, C. K., Cooper, Z. G. T., & Kinder, J. B. (2023). *Digital Energetics*. U of Minnesota Press.

Ramakrishna, D., & Shaik, M. A. (2024). A Comprehensive analysis of Cryptographic Algorithms: Evaluating Security, Efficiency, and Future Challenges. *IEEE Access : Practical Innovations, Open Solutions*.

Segate, R. V., & Daly, A. (2024). Encoding the enforcement of safety standards into smart robots to harness their computing sophistication and collaborative potential: A legal risk assessment for European Union policymakers. *European Journal of Risk Regulation, 15*(3), 665–704. DOI: 10.1017/err.2023.72

Shamo, S. A. (2024). Bridging the Quantum Divide: A Comprehensive Analysis of NIST and ISO Standards for Post-Quantum Cryptography and Strategies for Global Harmonization. *Available at SSRN* 4864519. DOI: 10.2139/ssrn.4864519

Shreedevi, K. S., Chayadevi, M. L., & Geetha, S. (2024). Advancing security in the modern digital era–A comprehensive exploration of elliptic curve cryptography. In *Computer Science Engineering* (pp. 252–261). CRC Press. DOI: 10.1201/9781003565024-28

Singh, S., & Sakk, E. (2024). Implementation and Analysis of Shor's Algorithm to Break RSA Cryptosystem Security. *Authorea Preprints*. DOI: 10.36227/techrxiv.170259160.05374043/v2

Singhal, N., Goyal, S., & Singhal, T. (2024). Emerging Trends in Regulatory and Legal Frameworks for Decentralized Insurance. *Potential, Risks, and Ethical Implications of Decentralized Insurance*, 211-260.

Sodiya, E. O., Umoga, U. J., Amoo, O. O., & Atadoga, A. (2024). Quantum computing and its potential impact on US cybersecurity: A review: Scrutinizing the challenges and opportunities presented by quantum technologies in safeguarding digital assets. *Global Journal of Engineering and Technology Advances, 18*(02), 049-064.

Sutradhar, M. S., Mondal, M. S., Bose, R., Dey, M. R. K., & Golder, M. S. S. (2025). *Securing the Future with Cyber Intelligence Innovations*. Authors Click Publishing.

Tiwo, O. J., Adesokan-Imran, T. O., Babarinde, D. C., Oyekunle, S. M., Olutimehin, A. T., & Olaniyi, O. O. (2025). Advancing Security in Cloud-based Patient Information Systems with Quantum-resistant Encryption for Healthcare Data. *Asian Journal of Research in Computer Science*, *18*(4), 187–208. DOI: 10.9734/ajrcos/2025/v18i4615

Tom, J. J., Anebo, N. P., Onyekwelu, B. A., Wilfred, A., & Eyo, R. E. (2023). Quantum computers and algorithms: A threat to classical cryptographic systems. *International Journal of Engineering and Advanced Technology*, *12*(5), 25–38. DOI: 10.35940/ijeat.E4153.0612523

Tsohou, A., Diamantopoulou, V., Gritzalis, S., & Lambrinoudakis, C. (2023). Cyber insurance: State of the art, trends and future directions. *International Journal of Information Security*, *22*(3), 737–748. DOI: 10.1007/s10207-023-00660-8 PMID: 36684688

Wilkens, S., & Moorhouse, J. (2023). Quantum computing for financial risk measurement. *Quantum Information Processing*, *22*(1), 51. DOI: 10.1007/s11128-022-03777-2

Zornetta, A. (2024). Quantum-safe global encryption policy. *International Journal of Law and Information Technology*, *32*(1), eaae020. DOI: 10.1093/ijlit/eaae020

Chapter 4
AI-Driven Benchmarking and Standards in Cybersecurity Insurance

Muhammad Usman Tariq
https://orcid.org/0000-0002-7605-3040
Abu Dhabi University, UAE & University College Cork, Ireland

ABSTRACT

AI-Driven Benchmarking and Standards in Cybersecurity Insurance explores the integration of artificial intelligence (AI) technologies in enhancing the risk assessment, compliance, and underwriting processes of cybersecurity insurance. With the rapid escalation of cyber threats, traditional methods of assessing and insuring against cybersecurity risks have become increasingly inadequate. This chapter examines how AI, particularly through machine learning and natural language processing, can automate and refine the benchmarking of cybersecurity practices against established global standards such as ISO/IEC 27001, the NIST Cybersecurity Framework, and GDPR. AI-driven tools enable real-time risk analysis, adaptive benchmarking, and continuous compliance monitoring, ensuring that insurance policies accurately reflect an organization's current cybersecurity posture. The chapter also delves into how AI can facilitate cross-industry benchmarking, enabling insurers to evaluate an organization's cybersecurity maturity in relation to its peers and adjust premiums accordingly.

DOI: 10.4018/979-8-3373-5545-0.ch004

INTRODUCTION

Modern businesses belonging to all industries depend heavily on digital systems, yet they remain susceptible to cyberattacks that include data theft, ransomware intrusions, and system breaches. Cybersecurity insurance has developed over time to assist organizations in reducing financial damages stemming from cyber events. Risk assessment and policy underwriting practices extensively used by the industry commonly trail behind the rapid developments in cyber threats. The evaluation process known as benchmarking helps insurance companies measure organizational cybersecurity systems through the comparison of industry standards and best practices. The implementation of artificial intelligence (AI) makes benchmarking more effective by generating precise outcomes while it adjusts automatically to shifting cyber threats (Pandey & Katsikas, 2023). Cybersecurity insurance benchmarking fulfills three essential operations by evaluating business risks and then determining policy costs while promoting enhanced safety methods among policyholders. The level of protection organizations have against cyber threats becomes clear through standard industry comparisons conducted by insurers. Strong security systems together with standard compliance alongside active risk mitigation efforts help organizations secure reductions on insurance premiums, though organizations with inadequate security systems may need to pay elevated costs or obtain restricted policy coverage (Madhavan et al., 2025). The benchmarking process receives AI enhancement through its ability to analyze large datasets from cyber incidents, threat reports, and network activities, which allow insurers to develop more accurate measures of risk. By employing AI-driven benchmarking, organizations can monitor fresh security threats in real time, which enables automatic adjustments to their risk evaluation process. The evolution of security standards influences how the insurance business handles risk assessments (Salem et al., 2024).

At the start, cybersecurity insurance policies implemented basic IT security guidelines with their policies based upon manually executed risk evaluations. The National Institute of Standards and Technology (NIST) Cybersecurity Framework, together with ISO/IEC 27001 and the Center for Internet Security (CIS) benchmarks, now represent standardized evaluation tools for insurers to assess cybersecurity readiness (Madhavan et al., 2025). Security frameworks offer insurers organized threat management frameworks that define proper security practices, including risk management plus access controls alongside incident response protocols and data protection systems that help insurance providers establish policy standards based on recognized security standards. The implementation of such standards depends on an organization's ability to implement them successfully. AI-driven benchmarking makes compliance assessments more efficient because it conducts automated checks of security standards while detecting areas of non-compliance and generating improvement recommendations. AI-based platform constantly checks network vulnerabilities to create security risk scores that insurers obtain instantly for premium determination (Radanliev et al., 2024; Tariq, 2025). The major impact of AI in cybersecurity insurance benchmarking emerges from its capability to analyze massive datasets for identifying patterns that human analysts would miss. Cybersecurity analytics models trained with historical incident data recognize danger elements that link to business fields and organization dimensions and regional elements. AI-based systems recognize financial institutions are at a stronger risk for phishing attacks alongside healthcare organizations that become more vulnerable to ransomware attacks due to the value of their patient records. Insurance risk models benefit from machine learning algorithms, which allow insurers to update premium rates according to current security hazards instead of using outdated hypotheses. Through data analytics, insurers can create customized insurance coverages based on risk patterns rather than standardized industry figures (Pandey & Katsikas, 2023). The predictive abilities of cybersecurity insurance receive better performance through AI-based benchmarking systems. The traditional insurance analytics foundation of past data evaluation falls short in the fast-paced cybersecurity industry. AI systems possess the ability to examine current threat intelligence from new malware strains and software vulnerabilities and geopolitical events that create cyber dangers (Radanliev et al., 2024). Insurance companies can produce more advanced policy frameworks through the integration of real-time security information in their assessment processes. The detection by AI of a ransomware attack surge on a specific industry enables insurers to create immediate risk alerts that push policyholders toward enhanced protective measures or modified insurance coverage adjustments. The benchmarking capabilities of artificial intelligence during cybersecurity assessments deliver benefits through claims processing as well as fraud detection in addition to policy underwriting functions. Organizations must submit claims about their attacks and their damage extent together with their security protocols during the attack incident (Madhavan et al., 2025; Tariq, 2024).

BACKGROUND

The emerging field of AI-driven benchmarking and Standards in Cybersecurity Insurance combines artificial intelligence technologies with risk management strategies and cybersecurity insurance into one functional entity. The fusion enables improved risk assessment as well as security management practices, which sustain compliance standards and adhere to insurance regulations. The rapid growth of cyber threats together with advanced global cybersecurity risks alongside rising demand for dynamic insurance solutions increased the importance of this emerging field

(Radanliev et al., 2024). To meet rising cyber threat risks, the insurance industry has developed cybersecurity insurance programs over time. The traditional basis of cybersecurity insurance policies depended on general risk evaluations together with historical statistics and company-wide standards for protection. These conventional risk assessment practices proved insufficient to identify shifting cyber threats, so they led to inadequate policy protection along with pricing errors. Modern cybersecurity threats exist as intricate combined elements that include acts of data breaches, ransomware schemes, and internally generated threats alongside persistent threats (APTs). The changing cybersecurity insurance market needed updated strategies for evaluating risks as well as setting prices and creating policy structures. Benchmarking and standards powered by AI technology provide organizations with a superior data-based solution for these challenges (Radanliev et al., 2024). Artificial intelligence technologies, including machine learning (ML), along with natural language processing (NLP) and neural networks, enable benchmarking to evaluate security risks as well as practices in an organization. Due to AI system capabilities of handling large-scale data instantly, they identify patterns while detecting security issues and generating recommendation insights from recent data intelligence. The designed infrastructure assesses the cybersecurity maturity of organizations while performing evaluations based on established standards and best practices in the industry. Insurance providers obtain accurate risk assessments in real time through this method; therefore, they offer tailored premiums and coverage conditions to their clients (Bello et al., 2023; Tariq, 2025).

AI-driven benchmarking has several advantages when it comes to cybersecurity insurance. Instead of depending on static, historical risk assessments, it assists in assessing risks using up-to-date, real-time data. This method makes sure that insurance policies represent an organization's present cybersecurity posture by taking into consideration the dynamic nature of cyber threats. Furthermore, AI-powered solutions can track cybersecurity performance over time, enabling insurers to modify risk assessments and rates continually. Because of this, insurance solutions may be customized to meet the unique requirements of every company, improving the precision and efficacy of coverage (Radanliev et al., 2024). The application of cybersecurity standards is crucial to AI-driven benchmarking. These standards, which include the General Data Protection Regulation (GDPR), the NIST Cybersecurity Framework, and ISO/IEC 27001, offer the best practices and rules that enterprises should adhere to in order to safeguard confidential data and reduce cybersecurity threats. These guidelines provide a starting point for cybersecurity readiness and are essential to building confidence in the insurance sector. But historically, putting these standards into practice and evaluating them has required a lot of resources, frequently including manual audits, inspections, and reports. By automating the monitoring and assessment of adherence to certain criteria, artificial intelligence streamlines this procedure (Pandey & Katsikas, 2023). The use of AI in benchmarking has also been significantly influenced by the development of cybersecurity requirements. The standards created to defend against cyberattacks have evolved along with the threats themselves (Tariq, 2025). Prioritizing adherence to fundamental security procedures and legal requirements was the main emphasis of earlier cybersecurity standards. These standards now cover a wider range of issues, including incident response, threat intelligence, data security, risk management, and continuous improvement. Organizations find it difficult to maintain current cybersecurity procedures and ensure compliance due to the complexity of these changing regulations. By automating these procedures, artificial intelligence (AI) enables businesses to keep an eye on their compliance with these guidelines without needing to make regular manual adjustments (Bello et al., 2023).

Additionally, AI makes it possible to assess cybersecurity procedures across industries, which is crucial in the linked world of today. Although cybersecurity concerns vary by industry, the fundamentals of sound cybersecurity are universal. AI systems can assess cybersecurity procedures across industries, analyze data from several sectors, and spot trends. Comparing their cybersecurity maturity to that of their peers aids firms in identifying any possible weaknesses in their defenses. Insurers may also create more thorough risk models that take into consideration both generic cybersecurity hazards and industry-specific risks, thanks to this cross-industry benchmarking. AI-driven benchmarking, for instance, may be used to assess how well financial institutions comply with industry standards like the Payment Card Industry Data Security Standard (PCI DSS) or how well healthcare firms follow HIPAA guidelines. The insurance sector is not the only one to profit from AI-driven benchmarking. By identifying vulnerabilities, weaknesses, and places for development, organizations may use these technologies to enhance their cybersecurity procedures. To stay ahead of new threats, AI may assist enterprises in monitoring their progress in bolstering cybersecurity defenses. AI-driven benchmarking is a useful tool for businesses looking to improve their cybersecurity posture and guarantee adherence to industry standards because of this ongoing feedback loop (Radanliev et al., 2024). The use of AI in cybersecurity insurance is not without difficulties, despite its numerous benefits. The absence of common data formats and system compatibility is one of the main challenges. Because cybersecurity data is frequently kept in a variety of forms, it can be challenging for AI systems to compare and evaluate data from different businesses. Incompatible technology and inconsistent data standards might reduce the efficacy of AI-driven benchmarking and its capacity to produce reliable evaluations. To guarantee that AI technologies are utilized ethically and impartially, ethical issues pertaining to data utilization and algorithmic openness must also be addressed (Bello et al., 2023). AI-driven cybersecurity insurance benchmarking and standards present a bright future for both businesses and insurers. AI can assist businesses in better understanding and reducing their cybersecurity risks by automating compliance checks, improving risk assessments, and offering real-time evaluations, which may also help cybersecurity standards develop, making sure they stay applicable in the face of quickly evolving cyber threats. Even if there are obstacles to overcome, especially regarding data consistency and ethical issues, artificial intelligence has the potential to completely transform cybersecurity insurance. AI-driven benchmarking has the potential to become a key component of contemporary cybersecurity risk management and insurance procedures with sustained innovation and cross-sector cooperation (Deep et al., 2024; Tariq, 2025).

Importance of Benchmarking in Cybersecurity Insurance

Benchmarking in cybersecurity insurance functions as a basic method to review an organizational security position against industry benchmarks, mandatory legal requirements, and industry peers. Organizations use benchmarking as a method to compare their cybersecurity practices against specified standards or best practices from their industry sector. Through benchmarking, the insurance industry can verify organizational cybersecurity readiness independently, which subsequently determines cost eligibility for coverage. Systematic cybersecurity measure analysis enables insurers to determine how well security controls function and locate vulnerabilities while forecasting the potential for cyberattacks to happen. The underwriting process becomes more effective, which produces better risk assessments and creates insurance policies that properly match the security level achievements of each organization (Al Siam et al., 2025). Through benchmarking activities, insurers gain better insights that help them evaluate organizational risks when creating policies for cybersecurity insurance coverage. Insurance companies use records as their main method for forecasting potential damage rates (Sindiramutty, 2023). The continuous emergence of new security attack vectors throughout time makes past risk data ineffective for predicting modern threats. Benchmarking resolves this issue through current industry-specific risk comparison data that helps insurers evaluate organizational risk levels. Financial institutions that integrate their security elements into the National Institute of Standards and Technology (NIST) Cybersecurity Framework and ISO/IEC 27001 standards will receive lower risk evaluations than their security-astute competitors. Insurers employ this differentiation system to evaluate actual cybersecurity practices through trustworthy assessments instead of using historical incident reports (Deep et al., 2024).

Premium calculations greatly depend on benchmarking procedures. Risk scores developed through benchmarking exercises help insurers calculate policy premiums that must be paid by their customers. Strong cybersecurity measures combined with effective incident response plans and industry standards compliance lead organizations to receive reduced premium prices because these organizations demonstrate low-risk claims. Organizations that maintain insufficient security along with outdated protection systems can expect increased insurance costs up to complete denial of coverage (Sindiramutty, 2023). Operational healthcare providers who excel in data encryption standards and fully meet HIPAA requirements obtain better rates on their cybersecurity premiums than organizations that demonstrate repeated data exposure and non-compliance incidents. Organizations utilizing benchmarking data receive discounts on their premiums because it encourages them to actively enhance their cybersecurity capabilities instead of simply reacting to security threats (Al Siam et al., 2025). The benchmarking process helps insurers develop policies because it creates specific coverage boundaries. Organizational cybersecurity practices determine many exclusions and conditions included in their cyber insurance coverage. Insurance providers use benchmarking to create standardized security criteria for organization coverage qualification. Insurers demand policyholders perform regular security audits in addition to implementing employee cybersecurity training along with a multi-factor authentication framework to access underwriting before accepting policies. Using benchmarking data allows insurers to develop organized policies specifically designed for each organization's particular risk situation while providing both acceptable rates and long-lasting insurance coverage (Egho-Promise et al., 2024). Universal cybersecurity standards present a major obstacle because industry requirements and geographical areas across the world demonstrate different standards. The diverse cyber risks between different industries create obstacles when trying to use uniform benchmarking procedures. A business that procures computer technology while handling extensive consumer information data must defend against threats that differ from those experienced by manufacturing companies utilizing industrial control programs (Tariq, 2024). To achieve accurate sectoral risk assessment, the current requirement exists for established benchmarks to adapt to individual industry characteristics (Al Siam et al., 2025).

The process of benchmarking becomes harder to achieve because each jurisdiction maintains its specific regulatory standards. Structural data protection rules under the European Union's General Data Protection Regulation (GDPR) surpass guidelines from other regions that do not enforce such rigorous requirements. Different insurance regulations create such regulatory fragments that prevent insurers from creating standardized benchmarking models that can function universally across various markets. Security threats evolve at such high speeds that it requires the benchmarking criteria to be updated regularly. Static benchmark systems will eventually lose their effectiveness because threat actors develop new methods together with emerging security risks. Companies in the insurance sector need to develop flexible benchmarking systems with current threat intelligence and responsive risk measurement models. The combination of AI-driven benchmarking solutions enables insurers to track threat perspectives through updated risk models while generating analytics for developing precise policy structures. Using AI-automated benchmarking systems brings up multiple privacy-related issues and unknown biases in automated risk assessment operations (Egho-Promise et al., 2024). Although security insurance faces difficulties, benchmarking serves as the essential foundation that gives insurers and policyholders essential knowledge about risks and protective approaches. Sound benchmarking frameworks applied to cybersecurity insurance models help insurers conduct more precise risk assessments, which lead to better security practices and longer-lasting policy structures. The importance of benchmarking within cybersecurity insurance will increase in significance as digital threats transform, due to which the mechanism must adapt continually to maintain effectiveness in modern digital environments (Al Siam et al., 2025).

Role of AI in Benchmarking Cybersecurity Standards

The transformative power of AI in cybersecurity benchmarking emerges from automatic security framework analysis and faultless compliance assessments while facilitating the assessment of multiple industry cybersecurity levels. The current benchmarking methodologies depend substantially on human-led audits combined with self-reported data and history-based assessments that lead to problems with time consumption and imprecision as well as human mistakes (Radanliev, 2024). Benchmarking backed by artificial intelligence uses machine learning alongside natural language processing to deliver immediate data-based information about how organizations manage cybersecurity. AI enables insurers and both regulators and organizations to make informed decisions about policy structures and risk exposures through continuous security practice and compliance analysis (Egho-Promise et al., 2024). Machine learning algorithms perform comprehensive analysis on cybersecurity data, industry best practices, and threat intelligence records to detect security patterns for potential risk assessment. ML models differentiate from static benchmarking methods since they evolve by absorbing fresh threat intelligence to update their risk evaluation processes. An AI system that examines financial institutions' cybersecurity framework uses other banks' firewall controls and patch management plans and user permissions to evaluate compliance with industry norms. The system uses insights from AI to reveal possible regions of improvement that would include stronger authentication protocols together with improved intrusion detection capabilities (Rahman et al., 2024). Natural language processing technology enables the improvement of AI-driven benchmarking systems because it breaks down and analyzes security framework content containing policies and regulatory requirements along with best practices. The application of NLP by AI in compliance documents alongside security policies and audit reports permits machine learning to automate organizational standards assessment. The text analysis of ISO/IEC 27001 standards performed by AI systems verifies compliance gaps between that standard and organizations' cybersecurity policies. Organizations of all sizes implement this feature because AI enables them to identify and match security requirements that span across multiple regulatory frameworks (Egho-Promise et al., 2024).

The most critical use of AI in cybersecurity benchmarking involves the automation of compliance checks through established security frameworks, which include ISO/IEC 27001 as well as the NIST Cybersecurity Framework alongside the General Data Protection Regulation (GDPR). The common practice of performing audits through manual assessments necessitates time-consuming and inconsistent work from human inspectors (Radanliev, 2024). Information technology tools powered by AI provide automated cross-validation between the security control frameworks of the organization and current industry standards through ongoing monitoring systems. A governance risk and compliance (GRC) platform using artificial intelligence technology performs automatic scans of IT infrastructure to identify regulatory non-compliance and then produces simultaneous compliance verification reports. The automated system provides relief to security teams by making daily compliance updates, so they remain current with new regulatory changes (Rahman et al., 2024). The GDPR requires benchmarking analytics based on artificial intelligence to examine data operations and identify privacy risks to maintain compliance by following data protection standards. The tools function by identifying stored personal data that lacks encryption along with insufficient access controls so organizations may prevent penalties by fixing issues before regulatory action occurs. AI systems monitor healthcare facilities for HIPAA compliance through the evaluation of electronic health record security controls, which help detect weak spots that might result in data breaches (Model, 2024).

AI-Powered Tools for Cybersecurity Benchmarking

AI-based tools transformed cybersecurity benchmarking through their provision of real-time performance measurement and predictive analytics features and sustained monitoring of security flank points. The traditional methods of cybersecurity benchmarking used periodic audits, static risk assessments, and manual evaluations due to their lack of capability to track new risks effectively and update risk profiles. These limitations disappear with AI-powered tools, which supply organizations with data-based dynamic benchmarking insights that establish their current cybersecurity maturity levels versus industry benchmarks, regulatory guidelines, and peer organizations. The combination of artificial intelligence algorithms alongside big data analytics and automated processes leads to greatly improved cybersecurity benchmarking capabilities, thus helping insurers, regulators, and businesses make risk-based decisions through current risk evaluations (Ejjami, 2024). The major contribution that AI brings to cybersecurity benchmarking is instant runtime assessment of organizational vulnerabilities. AI platforms monitor IT infrastructure consistently to locate security gaps by comparing organizations with NIST Cybersecurity Framework and both ISO/IEC 27001 requirements and GDPR rules. Organizations that use AI-based tools benefit from automated dataset analysis through machine learning, which predicts security vulnerabilities while detecting abnormal activity. Security-scanning tools using Artificial Intelligence technology automatically detect server misconfigurations in cloud setups while detecting obsolete software programs as well as security weaknesses in network protection systems to help businesses stay secure in line with industry requirements (Ejjami, 2024).

The recent years have observed multiple AI-based cybersecurity benchmarking platforms achieve popularity through their complete risk assessment and benchmarking intelligence abilities. SecureScorecard and BitSight monitor organizational external interfaces to evaluate attacks and supply chain risk as well as security practices for rating purposes. Some platforms evaluate publicly visible information together with network traffic patterns and threat intelligence feeds to determine security ratings, which insurers and businesses use for risk assessment. To produce an overall security grade, SecurityScorecard, for example, assesses variables including malware infestations, patching frequency, and domain security setups. This enables businesses to assess their cybersecurity performance against that of their peers in the sector and take preventative action to strengthen their defenses (Model, 2024). BitSight also provides cybersecurity risk evaluations to assist financial institutions and insurers in determining the cyber risk exposure of prospective policyholders or business partners. BitSight records cyber occurrences, continually monitors digital footprints, and offers benchmark comparisons against rivals in the same industry by utilizing AI-driven analytics. For instance, BitSight's evaluations may be used by a financial services company to assess if a possible (Model, 2024).

Integration of AI and Cybersecurity Standards

Today, organizations use artificial intelligence (AI) to make substantial improvements in their standards compliance approach while managing risk and industry-specific guideline adherence. Organizations use time-consuming manual methods along with human interpretation of rules in their traditional compliance activities because these methods produce inconsistent results. Real-time examination of regulatory rules and quick establishment of policy benchmarks and enhanced cybersecurity governance stem from AI technology through machine learning (ML) and natural language processing (NLP). These AI methods drive efficiency improvements in compliance reporting. The combination of artificial intelligence with machine learning leads organizations to higher compliance standards at lower operational costs while maintaining regulation adherence (Wall, 2021). AI delivers its most vital assistance to cybersecurity compliance by automatizing the reporting process. Organizations need to document their security practices fully, as well as their risk management strategies and data protection measures, because GDPR, the NIST Cybersecurity Framework, and PCI DSS set mandatory regulatory standards. The standard reporting procedures consist of extensive manual efforts where cybersecurity teams collect organizational data from multiple sources to prepare documents for auditors and regulators. AI-driven compliance tools achieve streamlined reporting through uninterrupted analysis of security logs and access control policies together with threat intelligence data, which yields up-to-date compliance reports (Achuthan et al., 2024). AI-specific GRC platforms conduct automatic security control assessments to validate how organizational measures conform to regulatory demands. The platforms implement NLP to review compliance documents; at the same time, they use ML algorithms to track any discrepancies with standards. HIPAA compliance requires healthcare organizations to use an AI-controlled system that monitors access logs to verify authorized personnel have accessed patient records. When unauthorized access occurs, the system launches alerts together with guidance for restoring organizational compliance standards (Wall, 2021).

AI actively participates in the vital process of identifying organizational policy relationships with mandatory cybersecurity benchmarks while operating in real time. Organizations throughout various industries execute ongoing monitoring of their security position because changing regulations demand it. Competent AI technology evaluates organizational security frameworks and then compares them to ISO/IEC 27001 and NIST Cybersecurity Framework standards in addition to Federal Financial Institutions Examination Council requirements designed for banking institutions (Achuthan et al., 2024). The major strength of AI applications in this area stems from their ability to conduct continuous checks that substitute traditional periodic audits. Through AI implementation, organizations can obtain immediate security status assessment rather than the typical annual or quarterly compliance assessment format. The combination of AI algorithms enables organizations to track network traffic so they can detect violations of security policies, such as data transfer policies or encryption rule violations. Upon identifying any non-compliant practice, AI systems can immediately propose solutions to enhance access security controls and update aged software systems (Achuthan et al., 2024). Multiple real-life implementations show the practical advantages that emerge from AI cybersecurity compliance integration. JPMorgan Chase deployed AI-based compliance monitoring software to boost its cybersecurity governance systems. The bank used AI to process big datasets of security and transaction information, which revealed various compliance risk indicators that safeguarded the organization. Automation practices in compliance monitoring at JPMorgan decreased manual audit requirements while continuously securing their financial operations through GLBA and SOX regulations (Wall, 2021).

The telecommunications industry uses AI to achieve GDPR compliance for the European Union. The AI system processes data access logs together with encryption protocols and user consent records to verify GDPR compliance for data protection. Any discrepancies detected, such as unprotected customer data located in non-compliant regions, resulted in notifications to the compliance team and automated steps for fixing the issue. The prepared strategy protected the company from costly fines through its proactive measures and maintained protection for customer data (Achuthan et al., 2024). The deployment of AI technology within cybersecurity compliance presents several obstacles, even though it delivers successful outcomes. The main disadvantage of AI-computed compliance reports involves their doubtful trustworthiness. The automation of compliance monitoring through AI depends on proper training of models with precise regulatory information that contains no bias while using current version data. The application of incorrect or old compliance rules during AI system training produces faulty recommendations, which create regulatory hazards for organizations. Organizations need to maintain updated AI-driven compliance systems, while people should verify AI-produced insights (Wall, 2021). Compliance assessments based on AI face difficulties in making their decision processes easily understandable. The interpretability of many AI-driven compliance tools remains low because their operation functions as black boxes that prevent organizations from identifying aspects of specific compliance scores or risk assessments. AI developers need to build explanation functionalities into their systems that give detailed reasons behind detected compliance violations. A tested AI system that detects non-compliant PCI DSS security protocols requires detailed explanations showing current encryption weaknesses and lacking firewall configuration elements. Through automated compliance reporting, AI and its benchmark mapping capabilities facilitate efficient real-time monitoring to drive accurate regulatory compliance operations. AI technologies will become more and more important in determining cybersecurity compliance in the future as they develop, assisting businesses in staying ahead of legal requirements and enhancing their overall security posture (Achuthan et al., 2024).

Challenges in AI-Driven Benchmarking

Artificial intelligence benchmarking tools for cybersecurity insurance functions to enhance the evaluation of security risks as well as insurance premiums and regulatory requirements monitoring capabilities. Although the benefits are substantial, the obstacles that block its widespread usage and effectiveness stand as major obstacles. AI-based assessment implementation faces technical restrictions together with moral obstacles as well as artificial intelligence assessment complexities. Multiple obstacles arise because of incompatible data standards between systems as well as data ethics and algorithm visibility requirements and struggles with AI-generated false positive and negative results in assessment processes. The emergence of AI benchmarking systems requires solutions to important problems to create dependable and unbiased systems that properly guide cybersecurity insurance determinations (Balan, 2022). The main hindrance for AI-driven benchmarking within cybersecurity insurance arises from systems that do not align with standardized data formats and lack interoperability between their systems. The evaluation of cybersecurity threats through risk assessments needs information from various platforms, which includes security logs together with compliance reports, as well as threat intelligence feeds and incident response documentation. Multiple data sources maintain independent data structures that prevent successful combination and comprehensive analysis of their information. The different organizations employ distinct data systems, including proprietary programs and open-source tools, which results in incompatible ways to track security information (Heinl et al., 2024).

Without universal data format standards, AI finds it challenging to build meaningful assessment frameworks that span various business industries and legal frameworks. The accuracy of AI risk assessments suffers because insurance providers use AI models to contrast business cybersecurity readiness compared to industry guidelines when data standards do not match. The reporting of security incidents between financial institutions and healthcare providers varies extensively because different industries need to meet separate regulatory standards, including GLBA for financials and HIPAA for healthcare. Standardization across industries proves difficult due to the present challenges in benchmarking (Balan, 2022). Standards development initiatives, including the National Institute of Standards and Technology (NIST) Cybersecurity Framework, along with the MITRE ATT&CK framework, try to resolve these inconsistent issues. The adoption of standardized frameworks spans industries to different degrees, with organizations changing these frameworks to fit their requirements, which complicates the use of AI in benchmarking activities. Standardized data formats remain essential because AI systems first need to dedicate major resources to normalize and translate information before performing meaningful benchmarking operations. Increasing complexity in benchmarking affects the performance benefits provided by AI technology for cybersecurity insurance assessments (Heinl et al., 2024).

The use of AI to benchmark operations faces severe hurdles because of raised ethical questions. To function properly, AI systems need extensive databases that help them detect trends and measure threats, then create standards. The process of gathering and managing data generates privacy issues because it potentially produces biases while remaining hard to track for users. Most organizations refrain from supplying extensive cybersecurity information to their insurers for concern about revealing security weaknesses that attackers or government authorities might use against them. Businesses that select to withhold information requirements limit AI models' access to fundamental data needed for correct benchmark development (Balan, 2022). The lack of clear algorithms remains an essential challenge during AI-based benchmark implementation. The business community alongside insurance organizations must comprehend the reasoning procedures of AI algorithms, specifically when these assessments determine insurance rates and policy acceptability. Some AI models function with "black box" characteristics, which limit understanding of why particular organizations obtain different cybersecurity risk assessments from one another. Some insurance providers and cybersecurity customers lack trust in AI benchmarks because of insufficient clarity, which also raises questions about fairness within insurance coverage of cybersecurity risks (Rehan, 2024).

An AI system uses historical incident reports to determine whether a financial institution holds a high data breach risk factor. The institution faces difficulties pinpointing which vulnerabilities and factors enhance their high-risk assessment when specific explanations are not provided. The inability to interpret AI processing hinders organizations from taking proper security improvements because they lack a clear understanding of security weaknesses (Heinl et al., 2024). AI-driven benchmarking tools should integrate explainability components that let users see how AI generates its evaluations. Organizations gain improved transparency of AI decisions by using SHAP (SHapley Additive Explanations) and LIME (Local Interpretable Model-Agnostic Explanations) techniques, which provide explanations for risk scores and compliance evaluations. The European Union's AI Act and the U.S. National AI Initiative require organizations to implement responsible AI governance through cybersecurity benchmarking by setting strong ethical AI practice requirements (Rehan, 2024). The integration of AI systems into benchmarking operations faces two major operational challenges related to the correct identification of positive and negative outcomes. AI systems create two types of errors that affect cybersecurity risk detection: they establish false positives by incorrectly marking nonexistent risks and false negatives through the non-detection of actual security risks. The use of AI-driven benchmarking for cybersecurity assessment leads organizations to face major consequences in both false positive and false negative circumstances (Glintschert, 2020).

False positive outcomes make organizations spend money on unnecessary security protocols while wasting their operational capabilities along with their budget expenditures. An incorrect identification by an AI compliance tool leads organizations to spend excessive resources on changing their encryption protocols even though

GDPR standards have not been violated. Rapidly growing numbers of false alarms sometimes create "alert fatigue," which makes security staff ignore authentic security risks (Rehan, 2024). Conversely, false negative results might be considerably more harmful. A business may believe it is safe when, in fact, it is still vulnerable to cyberattacks if an AI system is unable to spot a serious vulnerability or compliance gap. The 2017 Equifax data breach serves as an example in which cybersecurity precautions failed to identify a known vulnerability in the Apache Struts framework. AI-driven benchmarking tools would have provided Equifax with a false feeling of security and allowed the attack to happen if they had been used but had missed the vulnerability (Glintschert, 2020). The caliber of training data required to create AI models is one factor contributing to false positives and negatives in AI-driven benchmarking. Real-time threat intelligence and a variety of datasets must be used to continually update the models of AI-driven benchmarking systems to address these issues. Businesses can also use a hybrid strategy that blends human supervision with AI-driven benchmarking. AI-generated tests may be reviewed by cybersecurity specialists to confirm results, lowering the possibility of false positives and false negatives. Moreover, feedback loops must be incorporated into AI models so that businesses may gradually increase the precision of their benchmarks (Glintschert, 2020). Notwithstanding these difficulties, AI-driven benchmarking is still a potent instrument for enhancing cybersecurity risk assessments and compliance analyses. It will be essential to address the problems of data standardization, ethical openness, and accuracy if AI is to be widely used in cybersecurity insurance and regulatory compliance. Organizations may fully utilize AI-driven benchmarking while guaranteeing fairness, dependability, and credibility in cybersecurity assessments by putting in place standardized data formats, enforcing ethical AI practices, and improving AI models to reduce false positives and negatives (Glintschert, 2020).

Case Studies of AI in Cybersecurity Insurance Benchmarking

Artificial Intelligence-powered benchmarking systems emerged as an essential instrument in cybersecurity insurance, which lets companies evaluate risks while strengthening compliance and bettering their security expectations. Artificial intelligence allows companies to process extensive cybersecurity data, which enables them to automate compliance auditing and create universal industrial risk evaluation frameworks. AI-driven benchmarking assessments generate significant practical effects across various sectors but first require studying exclusive examples of its usage in real-world situations. The following research examines payment system security through the Payment Card Industry Data Security Standard (PCI DSS) compliance in financial institutions, together with Health Insurance Portability and Accountability Act (HIPAA) compliance in healthcare organizations through AI analytics implementation. The examined cases demonstrate how AI benchmarking brings both opportunities and difficulties for organizations and reveals established practices that enhance performance at executive levels (Almansoori, 2024). Financial institutions need AI-driven benchmarking to monitor their compliance with the Payment Card Industry Data Security Standard (PCI DSS), as it stands as a primary focus in cybersecurity insurance. The PCI DSS contains security standards that were developed to defend payment card operations and customer information. Organizations that fail to maintain PCI DSS compliance face financial consequences together with reputational loss, while paying higher cybersecurity insurance expenses. Financial institutions continually introduce AI-driven benchmarking technologies to execute automated compliance checks, which strengthen their security status (Gawankar et al., 2024).

The security standards of PCI DSS presented challenges to a major international banking institution because they had numerous locations throughout multiple channels. The organization faced difficulties conducting manual audits because they were both time-consuming and inconsistent and easily affected by human mistakes. The bank experienced difficulties in security vulnerability tracking and payment system compliance with PCI DSS standards. So, the institution developed an AI benchmarking tool that applied natural language processing and machine learning to analyze security records, payment transactions, and compliance documents. This AI system tracked real-time network traffic while it detected irregularities and located security weak points that might result in non-compliance. Through industry benchmark assessments, the AI system gave immediate findings about which security controls needed strengthening (Almansoori, 2024). Through its AI-based benchmarking methodology, the system effectively identified delicate security weaknesses that traditional human audits failed to discover. The AI system identified the aged encryption protocols used by the bank's payment processing legacy systems, during which data breaches became a significant risk. The bank recognized this issue, which enabled an early security upgrade of encryption standards to prevent potential penalties for non-compliance (Gawankar et al., 2024).

The Bank used the AI-driven benchmarking tool to improve its cybersecurity insurance premiums as it showed enhanced performance capabilities in risk management. The bank proved its commitment to PCI DSS standards and advanced security practices, which earned it reduced insurance costs from its provider. The insurer gave better risk evaluation to the bank because they recognized that data breaches and fraud incidents were less likely (Gawankar et al., 2024). The case study demonstrates the successes of AI-driven benchmarking yet exposes various obstacles that companies need to address with such practices. The accuracy of AI-generated compliance reports remained the main issue that needed proper attention. The bank encountered problems with its cybersecurity team understanding the AI-generated risk scores that produced incorrect compliance assessment results. The bank resolved this problem through a dual strategy that integrated AI analytics with human checks of findings until making security decisions. The HIPAA privacy legislation sets rigid security measures that healthcare institutions must follow to defend patient information. Abiding by HIPAA regulations prevents healthcare organizations from encountering significant fines and legal problems while causing insurance costs to rise (Almansoori, 2024).

This AI system tracked real-time network traffic while it detected irregularities and located security weak points that might result in non-compliance. The AI system analyzed bank security controls against industry best practices to deliver live information about protection limitation zones. AI-driven benchmarking technology exceeded manual audit capabilities by discovering fragile security weaknesses that human auditors had failed to notice previously. The AI system detected the outdated encryption protocols in the bank's outdated payment systems, putting data at risk of data breaches. The bank recognized this issue, which enabled an early security upgrade of encryption standards to prevent potential penalties for non-compliance (Hassan et al., 2023). The Bank used the AI-driven benchmarking tool to improve its cybersecurity insurance premiums as it showed enhanced performance capabilities in risk management. The bank proved its commitment to PCI DSS standards and advanced security practices, which earned it reduced insurance costs from its provider. The insurer gave better risk evaluation to the bank because they recognized that data breaches and fraud incidents were less likely (Tiwari et al., 2020).

Although the case study shows progressive outcomes of AI-driven benchmarking, there are still issues that accompany its use. The accuracy of AI-generated compliance reports remained the main issue that needed proper attention. The bank encountered problems with its cybersecurity team understanding the AI-generated risk scores that produced incorrect compliance assessment results. The bank resolved this problem through a dual strategy that integrated AI analytics with human checks of findings until making security decisions. HIPAA imposes rigorous safety protocols and privacy measures, which healthcare organizations need to implement to maintain patient information security. Abiding by HIPAA regulations prevents healthcare organizations from encountering significant fines and legal problems while causing insurance costs to rise (Hassan et al., 2023). The implementation process of healthcare AI benchmarking tools brought about multiple implementation difficulties. Security assessments encountered problems because of possible biases present within their algorithmic processes. The artificial intelligence system faced problems distinguishing between ordinary staff behavior variations and real compliance violations during its initial phase of operation. The incorrect identification of valid user access attempts as potential security threats increased because of this implementation. To solve this issue, the hospital worked hand in hand with

AI developers to enhance the benchmarking algorithms while adding contextual assessment features to security evaluations (Tiwari et al., 2020).

The implementation of artificial intelligence benchmarking in financial services and medical institutions presents useful insights that assist foremost executives in their security framework improvement. AI-driven benchmarking achieves its best results when people work alongside AI systems. Human developers need to analyze AI-generated insights because artificial intelligence succeeds at big data processing along with risk discovery, but human decision-makers must assess these findings to make security choices effectively. The adoption of a system that merges AI automation with expert human evaluation leads to maximum security results for organizations (Tiwari et al., 2020). These case studies demonstrate how AI benchmarking technology optimizes the process of obtaining cybersecurity insurance protection. Organizations achieve better insurance policy terms at reduced premiums by supplying insurers with current compliance statistics and risk evaluations in real time. This cost-reduction mechanism improves organizational motivation to achieve strict security criteria (Hassan et al., 2023).

Organizations need to resolve two major difficulties in AI-driven benchmarking, which include challenges related to algorithmic transparency and algorithmic bias. Adequate explanations from AI models in risk assessment and compliance evaluation processes are vital to establishing stakeholder trust. Software developers involved in AI creation should develop transparent risk assessment systems for business entities to examine their score computation process while adapting accordingly to environment-specific conditions. Lastly, interoperability and data standards continue to be essential components of AI-driven benchmarking success. Industry-wide standards that provide smooth data integration across various security frameworks should be promoted by organizations. Organizations may improve the precision and dependability of AI-driven benchmarking tools by using standardized data formats and working with industry regulators (Tiwari et al., 2020). By automating compliance checks, enhancing risk assessments, and maximizing insurance coverage, AI-driven benchmarking is revolutionizing cybersecurity insurance. The advantages and difficulties of AI-driven benchmarking in practical applications are illustrated by the case studies of financial and healthcare institutions. Organizations may fully utilize AI-driven benchmarking to improve cybersecurity resilience and regulatory compliance by addressing algorithmic transparency, promoting data consistency, and integrating AI capabilities with human supervision (Tiwari et al., 2020).

Future Directions in AI for Cybersecurity Benchmarking

AI-based benchmarking stands ready to expand its vital position in cybersecurity insurance operations because modernizing technologies continue to boost its functionalities. Technological developments in cyber threats require modern solutions better than conventional risk assessment processes and compliance standards. AI-driven benchmarking will obtain substantial benefits from advances in generative AI alongside federated learning and adaptive benchmarking because it aids insurers and organizations with cybersecurity assessment. The innovations deliver three improvements by refining risk models through better data privacy capabilities and enhancing insurer-organizational-regulatory body partnership connections (Alqahtani & Kumar, 2024). Generating AI systems has emerged as the most influential advancement in AI-driven benchmarking. Utility testing with generative AI differs from typical machine learning, which handles existing information by allowing it to produce simulated attack simulations with synthesized datasets for assessment benchmarks. Insurers and organizations benefit from this approach by measuring their security preparedness against unconventional cyber threats, which currently remain absent from actual data records. Cybersecurity insurers now use generative AI as part of their penetration testing, which includes threat simulation. AI-driven systems enable creators to develop modern, advanced attack approaches that emerge from current developments in cybercriminal activity. Through this method, insurers use hypothetical plausible threats to measure the effectiveness of the security controls of organizations during risk assessment. Under traditional benchmarking procedures, organizations primarily demonstrate security through previous experiences of phishing attacks alongside ransomware cases. A newly developed AI system can duplicate complex criminal hacking methods, including artificial intelligence-assisted deepfake social manipulation techniques. This simulation testing enables insurance companies to evaluate the institution's real risk factors so they can create customized policy terms (Alqahtani & Kumar, 2024). Generative AI provides multiple benefits, but it creates new difficulties for users to handle. The main worry regarding the utilization of AI-generated cyber threats is their ethical acceptance. The improper application of these AI models may create opportunities for cyber criminals since they deliver plans for complex cyber assaults. Therefore, standards for the appropriate use of generative AI in cybersecurity benchmarking must be established by industry authorities and AI developers.

Policy Recommendations

AI-driven benchmarking within cybersecurity insurance continues to transform the assessment of risks as well as the structure of policies and the maintenance of compliance due to progressing emerging technologies. AI's complete utilization requires the creation of complete policy recommendations that unite industrial needs with benchmarking solutions and overcome essential obstacles. AI integration into cybersecurity insurance frameworks requires policies that help subscribers operate through altered industry standards and enhance international standardization and collaborative efforts (Benzaid & Taleb, 2020). Creating regulatory structures stands as one key policy recommendation for implementing AI-based benchmarking into the cybersecurity insurance system. Insurance providers working together with regulatory entities need to create specific rules defining AI usage for cybersecurity risk evaluations to deliver clear underwriting policy standards. Risk assessments must utilize AI benchmarking together with present-day analytics tools that measure the security status of organizations. Insurers should establish premiums for insurance based on current security metrics through objective and continuous updates instead of using old-fashioned risk models (Alqahtani & Kumar, 2024).

Insurers must require AI-driven benchmarking tools to provide services to sensitive data-handling companies such as financial institutions, healthcare providers, and government agencies. Standardized AI-driven assessments as a part of insurance procedures enable insurers to confirm that organizations maintain strong cybersecurity preparedness levels (Benzaid & Taleb, 2020). The regulatory bodies must team up with government organizations to establish rules making mandatory AI security audits for businesses that parallel credit scoring processes adopted by financial entities. At the same time, insurance coverage should adapt to continuously shifting cybersecurity risks. The calculation of insurance premiums under traditional models uses historical data, though present-day cyber threats exceed past patterns of cyber incidents. AI benchmarking technology provides live risk evaluation, which enables insurers to make immediate changes to their coverage plans and pricing structures. By lowering rates for companies that satisfy strict cybersecurity standards, insurers could enact rules that encourage businesses to take proactive security steps (Alqahtani & Kumar, 2024). For example, businesses may be eligible for reduced insurance costs if they include AI-driven security analytics in their cybersecurity frameworks. This would motivate businesses to spend money on AI-powered security solutions that keep an eye on networks, spot irregularities, and neutralize threats before they become more serious. Such a strategy improves overall cybersecurity resilience in addition to helping insurers by lowering claims (Bahuguna et al., 2020).

The necessity for insurers to match AI-driven benchmarking with changing industry norms is another important policy proposal. Best practices for risk management and data protection are established by cybersecurity frameworks, including the GDPR, ISO/IEC 27001, and the NIST Cybersecurity Framework. Insurance policies need to evolve in step with changing industry standards since the cybersecurity environment continuously evolves (Bahuguna et al., 2020). The established policy fails to represent properly the increasing security risks that develop in an environment of changing threats. Insurance companies should develop adaptable policy structures that consider rapid market shifts throughout the cybersecurity sector and the insurance market. Insurers can reach this goal through the integration of threat intelligence systems with dynamic benchmarks, as explained in an earlier section. Insurance companies should team up with cybersecurity specialists and researchers to maintain their knowledge of new cyber threats and protective methods and weaknesses. An ongoing partnership between insurers and experts enables businesses to develop relevant and complete insurance policies that combat developing risks (Benzaid & Taleb, 2020). Insurance companies should reward businesses for their cybersecurity progress through premium discount programs that reward organizations that actively strengthen their cybersecurity capabilities. An insurer gives premium discounts to businesses that perform routine penetration tests, establish data encrypting standards, or join industry-wide cybersecurity information sharing networks. When they reward organizations for taking proactive actions, insurers develop a continuous improvement culture that makes organizations view cybersecurity as an ongoing investment instead of a single expense (Bahuguna et al., 2020).

Several insurers now use cybersecurity maturity models to develop their pricing systems for coverage. Insurance organizations utilize these frameworks for evaluating the cybersecurity preparedness of companies through maturity levels, which influence premium rates. The models can be updated to follow new cybersecurity best practices and emerging threats while ensuring the policies effectively manage current dangers because of standard evolution. Insurance companies should update their policies while creating better alliances between cybersecurity solution providers, data analysts, and threat intelligence companies. Through proper collaboration, insurers can create thorough data-based insurance policies that adhere to present-day industry requirements. The alliance between insurance companies and cybersecurity vendors enables insurers to acquire detailed client vulnerability and threat exposure data they can use to structure more efficient policies (Kiranbabu et al., 2025). The creation of an integrated risk management ecosystem demands worldwide standardization together with AI application collaboration at the scale of the entire cybersecurity insurance industry. The global nature of cybersecurity threats demands that businesses and regulators, together with insurers, establish international partnerships and work strategies on a worldwide scale. A single standardized method for AI-driven cybersecurity insurance will decrease the existing variations between territories regarding coverage levels and insurance costs. Detected security insurance will require a standardization of AI applications through security insurance to enable all parties to conduct business with uniform core assets (Freitas et al., 2024). The application of AI for risk assessment requires consistent approaches that need global standards to define how data collection and analysis should be done, along with interpretation protocols according to specified guidelines. Standardized risk assessment guidelines created by the industry would facilitate international insurance operations because they would define consistent criteria for risk evaluation in multiple markets. The use of global cooperation enables insurers to develop standard best practices that satisfy different data privacy laws for AI risk management applications (Freitas et al., 2024).

The International Association of Insurance Supervisors (IAIS) should take the lead in building structures through which they can enable this partnership by creating standards between innovation and regulation when employing AI in cybersecurity insurance (McIntosh et al., 2024). The implementation of global collaboration encounters three main barriers because countries have various sets of regulations and technology development rates alongside distinct cultural risk perception norms. The implementation of AI-driven benchmarks becomes difficult for jurisdictions with minimal cybersecurity infrastructure since they struggle to adopt standards effective for their circumstances. Standardization initiatives worldwide need to respect different settings across nations by enabling adaptability within AI application methods as they work to maintain insurance system integrity and security (Kiranbabu et al., 2025). The implementation of AI benchmarking with cybersecurity insurance frameworks, together with dynamic industry standards alignment and global cooperation, modifies the effective protection of cybersecurity insurance against emerging security risks. Insurers who adopt these recommendations will develop customized policies that suit business risk profiles and simultaneously strengthen continuous cybersecurity practice development for their customers. The success and fairness of these initiatives depend on resolving the issues involving AI bias together with data privacy matters and regulatory standard discrepancies across the globe. The complete harnessing of AI capabilities in cybersecurity insurance depends on worldwide stakeholder partnerships along with uniformed methods of implementation (McIntosh et al., 2024).

CONCLUSION

The adoption of AI-driven benchmarking for cybersecurity insurance brings essential changes to organizational risk management strategies and compliance requirements as well as resilience against cyber threats. Defining risk assessment methods through AI enables insurers to progress past previous evaluation tactics that function with static historical information until they reach present-time dynamic evaluations. The innovative system produces enhanced, individualized evaluation results that demonstrate how cyber dangers are developing. The promising nature of this transition requires organizations to navigate various ethical and technical barriers in addition to regulatory concerns. AI boosts cybersecurity insurance through improved risk evaluation capability, which includes the detection of multiple variables plus instant threat data analysis and organization development monitoring. AI-driven tools, through automation, enable businesses to ensure both policy currency and practice compliance by following the standards of ISO/IEC 27001, NIST, and GDPR. The feedback system maintains active security enhancements through which insurers deliver customized insurance policies that better represent policyholder exposure to risks.

AI achieves its most important advantage through global data set mapping across industries and areas, which provides comprehensive risk insights for cybersecurity. The elimination of national boundaries by cyber threats necessitates benchmarking programs that unite different industries worldwide. The acceptance of AI enables cybersecurity insurance to develop into a standardized, more transparent, and equitable sector that can establish and constantly refine international standards to respond to contemporary threats. The necessary capability to monitor risk development alongside assessing them as well as making necessary adjustments exists because cyberattacks have become more complex and abundant. Additionally, we should recognize multiple problems which AI benchmarking technologies can create. Security insurance benefits from AI only to a limited extent because complex data standardization issues and obstacles with interoperability limit its effectiveness and raise serious doubts about AI algorithm transparency and fairness. AI evaluation standards need to exist because they prevent inconsistencies from appearing in risk assessments, thereby causing unfair price adjustments for customers. The ethical problems arising from the application of AI for benchmarking require proper examination. Traffic between the insurance process and the policyholder depends on preserving transparency in algorithms alongside clearing assessments of risk biases. AI developers need to integrate data privacy standards along with consent protocols and discrimination protocols during their product creation because otherwise existing cybersecurity preparedness inequalities may become worse. AI-driven assessments face the challenge of correctly dealing with instances where AI makes incorrect positive and negative analysis. Incorrect risk assessments created by these errors result in either underestimating or correctly determining the security state of organizational systems. AI models require design features that allow them to learn from their experiences, so they enhance accuracy levels during operation. The regular inspection of AI algorithms by humans together with system audits should be established to maintain the reliability and performance capability of AI tools.

The prospect of AI in cybersecurity insurance demonstrates positive development through emerging technologies that will improve risk assessment capability along with compliance checking abilities. These technologies continue to advance toward implementing progressive benchmarking systems which combine secure practices with data privacy measures and adaptive capabilities against emerging security threats. In the end, incorporating AI into cybersecurity insurance frameworks successfully necessitates a well-rounded strategy that considers both the technological promise and the practical, ethical, and legal issues it raises. AI has the potential to revolutionize the assessment and insurance of cybersecurity risks by emphasizing standardization, openness, and cooperation, which will have a substantial positive impact on both insurers and businesses. To guarantee that the promise of AI-driven cybersecurity insurance is fulfilled in a way that improves overall security and equity, however, much thought must be paid to the difficulties and complexity involved. AI has the potential to significantly alter cybersecurity insurance in the future by ensuring that it is robust and flexible in the face of constantly changing cyberthreats, provided that the appropriate regulations, instruments, and tactics are in place.

REFERENCES

Achuthan, K., Ramanathan, S., Srinivas, S., & Raman, R. (2024). Advancing cybersecurity and privacy with artificial intelligence: Current trends and future research directions. *Frontiers in Big Data*, *7*, 1497535. DOI: 10.3389/fdata.2024.1497535 PMID: 39703783

Al Mansoori, M. (2024). *AI-driven anomaly detection in cybersecurity* (Master's thesis, Rochester Institute of Technology).

Al Siam, A., Alazab, M., Awajan, A., & Faruqui, N. (2025). A comprehensive review of AI's current impact and future prospects in cybersecurity. *IEEE Access : Practical Innovations, Open Solutions*, *13*, 14029–14050. DOI: 10.1109/ACCESS.2025.3528114

Alqahtani, H., & Kumar, G. (2024). Cybersecurity in electric and flying vehicles: Threats, challenges, AI solutions & future directions. *ACM Computing Surveys*, *57*(4), 1–34. DOI: 10.1145/3697830

Bahuguna, A., Bisht, R. K., & Pande, J. (2020). Country-level cybersecurity posture assessment: Study and analysis of practices. *Information Security Journal: A Global Perspective, 29*(5), 250–266.

Balan, M. (2022). *AI-powered IAM and threat intelligence: Safeguarding patient data in the age of cybersecurity breaches.*

Benzaid, C., & Taleb, T. (2020). AI-driven zero touch network and service management in 5G and beyond: Challenges and research directions. *IEEE Network*, *34*(2), 186–194. DOI: 10.1109/MNET.001.1900252

Deep, S., Kumar, S., & Kalra, P. (2024). AI-driven data security in healthcare: Safeguarding data and financial transactions. *International Journal of Novel Research and Development.*

Egho-Promise, E., Lyada, E., & Aina, F. (2024). Towards improved vulnerability management in digital environments: A comprehensive framework for cybersecurity enhancement. *International Research Journal of Computer Science*, *11*(5), 441–449. DOI: 10.26562/irjcs.2024.v1105.01

Ejjami, R. (2024). Enhancing cybersecurity through artificial intelligence: Techniques, applications, and future perspectives. *Journal of Next-Generation Research, 5.0.*

Freitas, S., Kalajdjieski, J., Gharib, A., & McCann, R. (2024). AI-driven guided response for security operation centers with Microsoft Copilot for security. *arXiv preprint arXiv:2407.09017.*

Gawankar, S., Nair, S., Pawar, V., Vhatkar, A., & Chavan, P. (2024, August). Patient privacy and data security in the era of AI-driven healthcare. In *2024 8th International Conference on Computing, Communication, Control and Automation (ICCUBEA)* (pp. 1–6). IEEE. DOI: 10.1109/ICCUBEA61740.2024.10775004

Glintschert, M. (2020). AI-driven IT and its potentials–a state-of-the-art approach. *Available at SSRN* 3576417. DOI: 10.2139/ssrn.3576417

Hassan, M. M., Abrar, M. F., & Hasan, M. (2023). An explainable AI-driven machine learning framework for cybersecurity anomaly detection. In *Cyber Security and Business Intelligence* (pp. 197–219). Routledge. DOI: 10.4324/9781003285854-13

Heinl, P., Patapovas, A., & Pilgermann, M. (2024). Towards AI-enabled cyber threat assessment in the health sector. *arXiv preprint arXiv:2409.12765.*

Kiranbabu, M. N. V., Viji, A. J., Chandanan, A. K., Birchha, V., Pandey, T. K., & Sar, S. K. (2025). The challenge of adversarial attacks on AI-driven cybersecurity systems. *Journal of Cybersecurity & Information Management*, *15*(1).

Madhavan, K., Yazdinejad, A., Zarrinkalam, F., & Dehghantanha, A. (2025). Quantifying security vulnerabilities: A metric-driven security analysis of gaps in current AI standards. *arXiv preprint arXiv:2502.08610.*

McIntosh, T. R., Susnjak, T., Liu, T., Watters, P., Xu, D., Liu, D., Nowrozy, R., & Halgamuge, M. N. (2024). From COBIT to ISO 42001: Evaluating cybersecurity frameworks for opportunities, risks, and regulatory compliance in commercializing large language models. *Computers & Security*, *144*, 103964. DOI: 10.1016/j.cose.2024.103964

Pandey, P., & Katsikas, S. (2023). The future of cyber risk management: AI and DLT for automated cyber risk modelling, decision making, and risk transfer. In *Handbook of Research on Artificial Intelligence, Innovation and Entrepreneurship* (pp. 272–290). Edward Elgar Publishing.

Radanliev, P. (2024). Cyber diplomacy: Defining the opportunities for cybersecurity and risks from artificial intelligence, IoT, blockchains, and quantum computing. *Journal of Cyber Security Technology*, *1*, 1–51.

Radanliev, P., De Roure, D., Maple, C., Nurse, J. R., Nicolescu, R., & Ani, U. (2024). AI security and cyber risk in IoT systems. *Frontiers in Big Data*, *7*, 1402745. DOI: 10.3389/fdata.2024.1402745 PMID: 39449740

Rahman, M. M., Pokharel, B. P., Sayeed, S. A., Bhowmik, S. K., Kshetri, N., & Eashrak, N. (2024). riskAIchain: AI-driven IT infrastructure—blockchain-backed approach for enhanced risk management. *Risks*, *12*(12), 206. DOI: 10.3390/risks12120206

Rehan, H. (2024). AI-driven cloud security: The future of safeguarding sensitive data in the digital age. [JAIGS]. *Journal of Artificial Intelligence General Science*, *1*(1), 132–151.

Salem, A. H., Azzam, S. M., Emam, O. E., & Abohany, A. A. (2024). Advancing cybersecurity: A comprehensive review of AI-driven detection techniques. *Journal of Big Data*, *11*(1), 105. DOI: 10.1186/s40537-024-00957-y

Sindiramutty, S. R. (2023). Autonomous threat hunting: A future paradigm for AI-driven threat intelligence. *arXiv preprint arXiv:2401.00286.*

Stettinger, G., Weissensteiner, P., & Khastgir, S. (2024). Trustworthiness assurance assessment for high-risk AI-based systems. *IEEE Access : Practical Innovations, Open Solutions*, *12*, 22718–22745. DOI: 10.1109/ACCESS.2024.3364387

Tariq, M. U. (2024). Leveraging AI for Entrepreneurial Innovation in Healthcare. In Özsungur, F. (Ed.), *Generating Entrepreneurial Ideas With AI* (pp. 192–216). IGI Global., DOI: 10.4018/979-8-3693-3498-0.ch009

Tariq, M. U. (2024). The role of AI in skilling, upskilling, and reskilling the workforce. In Doshi, R., Dadhich, M., Poddar, S., & Hiran, K. (Eds.), *Integrating generative AI in education to achieve sustainable development goals* (pp. 421–433). IGI Global., DOI: 10.4018/979-8-3693-2440-0.ch023

Tariq, M. U. (2025). AI-Driven Research Methodologies: Revolutionizing Data-Driven Discoveries in Engineering and Physical Sciences. In Basha, J., Alade, T., Al Khazimi, M., Vasudevan, R., & Khan, J. (Eds.), *Optimizing Research Techniques and Learning Strategies With Digital Technologies* (pp. 97–122). IGI Global Scientific Publishing., DOI: 10.4018/979-8-3693-7863-2.ch004

Tariq, M. U. (2025). Navigating the Convergence of IoMT and Generative AI in Global Healthcare: Opportunities, Challenges, and Ethical Considerations. In Kumar, V., Katina, P., & Zhao, J. (Eds.), *Convergence of Internet of Medical Things (IoMT) and Generative AI* (pp. 513–534). IGI Global Scientific Publishing., DOI: 10.4018/979-8-3693-6180-1.ch022

Tariq, M. U. (2025). Leveraging Artificial Intelligence to Enhance Diversity and Drive Business Innovation. In Margaretha van der Poll, H., Andrew van der Poll, J., & Ngwakwe, C. (Eds.), *Diversity, AI, and Sustainability for Financial Growth* (pp. 79–96). IGI Global Scientific Publishing., DOI: 10.4018/979-8-3693-6011-8.ch004

Tiwari, S., Sresth, V., & Srivastava, A. (2020). The role of explainable AI in cybersecurity: Addressing transparency challenges in autonomous defense systems. *International Journal of Innovative Research in Science, Engineering and Technology*, *9*(3), 718–733. DOI: 10.15680/IJIRSET.2020.0903165

Wall, A. M. (2021). *Guidelines for artificial intelligence-driven enterprise compliance management systems* (Doctoral dissertation).

KEY TERMS AND DEFINITIONS

AI-Powered Risk Assessment: The use of artificial intelligence to analyze and predict cybersecurity risks based on historical and real-time data.

Compliance Automation: The application of AI and machine learning to streamline adherence to cybersecurity regulations and standards.

Cybersecurity Benchmarking: The process of evaluating an organization's cybersecurity measures against established industry standards and best practices.

Predictive Analytics in Cybersecurity: The use of AI-driven data analysis to anticipate potential cyber threats and vulnerabilities.

Regulatory Cybersecurity Standards: Frameworks and guidelines such as ISO/IEC 27001 and the NIST Cybersecurity Framework that define best practices for managing cybersecurity risks.

Chapter 5

Leveraging AI to Establish Cybersecurity Insurance Benchmarks and Guidelines:

Standards in Cybersecurity Insurance

Nabeel Alassaf
https://orcid.org/0000-0001-9409-2353
Universiti Sains Malaysia, Malaysia

Selvakumar Manickam
https://orcid.org/0000-0003-4378-1954
Cybersecurity Research Centre, Malaysia

Ammar Odeh
https://orcid.org/0000-0002-9929-2116
Princess Sumaya University for Technology, Jordan

Shams ul Arfeen Laghari
School of ICT, Faculty of Engineering Design Information and Communications Technology, Bahrain

Mohammed Anbar
Cybersecurity Research Centre, Malaysia

Abobakr Aboshgifa
The Libyan Higher Technical Center for Training and Production, Libya

Nabil Belhaj
Libyan Higher Technical Center for Training and Production, Libya

ABSTRACT

Cybersecurity insurance is a vital risk mitigation tool as cyber threats grow in complexity. However, the absence of standardized evaluation metrics and benchmarking frameworks creates challenges in assessing cybersecurity risks and determining

DOI: 10.4018/979-8-3373-5545-0.ch005

policy premiums. Artificial Intelligence (AI) is transforming this field by enabling data-driven risk assessment, automated underwriting, and predictive analytics. This chapter examines AI's role in establishing benchmarking methodologies and driving standardization in cybersecurity insurance. It explores how AI models utilize historical data, threat intelligence, and real-time monitoring to assess cyber risk, automate compliance checks, detect fraud, and enable adaptive insurance pricing. Additionally, it addresses key challenges, including ethical considerations, data privacy, and regulatory compliance. By integrating AI into cybersecurity insurance frameworks, insurers can enhance risk quantification, streamline claims processing, and promote industry-wide standards.

1. INTRODUCTION

Cybersecurity threats are evolving at an unprecedented rate, posing significant financial and operational risks to organizations across all industries. With the increasing frequency and sophistication of cyberattacks, businesses and institutions face mounting challenges in safeguarding their digital assets, maintaining regulatory compliance, and ensuring business continuity. These risks extend beyond direct financial losses, often leading to reputational damage, legal liabilities, and operational disruptions. As cybercriminal tactics become more advanced, traditional security measures can no longer mitigate the ever-growing threat landscape. Organizations must explore additional protective measures, including cybersecurity insurance, to cushion the financial impact of potential breaches and attacks (Dhieb, Ghazzai, Besbes, & Massoud, 2020).

The rise of cybersecurity insurance has provided a crucial safety net, offering financial compensation and support in the event of cyber incidents. However, the traditional insurance models in this domain face significant challenges, primarily due to the difficulty of accurately quantifying cyber risks. Unlike conventional insurance sectors, where risks such as natural disasters or automobile accidents are backed by extensive historical data and well-defined actuarial models, cybersecurity insurance struggles with cyber threats' unpredictability and evolving nature. Standardizing policies, assessing coverage requirements, and setting fair pricing models is difficult. Insurers often rely on subjective assessments, generalized risk factors, and limited datasets, leading to inconsistencies in policy terms and premium structures. These gaps have created an urgent need for more accurate, data-driven risk assessment mechanisms to enhance underwriting processes and optimize coverage decisions (Arefin & Simcox, 2024; Jawhar, Kimble, Miller, & Bitar, 2024).

AI-driven benchmarking presents a transformative solution to these challenges by leveraging artificial intelligence and machine learning for real-time risk assessment, automated policy management, and claims processing. AI-driven models can provide standardized cybersecurity maturity evaluations by analyzing vast datasets of cyber incidents, threat intelligence feeds, and organizational security postures. This allows insurers to objectively assess an organization's security framework, ensuring that coverage and premium structures align with actual risk exposure (Shahidi, Darmel, Jalalzai, & Amiri, 2024). Moreover, AI-driven analytics can detect emerging threats, predict potential vulnerabilities, and recommend proactive mitigation strategies, enhancing overall cybersecurity resilience. Such advancements reduce human bias in underwriting decisions, enable dynamic policy adjustments, and streamline claims verification, ultimately leading to a more efficient and fair insurance ecosystem (Deshpande, 2024; Parveen, 2024).

As AI adoption in cybersecurity insurance expands, it is poised to play a pivotal role in shaping industry standards and enhancing risk management strategies. By integrating AI-powered risk modeling, insurers can move towards a more predictive and preventive approach rather than a reactive one. This Shift will enable organizations to adopt more comprehensive cybersecurity strategies, incentivizing investments in proactive security measures to lower insurance costs. Furthermore, AI-driven solutions can facilitate collaboration between insurers, cybersecurity firms, and regulatory bodies to establish standardized frameworks for cyber risk evaluation and incident response. As a result, AI will drive the evolution of cybersecurity insurance, ensuring that policies remain adaptive to emerging threats while providing organizations with robust financial protection (Rangaraju, 2023).

Ultimately, the convergence of AI and cybersecurity insurance will redefine the future of cyber resilience. Organizations that embrace AI-driven benchmarking will benefit from enhanced threat intelligence, improved incident response capabilities, and optimized financial protection against cyber risks. As the industry matures, AI-powered innovations will refine insurance practices and foster a more secure digital ecosystem where businesses, governments, and insurers work together to combat cyber threats. By leveraging AI's potential, the cybersecurity insurance sector can evolve into a more precise, efficient, and equitable system, ensuring long-term sustainability and resilience in an increasingly digitized world (Odeh, Taleb, Alhajahjeh, & Aparicio-Navarro, 2024; Reddy, 2023).

Cybersecurity threats continue to evolve, presenting financial and operational risks for organizations across all sectors. The rise of cybersecurity insurance has provided a critical safety net, but traditional insurance models struggle with risk quantification, policy standardization, and fair pricing. AI-driven benchmarking offers a transformative solution by enabling real-time risk assessment, standardized cybersecurity maturity evaluation, and automation of claims processing. As

AI adoption in cybersecurity insurance grows, it will play a pivotal role in shaping industry standards, enhancing risk management strategies, and driving the future of cyber resilience.

1.1. Overview of Cybersecurity Threats and Their Financial Implications

In an increasingly digital world, cyber threats have become one of the most significant risks facing businesses, governments, and individuals. The growing reliance on cloud computing, interconnected devices, and online transactions has expanded the attack surface for malicious actors. Cybercriminals exploit software, networks, and human behavior vulnerabilities to carry out sophisticated attacks, ranging from ransomware to advanced persistent threats (APTs). The financial and reputational damages caused by these incidents have escalated, making cybersecurity an essential component of risk management for organizations worldwide (Kamuangu, 2024).

The financial implications of cyber threats are vast and continue to rise. According to recent reports, global cybercrime damages are projected to reach $10.5 trillion annually by 2025, making it more lucrative than the international drug trade. Data breaches alone cost companies an average of $4.45 million per incident, stemming from regulatory fines, legal fees, reputational damage, and loss of business. High-profile cyberattacks, such as the SolarWinds attack, the Colonial Pipeline ransomware incident, and breaches at major financial institutions, demonstrate the magnitude of the risk. Moreover, supply chain vulnerabilities and the proliferation of zero-day exploits make it difficult for traditional cybersecurity measures to keep pace with evolving threats (Pandey & Kapoor, 2025).

In addition to financial losses, cyberattacks have long-term effects on businesses and critical infrastructure. Organizations suffer from operational disruptions, intellectual property theft, and erosion of customer trust. Governments and policymakers recognize cybersecurity as a national security concern, emphasizing the need for robust risk management strategies. However, organizations remain vulnerable to sophisticated attacks despite increased investments in cybersecurity tools and policies. Given the unpredictability and growing frequency of cyber incidents, businesses are increasingly seeking financial protection through cybersecurity insurance to mitigate potential losses.

1.2. Rise of Cybersecurity Insurance as a Response to Increasing Cyber Risks

Organizations face uncertainty in effectively estimating and managing cyber risks as cyber threats evolve. This uncertainty has fueled the rise of cybersecurity insurance, a financial instrument designed to protect businesses from the economic and legal consequences of cyberattacks. Cyber insurance policies typically cover a range of expenses, including incident response costs, legal fees, regulatory fines, business interruption losses, and customer compensation in the event of a cyber incident (Pandey & Kapoor, 2025).

The cybersecurity insurance market has witnessed exponential growth in recent years. In 2020, the global cyber insurance market was valued at approximately $7.8 billion and is projected to reach over $20 billion by 2025, driven by increased cyber threats and regulatory requirements. Industries such as finance, healthcare, retail, and manufacturing, which handle vast amounts of sensitive data, are among the primary adopters of cybersecurity insurance.

Governments and regulatory bodies have also played a crucial role in shaping the cybersecurity insurance landscape. Data protection laws such as the General Data Protection Regulation (GDPR) and the California Consumer Privacy Act (CCPA) impose strict requirements on organizations to safeguard user data. Non-compliance can result in hefty fines, making cybersecurity insurance a valuable risk transfer mechanism for organizations striving to meet regulatory standards (Bonta, 2022).

Despite its growing adoption, cybersecurity insurance remains a complex domain. Unlike traditional insurance models (e.g., property or health insurance), cyber risks are dynamic and difficult to quantify. The evolving nature of cyber threats and the lack of historical data make risk assessment and policy pricing challenging for insurers. These complexities have led to gaps in coverage, inconsistent underwriting practices, and challenges in claims processing.

1.3. Challenges in Traditional Cybersecurity Insurance Models

While cybersecurity insurance offers financial protection against cyber risks, traditional insurance models struggle to keep pace with the rapidly evolving threat landscape. Several key challenges exist in the current cybersecurity insurance framework:

1.3.1. Difficulty in Cyber Risk Quantification

Cyber risks are inherently intangible and continuously evolving, making their accurate assessment a persistent challenge for insurers, businesses, and cybersecurity professionals. Unlike risks associated with natural disasters, where the frequency, severity, and financial impact can be estimated based on centuries of historical data and geological patterns, or health-related risks, which rely on well-established epidemiological studies and actuarial models, cyber threats do not follow predictable patterns. Instead, they are driven by human ingenuity, technological advancements, and ever-changing attack methodologies. The dynamic nature of the cyber threat landscape means that new vulnerabilities, attack vectors, and malicious strategies emerge at an alarming rate, often outpacing the development of defensive measures (Woods & Böhme, 2021).

One of the primary difficulties in assessing cyber risks stems from the adaptability and innovation of cybercriminals. Unlike hurricanes or earthquakes, which follow scientific principles and established probability models, cyberattacks are intentional, strategic, and continuously evolving. Threat actors, including state-sponsored hackers, cybercriminal organizations, and opportunistic attackers, constantly refine their tactics, techniques, and procedures (TTPs) to exploit emerging vulnerabilities. The proliferation of ransomware-as-a-service (RaaS), phishing-as-a-service (PhaaS), and other cybercrime business models has complicated risk assessment by making sophisticated attack tools readily available to a broader range of threat actors. This level of unpredictability means that relying on historical data alone is insufficient for accurately underwriting cyber insurance policies.

Additionally, the rapid pace of technological innovation adds another layer of complexity to cyber risk evaluation. New security vulnerabilities emerge as organizations adopt emerging technologies such as cloud computing, Internet of Things (IoT) devices, artificial intelligence, and blockchain. Each technological advancement introduces novel risks that may not have been previously encountered, making it difficult for insurers to develop standardized risk models. For instance, IoT devices often lack robust security features, creating potential entry points for cybercriminals, while artificial intelligence systems may be susceptible to adversarial attacks. The interconnected nature of modern digital ecosystems amplifies these risks, as a single weak point in a supply chain or cloud infrastructure can lead to widespread security breaches affecting multiple entities (Georgiadou, Mouzakitis, & Askounis, 2021).

Furthermore, cyber risk assessment is complicated by the lack of transparency and uniformity in incident reporting. Unlike physical disasters or medical conditions, where data is systematically collected and analyzed over time, cyber incidents often go unreported or are inconsistently documented due to reputational concerns, legal implications, and regulatory disparities across different jurisdictions. Many organizations are reluctant to disclose cyberattacks for fear of damaging their brand reputation, losing customer trust, or facing regulatory scrutiny. This underreporting skews available data, making establishing accurate probability models for cyber threats difficult. Even when cyber incidents are reported, the level of detail and standardization varies, limiting the ability of insurers and researchers to derive meaningful insights for risk quantification.

Given these challenges, traditional actuarial methods used in other insurance domains fail to provide a reliable framework for cyber risk assessment. Unlike property or life insurance, where risks can be assessed based on fixed variables such as geographic location, building materials, or medical history, cyber risks are fluid, contextual, and highly dependent on an organization's security posture, employee awareness, third-party relationships, and regulatory environment. The absence of a universally accepted cyber risk rating system further complicates underwriting decisions, as insurers must rely on a combination of security assessments, threat intelligence reports, and qualitative evaluations to determine coverage and pricing.

Insurers and cybersecurity experts increasingly turn to artificial intelligence, machine learning, and advanced analytics to address these complexities and enhance cyber risk assessment. AI-driven risk modeling can analyze vast datasets, detect patterns in cyber incidents, and predict emerging threats more accurately than traditional methods. By leveraging real-time threat intelligence, automated security assessments, and predictive analytics, insurers can move toward more dynamic underwriting processes that account for the evolving nature of cyber threats. Additionally, adopting standardized cybersecurity frameworks, such as the National Institute of Standards and Technology (NIST) Cybersecurity Framework or the ISO/IEC 27001 standard, can provide a more structured approach to evaluating organizational security postures and quantifying cyber risk exposure (Koza, 2022).

Ultimately, the unpredictable nature of cyber risks underscores the need for continuous adaptation and innovation in risk assessment methodologies. As cyber threats evolve, insurers, businesses, and policymakers must collaborate to develop more robust, data-driven approaches to cyber risk quantification. By integrating advanced technologies, improving incident reporting mechanisms, and fostering greater transparency in cybersecurity practices, the industry can work toward more accurate, fair, and effective cyber insurance models that provide meaningful protection in an increasingly digital world.

1.3.2. High Variability in Policy Coverage

Cyber insurance policies lack standardization, leading to inconsistencies in coverage. Some policies cover business interruption costs, while others exclude them. Similarly, coverage for ransomware payments, regulatory fines, and third-party liabilities varies across insurers. This lack of uniformity makes it challenging for businesses to compare policies and assess their true protection levels (Kolluru et al., 2024).

Cyber insurance policies suffer from a critical lack of standardization, leading to significant inconsistencies in coverage, policy terms, and claims processing. Unlike more established insurance markets, such as auto, health, or property insurance, where standardized guidelines and actuarial data help create uniform coverage options, cyber insurance remains a relatively nascent and rapidly evolving field. The absence of universally accepted industry standards results in substantial variations between policies, making it difficult for organizations to navigate the landscape effectively. As cyber threats continue to increase in frequency and sophistication, the lack of consistency in cyber insurance coverage creates uncertainty for businesses seeking financial protection against potential cyber incidents (Deshpande, 2024; Jawhar et al., 2024; Kamuangu, 2024).

One of the most glaring inconsistencies among cyber insurance policies is the scope of coverage for business interruption costs. Some insurers offer comprehensive policies that cover lost revenue, recovery expenses, and operational downtime caused by cyberattacks, while others exclude these provisions or impose strict conditions for eligibility. Since cyber incidents can disrupt critical business operations—sometimes for weeks or months—having adequate business interruption coverage is essential. However, the disparity in policy offerings forces organizations to scrutinize policy details meticulously, often requiring legal and cybersecurity expertise to understand the full extent of their protection. Many businesses may assume they are covered for operational losses without a standardized approach, only to discover gaps in their policies when a cyber incident occurs (Vose et al., 2021).

Similarly, coverage for ransomware attacks is highly inconsistent across insurers. Ransomware has emerged as one of the most prevalent and financially damaging cyber threats, with attackers encrypting business-critical data and demanding payments for its release. Some policies explicitly cover ransomware payments, incident response services, and data restoration costs, while others exclude ransom payments altogether or impose restrictive conditions that limit reimbursement. Given the rise of ransomware-as-a-service (RaaS) and the growing sophistication of cyber extortion tactics, businesses need clear guidance on whether their insurance policies provide adequate protection. The lack of standardization in ransomware coverage leads to uncertainty, making it difficult for organizations to determine whether they should rely on cyber insurance or invest in alternative risk mitigation strategies.

Regulatory fines and compliance-related costs also represent a major variation in cyber insurance policies. As governments and regulatory bodies implement stricter data protection laws—such as the General Data Protection Regulation (GDPR) in Europe and the California Consumer Privacy Act (CCPA) in the United States—

businesses face significant financial penalties for failing to safeguard sensitive customer information. Some cyber insurance policies include coverage for regulatory fines, legal defense costs, and compliance-related expenses, while others explicitly exclude them. This discrepancy is particularly concerning for businesses operating across multiple jurisdictions, as they may face different regulatory requirements and financial exposures depending on where a data breach occurs. Companies must carefully evaluate policy terms without a standardized approach to ensure they are adequately protected against legal and regulatory risks (Khatam, 2022).

Another area of inconsistency is third-party liability coverage. Cyber incidents often have ripple effects that impact business partners, customers, and service providers. Some cyber insurance policies cover third-party claims, including lawsuits resulting from data breaches, contractual disputes, and reputational damage. Others focus solely on first-party losses, exposing businesses to financial liabilities arising from legal actions or customer compensation demands. Given the interconnected nature of modern business ecosystems, third-party liability coverage is crucial to cyber insurance, yet its availability varies widely among insurers. This inconsistency makes it challenging for organizations to assess their true protection levels and determine whether additional liability coverage is necessary.

The lack of uniformity in cyber insurance policies creates challenges for businesses and insurers, brokers, and regulatory bodies. Organizations struggle to compare policies, assess risk exposure, and determine the most suitable coverage options for their needs. The absence of standard definitions, exclusions, and coverage frameworks further complicates the underwriting process, making it difficult for insurers to evaluate cyber risks consistently. Additionally, discrepancies in policy wording can lead to disputes over claims, prolonging the resolution process and reducing the effectiveness of cyber insurance as a risk management tool (Arefin & Simcox, 2024; Khatam, 2022; Odeh & Taleb, 2024; Odeh, Taleb, Alhajahjeh, Aparicio, et al., 2024; Pandey & Kapoor, 2025; Woods & Böhme, 2021).

To address these issues, the cyber insurance industry must work toward greater standardization and transparency in policy structures. Establishing industry-wide best practices, developing standardized coverage frameworks, and adopting clear definitions of cyber risks would help businesses make informed decisions when selecting insurance policies. Regulatory agencies and industry associations could play a pivotal role in creating guidelines that promote consistency in cyber insurance offerings, ensuring that businesses receive reliable and comprehensive protection. Furthermore, leveraging AI-driven risk assessment tools and data analytics could enhance underwriting accuracy, enabling insurers to provide more tailored, standardized policy options based on real-time risk intelligence.

Ultimately, the lack of standardization in cyber insurance policies remains a major barrier to effective risk management. As cyber threats evolve, businesses need clear, consistent, and reliable insurance coverage to protect against financial and operational disruptions. By working toward greater uniformity in policy structures, insurers can enhance trust in the cyber insurance market, provide businesses with a clearer understanding of their coverage, and contribute to a more resilient cybersecurity ecosystem.

1.3.3. Rising Premiums and Limited Coverage Capacity

The surge in cyberattacks has led insurers to increase premiums and limit coverage. Businesses with a high-risk profile (e.g., those in financial services or healthcare) often face difficulty obtaining affordable cyber insurance. In some cases, insurers impose strict cybersecurity requirements, such as multi-factor authentication (MFA) and endpoint detection and response (EDR), as prerequisites for coverage. Organizations that fail to meet these criteria may face higher premiums or outright rejection.

The rapid surge in cyberattacks has significantly impacted the cyber insurance industry, leading insurers to reevaluate their risk models, adjust policy terms, and impose stricter requirements on businesses seeking coverage. As the frequency and severity of cyber incidents continue to escalate—fueled by ransomware attacks, data breaches, and sophisticated supply chain intrusions—insurers are increasingly cautious about underwriting cyber policies. The growing financial impact of cyber threats has resulted in higher premiums, reduced coverage options, and more stringent eligibility criteria for businesses, particularly those operating in high-risk sectors. This Shift in the cyber insurance landscape has made it increasingly challenging for organizations to secure affordable and comprehensive policies, creating additional financial and operational burdens (Patterson & Doyle, 2021).

Businesses that fall into high-risk categories—financial services, healthcare, and critical infrastructure—face some of the greatest difficulties in obtaining cyber insurance. These industries handle large volumes of sensitive data, making them prime targets for cybercriminals. Financial institutions process vast amounts of transactional data, healthcare organizations manage confidential patient records, and energy providers operate critical systems that, if compromised, could lead to severe disruptions. Due to their increased exposure to cyber threats, insurers perceive these industries as high liability, often charging prohibitively expensive premiums or imposing restrictive conditions to mitigate their financial risks. This has resulted in many businesses struggling to find affordable cyber insurance, leaving them vulnerable to significant economic losses in the event of an attack (Arefin & Simcox, 2024; Georgiadou et al., 2021; Woods & Böhme, 2021).

In response to rising cyber risks, many insurers have introduced stringent cybersecurity prerequisites that organizations must meet before qualifying for coverage. Common requirements include implementing advanced security measures such as multi-factor authentication (MFA), endpoint detection and response (EDR), network segmentation, data encryption, and employee cybersecurity training programs. These controls are designed to minimize the likelihood of successful cyberattacks, ultimately reducing insurers' exposure to claims. However, meeting these security requirements can be costly and time-consuming, particularly for small and medium-sized businesses (SMBs) with limited cybersecurity budgets. Organizations that fail to implement these security measures may be subject to significantly higher premiums, reduced policy coverage, or outright denial of coverage, forcing them to invest heavily in cybersecurity enhancements or operate without insurance protection.

In some cases, insurers have exceeded security requirements and have begun mandating regular security assessments, penetration testing, and incident response plans as underwriting criteria. Businesses that lack robust security postures or fail to demonstrate proactive risk management strategies may find themselves ineligible for coverage altogether. Additionally, some insurers have introduced exclusions for certain types of cyber incidents, such as nation-state-sponsored attacks, exposing organizations to risks that may not be covered under their policies. The increasing complexity of policy terms and exclusions has made it difficult for businesses to fully understand the extent of their coverage, leading to potential gaps in protection.

The tightening of cyber insurance policies has also increased the focus on risk quantification and continuous monitoring. Many insurers now leverage AI-driven threat intelligence, real-time vulnerability assessments, and cyber risk scoring models to dynamically adjust policy pricing and coverage based on an organization's security posture. This approach enables insurers to tailor premiums more accurately, rewarding businesses with strong cybersecurity frameworks while penalizing those with inadequate defenses. While this Shift promotes better cybersecurity practices, it also creates a financial strain on companies that may struggle to meet evolving security expectations (Voolstra et al., 2021).

Ultimately, the rising costs and coverage limitations in the cyber insurance market highlight the need for businesses to adopt a proactive approach to cybersecurity risk management. Rather than relying solely on insurance as a financial safety net, organizations must prioritize investment in advanced security solutions, threat intelligence, and employee training programs to mitigate cyber risks effectively. Additionally, industry stakeholders, regulatory bodies, and insurers must collaborate to establish standardized security benchmarks, ensuring businesses have clear guidelines on the necessary cybersecurity measures for obtaining coverage.

As cyber threats evolve, the cyber insurance industry will likely see further adjustments in risk assessment methodologies, policy structures, and pricing models. While these changes may introduce challenges for businesses seeking coverage, they also underscore the growing recognition that cybersecurity is not just an IT concern but a fundamental component of risk management. By aligning insurance policies with strong cybersecurity practices, insurers and businesses can work together to create a more resilient and sustainable approach to managing cyber risks in an increasingly digital world.

1.3.4. Challenges in Claims Processing and Fraud Detection

Cyber insurance claims are complex and time-sensitive. Organizations filing claims after a cyberattack often struggle to prove the extent of their losses, leading to disputes between insurers and policyholders. Additionally, fraudulent claims have emerged as a concern, where businesses misrepresent cyber incidents to obtain payouts. Traditional claims processing methods rely on manual assessment, making them slow and prone to errors.

Cyber insurance claims are inherently complex, requiring swift and accurate processing to mitigate cyber incidents' financial and operational impact. Unlike traditional insurance claims—such as those related to property damage or automobile accidents—cyber claims involve intangible losses, making it challenging to quantify damages precisely. When organizations experience a cyberattack, they often face difficulties proving the extent of their financial, reputational, and operational losses, leading to prolonged disputes with insurers. These disputes can arise over business interruption costs, data recovery expenses, regulatory penalties, and legal liabilities. Without a standardized framework for evaluating cyber incident damages, insurers and policyholders frequently find themselves at odds over claim eligibility, reimbursement amounts, and policy exclusions.

One of the primary challenges in cyber insurance claims processing is the burden of proof placed on policyholders. Unlike physical damages, which can be visually inspected and assessed, cyber incidents require forensic investigations to determine the root cause, attack vector, and overall impact. Organizations must provide detailed documentation, including incident response reports, forensic analysis, financial statements, and evidence of compliance with policy requirements. The lack of uniform standards for assessing cyber damages further complicates this process, as different insurers may have varying criteria for validating claims. This often results in delayed claim approvals, forcing organizations to cover immediate recovery costs out of pocket while awaiting reimbursement. Given the urgency of cyber incident response, these delays can significantly hinder an organization's ability to resume normal operations promptly.

1.3.5. Lack of Benchmarking and Standardized Risk Assessment Models

A fundamental challenge in cybersecurity insurance is the absence of standardized risk assessment frameworks. Insurers rely on self-reported business data, leading to inconsistencies and potential misrepresentation. Insurers struggle to fairly evaluate cyber risks without a uniform benchmarking system, leading to inequitable policy pricing and coverage gaps.

Additionally, fraudulent claims have emerged as a growing concern in the cyber insurance industry. Some businesses, intentionally or due to misinterpretation of policy terms, may misrepresent cyber incidents to obtain payouts. For example, an organization might exaggerate the financial impact of a cyberattack, claim damages for pre-existing vulnerabilities, or even stage an incident to take advantage of insurance coverage. Such fraudulent activities increase financial risks for insurers and contribute to higher premiums and stricter policy terms for legitimate policyholders. To combat fraud, insurers have begun implementing more rigorous claim verification processes, requiring extensive evidence, independent cybersecurity audits, and forensic investigations before approving payouts. While these measures help prevent fraudulent claims, they add complexity to the claims process, further delaying settlements for businesses genuinely affected by cyber incidents (Odeh, Keshta, & Abdelfattah, 2021; Odeh & Taleb, 2023; Takamoto et al., 2022).

Traditional claims processing methods exacerbate these challenges, often relying on manual assessments, extensive paperwork, and subjective evaluations. The lack of automation in cyber insurance claims handling makes the process slow, labor-intensive, and prone to errors. Insurers must analyze vast amounts of data, verify technical reports, and assess compliance with policy requirements—all of which can introduce inconsistencies and delays. Manual processing also increases the risk of human bias and oversight, leading to discrepancies in claim approvals and settlement amounts. Given the rapidly evolving nature of cyber threats, insurers must modernize their claims-handling procedures to improve efficiency, accuracy, and fairness in claim resolutions.

To address these inefficiencies, the cyber insurance industry increasingly turns to artificial intelligence, machine learning, and automated claims processing solutions. AI-driven analytics can streamline claims verification by analyzing real-time cyber incident reports, financial impact assessments, and policyholder compliance data. Automated tools can cross-reference claims with historical cyberattack patterns, threat intelligence feeds, and digital forensics findings to validate the legitimacy of an incident. Additionally, blockchain technology is being explored to create transparent, immutable records of cyber incidents, ensuring that claims data is secure, verifiable, and tamper-proof. By integrating these technologies, insurers can enhance the speed and accuracy of claims processing, reducing disputes and improving the overall efficiency of cyber insurance settlements.

Improving the cyber insurance claims process requires collaboration between insurers, businesses, cybersecurity professionals, and regulatory bodies. Standardized frameworks for incident reporting, financial loss quantification, and forensic analysis can help create a more transparent and efficient claims ecosystem. Organizations must also take proactive steps to document their cybersecurity practices, incident response protocols, and risk mitigation efforts to facilitate smoother claims processing. As cyber threats continue to grow in complexity, the ability to swiftly and accurately assess cyber insurance claims will be critical in ensuring that businesses receive the financial support they need to recover from attacks. By leveraging technology, refining claims evaluation methodologies, and promoting greater transparency, the cyber insurance industry can enhance trust, efficiency, and resilience in an increasingly digital world.

1.4. The Need for AI-Driven Benchmarking to Improve Accuracy and Fairness

To overcome the limitations of traditional cybersecurity insurance models, there is a growing need for AI-driven benchmarking and risk assessment frameworks. AI has the potential to transform cybersecurity insurance by improving the accuracy of risk evaluations, streamlining underwriting processes, and enhancing claims processing efficiency.

1.4.1. AI for Real-Time Risk Assessment

AI-powered models analyze vast amounts of cyber threat intelligence data to assess an organization's cybersecurity posture. By monitoring network traffic, identifying vulnerabilities, and detecting anomalies, AI can generate dynamic risk scores that reflect an organization's real-time cyber risk exposure. This data-driven approach provides insurers objective and consistent risk evaluations, reducing reliance on subjective assessments (Kaul, 2021).

1.4.2. AI-Powered Benchmarking for Standardized Risk Evaluation

AI-driven benchmarking enables insurers to compare an organization's cybersecurity maturity against industry standards and best practices. To establish standardized benchmarks, machine learning models analyze historical breach data, compliance records, and security policies. These benchmarks help insurers fairly price policies while allowing businesses to understand their cyber resilience relative to their industry peers (Moolchandani, 2025).

1.4.3. Automation of Claims Processing and Fraud Detection

AI streamlines claim processing by automating incident verification and loss assessment. Natural Language Processing (NLP) algorithms analyze forensic reports, security logs, and breach notifications to validate claims. AI-based fraud detection models also identify anomalies and suspicious claims, reducing fraudulent payouts and ensuring policyholder accountability (Faheem, 2021).

1.4.4. Enhancing Transparency and Trust in Cyber Insurance

AI-driven benchmarking fosters transparency in cybersecurity insurance by eliminating bias and subjectivity in underwriting. Businesses benefit from clearer risk evaluations, insurers gain more reliable underwriting models, and regulators can enforce standardized cybersecurity practices.

2. THE ROLE OF AI IN CYBERSECURITY INSURANCE

Integrating Artificial Intelligence (AI) into cybersecurity insurance is transforming how insurers assess risk, price policies, and process claims. Traditional insurance models rely on historical data and static risk assessment frameworks, which struggle to keep pace with the rapidly evolving cyber threat landscape. AI-driven solutions offer data-driven insights, real-time risk evaluations, and automated decision-making, making cybersecurity insurance more accurate, efficient, and fair (Adriko & Nurse, 2024).

2.1. AI in Risk Assessment and Underwriting

AI is crucial in three key areas: risk assessment and underwriting, policy pricing and premium calculation, claims processing, and fraud detection. By leveraging machine learning, predictive analytics, and natural language processing (NLP), insurers can enhance risk quantification, improve underwriting accuracy, and reduce fraud. This section explores how AI is revolutionizing cybersecurity insurance in each domain.

2.2. AI Models for Analyzing Historical Breach Data

One of the primary applications of AI in cybersecurity insurance is its ability to analyze historical breach data and identify patterns in cyberattacks. Traditional underwriting relies on self-reported security practices and past incidents, which may not provide a complete picture of an organization's cyber risk exposure. AI-driven systems, however, can ingest vast amounts of historical cyber breach data, including:

- Publicly available breach reports
- Threat intelligence feeds
- Dark web activity monitoring
- Security logs from enterprises

Using machine learning (ML) models, insurers can identify correlations between specific security practices and breach likelihood, enabling more data-driven underwriting decisions.

2.3. Machine Learning Algorithms for Predicting Cyber Threats

AI enhances predictive modeling in cybersecurity insurance by utilizing ML algorithms to forecast potential cyber risks. Instead of relying solely on past breaches, AI analyzes network traffic anomalies, system vulnerabilities, and cybercriminal tactics to predict the likelihood of an attack.

For example:

- Supervised learning models use labeled datasets to predict attack vectors and industry-specific risks.
- Unsupervised learning detects anomalous behaviors, identifying organizations at higher risk of an attack.
- Reinforcement learning continuously adapts to new cyber threats by learning from real-time cyber incidents.

These AI-powered predictive risk models enable insurers to adjust coverage in real time, providing more accurate risk assessments than static historical data-based methods.

2.4. Risk Scoring Methodologies and AI-Based Quantification

AI enhances cyber risk scoring by evaluating an organization's cybersecurity maturity, network hygiene, and real-time vulnerabilities. AI-driven risk quantification models assess (Faheem, 2021):

1. External Attack Surface – AI scans publicly accessible digital assets to identify exposed vulnerabilities (e.g., unpatched software, open ports).
2. Internal Security Practices – AI evaluates an organization's incident response capabilities, compliance adherence, and access control policies.
3. Behavioral Analytics – AI tracks user behavior to detect abnormal access patterns, insider threats, and potential data breaches.

These AI-generated risk scores provide insurers with objective and consistent assessments, ensuring fair and accurate underwriting.

2.5. AI in Policy Pricing and Premium Calculation

2.5.1 Real-Time Risk Assessment and Dynamic Pricing Models

Traditional cyber insurance pricing relies on static assessments and predefined risk categories. However, cyber threats are dynamic, meaning an organization's risk exposure can change rapidly. AI-powered real-time risk assessment models enable insurers to:

- Continuously monitor cyber risks through threat intelligence feeds.
- Adjust policy premiums dynamically based on real-time cybersecurity practices.
- Provide discounts for proactive security measures (e.g., implementing zero-trust architecture, using endpoint detection and response tools).

By integrating AI-driven dynamic pricing models, insurers can move towards usage-based cyber insurance policies, where premiums fluctuate based on ongoing cybersecurity posture.

2.5.2 Use of Behavioral Analytics in Determining Risk Exposure

AI enhances risk assessment by leveraging behavioral analytics, which studies how users, employees, and external attackers interact with an organization's systems. Behavioral AI models:

- Identify suspicious login attempts and credential misuse.
- Analyze data access patterns to detect unauthorized activities.
- Flag high-risk behaviors, such as employees ignoring phishing warnings or using weak passwords.

By incorporating behavior-based risk indicators, insurers can offer personalized policy pricing, rewarding companies demonstrating strong cybersecurity awareness and compliance (Challoumis, 2023).

2.6. AI-Driven Fraud Detection in Applications

Insurance fraud is a growing concern, and AI is instrumental in detecting fraudulent cyber insurance applications. AI-driven anomaly detection helps insurers (Thilagavathi et al., 2024):

- Identify businesses that misrepresent their cybersecurity readiness to secure lower premiums.
- Detect fake cyber incidents used to claim insurance payouts dishonestly.
- Verify policyholder compliance with required security controls through real-time monitoring.

By leveraging AI-driven fraud detection, insurers can ensure fair pricing and accurate risk assessment while reducing financial losses due to fraudulent claims.

2.7. AI in Claims Processing and Fraud Detection

2.7.1 Automated Claims Verification and Processing Using AI

Traditional claims processing in cyber insurance is manual, time-consuming, and prone to human errors. AI-powered automation accelerates claims verification by:

- Extracting relevant information from cyber incident reports using Natural Language Processing (NLP).
- Cross-referencing claims with real-time cybersecurity event logs and forensic data.
- Determining claim validity by detecting inconsistencies or missing evidence.

AI-driven claims automation reduces processing time, enhances accuracy, and minimizes disputes between insurers and policyholders (Hasan & Rizvi, 2022).

2.7.2 Role of AI in Identifying Fraudulent Claims

Cyber insurance fraud is increasingly sophisticated, with policyholders attempting to exploit insurance policies by fabricating cyber incidents. AI combats fraud by:

- Analyzing historical claims data to identify suspicious claim patterns.
- Using machine learning models to detect anomalies in reported cyber events.
- Validating claims against threat intelligence databases to confirm the legitimacy of reported cyberattacks.

For instance, AI can detect if a ransomware attack was staged by analyzing encryption patterns and verifying whether the malware exists in known threat databases.

2.7.3 Use of NLP and Deep Learning in Claims Analysis

AI-driven Natural Language Processing (NLP) and deep learning models enhance claims analysis by:

- Extracting insights from unstructured cyber incident reports.
- Identifying inconsistencies in forensic investigations.
- Automatically classifying claims based on severity and impact levels.

By incorporating AI-powered NLP, insurers can streamline claims processing and reduce fraudulent payouts, ensuring a fair and transparent claims system (Hasan & Rizvi, 2022).

AI revolutionizes cybersecurity insurance by transforming risk assessment, policy pricing, and claims processing. AI models analyze vast datasets to predict cyber risks, ensuring more accurate underwriting decisions. In pricing, AI-driven dynamic risk assessment models enable insurers to adjust premiums in real-time, rewarding companies that proactively enhance their cybersecurity posture. Additionally, AI streamlines claims verification and fraud detection, reducing financial losses for insurers while improving trust and efficiency in cyber insurance markets.

As cyber threats evolve, AI will play an increasingly critical role in cybersecurity insurance, paving the way for more adaptive, data-driven, and fair insurance models that benefit insurers and policyholders.

3. AI-DRIVEN BENCHMARKING IN CYBERSECURITY INSURANCE

3.1 Definition and Importance of Benchmarking

Standardized Metrics for Assessing Cybersecurity Readiness Benchmarking in cybersecurity insurance refers to establishing standardized metrics to evaluate an organization's cybersecurity maturity, resilience, and preparedness against cyber threats. Traditional cybersecurity assessments rely on qualitative evaluations, subjective audits, and industry best practices. However, these methods lack consistency and fail to provide accurate, data-driven insights into an organization's cyber risk exposure. AI-driven benchmarking offers a more objective, real-time, and scalable approach to cyber risk evaluation.

Key metrics used in cybersecurity benchmarking include:

- Incident Response Efficiency – Time taken to detect, contain, and remediate security incidents.
- Vulnerability Management – Number of unresolved security vulnerabilities and their severity.
- Network Security Posture – Firewall configurations, intrusion detection/prevention systems (IDPS), and endpoint security controls.
- Compliance Adherence – Alignment with regulatory frameworks such as GDPR, NIST, and ISO 27001.
- User Behavior Analytics – Insider threat risk assessment based on employee interaction with systems.

How AI Facilitates Objective and Consistent Benchmarking AI enhances cybersecurity benchmarking by automating data collection, normalization, and analysis. Machine learning models can:

- Continuously monitor security logs, threat intelligence feeds, and network activity.
- Compare an organization's security performance against industry benchmarks and historical attack trends.
- Identify weaknesses and recommend security enhancements based on real-time threat intelligence.

By leveraging AI-driven benchmarking, insurers can improve risk assessment accuracy, enabling more transparent underwriting and fair premium pricing (Kwame & Petrucka, 2021).

3.2 AI Models for Benchmarking Cybersecurity Maturity

Comparison of Different AI-Driven Benchmarking Frameworks Various AI models have been developed for cybersecurity benchmarking, including:

- Supervised Machine Learning – Uses historical breach data to predict an organization's likelihood of experiencing a cyberattack.
- Unsupervised Learning (Anomaly Detection) – Identifies deviations from normal network behavior, detecting unknown vulnerabilities.
- Reinforcement Learning – Continuously updates risk benchmarks based on new attack patterns and policy changes.

Use of Anomaly Detection in Benchmarking Cyber Resilience Anomaly detection plays a critical role in cybersecurity benchmarking by identifying deviations from normal security operations. AI-powered systems analyze network traffic, endpoint activities, and user behavior to detect:

- Unusual login attempts or privilege escalations.
- Unexpected file modifications suggest potential ransomware activity.
- Changes in encryption patterns indicative of data exfiltration.

By incorporating anomaly detection into benchmarking, AI can provide dynamic and real-time cybersecurity risk-scoring models (Rao et al., 2022).

3.3 Industry-Wide Adoption and Challenges

Variability in Cybersecurity Postures Across Industries have varying cybersecurity maturity levels, making uniform benchmarking challenging. For instance:

- Financial institutions have strict regulatory requirements (e.g., PCI-DSS, Basel III), ensuring higher cybersecurity resilience.
- Small businesses often lack advanced cybersecurity measures, increasing their risk exposure.
- Healthcare organizations handle highly sensitive data, requiring more stringent security controls.

AI-driven benchmarking frameworks must consider industry-specific threat landscapes and regulatory environments to address these disparities.

Ethical Concerns in AI-Driven Benchmarking Despite its advantages, AI-driven benchmarking raises several ethical concerns:

- Bias in AI Models – Training datasets may favor certain industries or geographies, leading to skewed risk assessments.
- Transparency Issues – AI-based risk scoring models must be explainable to avoid unfair premium pricing decisions.
- Privacy Risks – Data collection for benchmarking must comply with GDPR, CCPA, and other privacy laws to prevent misuse.

Addressing these challenges requires greater regulatory oversight, transparency in AI decision-making, and robust privacy safeguards (Strich, Mayer, & Fiedler, 2021).

4. DEVELOPMENT OF STANDARDS IN AI-DRIVEN CYBERSECURITY INSURANCE

4.1 Need for Standardized Cyber Risk Metrics

Lack of Consistency in Current Cybersecurity Insurance Models One of the biggest challenges in cybersecurity insurance is the absence of standardized risk assessment frameworks. Currently, different insurers:

- Use varying methodologies for underwriting policies.
- Have inconsistent definitions for cyber incidents and claim eligibility.
- Lack of a common scoring system to evaluate cybersecurity maturity.

The absence of standardization creates disparities in policy coverage and pricing, leading to unfair risk assessments for organizations. The Role of Regulatory Bodies and Industry Coalitions To address these issues, regulatory bodies, and industry coalitions are working on establishing universal cybersecurity risk metrics (Zirar, Ali, & Islam, 2023). Key stakeholders include:

- National Institute of Standards and Technology (NIST) – Provides risk management frameworks widely adopted by enterprises.
- International Organization for Standardization (ISO 27001) – Offers guidelines for information security management.
- Cybersecurity & Infrastructure Security Agency (CISA) – Focuses on critical infrastructure protection.
- Insurance Regulators – Require AI-driven underwriting models to comply with ethical and non-discriminatory guidelines.

4.2 AI and International Cybersecurity Standards

Existing Frameworks (NIST, ISO 27001, GDPR, etc.) Several cybersecurity standards provide foundational guidelines for risk assessment and compliance:

- NIST Cybersecurity Framework – Focuses on risk identification, protection, detection, response, and recovery.
- ISO 27001 – Establishes information security best practices for enterprises.
- General Data Protection Regulation (GDPR) – Enforces data privacy and security standards.
- California Consumer Privacy Act (CCPA) – Regulates how organizations handle personal data.

AI-Driven Enhancements to Regulatory Compliance AI enhances compliance with these standards by:

- Automating compliance monitoring and generating real-time risk reports.
- Identifying security gaps that may lead to non-compliance penalties.
- Enhancing security audit accuracy by analyzing historical cybersecurity incidents.

By integrating AI-driven compliance tools, insurers can ensure policyholders meet cybersecurity requirements, reducing policy risks and potential financial liabilities (Sorensen et al., 2021).

4.3 Ethical Considerations and Bias in AI Benchmarking

Bias in AI Models and Its Impact on Cybersecurity Insurance Bias in AI-driven benchmarking arises due to:

- Unbalanced training data leads to inaccurate risk assessments for small businesses or minority sectors.
- Algorithmic discrimination is when certain industries face higher premium rates based on past breach trends rather than current cybersecurity maturity.
- Opaque AI decision-making makes it difficult for businesses to contest high-risk classifications.

4.3.1 Mitigating Risks Through Transparency and Explainability in AI

To ensure fairness in AI-driven cybersecurity insurance, insurers must:

- Implement explainable AI (XAI) techniques to clarify how risk scores are calculated.
- Audit AI models regularly to detect and correct bias.
- Adopt AI governance frameworks to align with regulatory standards.

By prioritizing transparency, AI-driven cybersecurity insurance models can achieve greater industry trust and regulatory approval.

5. CASE STUDIES OF AI IMPLEMENTATION IN CYBERSECURITY INSURANCE

Integrating artificial intelligence (AI) into cybersecurity insurance has revolutionized risk assessment, claims processing, and fraud detection. This section explores real-world applications of AI in the industry, highlighting successes, challenges, and key lessons learned.

5.1 AI-Based Cyber Risk Scoring Models in Action

Cyber risk scoring models powered by AI enable insurers to quantify threats with unprecedented precision. These models predict the likelihood and financial impact of cyber incidents by analyzing vast datasets—from network vulnerabilities to industry-wide breach trends (Faheem, 2021).

Real-World Examples:

1. **Guidewire (Cyence):**

Acquired by Guidewire in 2017, Cyence uses AI to model cyber risk scenarios. Its platform ingests data from 150+ sources, including dark web activity and software vulnerabilities, to generate dynamic risk scores. For example, a mid-sized insurer using Cyence reduced claims payouts by 22% within a year by adjusting premiums based on real-time risk assessments during the 2020 SolarWinds breach.

2. **Corax:**

Corax's AI-driven platform evaluates clients' security posture by analyzing internal data (e.g., firewall configurations) and external threats (e.g., phishing campaigns). A case study with a Fortune 500 retailer revealed that Corax's model identified a 40% higher risk of ransomware due to outdated endpoints, prompting preemptive mitigation that averted a $3M potential loss.

3. **CyberCube:**

Specializing in catastrophic cyber risks, CyberCube's AI models simulate scenarios like cloud provider outages. After a major insurer used CyberCube to assess a tech client's exposure to AWS outages, they revised coverage terms, avoiding $50M in losses during a 2022 regional AWS outage.

AI risk scoring enhances underwriting accuracy and enables proactive risk management. However, reliance on external data sources can introduce blind spots, as seen in a 2021 case where an insurer overlooked a client's poor employee training practices, leading to a costly phishing-related claim.

5.2 Automated Cyber Insurance Claim Processing

AI streamlines claim processing by automating documentation, fraud detection, and payout calculations, reducing processing times from weeks to hours (Devaraj, 2023).

AI-Driven Fraud Detection:

- **Shift Technology:**

This firm's AI analyzes claims for inconsistencies, such as mismatched timestamps or exaggerated losses. A European insurer using Shift reduced fraudulent claim approvals by 35% in 2023, saving €12M annually. In one instance, the system flagged a $2M ransomware claim as suspicious due to duplicated invoice amounts, uncovering a fabricated incident.

- **Lemonade:**

Lemonade's AI chatbot, "AI Jim," resolves claims in seconds by cross-referencing policy details with incident data. During a 2023 DNS attack affecting 200+ small businesses, AI Jim processed 90% of claims autonomously, with an average resolution time of 8 minutes.

Challenges and Innovations:

While automation boosts efficiency, limitations persist. For example, a US insurer faced backlash in 2022 when its AI denied legitimate claims due to overly strict anomaly detection thresholds. To address this, leading firms now combine AI with human audits, ensuring accuracy without sacrificing speed.

5.3 Lessons Learned from AI Integration

Success Stories:

- **Proactive Risk Mitigation:**

AIG's partnership with IBM Watson for predictive analytics reduced clients' breach likelihood by 30% through tailored security recommendations.

- **Cost Efficiency:**

Zurich Insurance reported a 25% reduction in operational costs after automating 70% of routine underwriting tasks with AI.

Failures and Pitfalls:

- **Bias in Data:**

In 2021, an insurer's AI model unfairly penalized SMEs in the healthcare sector due to training data skewed toward large corporations. Remediation required overhauling datasets and incorporating fairness algorithms.

- **Over-Reliance on Automation:**

A startup insurer faced regulatory fines after its AI misinterpreted regulatory filings, highlighting the need for human oversight.

Key Takeaways:

1. **Hybrid Models Work Best:** Combining AI speed with human expertise balances efficiency and accuracy.
2. **Transparency Builds Trust:** Insurers like AXA now provide "explainable AI" dashboards to clarify risk assessments for clients.
3. **Continuous Learning is Critical:** Regularly updating AI models with fresh data prevents obsolescence amid evolving threats.

AI is reshaping cybersecurity insurance, offering tools to predict risks, combat fraud, and streamline operations. While data bias and integration hurdles persist, the industry's iterative approach—learning from triumphs and missteps—paves the way for resilient, AI-driven solutions. As threats evolve, insurers must prioritize adaptability, transparency, and collaboration to harness AI's full potential.

6. FUTURE DIRECTIONS AND CHALLENGES IN AI-DRIVEN CYBERSECURITY INSURANCE

The rapid advancement of AI in cybersecurity insurance promises transformative benefits but also introduces complex challenges. This section explores emerging trends, regulatory hurdles, and the push for global standards to shape the industry's future.

6.1 AI Evolution in Cyber Insurance

6.1.1 Trends in Predictive Cybersecurity Risk Modeling

AI is evolving beyond traditional risk assessment to anticipate novel threats through:

- Real-Time Threat Intelligence: Insurers like Coalition integrate AI with live data feeds from network sensors and threat intelligence platforms, enabling dynamic risk scoring. For example, during the 2023 MGM Resorts breach, Coalition's AI flagged vulnerabilities in API security days before the attack, allowing clients to patch systems.
- Generative AI for Scenario Simulation: Tools like Darktrace's Cyber AI Analyst simulate sophisticated attack vectors, such as AI-generated phishing campaigns, to stress-test policies. A reinsurer used this to model a $200M loss scenario from a generative AI-driven supply chain attack, refining coverage terms proactively.
- Behavioral Analytics: Startups like Balbix leverage AI to analyze user behavior patterns, predicting insider threats. A financial services firm reduced breaches by 45% after adopting Balbix's risk predictions (George, 2024).

6.1.2 Role of Federated Learning and Privacy-Preserving AI

To address data privacy concerns, insurers are adopting:

- **Federated Learning: Beazley** collaborates with clients to train AI models on decentralized data without sharing sensitive information. This approach helped a healthcare consortium improve ransomware predictions by 30% while complying with HIPAA.
- **Homomorphic Encryption: Enveil** uses this technology to analyze encrypted data, enabling insurers to assess risks in financial transactions without

exposing personal data. A European bank leveraged this to secure cyber insurance for digital payment systems.

- **Synthetic Data: Cybersyn** generates synthetic datasets mimicking real-world breaches, allowing insurers to train models without privacy risks (Dash, Sharma, & Ali, 2022).

Challenges:

- **Data Fragmentation:** Differing data formats across organizations hinder federated learning scalability.
- **Computational Overheads:** Privacy-preserving techniques like homomorphic encryption slow processing speeds, impacting real-time analytics.

6.2 Regulatory and Compliance Challenges

6.2.1 Evolving Cybersecurity Insurance Laws

Regulatory frameworks struggle to keep pace with AI innovation:

- **EU's AI Act:** Classifies insurance risk models as "high-risk," mandating transparency audits and human oversight. Insurers like **Allianz** now invest in "explainable AI" tools to comply.
- **U.S. State-Level Variability:** New York's DFS 500 regulation requires insurers to validate AI models for bias, while California's Privacy Rights Act limits data usage. A 2023 lawsuit against a Midwest insurer highlighted penalties for AI-driven discriminatory pricing in SMEs.

6.2.2 Balancing Innovation with Ethical AI Practices

Key ethical concerns include:

- **Bias in Risk Scoring:** A 2022 study found AI models penalized rural healthcare providers due to training data skewed toward urban breaches. Remedies include fairness-aware algorithms and diverse data sampling.
- **Transparency Gaps:** The **National Association of Insurance Commissioners (NAIC)** now requires insurers to disclose AI use in policy decisions. Lemonade faced scrutiny in 2023 for opaque claim denials, prompting reforms.

- **Accountability:** The EU's proposed Cyber Resilience Act mandates AI vendors to assume liability for flawed models, shifting risk from insurers to developers (Yanamala, Suryadevara, & Kalli, 2024).

Innovative Solutions:

- **Ethical AI Audits:** Firms like **Fairly AI** offer third-party audits to certify compliance with regulations like GDPR.
- **Regulatory Sandboxes:** The UK's FCA permits insurers to test AI innovations in controlled environments, fostering compliance without stifling growth.

6.3 The Future of AI-Driven Benchmarking and Standards

6.3.1 Emerging Technologies Shaping Benchmarking

- **Blockchain for Data Integrity:** Etherisc uses blockchain to create tamper-proof incident records, improving claims transparency. A pilot with Lloyds of London reduced dispute resolution time by 50%.
- **Quantum Computing:** While threatening current encryption, quantum-resistant AI algorithms (e.g., lattice-based cryptography) are being tested by IBM and Chubb to future-proof policies.
- **AI Auditing Tools:** Platforms like Arthur AI monitor model performance, detecting drift in risk predictions for ISO 27103 compliance (Neethirajan, 2023).

6.3.2 Global Standardization Efforts

- **ISO 27103:** This emerging standard for cybersecurity insurance frameworks mandates AI model transparency and regular updates.
- **NIST's AI Risk Management Framework:** Guides insurers in aligning AI practices with international norms, addressing 60% of compliance challenges reported in a 2023 industry survey.
- **Cross-Border Collaborations:** The **Global Cyber Alliance** and **Cyber Threat Alliance** advocate for unified benchmarks, though geopolitical tensions (e.g., U.S.-China data laws) complicate adoption.

Challenges to Standardization:

- **Divergent Regulations:** The EU's strict privacy laws conflict with China's data localization requirements, complicating multinational policy underwriting.
- **Rapid Technological Change:** Standards risk obsolescence as AI evolves; continuous stakeholder collaboration is critical.

The future of AI in cybersecurity insurance hinges on balancing innovation with ethical and regulatory guardrails. Predictive AI, federated learning, and quantum-ready encryption will redefine risk management, while global standards and adaptive regulations must address fairness and interoperability. Insurers, regulators, and tech providers must collaborate to build resilient frameworks that harness AI's potential without compromising trust. As threats grow in sophistication, the industry's ability to innovate responsibly will determine its success in safeguarding the digital ecosystem.

7. CONCLUSION

Integrating artificial intelligence (AI) into cybersecurity insurance has reshaped the industry, offering unprecedented capabilities in risk prediction, claims automation, and fraud mitigation. As cyber threats grow in scale and sophistication, AI has emerged as both a shield and a strategic asset, enabling insurers to transition from reactive payers to proactive partners in cyber resilience. This concluding chapter synthesizes AI's transformative impact, underscores the urgency of standardized frameworks, and reflects on the future trajectory of AI in risk assessment.

AI has revolutionized cybersecurity insurance across three key dimensions:

7.1. Enhanced Risk Assessment and Underwriting

AI-powered risk scoring models like Guidewire's Cyence and CyberCube have replaced static, manual evaluations with dynamic, data-driven insights. These tools accurately predict risks by analyzing dark web activity, software vulnerabilities, and historical breach patterns. For example, Corax's AI identified a 40% higher ransomware risk for a Fortune 500 retailer, enabling preemptive mitigation and averting $3M in losses. Such precision has allowed insurers to tailor premiums, reduce claim payouts, and incentivize clients to adopt stronger cybersecurity practices (Shen, 2025).

7.2. Streamlined Claims Processing and Fraud Detection

Automation tools like Shift Technology and Lemonade's AI Jim have slashed claim processing times from weeks to minutes. During the 2023 DNS attack, Lemonade's AI autonomously resolved 90% of claims, demonstrating scalability in crises. Meanwhile, AI-driven fraud detection systems saved insurers like Shift's European client €12M annually by flagging anomalies such as duplicated invoices or mismatched timestamps. These advancements highlight AI's dual role in improving efficiency and safeguarding profitability.

7.3. Proactive Threat Mitigation

Insurers are no longer passive stakeholders. Tools like AIG's IBM Watson partnership and Darktrace's Cyber AI Analyst provide clients with actionable recommendations, such as patching vulnerabilities or updating employee training. This Shift has reduced breach likelihood by 30% for AIG's clients, illustrating AI's capacity to transform insurers into cybersecurity allies (Odeh & Abu Taleb, 2023; Odeh, Al-Haija, Aref, & Taleb, 2023).

7.3.1 Challenges and Limitations

Despite these successes, AI adoption has faced hurdles:

- **Bias in Data:** Models trained on skewed datasets, such as urban-centric breach records, have unfairly penalized rural healthcare providers.
- **Over-Reliance on Automation:** Instances like the 2022 AI claim denials in the US underscore the need for human oversight.
- **Transparency Gaps:** Opaque "black-box" models have eroded trust, prompting regulators like the NAIC to mandate disclosure of AI use in policy decisions.

7.3.2 Importance of AI-Driven Benchmarking and Standardized Frameworks

The lack of universal standards poses one of the most significant barriers to AI's sustainable growth in cybersecurity insurance.

AI-driven benchmarking is transforming the insurance industry by providing insurers with powerful tools to assess and refine their risk models. Platforms such as Arthur AI play a crucial role in auditing model performance, identifying prediction drift, and ensuring that risk assessments remain aligned with evolving threats.

These platforms continuously monitor AI-driven underwriting and fraud detection mechanisms, ensuring that insurers maintain accuracy and reliability in a dynamic risk landscape.

In addition to model performance auditing, the validation of data sources is another essential aspect of AI benchmarking. Blockchain-based systems, such as Etherisc's tamper-proof incident logs, enhance transparency and reliability in claims processing. By leveraging blockchain's immutable ledger, insurers can verify the authenticity of claims, reduce fraudulent activities, and streamline compensation processes. This fosters trust between insurers and policyholders while ensuring regulatory compliance.

Beyond risk model comparison and data validation, AI-driven benchmarking also plays a key role in measuring return on investment (ROI). For example, Zurich Insurance reported a 25% reduction in operational costs after automating underwriting tasks. This demonstrates the tangible financial benefits of AI integration in the insurance sector, where automation leads to faster decision-making, reduced overhead costs, and improved overall efficiency.

7.3.3 The Push for Global Standardization

As AI continues to reshape the insurance landscape, the lack of global regulatory cohesion presents significant challenges. Divergent regulations and fragmented data practices across different jurisdictions necessitate the development of cohesive frameworks to guide AI adoption in the industry. One such effort is ISO 27103, an emerging standard that mandates transparency in AI-driven decision-making and requires regular updates to address newly discovered threats. By enforcing such transparency measures, insurers can enhance the accountability of their AI systems and ensure fair treatment of policyholders.

To further streamline regulatory compliance, the National Institute of Standards and Technology (NIST) has introduced the AI Risk Management Framework. This framework provides insurers with structured guidelines for aligning their AI practices with international norms, addressing critical gaps in regulatory compliance. In 2023, it was reported that the adoption of NIST's framework helped insurers resolve 60% of their compliance challenges, underscoring the necessity of standardized AI governance.

Cross-border collaboration is also gaining traction, as initiatives like the Global Cyber Alliance advocate for unified AI benchmarks across different regulatory environments. However, geopolitical tensions often hinder widespread adoption. For instance, regulatory discrepancies between the European Union's General Data Protection Regulation (GDPR) and China's data security laws highlight the difficulties in establishing universal AI governance policies. Despite these obstacles, the push for global standardization remains a priority, as insurers seek to navigate complex legal landscapes while ensuring consistency in AI-driven risk assessment.

7.3.4 Privacy-Preserving Technologies

With growing concerns over data privacy and security, privacy-preserving technologies have become essential for insurers striving to balance innovation with compliance. Federated learning and homomorphic encryption are among the key techniques that enable AI-driven insurance solutions while safeguarding sensitive information.

One prominent example of federated learning in insurance is Beazley's decentralized training models, which improved ransomware prediction accuracy by 30% while maintaining full compliance with the Health Insurance Portability and Accountability Act (HIPAA). By training AI models across decentralized networks without exposing raw data, federated learning allows insurers to enhance their predictive capabilities without violating privacy regulations.

Similarly, homomorphic encryption has proven to be a game-changer in securing data-intensive insurance operations. Enveil, a leader in encrypted data analysis, successfully deployed its technology to secure cyber insurance offerings for a European bank's payment systems. This case demonstrated that privacy and efficiency can coexist, as encrypted analytics enabled real-time fraud detection without compromising the confidentiality of transaction data. As privacy regulations tighten globally, these advanced encryption techniques will become integral to maintaining compliance while leveraging AI for risk assessment and fraud detection.

7.3.5 Challenges to Standardization

Despite the advancements in AI-driven insurance solutions, several obstacles hinder the standardization of AI practices in the industry. One of the primary challenges is regulatory fragmentation. The European Union's AI Act, which imposes strict requirements on AI transparency and ethical use, often clashes with the decentralized regulatory landscape in the United States, where AI governance varies significantly across states. This misalignment creates compliance headaches for multinational insurers, who must navigate differing legal expectations in various markets.

Another pressing challenge is the rapid pace of technological evolution. AI advancements often outpace standardization efforts, making it difficult for regulatory bodies to establish fixed frameworks that remain relevant over time. To address this issue, insurers and regulators must adopt agile, iterative frameworks that evolve alongside technological innovations. The insurance sector can develop adaptable regulations that promote responsible AI adoption without stifling innovation by fostering continuous collaboration between industry stakeholders, policymakers, and AI researchers.

As insurers continue integrating AI into their operations, overcoming these challenges will be essential in ensuring a balanced approach that promotes efficiency, fairness, and regulatory compliance in the industry.

7.3.6 Final Thoughts on the Future of AI in Risk Assessment

The cybersecurity insurance industry stands at a pivotal crossroads, where technological advancements offer unprecedented opportunities and complex challenges. Artificial intelligence (AI) has the potential to revolutionize cyber risk management by predicting zero-day exploits, automating critical aspects of the trillion-dollar insurance market, and democratizing access to coverage for businesses of all sizes. By leveraging AI-driven threat intelligence, insurers can proactively assess vulnerabilities, refine underwriting models, and provide real-time risk assessments tailored to individual organizations. These advancements can lead to more precise policy pricing, faster claims processing, and comprehensive coverage options that align with the ever-evolving cyber threat landscape. However, while AI presents a transformative path forward, its promise will remain unfulfilled without ethical guardrails, regulatory oversight, and international cooperation. (Odeh, Abdelfattah, & Salameh, 2024; Odeh, Aboshgifa, & Belhaj, 2023)

One of the biggest challenges facing the integration of AI in cyber insurance is the ethical implications of automated decision-making. AI-driven risk assessment models rely on vast amounts of data, including sensitive corporate and personal information. Using AI in underwriting and claims processing without proper safeguards could lead to biases, privacy violations, and unintended consequences. For example, businesses with limited cybersecurity budgets may be unfairly classified as high-risk entities, leading to unaffordable premiums or outright policy denials. Additionally, the opaque nature of some AI algorithms raises concerns about transparency and accountability, making it difficult for policyholders to challenge risk assessments or coverage decisions. Insurers must champion transparency by adopting explainable AI models, implementing fairness-driven algorithms, and ensuring that AI-driven assessments are subject to human oversight.

Privacy-preserving technologies must also become a cornerstone of AI-driven cyber insurance. Insurers handle vast amounts of proprietary cybersecurity data, breach reports, and policyholder information, making them prime targets for cybercriminals. If AI-driven models are to be trusted, insurers must invest in privacy-enhancing techniques such as federated learning, homomorphic encryption, and differential privacy. These technologies allow AI systems to analyze cyber risks and detect emerging threats without exposing sensitive data to potential exploitation. By prioritizing data security, insurers can build trust among policyholders while ensuring compliance with stringent data protection regulations across different jurisdictions.

Global cooperation is another critical factor in shaping the future of AI-driven cybersecurity insurance. Cyber threats do not respect national borders, nor should the frameworks designed to mitigate them. As AI becomes more deeply integrated into the insurance sector, regulators, insurers, and cybersecurity experts must collaborate on standardized policies that promote fair risk assessment, ethical AI usage, and consistent coverage terms. Without unified regulatory standards, inconsistencies in AI-driven underwriting models could lead to disparities in coverage across regions, creating challenges for multinational organizations. Policymakers must work alongside industry leaders to establish guidelines that foster innovation while protecting businesses, consumers, and critical infrastructure from emerging cyber risks.

The cybersecurity insurance industry stands at a crossroads. AI offers tools to predict zero-day exploits, automate trillion-dollar markets, and democratize access to coverage. Yet, its promise will falter without ethical guardrails, global cooperation, and adaptive regulations. Insurers must champion transparency, invest in privacy-preserving technologies, and collaborate with policymakers to build frameworks that foster innovation while protecting vulnerable stakeholders.

As AI evolves, so too must our approach to risk. The future belongs to those who recognize that technology alone is not a panacea—the synergy of AI's computational power and human ingenuity will secure the digital frontier.

REFERENCES

Adriko, R., & Nurse, J. R. (2024). Cybersecurity, cyber insurance and small-to-medium-sized enterprises: A systematic Review. *Information and Computer Security, 32*(5), 691–710. DOI: 10.1108/ICS-01-2024-0025

Arefin, S., & Simcox, M. (2024). AI-Driven Solutions for Safeguarding Healthcare Data: Innovations in Cybersecurity. *International Business Research, 17*(6), 1–74. DOI: 10.5539/ibr.v17n6p74

Bonta, R. (2022). California consumer privacy act (CCPA). *Retrieved from State of California Department of Justice: https://oag. ca. gov/privacy/ccpa.*

Challoumis, C. (2023). Risk on the tax system of the EU from 2016 to 2022. *ECONOMICS-INNOVATIVE AND ECONOMICS RESEARCH JOURNAL, 11*(Sp. issue), 55-72.

Dash, B., Sharma, P., & Ali, A. (2022). Federated learning for privacy-preserving: A review of PII data analysis in Fintech. [IJSEA]. *International Journal of Software Engineering and Its Applications, 13*(4).

Deshpande, A. (2024). *Cybersecurity in Financial Services: Addressing AI-Related Threats and Vulnerabilities.* Paper presented at the 2024 International Conference on Knowledge Engineering and Communication Systems (ICKECS). DOI: 10.1109/ICKECS61492.2024.10616498

Devaraj, S. M. (2023). Ai And Cloud For Claims Processing Automation In Property And Casualty Insurance. *International Journal Of Engineering And Technology Research (Ijetr), 8*(1), 38–46.

Dhieb, N., Ghazzai, H., Besbes, H., & Massoud, Y. (2020). A secure ai-driven architecture for automated insurance systems: Fraud detection and risk measurement. *IEEE Access : Practical Innovations, Open Solutions, 8*, 58546–58558. DOI: 10.1109/ACCESS.2020.2983300

Faheem, M. A. (2021). AI-Driven Risk Assessment Models: Revolutionizing Credit Scoring and Default Prediction. *Iconic Research and Engineering Journals, 5*(3), 177–186.

George, A. S. (2024). Emerging Trends in AI-Driven Cybersecurity: An In-Depth Analysis. *Partners Universal Innovative Research Publication, 2*(4), 15–28.

Georgiadou, A., Mouzakitis, S., & Askounis, D. (2021). Assessing mitre att&ck risk using a cyber-security culture framework. *Sensors (Basel), 21*(9), 3267. DOI: 10.3390/s21093267 PMID: 34065086

Hasan, I., & Rizvi, S. (2022). *AI-driven fraud detection and mitigation in e-commerce transactions.* Paper presented at the Proceedings of Data Analytics and Management: ICDAM 2021, Volume 1. DOI: 10.1007/978-981-16-6289-8_34

Jawhar, S., Kimble, C. E., Miller, J. R., & Bitar, Z. (2024). *Enhancing cyber resilience with ai-powered cyber insurance risk assessment.* Paper presented at the 2024 IEEE 14th Annual Computing and Communication Workshop and Conference (CCWC). DOI: 10.1109/CCWC60891.2024.10427965

Kamuangu, P. (2024). A Review on Cybersecurity in Fintech: Threats, Solutions, and Future Trends. *Journal of Economics. Finance and Accounting Studies, 6*(1), 47–53.

Kaul, D. (2021). AI-Driven Dynamic Upsell in Hotel Reservation Systems Based on Cybersecurity Risk Scores. [IJCET]. *International Journal of Computer Engineering and Technology, 12*(3), 114–125.

Khatam, D. (2022). *Regulating Data Privacy in the Age of Surveillance Capitalism: The Making of the European General Data Protection Regulation and the California Consumer Privacy Act.* Stanford University.

Kolluru, V., John, R., Chen, J., Konkathi, P., Kolluru, S., Saraf, S., Henebry, G. M., Xiao, J., Jain, K., & Kussainova, M. (2024). Dominant role of grazing and snow cover variability on vegetation shifts in the drylands of Kazakhstan. *Communications Earth & Environment, 5*(1), 424. DOI: 10.1038/s43247-024-01587-1

Koza, E. (2022). Semantic analysis of ISO/IEC 27000 standard series and NIST cybersecurity framework to outline differences and consistencies in the context of operational and strategic information security. *Med. Eng. Themes, 2*, 26–39.

Kwame, A., & Petrucka, P. M. (2021). A literature-based study of patient-centered care and communication in nurse-patient interactions: Barriers, facilitators, and the way forward. *BMC Nursing, 20*(1), 158. DOI: 10.1186/s12912-021-00684-2 PMID: 34479560

Moolchandani, S. (2025). AI-driven risk platform automating data aggregation and risk insight generation. *International Journal of Science Engineering and Technology, 13*(1), 12.

Neethirajan, S. R. (2023). AI-driven climate neutrality in dairy farming: Benchmarking emissions for sustainable transformation: *Preprints.*

Odeh, A., Abdelfattah, E., & Salameh, W. (2024). Privacy-Preserving Data Sharing in Telehealth Services. *Applied Sciences (Basel, Switzerland), 14*(23), 10808. DOI: 10.3390/app142310808

Odeh, A., Aboshgifa, A., & Belhaj, N. (2023). *Mitigating DDoS Attacks in Cloud Computing Environments: Challenges and Strategies.* Paper presented at the 2023 International Conference on Electrical, Computer and Energy Technologies (ICECET). DOI: 10.1109/ICECET58911.2023.10389269

Odeh, A., & Abu Taleb, A. (2023). Ensemble-Based Deep Learning Models for Enhancing IoT Intrusion Detection. *Applied Sciences (Basel, Switzerland), 13*(21), 11985. DOI: 10.3390/app132111985

Odeh, A., Al-Haija, Q. A., Aref, A., & Taleb, A. A. (2023). Comparative study of catboost, xgboost, and lightgbm for enhanced URL phishing detection: A performance assessment. *Journal of Internet Services and Information Security, 13*(4), 1–11. DOI: 10.58346/JISIS.2023.I4.001

Odeh, A., Keshta, I., & Abdelfattah, E. (2021). *Machine learningtechniquesfor detection of website phishing: A review for promises and challenges.* Paper presented at the 2021 IEEE 11th Annual Computing and Communication Workshop and Conference (CCWC). DOI: 10.1109/CCWC51732.2021.9375997

Odeh, A., & Taleb, A. A. (2023). A Multi-Faceted Encryption Strategy for Securing Patient Information in Medical Imaging. *Journal of Wireless Mobile Networks, Ubiquitous Computing and Dependable Applications, 14*(4), 164–176. DOI: 10.58346/JOWUA.2023.I4.012

Odeh, A., & Taleb, A. A. (2024). Utilizing linear regression and random forest models for money laundering identification. *Telkomnika, 22*(6), 1573–1580. DOI: 10.12928/telkomnika.v22i6.26163

Odeh, A., Taleb, A. A., Alhajahjeh, T., Aparicio, F., Hamed, S., Al Daradkeh, N., & Al-Jarallah, N. A. (2024). *Data Privacy and Compliance in IoT Smart and Agile Cybersecurity for IoT and IIoT Environments.* IGI Global.

Odeh, A., Taleb, A. A., Alhajahjeh, T., & Aparicio-Navarro, F. (2024). *Cryptographic Solutions Smart and Agile Cybersecurity for IoT and IIoT Environments.* IGI Global.

Pandey, P., & Kapoor, A. (2025). CYBERCRIME IN THE DIGITAL ERA: IMPACTS, AWARENESS, AND STRATEGIC SOLUTIONS FOR A SECURE FUTURE. *Sachetas, 4*(1), 32–37. DOI: 10.55955/410004

Parveen, N. (2024). *Law and AI-Powered Actuarial Revolution: Navigating the Future of Insurance Risk Assessment Artificial Intelligence and Actuarial Science*. Chapman and Hall/CRC. DOI: 10.1201/9781003472551-19

Patterson, L. A., & Doyle, M. W. (2021). Measuring water affordability and the financial capability of utilities. *AWWA Water Science*, *3*(6), e1260. DOI: 10.1002/aws2.1260

Rangaraju, S. (2023). Secure by intelligence: Enhancing products with AI-driven security measures. *EPH-International Journal of Science And Engineering*, *9*(3), 36–41.

Rao, A. S., Radanovic, M., Liu, Y., Hu, S., Fang, Y., Khoshelham, K., Palaniswami, M., & Ngo, T. (2022). Real-time monitoring of construction sites: Sensors, methods, and applications. *Automation in Construction*, *136*, 104099. DOI: 10.1016/j.autcon.2021.104099

Reddy, A. S. (2023). *Future Proofing Insurance Operations: A Guidewire-Centric Approach to Cloud*. Cybersecurity, and Generative AI.

Shahidi, S., Darmel, F. A., Jalalzai, S., & Amiri, G. A. (2024). Opportunities and Challenges in AI-Driven Cybersecurity: A Systematic Literature. *Journal of Social Science Utilizing Technology*, *2*(4), 516–530.

Shen, Y. (2025). Risk Quantification-based Underwriting Assessment Model. *Highlights in Business. Economics and Management*, *48*, 123–133.

Sorensen, G., Dennerlein, J. T., Peters, S. E., Sabbath, E. L., Kelly, E. L., & Wagner, G. R. (2021). The future of research on work, safety, health and wellbeing: A guiding conceptual framework. *Social Science & Medicine*, *269*, 113593. DOI: 10.1016/j.socscimed.2020.113593 PMID: 33341740

Strich, F., Mayer, A.-S., & Fiedler, M. (2021). What do I do in a world of artificial intelligence? Investigating the impact of substitutive decision-making AI systems on employees' professional role identity. *Journal of the Association for Information Systems*, *22*(2), 9. DOI: 10.17705/1jais.00663

Takamoto, M., Praditia, T., Leiteritz, R., MacKinlay, D., Alesiani, F., Pflüger, D., & Niepert, M. (2022). Pdebench: An extensive benchmark for scientific machine learning. *Advances in Neural Information Processing Systems*, *35*, 1596–1611.

Thilagavathi, M., Saranyadevi, R., Vijayakumar, N., Selvi, K., Anitha, L., & Sudharson, K. (2024). *AI-driven fraud detection in financial transactions with graph neural networks and anomaly detection.* Paper presented at the 2024 International Conference on Science Technology Engineering and Management (ICSTEM). DOI: 10.1109/ICSTEM61137.2024.10560838

Voolstra, C. R., Suggett, D. J., Peixoto, R. S., Parkinson, J. E., Quigley, K. M., Silveira, C. B., & Bourne, D. G. (2021). Extending the natural adaptive capacity of coral holobionts. *Nature Reviews. Earth & Environment, 2*(11), 747–762. DOI: 10.1038/s43017-021-00214-3

Vose, R., Huang, B., Yin, X., Arndt, D., Easterling, D., Lawrimore, J., . . . Zhang, H. (2021). Implementing full spatial coverage in NOAA's global temperature analysis. *Geophysical Research Letters, 48*(4), e2020GL090873.

Woods, D. W., & Böhme, R. (2021). *SoK: Quantifying cyber risk.* Paper presented at the 2021 IEEE Symposium on Security and Privacy (SP). DOI: 10.1109/SP40001.2021.00053

Yanamala, A. K. Y., Suryadevara, S., & Kalli, V. D. R. (2024). Balancing innovation and privacy: The intersection of data protection and artificial intelligence. *International Journal of Machine Learning Research in Cybersecurity and Artificial Intelligence, 15*(1), 1–43.

Zirar, A., Ali, S. I., & Islam, N. (2023). Worker and workplace Artificial Intelligence (AI) coexistence: Emerging themes and research agenda. *Technovation, 124*, 102747. DOI: 10.1016/j.technovation.2023.102747

Chapter 6
Emerging Trends and Innovations in Cybersecurity Insurance Policy Customization Using Generative AI Fraud Detection

Bhupinder Singh
https://orcid.org/0009-0006-4779-2553
Sharda University, India

Manmeet Kaur Kaur Arora
https://orcid.org/0009-0002-5071-117X
Sharda University, India

Namit Kumar Srivastava
School of Law, Christ University, Bangalore, India

Saurabh Chandra
https://orcid.org/0000-0003-4172-9968
Bennett University, Greater Noida, India

Thanarat Sonkla
Royal Thai Police, Thailand

Akash Bag
https://orcid.org/0000-0001-8820-171X
Adamas University, India

Avinash Krishna Goswami
School of Law, Sharda University, India

ABSTRACT

Generative AI is transforming policy customization and fraud detection. Cybersecurity insurance can be both a boon and a bane as the existing models for underwriting and assessment are relatively static in a world which is witnessing

DOI: 10.4018/979-8-3373-5545-0.ch006

a constant escalation between attack and defense mechanisms. By assessing huge datasets, spotting emerging pattern and predicting potential vulnerabilities in real time, generative AI introduces dynamic risk modeling. Help insurers design hyper-personalized cyber insurance products that are tailored to specific business profiles, operational risks and exposure levels to enhance coverage and premium accuracy. Generative AI helps in anomaly detection and identifying suspicious behaviour in insurance claims in fraud detection domain. Using legitimate claims scenarios to train AI model, fraud detection models can detect anomalies and fraud as never before. The intersection of expertise in cybersecurity, AI development and insurance will be key to creating strong, flexible and transparent insurance structures that can respond to the intricacies of today's cyber threats.

1. INTRODUCTION

Cybersecurity insurance, also known as cyber insurance, is a specialized type of insurance product designed to help organizations manage the financial risks associated with cyber incidents, including data breaches, ransomware attacks, and other types of cybercrime. With the digitalisation of businesses, the possibility of cyber threats has also increased manifold with traditional liability insurance proving to be insufficient to deal with the specific risks involved (Seethala, 2025). Cyber insurance fills this gap by covering costs that result from cyber incidents that are generally excluded from the standard coverage in a business insurance policy. An upsurge in cyberattacks, increasing in number and complexity, is driving demand for cybersecurity insurance. Data breaches can be extremely costly for organizations, leading to direct financial losses, legal liabilities, and reputational damage. For example, the average cost of a data breach has reached mind-boggling numbers, often in the millions, if you factor in fines, legal fees and remediation efforts (Narayan et al., 2025). Thus, cyber insurance has evolved into a critical part of the risk management programs of organizations of all sizes.

Cybersecurity insurance rapidly adapts due to escalating cyber threats and the complexity of contemporary cyber risk in a digitally connected world. Generative Artificial Intelligence (GenAI) is set to be one of the most disruptive new developments in this space, empowering cybersecurity insurance with highly accurate and predictive capabilities that aids in customizing insurance policies and fraud detection. Conventional insurance systems tend to be backward-looking and premised on static risk profiles that cannot adequately capture the dynamic and evolving challenges of cyber risk. GenAI transforms this framework by allowing insurance providers to sift through a large amount of structured and unstructured data, simulate different types of cyberattack scenarios, and devise specialized risk assessment models.

These models allow underwriters to tailor insurance policies to an organization's digital infrastructure, threat exposure, and behavioral risk metrics. Generative models provide new ways to detect fraud compared to traditional rule-based systems. They can commonly detect subtle differences, create synthetic data used in robust fraud detection algorithms, and create adversarial scenarios to enhance the claims verification processes.

1.1 Background of Study

Globally, the use of GenAI in cybersecurity insurance is being driven by regulatory changes, greater need for real-time cyber risk quantification, and the expansion of digital-first business ecosystems. Various nations in Europe, Asia, and North America are utilizing AI-based insurance technologies to strengthen national cybersecurity frameworks and decrease economic losses due to cybercrime. Insurance companies are teaming up with specialized companies in the area of cybersecurity to build continuous monitoring and risk mitigation services powered by GenAI tools as opposed to the reactive claims-based model but following a proactive prevention-first approach. Policy customization is further being pushed to new levels with innovations such as digital twins of IT systems, AI-based threat intelligence, and real-time behavioral biometrics. Leveraging GenAI, insurers can dynamically determine policy premiums, coverage terms, and exclusions by evaluating real-time cyber hygiene metrics and predictive threat landscapes. Such a personalization promotes higher visibility, effectiveness and trust between the insurers and the clients (Kulkarni et al., 2025).

1.2 Statement of Problem

Cyber threats are evolving and organizations' cybersecurity insurance policies need to be customized to their distinct needs.

Varied Risk Profiles: The risk profile of different organizations varies based on their industry, size, and digital maturity. For example, a financial institution will face a different set of cyber threats than those that a healthcare provider or retail business would. Insurers can address these unique risks effectively by customizing policies (Khan et al., 2025).
Potential Risks and Gaps, in Coverage, Specialized payment architectures can lead to standards of coverage that do not sufficiently address the specific needs of organizations, exposing them to significant financial consequences. Tailored policies can protect for specific risks for their organizations, including the first-party losses as direct losses sustained by the organization, as well

as third-party liabilities as losses sustained by customers or partners because of a breach.

Regulatory Compliance: Industries are often subject to strict regulations related to data protection and privacy. Tailored policies can assist businesses in coding with specific industries regulations, such as the Generalate Protection Regulation (GDPR) or the Health Insurance Portability and Accountability Act (HIPAA), which may require unique coverage needs.

Synergy with Cybersecurity Initiatives: Tailored cyber insurance policies can serve as a complementary force to an organization's existing cybersecurity safeguards and risk management practices. This ensures coverage is in step with an organization's security posture and incident response plans so businesses can bolster their overall resistance to cyber threats (Patil, 2024).

1.3 Generative AI in Cybersecurity Insurance: Overview and Relevance

A Transformative Approach Its usage in this area can greatly assist with policy personalization and create better fraud detection mechanisms. Risk Assessment and Underwriting: Generative AI can provide more accurate assessments of an organization's posture risk by processing vast amounts of data. AI models are also trained on historical data on breaches, vulnerabilities, and threat landscapes and can therefore help insurers assess the risk posed to customers, ultimately enhancing informed considerations around underwriting decisions and pricing on policies. For organizations in the same industry, this enables them to have targeted risk assessments relevant to their own specific environment (Saxena et al., 2024).

1.4 Empirical Literature Review

Dynamic policy adjustment, Generative AI's ability to process real-time data allows insurers to dynamically adjust policies as new threats arise or as an organization's risk profile changes. For instance, when an organization introduces new security measures or undergoes a significant operational shift, generative AI could suggest modifications to policy terms and coverage limits to reflect these changes (Vajjhala et al., 2025).

It would not be an exaggeration to say that the blockchain and GenAI symbiosis is proving to be the potent sauce for bringing transparency in claims processing and policy management process. It allows AI generated fraud detection rules to be programmed in smart contracts to automate claims adjudication resulting in reducing human error and fraudulent activities. AI frameworks are also increasingly incorporating ethical considerations (including compliance with data privacy laws such as the GDPR), and algorithmic explainability to foster regulatory alignment and accountability. As cyber threats become ever more complex and scaled, the need for intelligent, adaptive, and explainable insurance solutions is expected to grow. The convergence of cybersecurity insurance and Generative AI is more than an innovation it is a paradigm shift. It enables global insurers to harmonize towards intelligent, behavior-driven and fraud-resilient policy ecosystems, supplemented by behavioral models that go beyond traditional risk models (Saxena et al., 2024). Such a transition is essential to building digital trust and resilience for industries in an era increasingly characterized by uncertainty in cyber technologies and disruption.

Generative AI is critical to improving the fraud detection capabilities of cybersecurity insurance. AI systems are able to identify suspicious claims for additional checks through their analysis of behaviours in claims data, allowing them to spot anomalies that might mean a claim is fraudulent. Not only does this approach help insurers mitigate their risk, but also decreases the cost associated with insurance fraud (Pant, 2025). These systems learn from historical claims data over time, incorporating new fraud strategies and decreasing false positives. Also, machine learning and natural language processing (NLP) tools can analyze the claim reporting and documentation process to detect discrepancies or suspicious behavior that indicates possible fraud, allowing for earlier detection and removal of these incidents from the claims process. AI has the potential to transform the landscape of cybersecurity insurance by extending its ability to assess and adjust premiums and coverage policies dynamically.(Extended abstract not found) Therapeutically, as generative AI systems and software become more powerful, they also have the potential to transform the insurance industry, providing sharper security, better risk assessments, and more customized insurance packs (Dileep et al., 2025).

2. CONCEPTUAL FRAMEWORK ON CYBERSECURITY INSURANCE POLICY CUSTOMIZATION USING GENERATIVE AI FRAUD DETECTION

Generative AI is becoming a game changer in areas like cybersecurity insurance. This can help massive improvement in policy personalization and fraud detection mechanism in this sector. Assessment and Underwriting: Generative AI can process large datasets to more accurately assess an organization's cybersecurity posture. Through the analysis of historical data on breaches, vulnerabilities and threat landscapes, AI models can help insurers gather insights and information necessary for underwriting decisions and policy pricing. Such a background for analysis can lead to plant-specific risk assessments to a greater degree of accuracy (Porwal, 2025).

Dynamic Policy Adaptation: The real-time data processing capabilities of generative AI allow insurers to dynamically adjust policies as new threats arise or the risk profile of an organization evolves. For instance, if an organization introduces new security protocols or encounters a major shift in its operations, generative AI can then suggest appropriate adjustments to policy terms or coverage limits.

Fraud Detection: Within the context of cybersecurity insurance, generative AI significantly improves the ability to detect fraud. Generative AI can enhance the claims process by analysing claims data for patterns, identifying outliers that may point to fraud, and flagging suspicious claims for further investigation. Additional benefits include the following:

Enhanced Customer Experience: By augmenting the claims process, generative AI can automate documentation reviews and decision points. Such efficiency translates to quicker claims settlement times and greater customer satisfaction critical for keeping client relationships strong in an increasingly competitive marketplace.

Predictive analytics Generative AI can mine predictive analytics to predict future risks based on the current trends and historical data. This makes it possible for insurers to proactively converge their offerings and advise clients with bespoke solutions on how to mitigate against these newfound threats before they materialise as true incidents.

So, considering that the landscape of cyber threat continues to evolve as a dangerous risk to organizations globally, cybersecurity insurance is thus more than ever, an important avenue for financial protection against this danger. The ability to customize policies not only helps businesses get coverage tailored to their unique needs but also allows more accurate assessment of risks and fraud detection by insurers with the help of generative AI. All these measures can work to provide a robust framework for controlling cyber risk in the current digital age. This proactive strategy not only enables insurance companies to mitigate their risks, but it also decreases the costs incurred due to fraudulent claims (Mucskova, 2024).

3. MANAGERIAL IMPLICATIONS AND CRISIS COVERAGE IN CYBERSECURITY INSURANCE

To address this tightening landscape of risk from different cyber angles, cybersecurity insurance has become a critical in an organization's risk management strategy. For managers, this changing landscape requires a shift in how cybersecurity insurance is understood, acquired and used, but beyond simple compliance or as a financial safety net. Managerial implications encompass areas of risk identification, mitigation planning, and incident response coordination. Leaders must take a constructive position to integrate the cybersecurity insurance approach into the larger enterprise risk management systems. Now they're charged with making sure that insurance policies are not just in place but are tailored to suit the organization's risk exposure, digital setup and regulatory requirements. This ranges from working with IT and legal teams to conducting regular cybersecurity audits are followed to ensure policies and practices are aligned with current threats such as ransomware, data breaches, and supply chain attacks. insurers' ability to respond to real time incidents and offer legal and data forensic support, all post incident services should have depth and timeliness (Al Maqousi, 2025).

The other important dimension influencing the managerial decision-making process is crisis coverage. While many company owners focus solely on monetary losses, comprehensive cybersecurity insurance also encompasses crisis communication, reputation management, business interruption losses, and legal liabilities. Understand the breadth and limits of your coverage including exclusions, deductibles, and how long you have to report an incident. Crisis management plans that work in tandem with coverage can equate to less downtime, greater stakeholder trust, and improved business continuity. And policies are becoming increasingly inclusive of so-called pre-breach services in scope including employee training, phishing simulations and system assessments, allowing managers to pivot insurance away from reactive tool and into proactive coverage. The true-time aspects of contemporary cyber-attacks also require agile decision-making and pre-approved communications during a crisis.

At the global level, the incentive toward risk-based pricing and coverage customization requires managers to proactively demonstrate good cyber hygiene in order to obtain favorable terms with the market. This includes timely updates to cybersecurity measures, investments in advanced threat detection systems, and creating a culture of security within the organization. Insurers are beginning to evaluate the efficacy of the managerial oversight and governance frameworks for policies that they underwrite, and as a result, cyber resilience is becoming the new table stakes of enterprise leadership (Babu et al., 2025). To that degree, cybersecurity insurance now overlaps directly with strategic management and crisis preparedness." Managers need to import insurance into a live risk ecosystem, meaning that their organizations are prepared, resilient, agile, to act, and to adapt in an era of impending and growing cyber crises. This concrete shift in perspective is critical for operational integrity in the long run.

In recent years, the cybersecurity insurance landscape has transformed significantly due to increased cyber threat prevalence and regulatory changes, as well as a broader realization of how important it is to have tailored coverage. The few key trends in the cyber insurance market include growth, increasing cyberattack incidents and regulatory changes.

3.1 Cyber Insurance in Market Growth

The market for cyber insurance has grown dramatically, emerging as a key player in the risk management process at organizations in many different industries. With growing awareness of the financial burden resulting from cyber incidents, the demand for cyber insurance policies has skyrocketed over the previous decade. Industry reports suggest that the size of the global cyber insurance market is expected to surpass the $20 billion threshold by 2025 with over 25% compound annual growth rate from previous years.

4. FACTORS FOR ATTRIBUTING GROWTH

Increasing Awareness of Cyber Threats: Organizations are becoming increasingly feedback of the potential financial implications of cyberattacks. Hacking breaches, ransomware, and other high-profile incidents have exposed vulnerabilities, leading businesses to look for financial protection from such attacks.94% of organisations said they planned to increase investment in cyber security in the next year, meaning that they also understand the need for insurance to hedge risks against their measures. That's where cyber insurance comes into play it acts as a safety net to help cover costs incurred due to data breaches, legal liabilities, and recovery efforts (Mohapatra & Mishra, 2024).

Changing Threat Landscape: The sophistication and frequency of cyberattacks have skyrocketed. From ransomware–and phishing attacks–to advanced persistent threats (APTs), organizations are faced with thousands of threats. This changing environment requires innovative insurance solutions that help to accommodate emerging risks.

Increased Competition: The influx of new entrants into the cyber insurance market has created competitive dynamics that have spurred innovation in products and services. Market growth has also been spurred by an availability of specialized policies by insurers that are customized around industry specific needs and risk profiles.

Coverage Standardization: As the health insurance market mature, coverage options will start to standardize across provider networks. Standardizing terms helps organizations better understand their options and allows for comparisons between most policies. Insider Threats Insider threats are still a major risk as employees or contractors are often used as a vector to compromise security protocols either knowingly or unknowingly. This can also include data leak prevention measures that monitor user activity and alert the organization to potential threats.

Emerging Technologies; New tech such as cloud computing, IoT (internet of things) and artificial intelligence has costed new vulnerabilities available for attackers. Organizations are adopting these technologies within their operations but they should be cognizant of their impact on their cybersecurity posture.

5. REGULATORY CHANGES AND COMPLIANCE REQUIREMENTS

Cyber security best practices are evolving with cyber threats and new regulations are emerging to balance compliance with protection of sensitive data and hold organizations accountable in their cyber security practices. Regulatory changes help define cybersecurity insurance market: Increased Regulatory Scrutiny: First off, governments go all in with stricter policies for data protection or privacy. Regulations, like the General Data Protection Regulation (GDPR) in the EU, and state-level privacy laws like CCAP in the US, can carry hefty penalties for breaches and non-compliance.

Mandatory Cyber Insurance Requirements: Increasingly, certain jurisdictions are mandating that certain businesses acquire and maintain cyber insurance as part of their compliance framework. This trend is a sign of increasing awareness of the need for financial protection against cyber risks.

Notable Trends in Cybersecurity Compliance Regulations: Training on Incident Response Plans: Regulators have expressed a growing need for organizations to prepare contingency plans. Insurers may ask for proof of these plans before issuing policies or offering coverage at favourable rates. No longer do insurers have their heads in the sand. As they race to mitigate risk through the creation of tailored policies, the pressure for consistency in security practices across industries has increased. To be issued coverage, insurers may seek for businesses to have certain security practices in place multifactor authentication (MFA) or regular employee training, for example (Amirineni, 2024).

Collaboration between Regulators and Insurers: To encourage best practices around cybersecurity risk management, an increasing trend is in the direction of collaboration between regulators and insurers to set up guidelines. This partnership helps guarantee that organizations are well covered, while simultaneously promoting a culture of accountability in the industry.

6. INNOVATIONS IN POLICY CUSTOMIZATION

With the ever-evolving threat landscape around cyber, the need for cybersecurity insurance has been on the rise. Insurance companies are now looking into creative methods to tailor their policies to suit the particular requirements of organisations. Such customization is not only critical to providing proper coverage, but it also promotes a proactive risk management culture. In policy customization, some areas of innovation include customized coverage options, proactive services, and continuous monitoring tools for risk mitigation.

7. TAILORED COVERAGE OPTIONS

Custom coverage options lead the field of innovations in cybersecurity insurance. Unlike traditional insurance policies that provide blanket coverage, customized policies enable organizations to choose options that meet their unique risk and operational needs (Gopal et al, 2024). There are a number of reasons for this transition:

Varied Risk Profiles: Cybercrime threatens different organizations in different sectors. A healthcare provider, for example, may prioritize data protection in light of the sensitivity of patient information, while a financial institution may prioritize fraud prevention. Insurers, in response, are developing new coverage options that take these diverse needs into account, allowing businesses to purchase protection against relevant risks.

Dynamic Coverage Structures: Cyber threats are continuously evolving, which requires coverage policy structures to be adaptable as time goes on. They are now having insurers add clauses that give them the option to adjust coverage based on emerging risks or changes in an organization's activities. A company that is expanding its digital footprint might need coverage for new technologies or platforms.

Specific Incident Coverage: Insurers are also developing policies that specifically cover the costs associated with the rising threat of ransomware and targeted attacks. That includes costs such as ransom payments, legal fees or data recovery costs. Insurance providers can guide victims through the complexity of cyber incidents by providing coverage for specific incidents.

Bundled Services: Some insurers are now bundling cybersecurity police with IT security benefits into one package to meet both insurance and cybersecurity. This not only makes it easier to purchase insurance, it also incentivizes organizations to invest in preventive measures in addition to their insurance coverage (Vaish, 2025).

Insurers are using advanced technologies like artificial intelligence (AI) and machine learning (ML) to create custom risk assessments for clients. These assessments allow them to assess vulnerabilities and create unique policy options, ensuring that coverage is provided where it should be and aligned with their specific exposure to risk.

8. CHALLENGES AND CONSIDERATIONS

Although the introduction of generative AI into cybersecurity insurance has considerable benefits, it also has challenges that require attention:

Data Privacy: Large amounts of data can raise issues regarding data privacy and the protection of sensitive information. Insurers, for instance, need to ensure that they are compliant with regulations such as the General Data Protection Regulation (GDPR) regarding how they collect and use clients information.
Challenge is Algorithmic Bias, meaning there is a concern that generative AIs might unintentionally inject bias into risk assessments or underwriting decisions. Regular audits of their algorithms must also be conducted, to guarantee fair and accurate assessments.
Cyber Threat Complexity: Cyber threats are news every time, and keeping up with the latest attack vectors and methods used by cybercriminals can be difficult for generative AI solutions. As such, it will require constant updating of training data for these systems to remain effective.
Strategic Implementation: Implementing the social contact and potential AI technology into a legacy insurance organization can be a challenge. Old technology converts on new systems can be expensive and time-consuming often taking a lot of time to plan and execute.
Importance of Human Judgment: Even with generative AI's potential for efficiency, human judgment must be exercised in sensitive activities like claims adjudication and risk assessment. Insurers will have to balance automation and human judgment to maintain quality across the board (Challa, 2024).

9. MOVING TOWARDS MORE ETHICAL USE OF AI IN INSURANCE

Using generative AI in insurance also raises ethical dilemmas that companies must manage: Algorithmic Bias, Generative AI can unintentionally continue biases embedded in training datasets, resulting in disproportionate treatment of some demographics in risk assessment or claims review. Regular auditing of algorithms to detect biases and ensure fair outcomes for customers is imperative for insurers. The lack of transparency regarding the decision-making process of AI can create a deficit of trust between the insurer and insured. Consumers might not be cognizant of how their data is being used, or how decisions about coverage or claims are being made. Insurers must commit to transparency by making it clear how AI systems work and how they arrive at specific decisions. As insurers further deploy generative AI for a range of applications, obtaining informed consent for the use of such technologies will be paramount. The risks and their rights regarding data privacy. As the increasing need for automation continues, many are fearing the job displacement to insurance jobs. Generative AI can improve systems to create efficiency, but it also reduces demand for some functions that have previously been performed by humans. Insurers will need to be think about the impact on their workforce and invest in retraining initiatives to support employees transition into new roles.

10. STRIKING A BALANCE BETWEEN AUTOMATION AND HUMAN VIGILANCE

It is important to find the right balance between generative AI and the human touch despite the perks of automating the summarization workflow come at an efficiency and accuracy cost in some scenarios. While generative AI can produce results very quickly, you lose the ability to manually check if the results caught all the necessary details. Insurers should also leverage checks and balances built into their system that require human review at major inputs of the process such as claims adjudication or risk assessment (Nuhiu & Aliu, 2025).

Ethics and Morality, some situations may involve moral considerations that are complex for an automated system to navigate. Claims that involve individual extenuating circumstances might benefit from human involvement to consider specific factors that an algorithm might ignore, for instance.

Training Employees, as more insurers incorporate automation, training employees on how best to work with AI will become increasingly important. Employees need to know how to read AI-generated insights, and how to use those insights to make informed decisions, while ensuring that they remain accountable for final outcomes (Sindiramutty et al., 2025). As organizations become three times more aware of the need for custom-made coverage to address their Cyber risk, the Cyber insurance landscape is evolving rapidly. Heading forward, it is worth considering some of the implications of customisation of cyber insurance policies driven by an evolving threat landscape, regulatory headwinds and technological innovations.

11. CONCLUSION

The cyber insurance market forecast suggests that the market is projected to grow up to USD 92 billion by 2031, at a compound annual growth rate (CAGR) of around 25.4%. The rise is driven by the increased visibility of cyber threats and the cost of data and ransomware attacks. The growing need for tailored coverage options as businesses want to ensure that their insurance is in line with the specific risks they are facing. More insurers are selling customizable policies, where organizations can choose their coverage limits and types to meet their specific cyber threats, including costs related to data breaches and regulatory fines. This tailoring also includes additional services such as proactive assessments in cyber security and crisis management.

As regulations such as GDPR and CCPA become more stringent, the demand for cyber insurance that covers legal expenses and regulatory fines are rising. These rules have led insurers to encourage companies to be proactive about these safeguards in order to reduce the financial risk of penalties. AI technologies are getting integrated to enhance risk assessment and underwriting processes. AI tools allow insurers to process huge datasets for accurate risk assessments and premium adjustments according to real-time threat landscapes. This technology also enables ongoing monitoring tools that allow organizations to proactively manage their cyber risk. With identity-based attacks becoming more common, insurers are focusing on ensuring strong identity management protocols are embedded within their policies. Businesses are required by many insurers to take steps such as implementing multi-factor authentication (MFA) before they'll agree to coverage. This evolution emphasizes the increased risk posed by stolen credentials and serves as a call to action for organizations to improve their security posture.

12. FUTURE PROSPECTS ON CYBERSECURITY INSURANCE POLICIES CUSTOMIZATION

The evolving future of cybersecurity insurance policy customization will be driven by a handful of trends. When it comes to cyber threats, there is no shortage of demands, including comprehensive cover to combat a broader spectrum of risks. Insurers will need to adjust their offerings to include targeted protections against emerging threats such as ransomware and APTs (advanced persistent threats). The relationship between insurers and policyholders will become more cooperative as businesses look for advice on the best practices for risk management. Insurers will serve a critical function in educating clients on emerging threats and how companies can properly mitigate them. More focus on Proactive Risk Management:

Moving From Reactive to Proactive Risk Management Insurers will increasingly provide services to help organizations pinpoint vulnerabilities before they escalate into incidents, reducing the frequency and severity of claims.

Many industries operate in areas of risk where regulations are still evolving. Consequently, insurers will have to remain vigilant concerning the compliance requirements to which their policies are subject. This flexibility will be key to staying relevant in a fast-shifting regulatory landscape. These will be complemented by expansion of blockchains, and emerging technologies such as smart contracts will further encompass the policies along with billing protocols. This will lead to new advancements in underwriting procedures and streamline claims management.

REFERENCES

Al Maqousi, A. (2025). Cybersecurity in Smart. Examining Cybersecurity Risks Produced by Generative AI, 357.

Amirineni, S. (2024). Leveraging Machine Learning, Cloud Computing, and Artificial Intelligence for Fraud Detection and Prevention in Insurance: A Scalable Approach to Data-Driven Insights. *International Journal of Automation. Artificial Intelligence and Machine Learning*, *4*(2), 155–172. DOI: 10.61797/ijaaiml.v4i2.371

Babu, B. S., Umakanth, M., & Bhanumathi, P. (2025). Generative Artificial. *Organizational Sociology in the Digital Age*, 413.

Challa, K. (2024). Artificial Intelligence and Generative Neural Systems: Creating Smarter Customer Support Models for Digital Financial Services. *Journal of Computational Analysis and Applications*, *33*(8).

Gopal, M. K., Shetty, J., Yenduri, G., Maddikunta, P. K. R., Murugan, R., & Gadekallu, T. R. (2024). Experts Opinion on Generative AI: Adoption and Challenges in Actuarial Science. In *Artificial Intelligence and Actuarial Science* (pp. 21-36). Chapman and Hall/CRC.

Intaratat, K., Lomchavakarn, P., Boonsawad, P., Boonsiri, K., Kantaboon, K., Intaratat, D., & Kumar, R. Innovations in Smart Healthcare: Integrating Generative Artificial Intelligence with Federated Learning. In *Generative Artificial Intelligence in Healthcare* (pp. 224-246). CRC Press.

Khan, A., Jhanjhi, N., Hamid, D. H. H., Omar, H. A. H. B. H., Amsaad, F., & Wassan, S. (2025). Future Trends and Challenges in Cybersecurity and Generative AI. *Reshaping CyberSecurity With Generative AI Techniques*, 491-522.

Kulkarni, P., Pathak, P., Pillai, S., & Tigga, V. (2025). Role of Generative AI for Fraud Detection and Prevention. *Generative Artificial Intelligence in Finance: Large Language Models, Interfaces, and Industry Use Cases to Transform Accounting and Finance Processes*, 175-198.

Mohapatra, H., & Mishra, S. R. (2024). Analysis of Sector-Specific Responses of AI Generative. In Generative, A. I. (Ed.), *Current Trends and Applications* (pp. 167–184). Springer Nature Singapore. DOI: 10.1007/978-981-97-8460-8_9

Mucskova, M. (2024). Transforming Banking with Artificial Intelligence: Applications, Challenges, and Implications. *Trends Economics and Management*, *18*(42), 21–37. DOI: 10.13164/trends.2024.42.21

Narayan, M., Shukla, P., Dileep Kumar, M., & Mani, N. (2025). Generative AI in FinTech: Revolutionizing Fraud Detection, Personalized Advising, and Predictive Analytics. In *Generative AI in FinTech: Revolutionizing Finance Through Intelligent Algorithms* (pp. 137–154). Springer Nature Switzerland. DOI: 10.1007/978-3-031-76957-3_7

Nuhiu, A., & Aliu, F. (2025). The Transformative Role of Big Data Analytics and Generative AI in Redefining FinTech for New Business Models. In *Generative Artificial Intelligence (AI) Approaches for Industrial Applications* (pp. 281–304). Springer Nature Switzerland. DOI: 10.1007/978-3-031-76710-4_14

Pant, P. (2025). Revolutionizing Insurance Data Modernization: Enhancing Property and Casualty Insurance with Cloud Solutions, Data Lakes, and Real-Time Reporting to Propel Advanced Analytics, Ensure Unified Governance and Compliance, and Foster Innovation and Experimentation. *Journal of Computational Analysis and Applications*, *34*(5).

Patil, D. (2024). Artificial Intelligence In Financial Services: Advancements In Fraud Detection, Risk Management, And Algorithmic Trading Optimization. *Risk Management, And Algorithmic Trading Optimization (November 20, 2024).*

Porwal, P. D. (2025). Ethics and Laws: Governing Generative AI's Role in Financial Systems. Generative Artificial Intelligence in Finance: Large Language Models, Interfaces, and Industry Use Cases to Transform Accounting and Finance Processes, 283-298.

Saxena, A., Verma, S., & Mahajan, J. (2024). The Evolution of Insurance in the Digital Age. In *Generative AI in Banking Financial Services and Insurance: A Guide to Use Cases, Approaches, and Insights* (pp. 201–237). Apress. DOI: 10.1007/979-8-8688-0559-2_7

Saxena, A., Verma, S., & Mahajan, J. (2024). Evolution of Generative AI. In *Generative AI in Banking Financial Services and Insurance: A Guide to Use Cases, Approaches, and Insights* (pp. 3–24). Apress. DOI: 10.1007/979-8-8688-0559-2_1

Seethala, S. C. (2025). Revolutionizing Insurance with AI, Cloud, and Cybersecurity: A Strategic Guidewire Approach. *Cloud, and Cybersecurity: A Strategic Guidewire Approach (April 01, 2025).* in enhancing organizational resilience against cyber threats. *Cybersecurity Education Journal*, *5*(1), 35–50.

Sindiramutty, S. R., Prabagaran, K. R. V., Jhanjhi, N. Z., Murugesan, R. K., Brohi, S. N., & Masud, M. (2025). Generative AI in Network Security and Intrusion Detection. In *Reshaping CyberSecurity With Generative AI Techniques* (pp. 77–124). IGI Global.

Vaish, S., Singh, M., & Jha, A. K. (2025). Challenges for Responsible Implementation of Generative AI in Fintech. In *Generative AI in FinTech: Revolutionizing Finance Through Intelligent Algorithms* (pp. 325–344). Springer Nature Switzerland. DOI: 10.1007/978-3-031-76957-3_17

Vajjhala, N. R., Roy, S. S., Taşcı, B., & Chowdhury, M. E. H. (2025). Foundations and Emerging Trends in Generative Artificial Intelligence (AI) for Industrial Applications. *Generative Artificial Intelligence (AI) Approaches for Industrial Applications*, 1-18.

Chapter 7
Fraud Detection and Mitigation in Cybersecurity Insurance: AI-Driven Approaches and Best Practices

Muhammad Usman Tariq
https://orcid.org/0000-0002-7605-3040
Abu Dhabi University, UAE & University College Cork, Ireland

ABSTRACT

This chapter explores the pivotal role of artificial intelligence (AI) in transforming fraud detection and mitigation within the cybersecurity insurance industry. As cyber threats grow in complexity and frequency, the insurance sector faces mounting challenges to accurately identify and prevent fraudulent claims. The chapter delves into how AI technologies, particularly machine learning and predictive analytics, enable insurers to assess risk more effectively, detect anomalies in real-time, and improve the overall accuracy of claims assessments. It emphasizes the importance of data quality and volume, showcasing how historical claims data, incident reports, and threat intelligence databases fuel AI models to uncover potential fraud. Additionally, the chapter discusses the integration of AI systems with existing fraud detection workflows, balancing automation with human expertise. It examines best practices for designing AI-driven solutions that not only enhance detection accuracy but also maintain transparency, accountability, and regulatory compliance.

DOI: 10.4018/979-8-3373-5545-0.ch007

INTRODUCTION

The increasing problem of fraud in cybersecurity insurance causes substantial consequences for both insurance companies and their clients. The evolving nature of cyber threats necessitates a corresponding progression in fraudsters' methods of exploiting system vulnerabilities. The cybersecurity insurance field has experienced a significant rise in fraudulent activities because the insurance market expands rapidly while cybercriminals develop more advanced techniques. False claims constitute one type of fraud, while advanced schemes that utilize data manipulation in conjunction with identity theft represent another category of fraudulent activities. Insurers encounter difficulties in securing extensive coverage while they work to control fraudulent losses because this type of activity compromises their organizational financial health (Dhieb & Ghazzai, 2020). Fraud in the cybersecurity insurance industry shows increasing complexity in its current form. The adaptation of mature techniques used for evaluating and controlling risks stops being valid when confronted by modern fraudulent methods that use cutting-edge technological capabilities. Cybercriminals actively abuse both insurance policy weaknesses and claim evaluation methods because they understand these vulnerabilities. Ransomware attacks, along with data breaches and phishing schemes, present rising cyber threats that have made it more complex for insurers to detect actual claims from fraudulent ones. A cyberattack victim or business may present false evidence of significant cyber damage, or they might report being attacked to obtain insurance benefits although no actual cyberattacks occurred. These fraudulent claims create both monetary harm and damage credibility for the entire insurance sector, so insurers need stronger methods to detect fake claims (Bello & Folorunso, 2023).

Artificial intelligence functions as an advanced tool protecting cybersecurity insurance organizations from fraudulent activities (Tariq, 2024). AI efficiently processes massive data volumes, which makes it appropriate for detecting indicators of fraudulent behaviour through pattern recognition. Through the implementation of artificial intelligence into insurance fraud detection systems, insurers can utilize machine learning algorithms that pinpoint anomalies and evaluate risks alongside suspicious activity at higher accuracy rates compared to conventional detection methods. AI systems serve to inspect network events through comprehensive monitoring, which enables them to detect strange patterns in claim documentation when cyberattack details do not synchronize properly. AI systems that analyze historical data enable insurance providers to discover fraudulent patterns in claims so they can reformulate both their underwriting approaches and policy conditions (Dhieb & Ghazzai, 2020). AI-driven approaches in fraud detection matter in the current threat landscape for several reasons. The higher frequency and complexity of cyberattacks compel insurers to develop cutting-edge and flexible systems for their response. AI systems provide insurers with an extensive threat understanding through their processing of data stemming from social media platforms as well as dark web forums, along with network-based activities. With AI assistance, insurers can perform immediate decisions that help them respond effectively to new emerging fraud threats. Insurers can leverage machine learning models that identify phishing-related behavioral patterns, therefore enabling them to detect fraudulent claims during unfinished processing. The application of AI fostered collaborations between insurers and cybersecurity experts and law enforcement agencies for sharing information, which boosts their joint capabilities to combat cyber fraud (Bello & Folorunso, 2023).

The promising features of AI fraud detection coexist with traditional fraud detection systems within the cybersecurity insurance industry, although both have their respective limits. Traditional methods face their main difficulty because they depend on manual procedures along with rule-based systems that struggle to track modern cybercriminal approaches (Tariq, 2025). Most insurers maintain static databases containing fraud patterns even though these knowledge bases easily get outdated by changing methods used by criminals. The system's vulnerability leads to two problems: authorities deny proper claims but cannot recognize valid claims as legitimate when detected by system errors. Traditional approaches need extensive human involvement for their operation, which proves both slow and prone to human mistakes. AI-based detection systems minimize the requirement for human involvement by implementing automated processes while using new information to learn and maintain an effective fraud prevention system (Dhieb & Ghazzai, 2020). Traditionally, insurers struggle to identify new types of fraud since their established patterns are insufficient for uncovering novel scheming. The systems are falling victim to criminal manipulation due to cybercriminals' utilization of deepfake technology and social engineering. Deepfakes serve as a fraudulent method of producing fake videos or images that create obstacles in insurer authentication of claims. Current detection systems experience difficulties in detecting new fraud because their pre-established rules lack patterns that would represent modern types of deception. When compared to human investigators, AI has the capability of finding hidden inconsistencies and unusual patterns that appear beneath human detection. AI systems process large volumes of unstructured data using NLP and image recognition software to search for hidden fraudulent patterns that exist across emails, social media content, and multimedia media files (Bello & Folorunso, 2023). The progress made through AI-driven fraud detection continues to face barriers because of two main issues which include algorithmic bias that could result in discriminatory or unfair outcomes during detection evaluations.AI systems detect fraud with the same precision as their training datasets contain which means biased incomplete data during training can create erroneous false fraud alarms by missing other types of fraud activities. The training of AI models with primarily corporate data stops them from effectively detecting fraudulent insurance claims from small companies. To reduce this risk, AI systems should operate on broad datasets that reflect all groups of people, along with scheduled fairness inspections (Dhieb & Ghazzai, 2020). Traditional fraud detection methods must give way because swindlers within cybersecurity insurance continue their rise in numbers and professional dexterity. The application of artificial intelligence to fraud detection produces major potential gains in insurer capacities to address contemporary threats in fraud prevention while fighting future ones. The deployment of AI technology requires proper implementation standards because it needs to prevent algorithmic bias while maintaining balanced and effective detection systems. Insurers gain stronger fraud prevention abilities when they unite their human operatives with AI systems and repeatedly improve their detection capabilities to deliver improved security to their policyholders (Bello & Folorunso, 2023). The AI system architecture is provided in figure 1.

Figure 1. AI system architecture overview

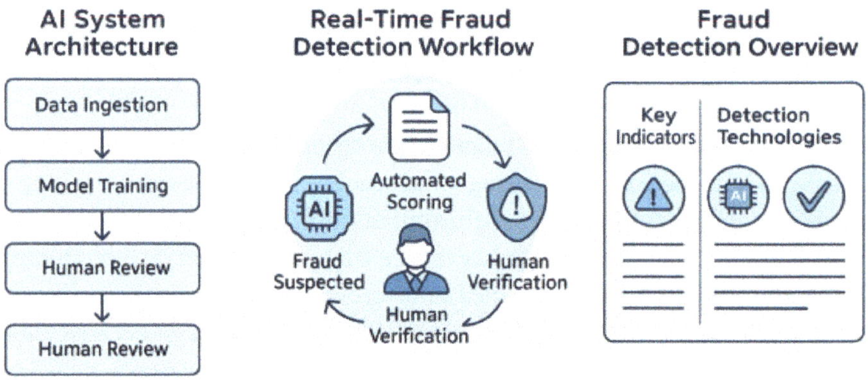

BACKGROUND

The cybercrime surge alongside worsening cyber threats in the industry has propelled cybersecurity insurance companies to focus primarily on fraud detection and prevention to remain protected. Insurance companies face escalating risk because cybersecurity insurance demand grows parallel to cyberattack occurrence frequency while they must guarantee full protection along with anti-fraud security measures. The amount of fraud affecting cybersecurity insurance continues to rise annually because cyber criminals constantly modify their scheming approaches to discover weaknesses in policy terms yet maintain claim procedures. The adoption of AI alongside advanced technologies has become essential because it has altered the way traditional fraud detection works, and therefore, more effective mitigation strategies need advancement (Pareek, 2023). The insurance industry created cybersecurity coverage to protect businesses during data breaches, ransomware attacks, and other cyber-attacks by paying for legal fees and data recovery expenses and damage to organizational reputation. The growth of complex cyberattacks led to improved fraudulent techniques employed by criminals seeking to trick insurance companies. Fraud takes different forms in the insurance field, such as individuals exaggerating or creating non-existent cyberattack damage and submitting attacks that never actually took place while manipulating attack origins (Tariq, 2025). Cybercriminals exploit the rising trend of companies underreporting cyber incidents to their reputations by filing deceptive claims that face minimal chances of detection (Hassan & Aziz, 2023). The occurrence of fraud within cybersecurity insurance coverage produces a range of negative effects. The financial expenses from deceptive claims in cyber insurance schemes total billions of dollars yearly for the industry, based on current estimates. The dishonest practices threaten both insurance companies' profitability levels and develop distrust between insurers and their policy-holding clients. The increase in insurance fraud demoralizes the entire cybersecurity insurance sector because insurance companies shy away from providing coverage to organizations while increasing policy premiums to their legitimate customers. Insurance premiums continue to increase due to rising cyberattack risks, so insurers need decisive action to combat fraud to protect both their profitability and market credibility (Bello & Olufemi, 2024).

The introduction of artificial intelligence represents a disruptive technological solution that aids cybersecurity insurance companies in fighting fraud. Its analytics processing capabilities AI identifies fraudulent insurance claims from unusual behavioural clues that otherwise would remain undetected. The subset of AI technology machine learning algorithms successfully interprets historical data patterns to find deviations from standard claim filing behaviour. An AI-driven system identifies suspicious behavior when a certain claimant submits frequent claims that correlate with significant cyber incidents that media reports disclose, so this behavior needs additional review (Hassan & Aziz, 2023). AI demonstrates its strength by processing new data, which enables fraud prevention efforts against developing fraud schemes. Business entities find their traditional prevention systems built from static rules and pre-defined patterns unable to prevent modern, sophisticated types of fraud (Tariq, 2024). Scammers benefit from deepfake technology to develop fake evidence of cyber incidents through the creation of seemingly genuine but fake images of ransomware communications and video footage demonstrating cyber attackers accessing protected information. The combination of sophisticated AI systems and advanced image recognition and natural language processing produces the detection of deceitful insurance claims by identifying data inconsistencies in fraudulent communications (Bello & Olufemi, 2024).

Real-time operation stands as a vital advantage of AI fraud detection because insurers can respond instantly to developing threats. Manual fraud detection via insurance systems faces challenges because there is both an increase in data volume and data variety. AI systems analyze claims submissions, network activities, and additional related information to detect suspicious actions in rapid time during the processing period. Insurers can begin blocking payments and start additional investigations by using this predictive method before issuing any fraudulent payouts (Hassan & Aziz, 2023). The implementation of AI programs for fraud detection presents multiple barriers that organizations must handle. The primary concern regarding algorithmic bias creates problems that result in improper and discriminatory outcomes during fraud detection activities. AI systems flag healthy claims as fraudulent and fail to recognize actual cases of fraud because they rely on data that includes errors and discriminatory biases during their training phase. An AI model that receives main training from large organizational data will demonstrate decreased effectiveness at stopping fraudulent activities submitted by smaller businesses or technologically challenged individuals. False positive errors would then occur to deny insurance coverage from genuine claimants. The detection process requires fair treatment, which can only be achieved through training AI systems with datasets that represent all types of users (Bello & Olufemi, 2024).

Using AI as a fraud detection tool brings significant benefits, yet organizations should understand its capabilities as an incomplete solution. The verification of claims legitimacy remains dependent on traditional audit methods together with expert investigations. The proper approach toward AI is to consider it as a supportive tool instead of seeking to replace traditional investigation methods. Modern algorithms require human supervision when dealing with complicated fraud investigations and when evaluating complicated claims that AI detection algorithms identify. Human investigators maintain an advantage over AI systems because they often understand contextual and judgmental elements that these technological systems cannot achieve

(Hassan & Aziz, 2023). Many insurance companies implement dual fraud detection methods that unite artificial intelligence with traditional techniques for developing a stronger total fraud prevention model. The combination of AI technology and human expertise presents insurers with enhanced capabilities to utilize the best attributes of both systems. AI rapidly evaluates big claims datasets for irregularities, but human investigators check unrealistic claims that AI systems detect for accuracy (Tariq, 2025). The best strategy to fight cyber insurance fraud involves uniting technological platforms with human expertise as an efficient method (Pareek, 2023). The implementation of AI-driven fraud detection faces multiple obstacles in its mission to reform the cybersecurity insurance sector. System designers need to pay equal attention to making AI algorithms reliable and unbiased and to including machine learning models in current fraud prevention protocols. The fight against cyber insurance fraud benefits greatly from AI-driven tools because of deepening cyber threat complexity and expanding fraudulent activity levels. AI's future development will boost its importance for fraud detection, which will enable insurers to protect themselves and their customers better from escalating cybercrimes (Pareek, 2023).

Understanding Fraud in Cybersecurity Insurance

Cybersecurity insurance fraud has emerged as a critical problem because it provides significant negative results for insurers and their policy subscribers. The growth of cybersecurity insurance continues to increase, and so does the number of sophisticated attacks of fraud. The purpose of cybersecurity insurance is to shield companies from the monetary losses caused by cyberattacks, which include data breaches along with ransomware attacks and network disruption events. The insurance industry expansion enables fraudsters to take advantage of system vulnerabilities, which allows them to falsify data claims for money they should not receive. The risks faced by insurers and their covered organizations because of this kind of fraud remain substantial, as viable fraud detection and prevention systems are essential to protect them (Ahmad, 2024). The submission of deceptive claims stands as the principal method of fraud that exists within cybersecurity insurance programs. Fraudsters will make up or amplify information regarding cyber incidents by falsely stating data breaches happened when there were none. It becomes challenging to detect this type of fraud because criminals produce phony evidence consisting of altered emails, tampered system logs, and deceitfully manufactured screenshots. Organizations file false claims under financial strain alongside loss management needs by believing the insurance provider will find their deceptive acts challenging to verify. Companies may initiate breach claims regarding incidents that stem from their internal mistakes. The U.S. healthcare provider made records falsely represent cyberattacks in 2021, while investigators proved the data breach stemmed from operational flaws (Ashfin, 2024). The cybersecurity insurance sector experiences prevalent fraud through companies that report exaggerated damage amounts or incident occurrences. Organizations that attempt to inflate claims they report about an actual event often aim to maximize their insurance payout potential. The attempt to obtain insurance compensation often includes methods of overstating ransomware attack effects and counting non-existent data breach victims. A cyberattack usually results in minimal infrastructure destruction according to actual events, but an organization may present stories of complete breakdowns. A multinational company gained media attention in 2020 after reporting hundreds of thousands of compromised records through fraudulent communications about their ransomware attack, which affected only limited files. The main purpose behind this insurance fraud is to obtain more compensation than the incident warrants, along with recovering expenses and fixing reputational harm (Ahmad, 2024).

Cybersecurity insurance industry fraudsters often adjust when incidents occur to achieve certain objectives. During fraudulent activities, organizations could modify the timing of a cyberattack, making it seem either precocious or delayed compared to its actual occurrence. Attack manipulation occurs frequently to hide organizational negligence and control the attack framework by altering when the cybersecurity event happened. Organizations delay breach reporting by months to avoid regulatory penalties for delayed submission and simultaneously present greater damage than occurred. The organization decides to fabricate events that never happened to create false stories that shield the organization from investigation or sanction for inadequate cybersecurity practices (Ashfin, 2024). The modification of event timelines proves challenging to identify because criminal offenders succeed at hiding evidence of their initial attack methods. The cybersecurity insurance sector demonstrates difficulties in criminal detection and prevention through the analysis of major criminal cases within the industry. A prominent insurance company sustained major financial problems in 2019 when multiple insurance claims submitted during cyberattack events later turned out to be founded on fraudulent statements. The international law firm made false claims about its data breach to receive a multi-million-dollar payout in a well-known case. A thorough examination revealed the insurance company fraud while they had already distributed a significant amount of funds. A financial services company filed false statements about the results of a cyberattack by saying their clients' essential data was stolen (Ahmad, 2024).

An official audit investigation showed that the organization had insufficient cybersecurity measures, leading to less damage than announced in their initial claims. The insecure state of the cybersecurity insurance industry becomes evident through cases of fraudulent claims, which both demonstrate insurers' difficulties in detecting such deceptions before making a commitment to payment (Ashfin, 2024). Insurance companies endure major financial losses and dual economic and reputational damage due to fraud occurrences. Unchecked false claims cause insurers to sustain major financial damage because insurers might have to pay out substantial amounts for illegitimate compensation requests. The direct financial costs of fraud produce additional expenses through regulatory scrutiny that forces insurers to pay increased premiums, which affect the whole market. Insurance premiums increase when insurers modify their risk models after fraud incidents because of heightened fraud vulnerability, thus requiring policyholders to pay higher rates. Insurance companies need to conduct protracted and pricey litigation to get back the money after fraud is uncovered during or after the payout period, thus affecting their financial capabilities. Insurance costs keep increasing because of this pattern, which ultimately impacts all components within the industry structure (Adeyeye & Akanbi, 2024). The damage to an insurer's reputation from fraud incidents remains as severe as other negative effects. Insurance companies losing credibility as risk assessors stands as an effect when they issue payment for false claims. Policyholders depend on insurers to validate coverage claims and distribute funds evenly in an open manner. Insurance policyholders distrust companies that cannot properly detect fraud, and they switch to different providers, causing business loss for insurers. Insurance organizations dealing in fraudulent claims receive broad market reputational repercussions because of which they encounter problems with regulatory organizations, investors, and peers. The present era demands strong recognition for comprehensive fraud prevention and risk management since insurers need both business retention and brand protection to succeed (Ashfin, 2024).

Insured organizations experience equally grave financial damage as well as negative impact on their reputation when fraud occurs. When organizations detect fraudulent claims, they might get punished by regulators and risk legal consequences and extra law enforcement monitoring. Submitting fraudulent claims results in damaging effects on an organization's reputation because such behaviour often becomes public knowledge. Insurers will cancel coverage entirely once they detect fraudulent activities that organizations participate in and deny policy renewal to these organizations. The organization will lose necessary protection for cyber events after termination of its coverage, which results in substantial financial vulnerabilities (Adeyeye & Akanbi, 2024). Fraud in cybersecurity insurance is a complicated and expanding issue that has detrimental effects on insurers' and insured companies' finances and reputations. The many forms of fraud, which include fabricated claims, inflated damages, and manipulated timetables, show how sophisticated fraudsters are and how hard it is for insurers to spot fraudulent activity. Prominent fraud instances draw attention to the dangers involved, and the harm done to insurers' and insured organizations' finances and reputations highlights the necessity of efficient fraud detection and prevention techniques. To handle the increasing risks posed by fraud in the sector, insurers must keep adjusting and improving their fraud mitigation strategies as the cybersecurity landscape changes (Adeyeye & Akanbi, 2024).

AI-Powered Fraud Detection Tools and Techniques

The detection along with mitigation of fraud within cybersecurity insurance grows more important due to Artificial intelligence (AI) involvement. Modern insurance methods fall short of defending insurers from financial losses while sustaining their reputation because fraudulent activities have grown sophisticated. The combination of AI tools and techniques delivers a superior method for detecting fraudulent behaviour, which then allows insurers to prevent fraud activities effectively and efficiently. Different Artificial Intelligence technologies, notably machine learning (ML) and natural language processing (NLP), along with predictive analytics, drive revolutionized fraud detection in the insurance industry. The analysis of extensive insurance data through these tools allows the identification of irregularities, which detects fraudulent claims before their impact on substantial financial losses becomes severe (George, 2024). Machine learning models provide companies with one of the most beneficial Artificial Intelligence techniques to identify abnormalities within claim data. By using large datasets, machine learning algorithms receive training so systems can identify and understand information patterns and relationships contained within the data. Through ongoing operation, these models detect irregularities that frequently signal cases of fraud. The insurance company uses a machine learning model to analyze historical claim data, including entire ranges of information about claim sizes and incident types, as well as customer records. New claims fall outside normal patterns when the model detects unusually high amounts of money claimed, as well as when policyholders file various claims during brief periods, along with inconsistencies in provided data. A quick and precise identification of anomalous claims through this process reduces the danger of making fraudulent payments to dishonest policyholders (Prakash & Deokar, 2025).

Large insurance firms such as AXA and Allianz currently use AI systems to fight fraud. The companies use machine learning algorithms to study insurance claim patterns, resulting in the identification of strange conduct. AXA employed machine learning to discover when policyholders made an excessive number of claims in a single situation. Analysis showed that multiple people engaged in a fraud ring submitted false claims through various fabricated identities. Through machine learning capabilities, AXA monitored fraudulent patterns to stop further fraudulent claims from being processed. Insurance companies receive dual advantages from automated detection, which leads to fewer expenses with quicker response times and precise fraud detection operations (George, 2024). The AI technology NLP demonstrates significant progress for fighting cybersecurity insurance fraud. The processing of human language through machines constitutes NLP because it enables systems to understand and analyse claim descriptions and other documentation and communication texts. Claims in the insurance field require multiple types of written reports, together with policyholder statements and supporting documentation. Through NLP algorithms, machines examine written content to detect signs of manipulation as well as inconsistencies in the data. An NLP model understands linguistic indicators of fraud by learning to detect the pairing of unclear content with conflicting statements and extensive claim details that differ from usual insurance reports (Okenwa et al., 2024). The analysis of claim descriptions alongside supporting documentation achieves its best results through NLP implementation. Through language processing analysis, NLP detects irregularities of policyholder wording that indicate potential fraud activity when details of an incident are manipulated to exaggerate damages or fabricate a breach. Detection systems flag claim reports for further checking when they contain technical terms that do not match the actual cyberattack details. Through text analysis, NLP identifies bogus documents that contain faked email evidence or image manipulations that would be detected through its examination for contradictory information (Prakash & Deokar, 2025).

NLP finds its application through IBM and SAS alongside other companies who created AI-powered fraud detection platforms for insurance claims analysis. The platforms perform large-scale text data analysis of email documents and claims forms by detecting dishonourable patterns and abnormal content. IBM's Watson for Cybersecurity system monitored claim descriptions during real-time processing to deny payments on incidents showing signs of fabrication or abuse (Okenwa et al., 2024). Several companies employ predictive analytics due to its rising use in fraud detection activities. Through predictive analysis, businesses use past information paired with statistical mathematical algorithms to produce future outcome forecasts. The application of predictive analytics in cybersecurity insurance lets companies recognize dangerous claims during preliminary review stages. Insurers build prediction models for fraudulent claims through the analysis of their prior claim records. The predictive models use specifications of cyber incident patterns along with claim value assessments and policyholder track records together with supporting contextual data (Okenwa et al., 2024). Predictive analytics creates models that identify systematic fraudulent patterns that occur during types of cyberattacks. Insurance claims from circumstances or sectors could trigger higher risk alarms because of historical statistical indicators. The analysis of policyholder behaviours becomes possible through predictive analytics practices used by insurers. Policyholders who file numerous expensive claims within a brief period receive suspect status as the analysis reveals fraudulent claim indicators (Okenwa et al., 2024). The analysis of historical data by these tools helps forecast potential insurance fraud through the investigation of factors involving claim frequency, policyholder characteristics, and incident classification. Insurers implemented predictive analytics, which detected multiple fraudulent claims when processed through their system. The analytical results showed that specific claims stemmed from a common group of people who depended on identical deceptive claim submission patterns. The insurer prevented substantial financial damages by observing these patterns before any significant harm occurred (Brokešová & Ondruška, 2025).

The evaluation of claims by Artificial Intelligence runs continuously when parties submit claims within the insurance process for detecting fraudulent activities. Traditional insurance systems review claims after submission, which exposes them to fraudulent payments before detecting the fraudulent nature of the claims. The analysis of claims through AI tools that operate in real-time helps identify potential frauds that lead to payment reduction, thus preventing financial losses. Integrated detection technology employing NLP and machine learning algorithms alongside predictive analytics functions to automatically detect troublesome claims while they are being submitted (Okenwa et al., 2024). Several insurance companies utilize AI systems to monitor claims for fraud indicators while customers submit their applications. Automated systems identify known suspicious conduct through their analysis of patterns that include claim duplicates along with contradictory customer data and unexpected payment values. The system identifies suspicious claims, which are then instantly directed toward additional investigation protocols before any payment transactions occur. Insurers maintain preventive measures through their proactive methods to stop fraudulent claims before processing, so they avoid experiencing avoidable financial losses (Brokešová & Ondruška, 2025). AI-based fraud detection tools, along with machine learning technologies with natural language processing, predictive analytics, and real-time detection capabilities, give insurance companies better results than their conventional fraud prevention methods. Using these modern technologies helps insurance companies locate and eliminate fraud while saving money and time and protecting their financial position along with their public image. Insurance companies can automate the detection process, examine enormous volumes of data, and spot fraudulent activity by using AI in fraud detection (George, 2024).

The Role of Data in AI-Driven Fraud Detection

AI-driven fraud detection in cybersecurity insurance heavily depends on the proper utilization of data for its operation. Successful detection of fraudulent claims by AI requires data with excellent quality and completeness, along with relevant information. The level of accuracy, together with performance in AI algorithms, depends on data quality and volume, which determines how effectively the system detects and predicts fraudulent activities. Running an industry such as cybersecurity insurance requires both the right data collection as well as its effective utilization because highly sophisticated fraudsters pose risks to the online security of fraud detection systems (Bokka, 2025). For AI tools to function optimally, the highest priority goes to data quality standards. AI models require data patterns for prediction, yet unreliable data produces subpar outcome quality from predictions. The incorrect accuracy or incomplete nature, as well as inconsistent elements in the dataset, can result in AI systems incorrectly detecting fraud along with failing to detect critical signs of fraud. An insurer's dataset containing claims data with incomplete information, together with incorrect timestamp data and inaccurate policyholder records, will cause their AI model to misunderstand claim details, making it generate incorrect fraud determination results. The improper processing of data results in both prevention failures for legitimate claims and acceptance failures for fraudulent ones (Parveen, 2024). Quality data enables AI models to identify actual fraud indicators hidden within the administrative and operational claims information. High-quality data contains precise elements that stay entire as well as current, thus giving Artificial Intelligence algorithms dependable information they require to make their predictions. To achieve successful fraud detection, insurers need to maintain updated datasets that contain important variables about policyholder conduct, along with claim records and incident traits. Accurate and current data delivered to a trained model enables it to recognize even faint indicators of fraud, such as atypical claim patterns combined with excessive benefit payments and untypical claims duration (Bokka, 2025).

The AI system functions from the base of collected data, which ensures successful fraud detection through the quality of gathered information. The amount of data available to AI-driven fraud detection systems matters as much as their data quality for achieving superior detection results. In Particular, machine learning models need extensive amounts of data during their training process to operate efficiently. Having insufficient data for training makes the model excessively specific to examples from the training phase, which results in poor prediction ability for new observations outside the initial data. The identification of diverse patterns becomes possible with large datasets because they enable the model to detect fraud across multiple circumstances. An AI system reaches superior levels of fraud claim discrimination when it accesses bigger and more diverse data sets (Parveen, 2024). AI-based fraud detection systems in cybersecurity insurance heavily rely on the analysis of historical claims throughout their operational process. The dataset consists of past claims data, which includes details regarding claim incidents as well as the amount paid and policyholder records, along with additional pertinent information. The typical patterns of legitimate claims become visible when AI algorithms process this information so they can detect deviations that could be indicators of fraud. Superior suspicion signals can be raised in insurance when a new policyholder submits a costly claim right after purchasing the policy. However, AI systems gain the capability to detect suspect actions by examining historical claims databases, which enables them to pinpoint these abnormal activities for more scrutiny (Bokka, 2025). Incident reports serve as important data sources that fraud detection teams utilize for their operations. The documents report crucial cyberattack and breach information, which details both the attack paths and the damage extent and policyholder response actions. AI models use incident reports to spot mismatches that exist between statements made in reports and compensation requests. The existence of ransomware in an incident report becomes crucial evidence when a policyholder reports a ransomware attack because the lack of ransomware evidence may indicate the claim is fraudulent. AI systems manage to review extensive incident report datasets to spot such inconsistencies, therefore outperforming traditional manual screening methods for fraud detection (Parveen, 2024).

Threat intelligence databases function as important data resources that insurers use to support their operations. Insurance organizations build their understanding of developing cyber risks through information databases that collect threat data together with vulnerability info and attack tendencies. Insurance companies achieve enhanced claim evaluation when they use threat intelligence data inside their fraud detection platforms. AI analyses policyholder claims submitted for specific cyberattacks through threat intelligence data to check both current attack prevalence and similarities across previous claims of the same kind. By investigating ongoing cyber risks, the insurer can evaluate claim legitimacy in relation to current threat patterns (Bokka, 2025). The implementation of fraud detection systems encounters multiple challenges when merging essential data sources despite their fundamental role in identification efforts. Organizations face a major challenge because different departmental or system databases operate independently from each other, which makes it hard to establish complete claims process visibility. Multiple organizations opt to place historical claims data within one technology system, though incident reports reside separately and threat intelligence data resides in external locations. Integrating data systems is essential because unsupported AI systems fail to perform optimally (Ramachandran et al., 2024).

AI systems require integrated data management to obtain all available data for making accurate fraud predictions. The process becomes delayed, which allows fraudulent claims to escape detection until later detection. Insurers need to establish solutions that will enable data to flow without interruption between various systems. Hospitals should establish a centralized data storage solution that enables real-time access to all important data sources. A cloud-based data repository would enable multiple information sources to integrate and get updated automatically. The implementation of centralized data storage enables insurers to provide their AI systems with the largest collection of current data required for precise fraud detection. A data integration platform helps organizations properly integrate external threat intelligence database information with their fraud detection systems (Ramachandran et al., 2024). Advanced data cleaning and preprocessing solutions work as a possible remedy to integration problems. Standardization and cleaning operations must occur before inserting data into AI models to maintain data consistency between datasets. Data cleaning operations include the identification of errors and associated corrections to prevent duplicate records along with value omission and format inconsistency. High-quality standardized data from multiple sources enables insurers to enhance their AI systems' detector performance because they work with reliable data inputs (Parveen, 2024). The use of data plays an essential role in AI-driven fraud detection for cybersecurity insurance because it determines how effectively detection systems operate. The identification of suspect fraudulent behaviour depends on AI algorithms being trained through powerful comprehensive databases. To guarantee smooth fraud detection, however, problems like data silos and integration problems must be resolved. Insurers may use artificial intelligence (AI) to identify fraud more correctly and efficiently by using a variety of data sources, including incident reports, threat intelligence, and historical claims, and successfully integrating these sources. This will eventually improve their capacity to safeguard against financial loss and reputational harm (Thapaliya, 2024).

Automating Fraud Detection: Workflow Integration

AI-based tools now direct cybersecurity insurers to dramatically change how they validate claims as part of their fraud detection systems. The implementation of automated processes through AI systems helps insurance companies detect fraud more quickly and accurately, as well as enhances process efficiency and reduces human investigator workload. Fraud detection automation delivers multiple benefits that combine to enhance operational procedures while minimizing human mistakes and fraud-related dangers. AI integration into workflows leads to two main issues concerning human investigator-AI system teamwork and ethical challenges stemming from excessive use of automated tools (Patil, 2024). The progress of automated fraud detection systems evolved through AI-driven tools that verify claim information. The tools run through extensive claim datasets to notice anomalous patterns that signal fraudulent conduct in addition to their ability to identify inconsistencies between different claims. The analysis of incoming claims against baselines built from historical data enables automatic flagging through AI models of any inconsistencies that exceed normal benchmarks. The combination of AI capabilities analyses three primary factors in claims assessment: historical records, incident nature, and temporal patterns compared to previous cases for genuine assessment. The AI system identifies suspicious behavior when claims payouts exceed normal payment ranges for comparable incidents while the policyholder owns a new insurance policy that faces a major claim shortly after purchase (Thapaliya, 2024).

The combination of artificial intelligence tools enables instant cross-referencing of claims through information from threat intelligence feeds, incident reports, and publicly accessible cybersecurity data. The system determines that a claim involving attacks through known documented threats by cross-referencing external data sources for vulnerability and attack vector information. AI systems will recognize suspicious attack methods that differ from those tracked by threat intelligence sources when detecting false insurance claims. This alert serves to initiate a proper investigation. The automated systems' fraud detection capabilities need human investigators to validate the accurate assessment of insurance claims. AI detection systems rapidly find irregularities yet lack the ability to make proper judgments about intricate insurance claims combined with truth and complexity and complex fraudulent methods. AI fails to detect several sophisticated fraud methods, including social engineering tricks combined with fake recreations of actual events, because it operates independently. The human investigators maintain their authority to review suspected cases in detail by talking with claimants and checking multiple resource points beyond AI's standards (Deep & Kumar, 2024). AI systems require human investigator collaboration to establish a fraud detection workflow that provides optimal performance. AI supports mass claim processing of volume data operations, but human investigators excel at making final assessments of complicated claims. An AI system detects suspicious claims through detecting inconsistent time sequences of reported incidents. A human investigator possesses the capabilities to differentiate genuine inconsistencies stemming from overlooked details from actual fraudulent claims in insurance reports. Legal investigators, along with AI's quick data analysis capacity, enable insurers to build a fraud detection system that achieves excellent accuracy and operational efficiency (Patil, 2024).

Real insurance business implementations demonstrate how automated fraud detection systems achieve integration within the insurance sector successfully. Major cybersecurity insurance providers leverage AI tools to automatically find fake ransomware claims by their customers. The analysis of thousands of past ransomware claims through machine learning allows insurers to create an automatic identification system that detects standard signs of fraudulent ransomware attacks that include lacking encryption verification and inconsistent payment records together with inconsistent attacker timelines. The AI system functions to identify suspicious claims automatically, which then decreases human investigators' manual work while they concentrate on reviewing priority cases that need multilayered evaluation. Artificial Intelligence tools process claims more quickly while enhancing fraud detection efficiencies (Hudson, 2024). In healthcare insurance, companies use AI tools to review cyberattack-related claims for authentication purposes as a new approach in the industry. NLP technology within these tools processes incident report text and other claim documents to detect damage inflation methods or timeline manipulation through the identification of suspicious patterns. AI systems examine claimed data breaches against existing system logs together with other available evidence to verify incidents as described, including alleged losses of patient records. Handing claim data to human experts becomes necessary when the system detects inconsistencies in the information submitted (Deep & Kumar, 2024).

Automated fraud detection faces multiple obstacles as part of its operation. The main concern arises from using AI tools too much since system inaccuracies might occur when updates or calibration are inadequate. An AI system that fails to obtain periodic updates from new information and developing fraud techniques will skip discovering newly detected fraudulent activities while showing false prediction results (Faisal & Nahar, 2024). The accuracy of AI systems depends completely on training data because flawed or biased datasets will prevent them from detecting fraud properly in specific circumstances. The effectiveness of AI-based fraud detection systems depends on continuous assessment and system updates performed by insurers to dictate their ability to detect fraudulent activity (Hudson, 2024). The increasing use of automation will not replace human investigator involvement in insurance fraud detection operations. AI systems currently work to fully comprehend fraud detection because this field needs to understand both data anomalies and contextual human behaviour in addition to clear identification of criminal objectives. Human judgment serves as the crucial factor to decide claim fraud because investigators need to evaluate background information as well as any available mitigating factors and external conditions beyond AI system capabilities. AI tools require partnership with human expertise to create accurate and fair processes in fraud detection systems (Faisal & Nahar, 2024). The cybersecurity insurance sector is experiencing a transformation through AI-driven fraud detection automation, which leads to accelerated, highly accurate, and efficient claims verification. A combination of AI processing capability for big data and human experts allows insurers to develop thorough fraud protection workflows that identify fraudulent claims better (Faisal & Nahar, 2024). These systems have shown their ability to combat fraud through practical implementation, which also improves the overall claims handling procedures. Insurance companies, however, need to be aware of the difficulties, especially the dangers of relying too much on AI and the necessity of preserving a human component in the ultimate decision-making process. Automation driven by AI has the potential to greatly improve cybersecurity insurance fraud detection when used properly (Deep & Kumar, 2024).

Ethical and Legal Considerations

The application of AI technology for detecting fraud in cybersecurity insurance requires careful examination of three major ethical and legal issues linked to privacy preservation, along with transparency requirements and compliance obligations. Primary matters focus on how customer data enables AI analysis systems. AI fraud detection systems need extensive datasets made up of sensitive client data to conduct accurate fraud detection operations effectively. Privacy issues emerge because customers remain unaware of the extent to which their data is utilized or what specific data is collected from them during the process of personal details extraction and incident report monitoring along with financial data management (Mbah & Evelyn, 2024). Insurers utilize analysis of customer historical claims data, personal contact information, and network activity while being at risk to misuse sensitive details when not properly managed. Privacy breaches could occur when data is gathered without consent from customers or if the information is distributed among third parties who do not divulge their activities to the customers. Customers need complete transparency regarding data usage practices because they should understand data collection purposes and protective measures and information about the ways data operators use their information (Salem & Azzam, 2024).

Fraud detection systems that utilize AI make decisions that produce unclear results to the affected parties. The hidden aspects of many AI models prevent customers from comprehending how their claims got flagged as suspicious and what behavioral markers led to their allegations being flagged as potentially fraudulent. The unclear decision-making process of automated systems produces unhappy customers because they cannot easily understand why they were targeted nor how to dispute machine-made decisions. This highlights how crucial it is to provide accountability and openness in an AI-based fraud detection system (Kapadiya et al., 2022). Insurers must be able to describe their algorithms, the data they employ, and the standards by which they reject or flag claims. In addition to giving people the chance to challenge or appeal decisions they feel were made incorrectly, this transparency fosters confidence between insurers and policyholders. Guaranteeing that AI systems are created with equity in mind also promotes ethical AI development by lowering the possibility of biased or discriminating results (Mbah & Evelyn, 2024). Additionally, a major challenge for insurers using AI to identify fraud is compliance with data privacy requirements. Strict guidelines on the collection, storage, and use of personal data are enforced by laws like the California Consumer Privacy Act (CCPA) in the US and the General Data Protection Regulation (GDPR) in the EU. These rules are intended to protect people's right to privacy and make businesses responsible for any violations or improper use of client information (Kapadiya et al., 2022). For instance, the GDPR gives people the right to seek access to or deletion of their data and requires businesses to have individuals' express consent before collecting it. In a similar vein, Californians are entitled under the CCPA to know what personal information is being gathered about them, why, and how they can choose not to have it used (Bansal & Bharatwal, 2024).

The international nature of cybersecurity insurance requires AI deployment to be evaluated through a proper regulatory framework across the world. GDPR established by the European Union set both requirements for explicit consent and individuals' right to know about automated decisions. The US CCPA maintains visible privacy standards alongside letting users opt out of processing, yet offers greater freedom for conducting algorithmic profiling. Several nations have adopted combined data protection systems that link consent authorization with specific risk-based exclusion protocols. Insurance companies base their fraud detection system design and deployment on existing regulatory rules between different jurisdictions. Developing regulations in emerging markets removes compliance requirements while exposing entities to amplified reputational alongside operational risks. Different jurisdictions emphasize the need for adaptable governance models that can maintain compliance throughout various jurisdictions.

Emerging Trends and Innovations in Fraud Detection

The methods used by insurers to detect and stop fraudulent activity are being drastically altered by new developments and trends in cybersecurity insurance fraud detection. The application of generative AI to model fraud situations is among the most exciting advancements. Generative AI enables insurers to train their models on a variety of potential fraud scenarios, including fraud kinds that have not yet been identified, by producing synthetic datasets that mimic different fraud patterns (Sharma & Mehta, 2024). This method improves AI systems' capacity to identify intricate and nuanced fraudulent activity that conventional datasets could miss. For example, insurers can simulate various fraudulent claim submission strategies using generative AI, which will assist fraud detection models in better distinguishing between genuine and fraudulent claims. Even though this technology has a lot of promise, its efficacy is mostly dependent on the caliber and variety of the synthetic data used for training; therefore, finding the ideal balance in data representation is crucial (Balcıoğlu, 2024). Another cutting-edge technique being investigated for insurance fraud prevention is blockchain technology. Blockchain can improve claim transparency by offering an unchangeable, visible record of transactions, making it almost impossible for fraudulent claims to remain undiscovered (Mohammed & Rahman, 2024). Real-time tracking of all claim-related interactions, such as policy issuance, claim submission, and payment, allows insurers to make sure that every step is safely documented and impervious to change or interference. In addition to lowering the possibility of fraud, this increases policyholder trust since they can confirm the veracity of claims. Although blockchain has many benefits in terms of security and transparency, integrating it into current insurance systems is difficult due to issues such as regulatory acceptability and the requirement for interoperability with traditional systems (Balcıoğlu, 2024). Another new development in preventing fraud is AI-driven risk rating. Insurers can identify people or organizations that may be more likely to file fraudulent claims by assigning risk ratings to policyholders based on an analysis of a variety of data elements, such as transaction history, customer behavior, and external threat information. Through a more thorough examination of high-risk claims or modifying coverage to better match recognized risks, this proactive strategy enables insurers to step in early (Mohammed & Rahman, 2024). However, if the algorithms are trained on historical data that could represent current discrepancies, the dependence on AI-driven risk rating may give rise to worries about potential biases in the models. For the industry, maintaining accuracy and fairness in risk-scoring algorithms is still a constant struggle (Sharma & Mehta, 2024).

Challenges and Limitations

While there are many advantages to AI-driven fraud detection, insurers also need to be aware of some of its drawbacks. The over-reliance on AI systems, which can result in false positives and false negatives, is one of the main issues. When valid claims are mistakenly reported as fraudulent, this is known as a false positive, which causes needless inquiries and delays for policyholders (Iseal et al., 2025). Conversely, false negatives occur when fraudulent claims are disregarded, which may enable fraudulent conduct to remain undiscovered. For instance, a claim including altered incident dates may be processed by AI algorithms intended to identify odd trends, which would be expensive for the insurer and compromise the efficacy of the fraud detection system (Adhikari & Hamal, 2024). It's important yet challenging to balance the sensitivity of AI models to reduce both kinds of mistakes since over-tuning the system to prevent false positives might result in more false negatives and vice versa (Iseal et al., 2025). AI systems' susceptibility to hostile assaults is another difficulty. Cybercriminals may trick AI systems by manipulating inputs, which makes it more difficult for fraud detection algorithms to identify illicit activity. For example, by changing claim documents or network activity logs, attackers may make small changes to the data utilized for fraud detection that AI algorithms can miss. In order to stay ahead of the game, fraud detection algorithms must be continuously adjusted and improved as AI systems and fraudsters' tactics get more complex (Adhikari & Hamal, 2024). Common issues include false positives arising from overfitting, integration challenges with legacy systems, and data quality problems stemming from incomplete or outdated records. For example, a pilot deployment by a mid-sized insurer failed when the model was trained exclusively on large enterprise data, resulting in systematic misclassification of SME claims. This was rectified by diversifying the training data and introducing human-in-the-loop review mechanisms. Lessons from such implementations underscore the necessity of iterative testing, robust validation frameworks, and ongoing model recalibration.

Recommendations and Best Practices

A hybrid strategy that combines AI and human experience is crucial to improving fraud detection in cybersecurity insurance. Though they are not perfect, AI-driven systems are capable of processing enormous volumes of data and identifying patterns that may otherwise go overlooked. By including human monitoring, the possibility of false positives or negatives is decreased since highlighted claims are examined contextually. For example, a human investigator can utilize their case expertise to assess if a genuine claim is real, even when AI may flag it as fraudulent based on odd patterns. By combining the speed and effectiveness of AI with the knowledge and discernment of human investigators, this synergy guarantees a more precise and nuanced approach (Ahmad, 2023). Another crucial suggestion is to create AI ecosystems that are safe and compliant. To protect sensitive data, insurers must implement strong security measures as AI models get more intricate. This entails using encryption, storing data securely, and making sure AI models are open and auditable. To avoid any legal ramifications, adherence to data protection laws like the CCPA or GDPR must also be given top priority. For instance, insurers should make sure AI systems ethically manage client data and provide people the legal right to see, update, or remove their data. Insurers can reduce the risk of regulatory fines and cultivate consumer trust by creating safe, open, and legal AI ecosystems (Gautam, 2023). Finally, maintaining the efficacy of AI fraud detection systems requires ongoing model training using real-world data. Since fraud trends are always changing, AI models need to be updated often to reflect new strategies employed by scammers (Gautam, 2023). Insurers can improve their AI models and make sure they continue to recognize new risks by using real-world data from past claims, threat intelligence feeds, and simulated fraud scenarios. By increasing detection accuracy and lowering the financial and reputational risks connected to fraudulent claims, this continuous training process aids insurers in staying one step ahead of fraudsters (Ahmad, 2023).

The successful deployment of AI-driven fraud detection systems requires a structured implementation roadmap. Initial phases should involve stakeholder engagement and a comprehensive needs assessment, followed by system integration planning, pilot testing, and phased rollouts. Integration with legacy systems and ongoing training for underwriting and fraud teams are essential to ensure operational continuity. For small-scale implementations, a 3–6 month timeline may suffice, whereas medium to large-scale deployments often span 9–18 months, depending on data readiness and organisational complexity. Clear change management protocols—covering communication, upskilling, and performance monitoring—are critical for fostering adoption and mitigating resistance.

CONCLUSION

By providing cutting-edge tools and methods that increase the speed, accuracy, and efficiency of identifying fraudulent claims, artificial intelligence (AI) has drastically changed fraud detection in cybersecurity insurance. AI technologies have completely changed how insurers evaluate risk and handle fraud, from machine learning models that can identify irregularities in claims data to natural language processing (NLP) tools that examine claim descriptions. These technologies lower the financial and reputational risks associated with fraud by assisting insurers in identifying suspicious activity that would be challenging or time-consuming to find using conventional approaches. For example, insurers may identify high-risk claims before they worsen by using AI-driven predictive analytics to find patterns and trends in claim data.

AI is a game-changer, but it is not without its difficulties. Continuous attention is needed to address problems like false positives, hostile assaults on AI systems, and the high implementation costs for smaller insurers. As a best practice, a hybrid method that blends AI and human knowledge enables insurers to take advantage of AI's speed and scalability while preserving the sophisticated judgment of human investigators. Furthermore, assuring the efficacy and moral use of AI in fraud detection requires the development of safe and legal AI ecosystems as well as the ongoing upgrading of fraud detection models using actual data. Future developments in AI-powered fraud detection might go in several directions. As AI systems develop, using increasingly sophisticated methods like blockchain to improve claim transparency and generative AI to simulate fraud situations might strengthen fraud prevention even further. AI-powered policyholder predictive risk scoring has the potential to advance, giving insurers the ability to evaluate fraud risks even before claims are filed. Future fraud detection in cybersecurity insurance has bright promise for lowering fraud and boosting sector integrity with ongoing AI developments, human skills, and ethical concerns.

REFERENCES

Adeyeye, O. J., Akanbi, I., Emeteveke, I., & Emehin, O. (2024). Leveraging secured AI-driven data analytics for cybersecurity: Safeguarding information and enhancing threat detection. *International Journal of Research and Publication and Reviews*, *5*(10), 3208–3223. DOI: 10.55248/gengpi.5.1024.2911

Adhikari, P., Hamal, P., & Jnr, F. B. (2024). Artificial intelligence in fraud detection: Revolutionizing financial security. *International Journal of Science and Research Archive*, *13*(01), 1457–1472. DOI: 10.30574/ijsra.2024.13.1.1860

Ahmad, A. S. (2023). Application of big data and artificial intelligence in strengthening fraud analytics and cybersecurity resilience in global financial markets. *International Journal of Advanced Cybersecurity Systems, Technologies, and Applications*, *7*(12), 11–23.

Ahmad, A. Y. A. B. (2024, April). Fraud prevention in insurance: Biometric identity verification and AI-based risk assessment. In *2024 International Conference on Knowledge Engineering and Communication Systems (ICKECS)* (Vol. 1, pp. 1–6). IEEE. DOI: 10.1109/ICKECS61492.2024.10616613

Ashfin, P. (2024). AI-driven threat detection and response in cybersecurity. *Bulletin of Engineering Science and Technology*, *1*(2), 125–143.

Balcıoğlu, Y. S. (2024). Revolutionizing risk management: AI and ML innovations in financial stability and fraud detection. In *Navigating the Future of Finance in the Age of AI* (pp. 109–138). IGI Global. DOI: 10.4018/979-8-3693-4382-1.ch006

Bansal, U., Bharatwal, S., Bagiyam, D. S., & Kismawadi, E. R. (2024). Fraud detection in the era of AI: Harnessing technology for a safer digital economy. In *AI-Driven Decentralized Finance and the Future of Finance* (pp. 139–160). IGI Global. DOI: 10.4018/979-8-3693-6321-8.ch006

Bello, O. A., Folorunso, A., Onwuchekwa, J., & Ejiofor, O. E. (2023). A comprehensive framework for strengthening USA financial cybersecurity: Integrating machine learning and AI in fraud detection systems. *European Journal of Computer Science and Information Technology*, *11*(6), 62–83.

Bello, O. A., & Olufemi, K. (2024). Artificial intelligence in fraud prevention: Exploring techniques and applications, challenges, and opportunities. *Computer Science & IT Research Journal*, *5*(6), 1505–1520. DOI: 10.51594/csitrj.v5i6.1252

Bokka, V. V. R. M. (2025). Crafting a comprehensive strategy to prevent fraud and enable recovery in mobile insurance in the USA.

Brokešová, Z., & Ondruška, T. (2025). Internal controls and insurance in Industry 5.0. In *Business Challenges and Opportunities in the Era of Industry 5.0* (pp. 195–213). Emerald Publishing Limited. DOI: 10.1108/978-1-83549-676-320251011

Deep, S., Kumar, S., & Kalra, P. (2024). AI-driven data security in healthcare: Safeguarding data and financial transactions. *International Journal of Novel Research and Development.*

Dhieb, N., Ghazzai, H., Besbes, H., & Massoud, Y. (2020). A secure AI-driven architecture for automated insurance systems: Fraud detection and risk measurement. *IEEE Access : Practical Innovations, Open Solutions*, *8*, 58546–58558. DOI: 10.1109/ACCESS.2020.2983300

Faisal, N. A., Nahar, J., Sultana, N., & Mintoo, A. A. (2024). Fraud detection in banking: Leveraging AI to identify and prevent fraudulent activities in real time. *Journal of Machine Learning. Data Engineering and Data Science*, *1*(01), 181–197.

Gautam, A. (2023). Evaluating the impact of artificial intelligence on risk management and fraud detection in the banking sector. *AI. IoT and the Fourth Industrial Revolution Review*, *13*(11), 9–18.

George, A. S. (2024). Emerging trends in AI-driven cybersecurity: An in-depth analysis. *Partners Universal Innovative Research Publication*, *2*(4), 15–28.

Hassan, M., Aziz, L. A. R., & Andriansyah, Y. (2023). The role of artificial intelligence in modern banking: An exploration of AI-driven approaches for enhanced fraud prevention, risk management, and regulatory compliance. *Reviews of Contemporary Business Analytics*, *6*(1), 110–132.

Hudson, J. (2024). *Artificial intelligence and cybersecurity integration: Modern database techniques for securing AI models.*

Isreal, S., Joseph, O., & Joseph, S. (2025). *AI in financial services: Using big data for risk assessment and fraud detection.*

Kapadiya, K., Patel, U., Gupta, R., Alshehri, M. D., Tanwar, S., Sharma, G., & Bokoro, P. N. (2022). Blockchain and AI-empowered healthcare insurance fraud detection: An analysis, architecture, and prospects. *IEEE Access : Practical Innovations, Open Solutions*, *10*, 79606–79627. DOI: 10.1109/ACCESS.2022.3194569

Mbah, G. O., & Evelyn, A. N. (2024). AI-powered cybersecurity: Strategic approaches to mitigate risk and safeguard data privacy.

Mohammed, A. F. A., & Rahman, H. M. A. A. (2024). The role of artificial intelligence (AI) in fraud detection in the private sector in Saudi Arabia. *Risk Management, 100*, 472–506.

Okenwa, C. D., David, O. D., Orelaja, A., & Akinwande, O. T. (2024). Exploring the role of explainable AI in compliance models for fraud prevention. *International Journal of Research and Scientific Innovation, 13*(5), 232–239.

Pareek, C. S. (2023). From detection to prevention: The evolution of fraud testing frameworks in insurance through AI. *Journal of Artificial Intelligence. Machine Learning & Data Science, 1*(2), 1805–1812.

Patil, D. (2024). Artificial intelligence in financial services: Advancements in fraud detection, risk management, and algorithmic trading optimization. *Risk Management.*

Prakash, V., & Deokar, R. (2025). Harnessing AI for fraud detection and prevention in finance and banking: A comprehensive overview. In *Real-World Applications of AI Innovation* (pp. 389–406).

Ramachandran, M. S., Sajithabanu, S., Ponmalar, A., Sithik, M. M., & Anand, A. J. (2024). Fraud detection and risk management using AI in business intelligence. In *Intersection of AI and Business Intelligence in Data-Driven Decision-Making* (pp. 117–150). IGI Global. DOI: 10.4018/979-8-3693-5288-5.ch005

Salem, A. H., Azzam, S. M., Emam, O. E., & Abohany, A. A. (2024). Advancing cybersecurity: A comprehensive review of AI-driven detection techniques. *Journal of Big Data, 11*(1), 105. DOI: 10.1186/s40537-024-00957-y

Sharma, R., Mehta, K., & Sharma, P. (2024). Role of artificial intelligence and machine learning in fraud detection and prevention. In *Risks and Challenges of AI-Driven Finance: Bias, Ethics, and Security* (pp. 90–120). IGI Global. DOI: 10.4018/979-8-3693-2185-0.ch005

Tariq, M. U. (2024). Leading Smart Technologies and Innovations for E-Business 5.0: Applications and Management Frameworks. In Popkova, E. (Ed.), *Smart Technologies and Innovations in E-Business* (pp. 25–46). IGI Global., DOI: 10.4018/978-1-6684-7840-0.ch002

Tariq, M. U. (2024). The role of AI ethics in cost and complexity reduction. In Tennin, K., Ray, S., & Sorg, J. (Eds.), *Cases on AI ethics in business* (pp. 59–78). IGI Global., DOI: 10.4018/979-8-3693-2643-5.ch004

Tariq, M. U. (2025). AI-Driven Research Methodologies: Revolutionizing Data-Driven Discoveries in Engineering and Physical Sciences. In Basha, J., Alade, T., Al Khazimi, M., Vasudevan, R., & Khan, J. (Eds.), *Optimizing Research Techniques and Learning Strategies With Digital Technologies* (pp. 97–122). IGI Global Scientific Publishing., DOI: 10.4018/979-8-3693-7863-2.ch004

Tariq, M. U. (2025). Leveraging Artificial Intelligence to Enhance Diversity and Drive Business Innovation. In Margaretha van der Poll, H., Andrew van der Poll, J., & Ngwakwe, C. (Eds.), *Diversity, AI, and Sustainability for Financial Growth* (pp. 79–96). IGI Global Scientific Publishing., DOI: 10.4018/979-8-3693-6011-8.ch004

Tariq, M. U. (2025). Quantum Algorithms and Predictive Analytics: Revolutionizing Consumer Insight. In Gajbhiye, P., Kannan, H., Rodriguez, R., & Rojas-Méndez, J. (Eds.), *The Quantum AI Era of Neuromarketing* (pp. 173–202). IGI Global Scientific Publishing., DOI: 10.4018/979-8-3693-7673-7.ch008

Thapaliya, S. (2024). Examining the influence of AI-driven cybersecurity in financial sector management. *The Batuk*, *10*(2), 129–144. DOI: 10.3126/batuk.v10i2.68147

KEY TERMS AND DEFINITIONS

Anomaly Detection: An AI-driven method of identifying deviations in claims data that may indicate fraudulent activity.

Blockchain for Fraud Prevention: A decentralized system that enhances claim transparency and reduces opportunities for fraudulent activities.

Fraud Detection in Cybersecurity Insurance: The process of identifying and preventing false or exaggerated claims using AI and data-driven techniques.

Natural Language Processing (NLP) for Fraud Analysis: AI technique used to assess claim descriptions and detect inconsistencies or manipulations.

Predictive Analytics in Fraud Prevention: The use of AI models to analyze historical claim patterns and predict potential fraud risks.

Chapter 8
Decrypting the Shadows Forensics and Investigation of Ransomware Attacks

Shashank Dave
Gujarat University, India

Kiran R. Dodiya
https://orcid.org/0009-0001-9409-7303
Gujarat University, India

Kapil Kumar
Coordinator, Department of Biochemistry and Forensic Science, Gujarat University, Ahmedabad, Gujarat, India

ABSTRACT

Ransomware encrypts critical files using algorithms like AES and RSA, demanding payment for decryption. Investigators struggle to recover data without the original keys, as attackers often erase logs and conceal activity. Securing backups is essential to reduce damage. Forensic experts examine network traffic, memory dumps, and system logs to trace ransomware behavior. Tools like Wireshark and NetFlow detect unusual C2 connections. Evidence is preserved using file carving, hash analysis, and imaging. Ransom notes, IPs, and cryptographic signatures help identify attackers. Blockchain analysis tracks crypto payments, aided by law enforcement and exchanges. Understanding exploits and social engineering boosts defense.

DOI: 10.4018/979-8-3373-5545-0.ch008

1. INTRODUCTION TO RANSOMWARE FORENSICS

1.1 Understanding Ransomware: A Primer

The role of ransomware has been such a significant cybercrime, as it uses malicious software to lock users out of their systems and even encrypt their files until payment in cryptocurrency is made for the decryption of said files. This initial infection, aside from inflicting data loss and economic cost, also damages the brand image of the business, which usually originates from phishing emails and malicious links. The practice of double extortion, which involves data thievery and threats of data exposure, has become widespread, thus intensifying the challenges victims face. System infiltration by ransomware results in strong algorithm-based file encryption followed by ransomware instructions for payment. The payment does not suggest recipients will get their files back.(*Ransomware Attack - What Is It and How Does It Work? - Check Point Software*, n.d.-a). Assailants who carry out cyberattacks are known to extract data that they can leverage for additional extortion. Ransomware released CryptoLocker in 2013 and WannaCry in 2017 to inflict massive harm on healthcare services and government institutions. Ransomware threats have become more sophisticated due to incidents targeting Colonial Pipeline and JBS Foods. Multiple defense methods are necessary to stop ransomware attacks from occurring. Online data backups stored offline serve to minimize damage, and employee training helps them detect phishing attempts. Systems free of software-related vulnerabilities protect against hacker attacks.(*Ransomware Attacks and Types | How Do Locky, Petya and Other Ransomware Differ?*, n.d.-a). Antivirus programs alongside endpoint detection systems and network segmentation boundaries can help mitigate the extent of ransomware attacks. Organizations need to put an incident response in place, which includes two steps: taking over infected networks, notifying all affected parties, and collaborating with authorities. Security advice strongly advises against paying ransom to perpetrators, as it only encourages them to continue their criminal practices. Most effectively, ransomware attacks can be prevented with active cybersecurity planning — specifically, by restoring old data, training employees, and updating all software. Understanding the evolution of threats and creating an incident readiness plan makes execution of those attacks less likely and minimizes their impact.

1.2 The Importance of Forensic Investigations

Not only could legitimate crime solutions beyond a reasonable doubt dispense justice, they would also increase immunity against cyber threats. Forensic evidence is the physical, along with digital or biological evidence, that experts analyze in order to collect facts and create evidence to support legal cases. Forensic professionals in criminal and civil legal matters identify potential criminals and establish chronological evidence and authenticated witness testimonies (*The Power of Cyber Forensics in Solving Crimes*, n.d.). Digital forensics has become essential in tracking cybercriminals while protecting sensitive data because cybercrime continues to expand. Digital forensics specialists retrieve data that is later examined from computing devices, as well as mobile phones and network servers. The electronic criminal activities of identity theft, combined with online fraud and ransomware attacks, produce traceable digital evidence. Digital forensic analysts use the recovered data to find attack perpetrators while exposing their attack procedures. Investigators obtain crucial crime-related information through examining network logs, email records, and system activities. The investigation process enables investigators to follow activity connections that might lead to the dismantling of entire cybercriminal organizations. Ransomware investigations are particularly complex. Specialists examine malware entry methods into systems along with their effects and discover strategies to retrieve encrypted files. The investigation of ransom payments enables authorities to trace down those responsible for cyber-crimes. The system assessments conducted by these investigations lead to better cybersecurity practices, which block upcoming security incidents. Securing investigations requires teams to establish points of infringement while working to retrieve stolen information, examine security weaknesses, and confirm proper legal implications. Malware systems are analysed and decrypted, and method information is always present and helpful for decryption or reverse engineering purposes.

The work carried out in conducting forensic investigations boosts organizational security. Reports derived by an issuer contain full detail and key court admissible evidence that can be tested against the rules of a court for relatedness. Collaborating with enforcement agencies strengthens the fight against cybercrime. This progress made through technological innovation enables forensic science to continue to play its role as a facilitator of justice delivery and defence of digital infrastructure. (*What Is a Cyber Crime Investigation?*, n.d.). With proactive measures such as backing up their systems, prepping employees, and monitoring their devices, organizations can protect themselves against these intrusive threats. An effective incident response plan allows organizations to initiate immediate remedial action as soon as a breach is detected, helping them minimize data losses and gain time to restore services. Digital technologies are creating a need for forensic investigations in order to locate evidence for legal processes whilst enhancing global cybersecurity efforts.

2. RANSOMWARE BEHAVIOUR ON ENCRYPTED NETWORK

2.1 How Ransomware Operates

Because the attacker uses it to break in, the system's infection vector is the first step of most ransomware attacks. Based on this, attackers hide their vector by wrapping their vector in phishing emails containing malicious URLs or sending malicious files and making a user download malicious files by purchasing from the corrupted sites, and using software vulnerabilities as entry points. Ransomware moves around silently in its target environments and uses standard system tools for privilege escalation and replication across network systems. Its primary malicious function involves file encryption, which means that it prevents access to essential data files and, consequently, leads to the breakdown of operations. The cybercriminals ask you to pay them in cryptocurrency and, thus, do not disclose their identity. (*What Are the Most Common Attack Vectors for Ransomware?*, n.d.) Another vital necessity for victims is to maintain their downtime period, keep their information, and conduct repayments as soon as possible when required.

Double extortion is just a deadly version of this scam. These killers first copy victim data and then start encryption, announcing that the stolen data will be disclosed publicly unless the ransom is paid. These attacks incur more damage through reputation damage and legal issues as well. Criminals who send the decryption to ransomware victims after paying ransom fees do not guarantee that the encryption key will be delivered, as they could ask for additional payments after cashing in the money. (Gallegos-Segovia et al., 2017). Typically, ransomware attacks have included backdoors through their code, giving an opportunity for illegal access to stay in the system and try their next attack. Wanting to remain in the network as long as possible leads to long-term problems, further delays the recovery of the system, and provides extended threat time.

Ransomware threats became more serious due to the establishment of Ransomware-as-a-Service (RaaS). Ransomware-as-a-Service providers give their affiliate members access to malicious tools and infrastructure through which they receive part of the demanded ransom payments. Technical challenges have been eliminated through this model, so unprofessional cybercriminals can now perform attacks. Affiliates access the dark web to buy and sell stolen data while conducting ransom deals and recruiting new members through its marketplace feature. The anonymity provided by the dark web lets criminals conduct their operations in a safe environment that decreases their chances of getting detected. (*What Is Ransomware-as-a-Service (RaaS)? | IBM*, n.d.). Organizations must adopt strong prevention systems, detection protocols, and incident response protocols because ransomware continues to develop as a significant cybersecurity threat against organizations of different sizes.

2.2 Advanced Encryption Technique: AES and RSA

The initial step of most ransomware attacks involves the system's infection vector because attackers use it to gain entry. Attackers conceal their vectors by disguising them as phishing emails containing malicious links or sending malicious attachments, making users download infected files from broken websites, and using software vulnerabilities as entrance points. Ransomware spreads across network systems and climbs the privilege ladder using standard system tools before it becomes dormant in its target environment. Some of the core nasty jobs this malware performs are encrypting files that prevent access to core files for firms, causing operational disruption. Cybercriminals remain anonymous online but demand that victims pay with cryptocurrency. Due to the reality that this is how long the period is between becoming contaminated and having your files stolen, victims are made to follow through with payments promptly to minimize the downtime period, together with holding onto their data. A more sinister iteration of this plan is double extortion. (*Ransomware Attacks and Types | How Do Locky, Petya and Other Ransomware Differ?*, n.d.-b). In a typical ransomware attack, the attackers first steal victim data. Then they follow the encryption process, stating that the public disclosure of stolen information will be done if payment is not reached to a certain amount. These attacks lead to losses from damage to reputation and legal issues. Ransomware victims who pay ransom fees cannot guarantee that the encryption key will be received, as the criminals may choose to demand more fees after extracting the money. In many cases, ransomware attacks introduce a backdoor in their code so that intruders can remain in the system while awaiting their next moves. By not abandoning the target, the attackers prolonged the problems, on one hand, hindering the efforts to recover the systems, and on the other hand, providing a prolonged security threat.

The rise of Ransomware-as-a-Service (RaaS) turned ransomware threats into a more pressing issue. Ransomware-as-a-Service (RaaS) affiliates receive a share of the ransom payments through malicious tools and infrastructure provided by RaaS operators. With this model, the technical challenges have been removed, and hence even unprofessional cybercriminals can perform the attacks. Through its dark web marketplace, affiliates buy and sell stolen data, conduct ransom deals, and even bring in new members into the fold. Criminals take advantage of the anonymity provided by the dark web to run their operations in a sterile environment that minimizes the risk of detection. (Zakaria et al., 2024). As ransomware evolves into a dominant cybersecurity threat against enterprises of all sizes, organizations should implement robust prevention systems, detection protocols, and incident response protocols.

3. THE ROLE OF BACKUP IN RANSOMWARE DEFENSE

3.1 Strategies for Securing Backups

Businesses are under constant pressure due to frequent and sophisticated ransomware threats, prompting organizations to create robust backup plans. It is the 3-2-1 backup rule where organizations will always have three copies of data, including one original file with two backup sets on different types of media (e.g., hard drive and cloud), and one backup at a different physical location. This multilayered backup approach is key to organizations, as it protects them from all three types of threats, such as ransomware, hardware failures, or human error. Because this data protection method allows an organization to restore data at multiple points in time and prevent permanent data loss, organizations deploy versioning to their backup implementations. A core backup protection strategy is to make your data immutable. Immutable backups protect you from ransomware encryption because they protect themselves from being deleted and modified. Native support for keeping backups immutable is included in specialized backup systems and cloud service providers, even though they are different services. Backups ensure complete protection in two steps — encryption during transmission and encryption for stored copies — both of which keep unwanted parties from accessing your data at rest. (*3-2-1 Backup Strategy Explained: Is It Effective?| Definition from TechTarget*, n.d.). Air-gapping techniques enable the isolation of backups, creating an additional layer of protection that prevents ransomware from attacking backup systems.

AI-powered technologies embedded in next-generation backup solutions make them highly secure. It is an automatic recovery processor that goes through AI systems, allowing them to recover core systems quickly and reduce the downtime of services easily. AI-Powered Ransomware Attack Signature Detection — Closer to real-time Ransomware attack detection allows the system to dynamically change backup policies based on how active the Ransomware attack is to provide the absolute most protection. By automating checksum comparisons with blockchain-based backup integrity solutions, Backup sets remain unaltered in an immutable way—backup Security Acts as a Dauntless Layer of a zero-trust framework. By Zero Trust principles, no matter how effective their network breaches have been, organizations will need to enforce secure access rules and sophisticated protocols for handling encryption keys to ensure that attackers cannot simply access backup data. Unlike their direct-attached data protection solutions, AWS, Azure, and Google Cloud offer cloud-native backup solutions that can scale reliably, with sophisticated geo-redundancy, snapshots, and automated validation. EDR and DLP solutions complement backup security to identify harmful ransomware infections before the threats can affect backup data (*What Are Air-Gapped Backups? - How Air-Gapped*

Backups Work, n.d.). Combining on-premise systems with cloud storage places your organization behind layers of backup redundancy in the event that either of those backup infrastructures becomes unavailable. Coupled with periodic exercises, taking backups to restore, it allows organizations to verify data integrity while preparing for a Ransomware strike.

Organizations significantly raise their ransomware resilience with layered backup strategies, adopt a Zero Trust security methodology, and implement AI and blockchain defense mechanisms. Regular testing processes and the implementation of advanced backup solutions result in corporate data security, less downtime, and ransomware avoidance.

3.2 Ensuring Backup Integrity Against Ransomware

Understanding the health of backup operations continues to be essential to defending against ransomware because these exploits both encrypt core data and coerce victims into paying ransom money for the decryption of that data. Basic backup systems are not serving any purpose without the required protection protocol amid the ever-rising ransomware threat level. Such backup systems become a direct target of attackers when the focus is on derailing recovery efforts as they encrypt, corrupt, or delete stored information to restrict recovery. When threat actors corrupt a backup, the organization experiences major disruptions and significant operational losses due to the inability to recover data. This proven backup approach, the 3-2-1 backup rule, suggests having three copies of data, each on two different kinds of devices, and kept on-site and off-site. This means additional redundancy, which acts as a layer of protection against ransomware threats. Immutable backups strengthen resilience with the defense capability of making a backup virtually impossible to change without proper permissions. Both customer-facing cloud service provider storage solutions and on-premises solutions include immutability, which blocks ransomware attacks from gaining access to data during an attack. This prevents ransomware from reaching backup data by physically or logically separating backups from the primary network through air-gapping and adding another layer of protection.

Setting up multi-factor authentication (MFA) is a good practice for additional backup protection. By maintaining multiple functional authentication methods, MFA acts as a security barrier that prevents unauthorized access even when attackers find access credentials. These measures, combined with rigorous access controls, further restrict backup exposure. (*Azure Backup and Restore Plan to Protect against Ransomware | Microsoft Learn*, n.d.) Encryption while in transit and when stored helps fortify backup security via cloud solutions, and ransomware monitoring alerts users about any suspicious actions.

An actively monitored backup solution system to detect ransomware infections is a godsend for users. It allows real-time detection of the abnormal changes that are indicative of ransomware, enabling organizations to take quick action. Checksums and data hash checks help verify the backup process automatically, and corrupted files can be identified and data integrity ensured further through regular hash checks. Regular software update and patch management implementation minimizes ransomware entry points.

Network downtime is costly, and proving your recovery readiness needs scheduled backup audits accompanied by scheduled restore tests to prove its validity. Disaster restoration work is contingent upon backup tests performed at regular intervals to confirm its quality as well as dependability in reopening preparations. Monitoring by a Committee-based platform should not only track backup systems but also monitor for utilization of storage space and, mainly, track all errors of the systems, as well as not miss any events to locate the problems before damage is caused. This process can be expanded with blockchain-based solutions that implement backup assurance — protecting backups by means of recorded damage-proof backups, where each backup transaction record is secured and verifiable. Many security measures need to be implemented to safeguard internal backup, such as backup dedicated protection, isolation, and access control up to MFA, continuous monitoring, and periodic verification checks and controls.(*Ransomware Data Recovery: How to Save Your Data*, n.d.)These layers of protection can help organizations ensure that their data can be recovered securely even in the case of a ransomware attack.

4. IDENTIFYING RANSOMWARE ATTACK

4.1 Analyzing Network Traffic and Logs

Network traffic and log analysis are essential for many cybersecurity practices, and organizations are able to identify the sources of phishing attempts, brute force attacks, and vulnerability exploitations through this method. The combination of system logs and network data assessments not only aids in quicker anomaly detection and incident response, which enhances current threat management approaches, but also improves operational performance. By creating insights for the analysis of network data packets, technicians discover issues on the network while extracting rare patterns of activity to accelerate operations. Network packets, their source/destination information, and the protocols used, along with their dimensional size measurements, help system operators gain this vital insight. With log analysis, you can monitor what system users do and what events are recorded, allowing the tool to refute typical behaviour as well as assign security breaches. Together, they offer cyber threat detection in near real-time, which minimizes damage and enables efficient network management. Current security tools employ algorithms based on machine learning to create behavioural baselines to ascertain the abnormal characteristics of a network that they deem possible security intrusions. Example: Security Information and Event Management (SIEM) systems are used to collect and aggregate logs/ data from various sources to correlate them in real time, and be able to alert the owner of the log when a problematic situation occurs. This gives rise to efficient incident detection and response operations. Deep Packet Inspection visually looks through the content of packets and recognizes harmful patterns hidden within encrypted traffic. (*Navigating the Cyber Security Landscape: A Comprehensive Review of Cyber-Attacks, Emerging Trends, and Recent Developments*, n.d.) DPI incorporates the best of both threat detection worlds, so its implementation requires closely considering privacy and cost.

4.2 Memory Dumps: A Window into Malicious Activity

A core dump or memory dump is like a snapshot of live memory that happens automatically at crashes. Still, a professional is able to write it manually for debugging and investigative purposes. A memory dump function serves as a data scope for fundamental insights into the system; it retains a volatile memory state needed for memory analysis until processes of the operating system clear their executions. Memory dumps run into any examination to know the system activity and are interpreted because some cyber spies try to hide some helpful content from disk investigation.

Memory dumps are significant and helpful for cybersecurity professionals as they provide information necessary for identifying advanced persistent threats (APTs), malware, and insider threats. APTs enter computer systems silently to gain long-term access and then blend into regular operating system operations. (What Is a Memory Dump ? - GeeksforGeeks, n.d.) Fileless malware infects legitimate system applications like svchost. Exe and explorer. Exe allows it to avoid detection by antivirus programs. Forensic investigators often make memory dumps to uncover hidden threats, identify suspicious processes, or reveal encrypted payloads.

Memory dumps act like a handy feature that provides you with all the details of the system states that run on an OS. In addition to revealing the operational processes with memory segments and loaded libraries, and even network connections, memory dumps can provide vital information to estimate possible attack chains for adversaries and identify connections to command and control (C2) servers. Evidence mainly consists of open ports, which correlate with DNS queries and active TCP/UDP connections, indicating malicious system activity. Since fileless threats run entirely in memory and leave no trace on the disk, they become the only type detectable via memory dumps. Analysts can study decrypted information along with credential theft activities and damaging actions using a memory dump obtained during an ongoing attack. Passwords in combination with session tokens are shown within memory dumps, which correlate to attackers gaining initial access and persistence. Nothing beats analysing some memory dumps while part of an incident response activity on an incident management team. With numerous snapshots of the attack points at different times, security analysts can identify when data was stolen and when and how a backdoor entry was breached. Through this evaluation method, organizations can avoid future attack impacts, discover weaknesses, and take necessary actions to strengthen their security systems.

The challenges faced by analysis in memory dumps and the massive volume of data preclude manual appraisal. Tools such as Volatility and Recall enable automation that streamlines the analytical process. By using these analysis tools, organizations gain actionable intelligence while consistently filtering data and automatically detecting anomalies, which reveal file hashes together with IP addresses and indicators of compromise data (IOC) (Miramirkhani et al., 2017). Specialized skills are necessary for cybersecurity analysts to interpret results correctly while analyzing memory dumps, although the tools simplify the process of identifying malicious activity. Organizations use memory dumps as essential components in contemporary cybersecurity to detect complex cyber-attacks. Memory dumps are indispensable because organizations can use them to identify malware while rebuilding attacks to stop future occurrences. (Aquilina, 2008) Memory dump analysis preserves its status as a core element for sound cybersecurity defense and incident response tactics because the prevalence of memory-resident threats is increasing.

Figure 1. Memory dump analysis: Key applications include threat identification, forensic analysis, system state insights, attack chain reconstruction, and automation tools for efficient cybersecurity investigations.

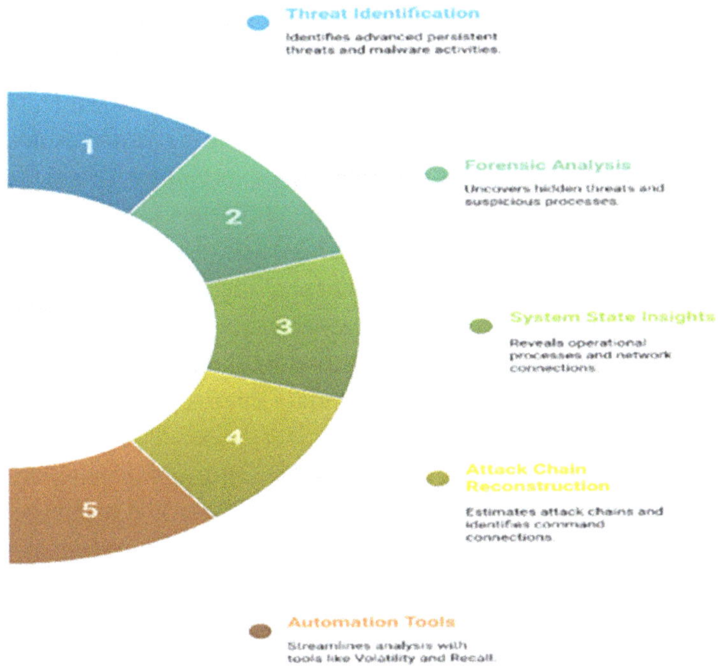

5. FORENSICS METHODS FOR EVIDENCE RECOVERY

5.1 File Carving Techniques

File carving operates as a critical forensic tool through which investigators retrieve deleted information from storage systems without depending on file system data. File carving becomes essential when directory entries or file allocation tables become corrupted or missing on formatted or damaged drives because it enables evidence retrieval. Carving tools recover files through byte-pattern analysis of distinct hexadecimal file headers that precede files and trailing footers that follow them without requiring metadata. The methodology works exceptionally well to retrieve images together with documents and specific file formats, which produce recognizable byte signatures. Data across multiple non-connected storage areas, referred to as fragmentation, creates difficulties during evidence recovery operations. The three advanced carving tools, Foremost, Scalpel, and PhotoRec, perform sector analysis to identify dispersed file patterns before reconstructing lost files. Complex forensic software bundles Autopsy and The Sleuth Kit let investigators analyze large forensic images, then group files by type and perform advanced investigation tasks. File carving is something that works well, but is limited. When the fragmentation becomes extreme or data becomes overwritten later, it is possible to recover individual partial or corrupted files. Because of this, file signature matching can yield false positives, where unrelated data chunks inadvertently resemble file signatures. Hash comparisons to verify file integrity or to delete irrelevant data from examinations are not used by investigators, and hence they minimize the accuracy of the investigation. So, despite all the analytical challenges associated with file carving (as we saw in the case of digital forensics research), it turns out that it remains a valuable and significant tool in investigative work-in-arms of the modern digital forensic researcher (File Carving vs. Metadata Recovery: What is the Difference?, n.d.). This type of extraction retrieves critical evidence from storage media, no matter the damage, to uncover evidence of tampering and incriminating actions or other pertinent information. Investigation success is marked when file carving joins forces with complementary forensic tools, allowing for reconstruction of the digital event with corresponding data, which can be used to support legal proceedings and investigations into the cybercrime.

5.2 Hash Analysis for Integrity Verification

File carving serves as an essential component of digital forensics by allowing investigators to recover deleted data from a storage medium based on the fact that it does not rely on file system details. When a drive is corrupt or damaged so that the directory entries or file allocation tables get corrupted or missing, file carving becomes mandatory for evidence recovery on the formatted volumes. File carving is a vital forensic technique where information deleted from storage systems is retrieved without relying on file system information. When directory Entries and file allocation tables become corrupted or missing on formatted or damaged drives, File carving becomes pivotal for evidence retrieval. Carving tools recover files through byte-pattern analysis of distinct hexadecimal file headers that precede files and trailing footers that follow them without requiring metadata. The methodology works exceptionally well to retrieve images together with documents and specific file formats, which produce recognizable byte signatures. Data across multiple non-connected storage areas, referred to as fragmentation, creates difficulties during evidence recovery operations. The three advanced carving tools, which include Foremost, Scalpel, and PhotoRec, perform sector analysis to identify dispersed file patterns before reconstructing lost files. (*File Carving | Infosec*, n.d.) Complex forensic software bundles, Autopsy and The Sleuth Kit, let investigators analyze large forensic images and group files by type and perform advanced investigation tasks.

File carving works well, yet there are limitations to this process. If fragmentation is very high or the data is overwritten later, then the recovery of complete or partial files is feasible. File signature matching can return false positives since completely unrelated data fragments could coincidentally be matched with a file signature. Many have claimed that hash comparisons are too easy to make and that malicious actors can omit hashes from their examinations. However, that is fallacious: Investigative accuracy relies on investigators using hash comparisons to verify file integrity and to eliminate unnecessary data from examinations. Some analytical problems complicate this field, but it can be an invaluable investigative tool for researchers in modern digital forensic work; file carving is therefore a critical yet challenging part of attention for almost all practitioners, including researchers. It extracts relevant artifacts from media, whether they are physically damaged or not, and it helps in revealing evidence with regard to any attempts of tampering involved or suspicious behaviour or other pertinent information. Investigators and cybercrime specialists can rebuild digital sequences — and comply with legal requirements to locate crucial evidence — with data recovered through file carving technology and other forensic disciplines.

5.3 Forensic Imaging: Preserving Digital Evidence

Initial recovery of digital evidence starts with forensic imaging that allows for deep examinations while keeping the original data untouched. A forensic investigator clones the suspect media at the single material level to acquire full proof details like erased data files and concealed framework data without altering the original evidence. This procedure will be inescapable as far as court-driven processes are concerned because, in the end, it is the integrity of the evidence that matters most. Imaging Process: Write-blockers are part of the imaging procedure that prevents any alteration to the source media (whether it be a hard drive, USB drive, particular drive, SD card, or other type). The tools for forensic image acquisition from the standard formats. E01, dd or. The best examples of AFF are FTK Imager, EnCase, and dd. These digital formats provide for data preservation and permanent records of metadata and evidence source documentation. Hash values give the ability to verify calculations of the accuracy of information prior to or immediately after imaging operations. Hash values act like digital signatures, ensuring that an imaging process has remained unchanged (Liu, 2009). This is where hash comparison comes in, as it is important in establishing forensic validity to help investigators safeguard the integrity of the evidence while making it suitable for a courtroom environment. After extracting the data, the forensic investigator generates an image to perform file carving and hash analysis. File carving techniques retrieve hidden data, whereas hash analysis demonstrates proof of unauthorized changes, which are the two disparate approaches in forensics. These techniques find hidden evidence and identify malicious behaviour, which in turn strengthens the investigative process. Forensic imaging is a basic digital forensic discipline applied to legal affairs due to its strict documentation techniques. The process of data preservation that is legally acceptable relies on the use of. dd, E01 or (*3 Methods to Preserve Digital Evidence for Computer Forensics*, n.d.). Formats with guaranteed granular data analysis are AFF. To address this requirement, the ability to ensure the integrity of evidence using forensic imaging tools, which yields impartial analysis necessary for legal courts, has motivated forensic analysts.

6. INVESTIGATING RANSOM NOTES AND COMMUNICATION

6.1 Analyzing Ransom Notes and Insights

The ransom note has both a threat value and an investigative value because it allows investigators to learn all about the attacker's processes, but also their motivations and identity. Ransom notes such as these from shut-down ransomware operations provide friction-related payment resources and quality, but play a crucial role in information exchange. Detailed technical analysis of these ransom notes assists investigators in understanding attacker motivations, whilst also providing insights into their skill level and psycho-cultural characteristics. One of the cornerstones of forensic linguistic investigation is the analysis of the ransom notes — how they are shaped, the kind of words and sentence structure used, and their verbal language. Nevertheless, a unique combination of language style use, slang usage, and cultural references can tell a lot about where the attacker is from and how far into their education they got. In the analysis, the quality of language, together with automated translation instruments, likely shows the experience of a non-native speaker. Stylometry — an analysis method that follows writing patterns to link notes with past cyberattacks. Ransom notes not typed or in particular typefaces usually include significant additional corroborating evidence

The analysis of metadata present in ransom notes provides investigators with significant resources for their investigations. The exact creation date and technical specifications, including timestamps together with software details or device identifiers, become identifiable metadata within notes (*GRIT Ransomware Report: July 2024 | GuidePoint Security*, n.d.). Computational forensic tools retain the ability to extract data from such sources and analyse it to discover attack relationships and their perpetrators. Modern ransom note forensics includes paper and ink elements and computer printer marks as part of its investigative methods. Ransom notes utilize standard formats as a practice, which RaaS groups commonly employ during operations. The attacker continues to use a fixed structural format but makes adjustments to the amount of ransom and payment deadline along with the cryptocurrency wallet details. Ransomware investigators can track an attacker's ancestral relationship by analyzing ransomware files against established families, including Ryuk, REvil, and Conti. Payment instructions are helpful for investigators because blockchain network records allow them to track cryptocurrency transactions, which could reveal the attackers' true identities.

The analysis of ransom notes requires equal attention to psychological evaluation techniques. The names used by attackers demonstrate their current emotional state through various tones from professional and calm to aggressive and mocking. Ransom demands that surpass normal values usually reveal both desperation among the criminals and their lack of experience, but rigorously planned messages show their deliberate approach. Such classifications help investigators determine which offenders might be involved in the crimes. Ransom note analysis receives additional benefits through the implementation of artificial intelligence (AI) and machine learning technologies. It identifies and analyses the linguistic variations and stylistic patterns that also surface across ransom notes in a number of ransomware incidents, using artificial intelligence (AI) algorithms. Automated tools run to parse the dark web and detect suspicious phrases with ransom templates to speed up detecting ransomware variants.

Figure 2. Cyber forensics techniques: Stylometry, Blockchain tracking, emotional tone assessment, and metadata extraction for analyzing threats and tracing attackers.

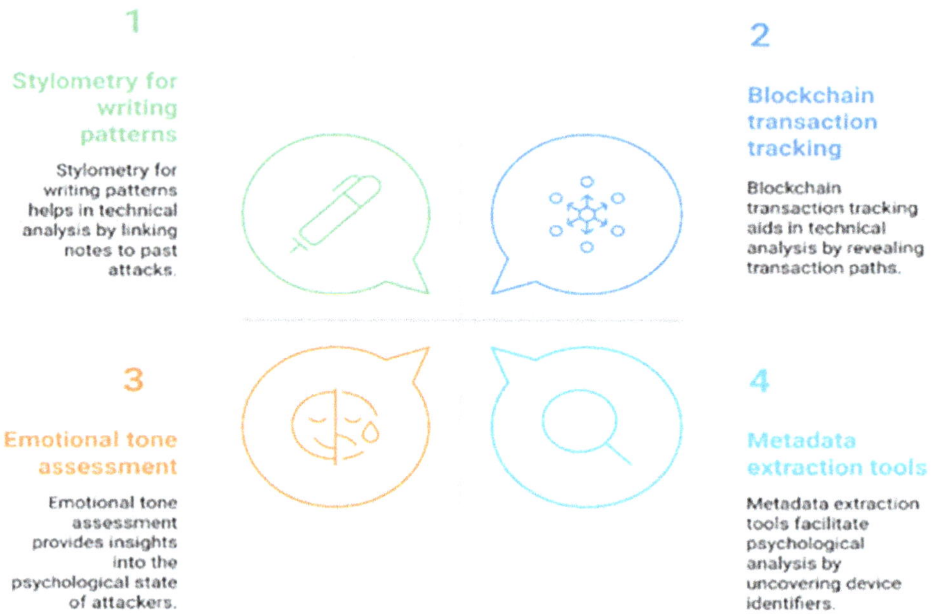

6.2 Tracing IP Addresses and Cryptographic Signature

Ransomware attacks are an increasing menace to cybersecurity as attackers are using file Encryption to demand a digital currency payment, mainly in the guise of cryptocurrency. Ransomware forensic investigations are essential for organizations battling against attacks, as they trace the attacks through tracing the perpetrator as well as understanding how they operate and tracking the money involved. An investigation into the details of the crime scene is what forms a good foundation for a cybercrime case—investigating IP addresses and looking into cryptographic signatures are good examples of forensic methods investigators employ to understand what an attacker did and where they came from, in the case of a ransomware case. A system breach by ransomware attackers results in file encryption using asymmetric encryption algorithms such as RSA and AES. The attackers place ransom notes, which include payment instructions, after the data encryption process. Studies of these notes help investigators gain knowledge about the attacker's methods and communication style as well as their understanding of technology. The identification of real perpetrators becomes challenging because criminals use anonymization tools like VPNs, proxies, and the Tor network to hide their authentic IP details. Even though obstacles exist, IP addresses function as critical indicators for investigation purposes. Such evidence reveals both the geographic source of attacks and identifies the Internet Service Provider and the specific devices involved. By examining IP addresses that fall across a number of different attack investigations, however, experts are able to identify links that in turn lead them to command and control (C&C) servers. These servers have associated IP addresses, and as the servers issue encryption keys and commands, investigators are able to link the servers to cybercriminal networks. Ransomware crypto signatures analysis is used by forensic analysts who investigate ransomware cases and their signed files and DLLS using this technique. Each strain of ransomware contains its unique cryptographic hash behavioral signatures, which help it get identified. The forensic analysis of these signatures allows investigators to identify the strain of ransomware leveraged, uncover similarities to previous intrusions, and trace back to specific cybercriminal groups. This means when you are operating with digital signatures, you are protecting yourself against illicit changes to the software. Investigators are able to determine both the origin of the malware and whether or not it is trustworthy by examining these signatures(*Ransomware Attack - What Is It and How Does It Work? - Check Point Software*, n.d.-b). To combat the perpetrators asking for ransom in cryptocurrency, blockchain forensic investigation is one of the most necessary techniques within a digital forensic investigation. While they offer anonymous payment services, transactions are transformed into public records when done with cryptocurrencies. Analysts decipher cryptocurrency wallet routes to find out if the criminals would contact either the attackers or the victims, or if they were connected to the money systems to be legal. This allows us to create the digital breadcrumbs that lead back to an attacker when IP address information is tied in with these security insights.

Investigators face challenges in their work when it comes to ransomware forensics. To evade detection, attackers employ code morphing malware in addition to their evasion techniques on each of their attempts to infect a target. This makes analyzing much harder as attackers use dynamic IP addresses and encryption to cover their tracks. Since tackling these tactics involves multiple investigative approaches, investigators use reverse engineering, network traffic analysis, and data point correlation as investigative tools to counter these tactics. The combination of IP address tracing with the analysis of the same kills most ransomware investigations in their tracks. When a particular IP is associated with known C&C servers and a ransomware signature matches, investigators can associate the activity with a threat actor. (Kogias et al., 2024). This large-scale approach works successfully with attack attribution and dismantling the criminal infrastructure, and serves as a shield against future attacks. They use both metadata and timestamp data in digital evidence by way of the ransom notes, which provide multiple investigative leads. In the same manner, unique traits in style, language patterns, and even coding errors can offer evidence for investigators to track down the attacker (or at least his affiliation). The vast network of agencies, plus the partnership with threat intelligence systems, allows competing forces around cybersecurity to track real-time active crimes and new releases of ransomware.

7. CHALLENGES IN RANSOMWARE FORENSICS

7.1 Evasion Techniques Employed by Attackers

Because the methods used by the attackers to breach systems are also used as barriers for forensic investigators, phishing, social media manipulation, and pretexting social engineering methods are used to convince users to execute malware or publish their credentials. The human factor is still vulnerable to these attacks, making wide-ranging training programmes essential to mitigate exposure. All ransomware attackers go through a series of steps — gaining network access, escalating privileges, stealing data, and then deploying ransomware. Attackers who gain control of their targets hit organizations harder to extract a ransom payment from those who have lost access to their data. These security evasion techniques range from log forgery to data destruction, along with rootkits that hide malignant activities, making the attacks undetected. By destroying and tampering with the log, the attackers create a subtle trail for the investigators to follow, leading to extraordinarily complex investigations. It is this very fact that systems attackers leverage to exploit software vulnerabilities, making frequent system maintenance imperative since the absence of updates will lead to exploitable weaknesses (*What Is Social Engineering | Attack Techniques & Prevention Methods | Imperva*, n.d.). Other groups have utilized Domain Generation Algorithms to create random commands and control domain names, which allow for a much more difficult time of detection and stopping. A fileless malware, leveraging system memory via genuine tools such as PowerShell, that eludes the traditional file detection engines.

As the RaaS sector has evolved, so has the ransomware kit, which is specifically focused on defeating your security defences. It is these platforms that allow basic users with no technical experience to carry out significant ransomware attacks, which is pushing the number of ransomware attacks higher and higher. To combat ever-evolving threats, improving cybersecurity resilience and implementation is possible only with the establishment of advanced monitoring systems, running training for employees, and putting in place plans for a comprehensive incident response, with the onus of cybersecurity resting on top of the organisation as the first point of compliance in the company.

Figure 3. Ransomware attack stages: Privilege escalation, data theft, ransomware deployment, and evasion techniques.

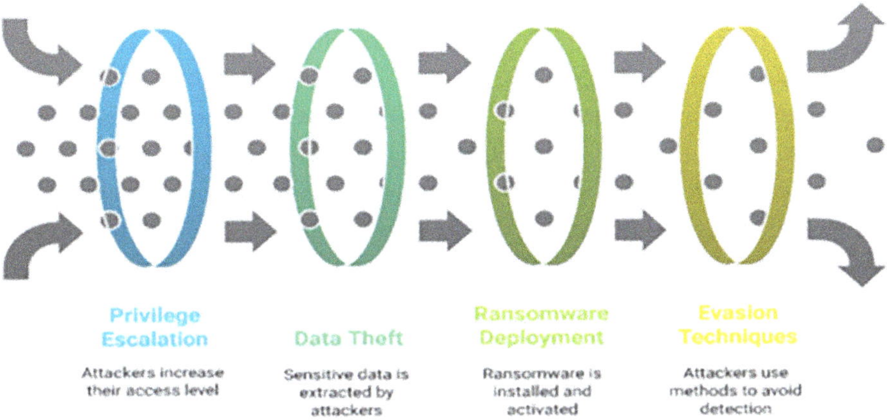

7.2 Containment Strategies in Rapidly Spreading Attacks

If done correctly, companies can recover their business quickly from recovery strategies, while avoiding ransom payouts. Ransomware Detectors are those employees who get appropriate training and are involved in defending against threats before they lead to a significant loss. To reduce organizations' exposure to social engineering attacks, such as phishing types, chosen personnel must receive continuous guidance on recent phishing methods, techniques, and cybersecurity policies. A feature for detecting anomalies indicative of possible ransomware in network activity enhances protection with sophisticated security tools, IDS, and SIEM platforms. Prevention of ransomware propagation between systems relies on organizations establishing defined access restrictions paired with network segmentation strategies. By keeping malicious activity isolated into separate segments, network segmentation minimizes exposure opportunities and time-to-containment (*How to Prevent Ransomware Attacks: Top 10 Best Practices | UpGuard*, n.d.). Timely measures make a difference, as these include isolating the ransomware-infected devices and segregating contaminated equipment to minimize the damage. Implementing IP address blocking along with suspicious activity monitoring must be the two primary core methods organizations use to prevent the spread of ransomware.

The backbone of endpoint protection software and its accompanying antivirus and anti-malware components, these prevention and response technologies provide a first line of defense to end users. Consistent data backups — both offline and in safe locations — can contribute to operational resilience, giving organizations a far better alternative than paying ransom. An incident response plan from Music City School describes who does what and when they communicate, in addition to recovery sequences; this plan must be consistently tested and adapted to remain operationally ready. Sharing threat intelligence with competitors gives insight into the current tactics that hackers use to target organizations, which often lead to a successful cyberattack, and therefore better protects the assets of the organization. Organizations actively engage in threat hunting and assessment to reduce their attack surface to prevent attacks and assess vulnerabilities. Investigating ransomware works within a challenging environment (due to evolving threats and encryption as well as data differences and variations). Still, there is a need for quick identification and rapid response activities. An adequate ransomware protection relies on appropriate segmentation of your networks, profound user awareness, constant monitoring, and full action playbooks. By employing these prevention techniques, companies build resilience to ransomware attacks, while reducing the likelihood of damage being done.

7.3 Ransomware Forensics: International Legal and Policy Frameworks

The ransomware attack is a worldwide threat that requires cross-border legal cooperation. International data protection and privacy laws, standards for evidence, and cybercrime treaties vary widely from jurisdiction to jurisdiction, and digital forensic investigations must respect these differences.

In the EU, the General Data Protection Regulation (GDPR) makes it mandatory for organizations to report data breaches involving personal data to their national supervisory authority and, where applicable, to affected data subjects without undue delay and, where feasible, within 72 hours of becoming aware of the breach. However, these new rules regarding data transfer and user consent can result in limitations when it comes to cross-border access to forensic data, even in criminal investigations, because they can restrict the sharing of data. In the United States, investigators can leverage statutes like the Computer Fraud and Abuse Act (CFAA) and Stored Communications Act (SCA), which provide for greater access between law enforcement and digital evidence. While on the one hand, there is the move towards regulations like GDPR, on the other hand, privacy-oriented regulations like California's CCPA have started to align with GDPR as far as processing personal data is concerned, which necessitates maintaining special care when forensic investigations are being performed.

At the international level, the Budapest Convention on Cybercrime fosters inter-State co-operation among its Parties in the preservation and exchange of computer-related evidence. Unfortunately, though, some nations, such as Russia and China, are not party to those agreements, which complicates the enforcement of ransomware actors operating from jurisdictions with little or no extradition treaties or inconsistent cyber laws between jurisdictions.

The international forensics challenge of ransomware has three main aspects:

1. Jurisdictional issues regarding the cross-border tracking of attacks
2. Admissibility of digital evidence – definition varies
3. Limitations on places where you could be forced to unlock your phone, encrypted communication, or anything you might store in the cloud
4. Absence of unified data breach reporting requirements

Strategic recommendations:

1. Improve MLATs for speedier cross-border assistance
2. Create standards for digital evidence handling around the world
3. Aidocracy: All the policy tools to develop blockchain tracing legislation
4. Encourage training initiatives in states that lack infrastructure for cyber enforcement

Having a national scheme of things in sync with international Ransomware legal policies will ensure quick investigation of Ransomware, effective prosecution of actions, and better deterrence of Ransomware in its entirety.

8. TOOLS FOR RANSOMWARE INVESTIGATION

8.1 Network Traffic Analysis with Wireshark and Netflow

Ransomware analysis needs network traffic because it provides crucial data about how, when, and where an attack started and how it propagates in the system. Wireshark and NetFlow combined can minimize maloperation by analyzing the flow of the network traffic over time. Wireshark provides investigators deep packet-level visibility, which helps them detect irregular HTTP requests, encrypted communications, and server connections to C2 command-and-control servers. NetFlow creates generalized traffic pattern views which permit analysts to detect data transfer anomalies as well as significant changes in outbound connections and unexpected DNS requests that signal ransomware threats.

Threat actors deploy numerous advanced methods that include both data removal capabilities and system spread activities to avoid being tracked. NetFlow data tracks ransomware movements by showing security teams which systems got compromised and revealing suspicious attempts to steal information. Wireshark allows analysts to precisely monitor packet data that exposes malicious payloads together with encrypted communication contents. Real-time ransomware detection becomes possible through tcpdump tools, which capture network packets while attacks occur. Security Information and Event Management solutions, together with Intrusion Detection Systems, can achieve better threat detection when NetFlow is integrated into their frameworks. The analysis benefits from FakeNet-NG and Network Miner because they help both observe malicious domains and extract malware payloads. (*Master Network Traffic Analysis with Wireshark | LevelBlue*, n.d.). FakeNet-NG provides an artificial network environment through which ransomware communications can be intercepted while Network Miner recovers network files for in-depth analysis. Through their analysis of the attack sequence, analysts gain knowledge about the point where the infection occurred and access to both command-and-control communications and information about what regions were disrupted. The constructed timeline functions as an important toolkit for teams who perform incident response and damage mitigation. Ransomware variants implement encrypted communication channels for C2 traffic, which results in increased difficulty of detection. Traffic patterns that reveal unusual encrypted data communication patterns or persistent connections leading to unknown IPs serve as indicators of possible malicious activity. (*Wireshark: An Effective Tool for Network Analysis*, n.d.) Organizations can limit ransomware's impact and stop data loss through Wireshark and NetFlow, which deliver valuable information to guide cybersecurity defense enhancements. Company resistance to future ransomware attacks increases when they actively monitor their network traffic to reduce ransomware damage.

8.2 Encrypted Communications: Techniques and Tools

The communication encryption protocols Signal Protocol together with Off-the-Record Messaging (OTR) ensure full end-to-end encryption, which makes messages accessible only to intended recipients. Current real-time message protection methods through encryption protocols succeed at their goal, but organizations struggle with key management when dealing with large encryption key datasets. The prevention of compromises depends on secure storage and proper distribution systems. The requirement by governments for access to encrypted content creates major privacy threats, which reduce encryption protocol quality levels and make user information vulnerable.

Encryption protocols are the key to fending off ransomware. Cybercriminals make use of cryptography to lock up computer files and later hold them to ransom for decryption methods. Organizations obtain protection against these threats in backups when they encrypt files before sending them to a cloud or off-site solution.

When the main files get corrupted or destroyed, there is a backup system that helps ensure seamless access to the files. Since many modern ransomware programs utilize encrypted communication for the transfer of stolen data and the control of command-and-control servers, NSM allows security detection of ransomware activities by monitoring encrypted traffic on networks. When unusual behaviour in software happens, security systems immediately respond, identifying patterns in the flows of encrypted data (DECEPTION).

Network segmentation is important for ransomware protection because it contains malware across networks while separating infected machines from the rest of the organization. Internal communications are protected through encryption from attackers who may access critical data that may be contained in recovery plans (Ermoshina & Musiani, 2019)—regular phishing awareness training, including avoiding harmful links. Education based on information gives users insight that reduces the chance of being attacked via ransomware using social engineering methods. Encryption as Cybersecurity Bullet: Needs Fine-tuning Through Cost: Benefit Calculation Algorithms that take up less system resource are very important for Mobile vehicles that operate under a limited capacity situation. Throughout this process, system performance is optimized while balancing the need for security. The continuing tension between the state, seeking regulated access to private, secure data, and civil liberties remains a hot topic in the public square. A more complicated answer is required for a better balance between having the possibility for lawful access while also keeping private information safe from exploitation. Encryption is still as important as it allows the intellectual property to be protected and preserves the confidentiality of the data while protecting the integrity of digital communication. Strong encryption with proactive detection and incident response enables organizations to defend against both ransomware attacks and operational threats more effectively (*Network Segmentation and How It Can Prevent Ransomware*, n.d.). Better Encryption Hashes: Cybersecurity will evolve to improve crypto, protect customers, and combat new cyber threats.

9. MALWARE ANALYSIS AND REVERSE ENGINEERING

9.1 Understanding Ransomware Behaviour Through Analysis

Ransomware is a special type of malicious software and application based on an encryption mechanism, where its targets are forced to pay criminals and unidentifiable attackers to set the proper encryption key to read their lost files and pay ransom in exchange only in cryptocurrency form. After infecting the system, ransomware begins encrypting your files with RSA or AES, or both strong encryption algorithms, which makes the file encryption irreversible without the attacker's decryption key. File encryption by this malware specifically selects file formats (usually documents, images, and databases) without changing the code of system files. Among ransomware variations, some strains specifically attack backup systems as well as network locations to block data retrieval without payment of the ransom. A ransomware note emerges following encryption as the cyber attacker demands cryptocurrency payments for decryption keys, but threatens to permanently lose data or discard stolen information if payment deadlines remain unmet. Ransomware analysis requires a complete understanding because it forms the basis for preventing infections and minimizing their destructive consequences. Analysis through dynamic and static techniques helps analysts to determine both infection entry points and methods of encryption. Also, it detects the patterns used in ransom alerts and activities that occur after successful infiltration. Ransomware is distributed through phishing emails along with malicious attachments, and by taking advantage of weaknesses in out-of-date computer programs, human interaction is targeted using social engineering techniques. (Albshaier et al., 2024) Advanced variants employ lateral movement techniques that allow them to spread across multiple systems throughout networks, making containment operations much more difficult. Behaviour-based detection systems need to examine abnormal file encryption patterns to discover new types of ransomware during their initial stages.

Once inside the attacked system, this incoming ransomware employs two significant strategies to mask itself from detection: one, to turn off security tools while also changing system configuration, and two, to make the injected malicious payload either obfuscated or encrypted via many anti-detection techniques. One is encryption for files (and information theft), and the other is combined into one “double extortion” threat, where this is nothing but public data exposure if not paid what the demands of the victims to comply. In an effort to fly under the radar, some of the newer ransomware variants are using fileless attacks since their malicious code does not generate any files on the hard disk. If a ransomware infection sends information to external servers to exchange keys or transfer data, then a thorough assessment of the network activity becomes a necessity. By identifying patterns of lateral movement on the network, the network administrator is able to isolate infected machines and prevent the ransomware from propagating to other devices. This leads us to an aspect of ransomware payloads that is ultimately of most interest to forensics analysts — the triggers that cause encryption to activate, the undesirable attributes and characteristics of the threats, and how the threat can be decrypted. Information on these behaviours enables organizations to develop better defense mechanisms that include not only reliable backup systems but also distributed networks and endpoint security. In addition to scheduling tasks and using system services, ransomware applies some locking persistence methods by changing system registry keys to keep running in the background. Techniques identified by cybersecurity professionals in their analysis lead to the creation of tools to detect and establish some of the strongest security protocols. (*What Is a Lateral Movement? Prevention and Detection Methods | Fortinet*, n.d.). By conducting behavioural analysis of ransomware, system weaknesses are identified and documented, resulting in an opportunity for cybersecurity professionals to produce superior threat intelligence that assists in the creation of prevention methods and strategies against future attempts with ransomware.

9.2 Key Management Processes and Operator Communication

The advanced cryptographic technology behind Ransomware attacks locks victim data before its release becomes possible only through payment of a requested ransom. The process of asymmetric encryption allows ransomware to encrypt files using public keys, but victims must have the private keys provided by attackers for data decryption. The attackers distribute separate encryption keys to their victims, which prevents them from unlocking target files without active participation. The complicated data retrieval process pushes victims toward paying ransom payments to attackers. Malware analysts solve key management problems through their investigation of ransomware code and network traffic interception alongside the review of ransomware binary code. The encryption keys, along with private key information, frequently hide within code that uses obfuscated techniques. To seek both keys and vulnerabilities, analysts inspect ransomware memory through programming tools during its runtime operations (Enomoto et al., 2024). Organizations can execute ransomware decryption without conducting ransom payments when scientists identify vulnerabilities or issues in encryption methodologies or key generation systems. Ransomware sends encryption keys through highly secure TOR networks, which makes the analysis process more challenging.

Understanding ransomware key distribution mechanisms plays an essential role in identifying the methods used for C&C server communication. Attackers establish anonymous communication through encryption because they want to stay hidden from security detection. C&C servers establish encryption communications, which malware analysts track to find potential flaws in key exchange protocols, as they could lead to data recovery. The attackers sometimes embed keys directly into the malware, but these embedded components often reveal locations for decryption analysis. Payments from victims enable access to decryption keys, which are transmitted through the command-and-control infrastructure. Security researchers review the decryption steps used by attackers to discover further vulnerabilities. (Xia et al., 2018). The information exchange between cybersecurity teams allows them to speed up the development of decryption tools while fighting ransomware threats as a collective group. The disruption of ransomware attacks heavily depends on our understanding of how ransomware keys function and operate. Cybersecurity experts who spot weaknesses within key storage, generation, or distribution systems can successfully counteract ransomware attacks by making their defences more resistant to new threats.

Figure 4. Ransomware mitigation: A layered process from attack initiation to key distribution, analysis, vulnerability identification, and decryption without ransom.

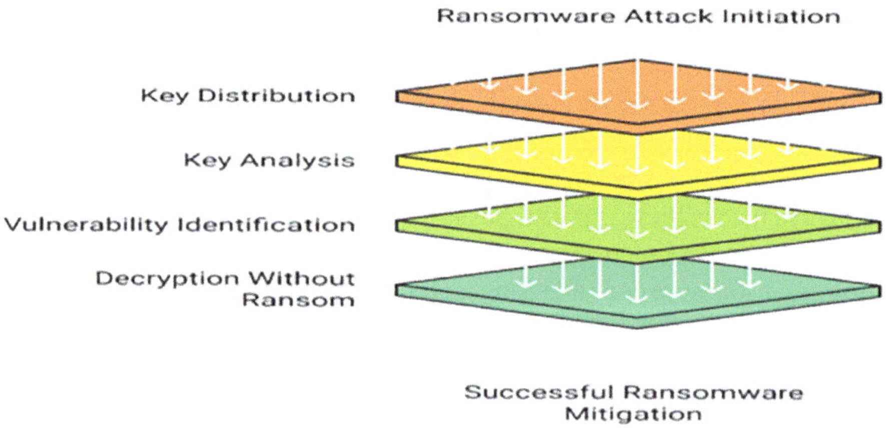

10. THE ROLE OF CRYPTOCURRENCY IN RANSOMWARE OPERATIONS

10.1 Analyzing Ransom Notes for Blockchain Addresses

Blockchain addresses serve as a significant security threat since attackers use them to collect anonymous payments through growing ransomware attacks. The files belonging to victims are encrypted, while ransom notes contain both payment details and cryptocurrency wallet addresses. Blockchain analysis supports investigators because Bitcoin transactions remain transparent while the system provides limited user anonymity. To start, investigators take the wallet address of the attacker from ransom notes found during the investigation. Financial institutions focus on discovering where the payment comes from by tracking money transfers "inside and outside" of both mixing services and decentralized exchanges through blockchain exploration tools. This means its traceability is complicated when mixing services merge different transactions into one movement process. Chain analysis and Elliptic combined supported tracking technology with Cipher Trace, which allows users to trace digital money transactions while also hiding the schemes. Using blockchain observer systems, operators (or people) follow the funds from one network to another and cryptocurrency due to this manipulation process and extract some key information from each hacking operation.(Meng Jun et al., 2024). Verification procedures introduced by some exchanges may reveal the identities of identified criminals. However, some challenges still exist. Similar to other privacy-related coins, Monero has transaction information that cannot be traced, ensuring that Monero is just as private as it feels. The prevalent location-based laws for international transactions erect enormous obstacles to tracking by law enforcement. Criminals protect their actions by using complex methods such as coin joining operations that are complicated to trace and secret wallet addresses hidden inside the message of ransom. (*The Role of Cryptocurrency in Ransomware Attacks*, n.d.). Blockchain analysis provides the ability to seize in forensic investigations of ransomware. Ransomware crime detection works best through the joint effort of investigators working with cybersecurity teams and financial institutions. Tracking the blockchain allows authorities to gain enough insight to identify patterns, disrupt laundering schemes, and in some cases recover ransom payment funds. National entities, along with enhanced blockchain analytic tools, have promised to mitigate the ransomware threat while reducing the ability of hackers to collect payments and helping to prevent future attacks.

Figure 5. Ransomware payment tracking: Extract wallet addresses, track transactions, identify mixing services, overcome legal challenges, and collaborate with agencies.

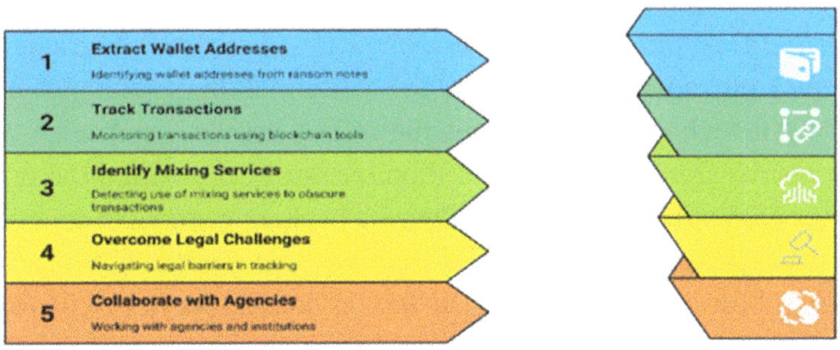

10.2 Collaborating with Exchanges and Law Enforcement

Ransomware has emerged as a new wave of a cybersecurity threat that entails data encryption and then a demand for payment in cryptocurrency. Blockchain works on the anonymity feature, which is the way cyber attackers can avoid discovery. As a result, this can prevent cryptocurrency payments because blockchain has a transparent transaction system where the investigators can identify cryptocurrency payments. Until all exchanges are cooperating with law enforcement units and specialized forensic firms at the same level, ransomware activity cannot be distinguished. Ransomware Research Report Final Report: Embassy of Crypto EXCHANGE CURRENCYembassyOfCryptoCoinJan 25, 2022 · 12:47 AM 6 min read Ransomware investigations are primarily reliant on cryptocurrency exchanges as they are the critical service enabling illegal proceeds to flow through the whole financial ecosystem, converting the funds originating from the predicate crimes to fiat. Most of the other cryptocurrency exchange systems manage to implement KYC. At the same time, they initiate a series of AML procedures to reach some necessary impressions of the user data collection that help them detect any suspicious behaviour and harmful activity—exchanges need to be able to stop the funds from moving further due to these ransomware payment detections. Criminal investigations are initiated after the exchanges share the transaction data with law enforcement. Although payment regulations are not designed primarily for crime prevention, they can help forensic investigators recognize the ransom payments. Agencies that conduct law enforcement, analyze cryptocurrency transactions easily with the help of blockchain analytics that track where the cryptocurrency actually goes; in this manner, they reveal high-risk wallet destinations for ransomware attackers. Because many of these groups operate domestically and internationally, the fight against ransomware will require international police cooperation (*Ransomware: Paying Cyber Extortion Demands in Cryptocurrency | Marsh*, n.d.). Public safety agencies are able to track ransom payments through a combination of exchange cooperation and data analysis technology that helps them find attackers and seize their assets. The blatant results from the Colonical Pipeline attack illustrated the effectiveness of this cooperation when in a matter of weeks hackers were able to recover stolen Bitcoin payments, and cripple some of the more malicious aspects of organized crime.

We also see obfuscation techniques, such as combining services with privacy coins like Monero to hide the attacker's financial trail further. These are the techniques that make the detection of funds harder. Rising scientific developments in blockchain tracing functions, along with high adherence to the function of the Financial Action Task Force (FATF) Travel Rule, result in improved overall performance of the monetary crime investigations. Even the identification of loopholes must become part of compliance standards and exchange regulation adherence enforcement, branded as the necessary element of effective management. (*Crypto Currency Regulation and Law Enforcement Perspectives*, n.d.). Public-private partnerships between organizations strengthen ransomware prevention and response protocols. The cybersecurity sector continues to work with financial service institutions and law enforcement agencies to develop decryption tools while they exchange threat information during the security implementation process. Ransomware prevention steps practiced regularly have been showing fruit in light of continuous public campaigns teaching everyone about data backup security and phishing attack techniques.

11. THE ATTACK LIFECYCLE: FROM INFECTION TO RECOVERY

Figure 6. Ransomware attack lifecycle

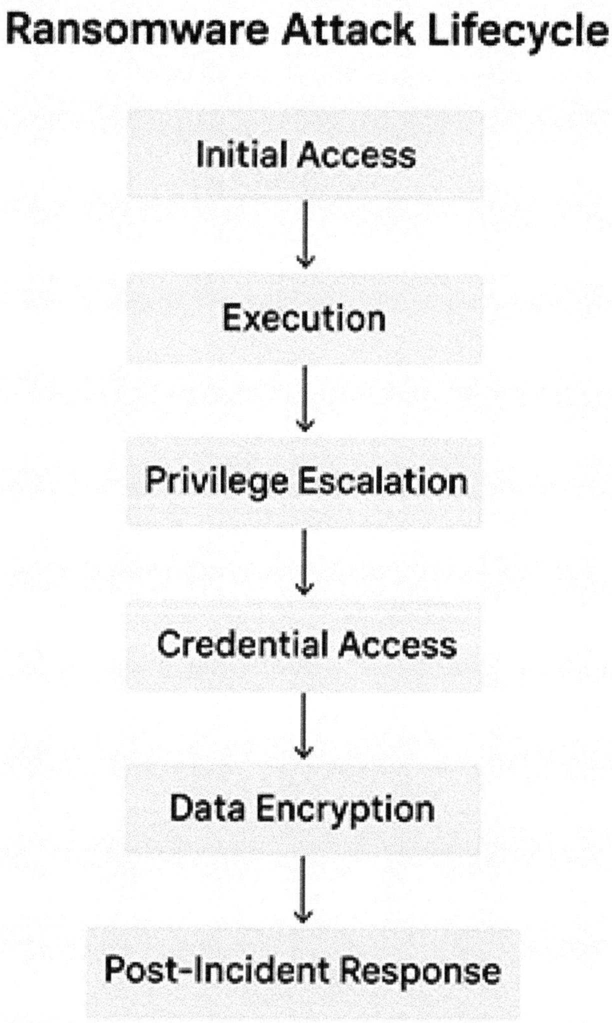

11.1 Mapping the Ransomware Attack Path

Ransomware stands as one of the most dangerous cybersecurity threats because it targets businesses as well as state agencies and private individuals. The malicious programs used in these attacks encrypt vital files, so victims must pay a ransom for access to their data. The attack sequence follows initial access, followed by execution, then lateral movement, and afterwards data encryption, and finally ransom demands and decryption together with recovery procedures, along with post-attack activities. Knowledge of these various action sequences becomes vital to stop such attacks before they occur and adequately respond to them. The first stage of the attack requires attackers to reach the target system through phishing emails, software vulnerabilities, and brute-force RDP attacks. Officials use Mimikatz to acquire user credentials and enhance their system privileges, thus evading security systems. Control over a system is granted to attackers through the essential step of privilege escalation.

The next step of attackers involves the movement of ransomware throughout networks when they exploit authentications of trust and stolen passwords. They collect sensitive information first so as to practice their double extortion methods, whereby they make ransom demands based on threats. Crooks have been covert during the encryption step, during which they convey SCYB/CRYB to vital data files and encrypt them with the aid of AES cryptography while they mount file extensions like. Crypt or. locked (*26 Ransomware Examples Explained in 2025*, n.d.). The victim is shown a ransom note, displayed with a message demanding payment in cryptocurrency, including Bitcoin, while also threatening public exposure and permanent destruction of data if the payment is not made. The choice between paying the criminals, which makes no guarantees that the decryption key will be provided, or restoring from backups falls to the victims' management teams. Preventing complete data loss will be most effective by using separate backups that are located offline. Which means victims have to choose between handing over money to the intruders with no guarantee of them providing the decryption key or attempting to restore data from backups. The most secure way to avoid complete data loss is to keep backups separately offline.

Figure 7. Ransomware attack sequence: Initial access, lateral movement, ransom demands, data encryption, and post-attack activities.

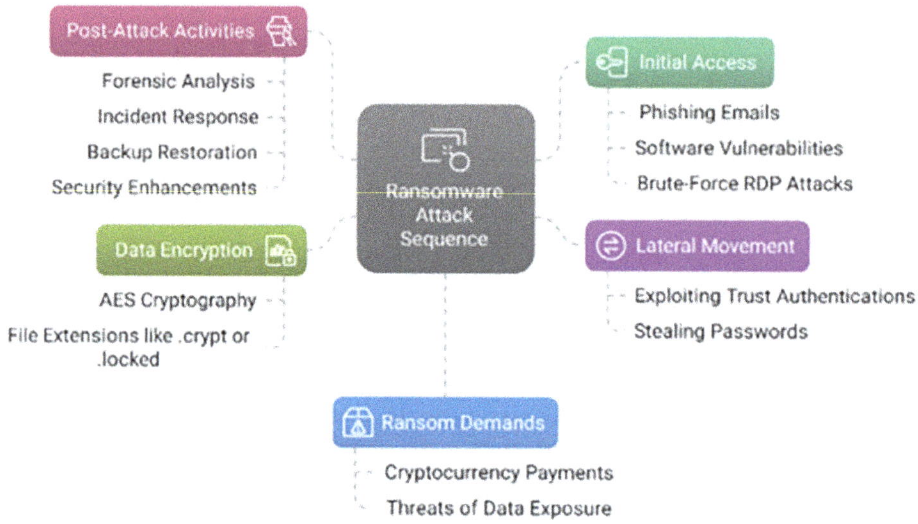

11.2 Vulnerability Exploitation and Lateral Propagation

Ransomware: Cybersecurity Threat Toping at Human Level Cybersecurity Best Practice—Overcoming System Vulnerabilities That National hesitate one Combination of exploit, such as Outdated software, weak authentication, and misconfigured service. These compromise routes that attackers utilize include things like social engineering, malicious websites, as well as standard software programs still with recognized vulnerabilities left unpatched. Cyberattacks play in the system with owned passwords and authentic admin tools, including PowerShell and PS Exec, prior to lateral movement between networks using actual network file traffic. These cybercriminals employ "living off the land" techniques as their methods become non-obtrusive system operations, which makes it difficult for them to be picked up. The current job of forensic investigators is to establish where attacks begin, pinpoint the entry points that the adversary took advantage of, and investigate their path between systems.(Aslan et al., 2023)The team's grafters compare treachery with its ambiguity, containing application logs alongside body language signals and memory segments, to spot malware survivors spreading through a hacker's target timing and abnormal file changing time. Security researchers use the abuse tool Mimikatz to identify how attackers encrypt sensitive data.

To pay or not to pay, victims of ransomware face the dilemma of either paying the amount demanded by the hacker or taking the risk of losing their data when the ransom is paid. The modern encryption algorithms are pretty advanced and complex, which also makes it almost impossible for victims to recover without paying the ransom demanded. Organizations battling these threats need to deploy a three-tiered layered defense system: routine software patching, stringent multi-factor authentication policies for remote access, and network firewall segmentation. (Cartwright et al., 2019)Two main strategies are needed to protect the business: employees should be trained to spot phishing attacks, and companies should keep backup data locked in an offline state.

12. PSYCHOLOGICAL TACTICS OF RANSOMWARE ATTACKER

12.1 Manipulating Victims: Understanding the Psychology

Ransomware is not merely an information security compromise; however, it is a method of psychological harassment that takes advantage of one of humanity's greatest fears as its access point. Furthermore, cybercriminals have many more apparitions than just encrypted data, which causes hysteria in victims. It is the ransom note that threatens irretrievable data loss and exposure of sensitive information, while using time-strapped self-evolving countdowns that force fast payment without a second to lose. These criminals try to alleviate the stress of victims by showing small file decryptions (which they call 'proof-of-life') to imply that payments will rest until all is decrypted — without actually saying so, of course. They claim that by exploiting our social nature and saying that many have paid, victims see it as a regular practice. (McIntyre & Frank, 2021) Offenders sometimes offer minor boons to create a sensation of obligation, a principle described as reciprocity. In the healthcare industry, the tactic of moral duty appeals comes to the forefront in persuading payment because victims are convinced the money will keep the funds away from other patients, who might then also suffer the same painful experience.

The combination of anxiety with false assertions of urgency results in victims hurriedly making decisions that destroy key forensic evidence that could assist authorities in arresting the molesters. Suppose victims act rashly with these psychological techniques. In that case, it leads to obfuscation for law enforcement because the digital data needed to ascertain the complete scope of the compromise becomes challenging to follow. (*The Psychology of Ransomware: Tactics of Manipulation*

Used by Cybercriminals – Best Recipes Ever, n.d.) One way to prevent this type of attack is for people to understand how malefactors carry it out. Exposing the attacker's emotional traps allows victims and forensic firms to make calculated decisions that reduce the total attack impact.

12.2 Enhancing Security Posture through Awareness Training

Widespread cybersecurity threat due to ransomware — the psychology of people is that they use emotions. Employing the psychology of fear, urgency, and trust, attackers threaten the victim by revealing sensitive data or threatening them with criminal prosecution or legal consequences in order to force them to make quick ransom payments. Not only does this compromise their reputation, but it also compromises their finances and personal well-being. However, mitigating these risks requires that the entire user training be executed. Human factor: Phishing starts with teaching team members to identify fake emails, verify any suspicious messages, and recognize untrusted links. With real-world simulations, users develop this readiness through mock phishing and ransomware exercises, so they are set to act without crisis, know the best way to disconnect their network from harm, and know how to contact IT support in no time. A culture of security should be embedded into organizations. Best practice promotion helps leadership elevate cybersecurity importance, which, in turn, drives safer digital habits amongst employees. (Maccoll et al., n.d.) Deep awareness training creates effective user behaviour change that contributes to lower ransomware attack probability and enhances overall cyber defense hardware capabilities.

13. CONCLUSION: THE FUTURE OF RANSOMWARE FORENSICS

13.1 Lessons Learned and Best Practices

Ransomware attacks have developed into a significant cybersecurity threat that takes away data, indirectly disrupts the functioning of the operations, and costs very high in terms of efforts, time, resources, and reputation. To combat this growing threat, organizations need to decode attack methods and leverage lessons from past incidents to develop proven best practices that are supported by forensic evidence. Best practices that operate within unique parameters and lessons learned have different objectives for enhancing organizational ransomware-response capabilities. Reflective insights drawn from analysis of experience allow organizations to improve future actions, and best practices morph into established effective methods and eventually into formal guidelines, policies, and frameworks. It takes both of those elements in order for organizations to keep ransomware attacks at bay (as well as take notice of their occurrence, deal with the attack, and recover). The critical insights gleaned from investigating ransomware attacks help reinforce organizational cybersecurity defences. Organizations become more conscious of how they can build resistance to attacks by taking a deep dive into each element of the threat, such as ingress points, as well as the methods of attack with associated threat actor TTPs. Since first-class ransomware-as-a-service tools provide a low-entry barrier for novice hackers to get started, organizations have to be ready for new threats. Organizations need to maintain basic forensic rules: evidence capture that maintains integrity, a fusion of endpoint detection and response tools (EDR) for rapid identification, plus continuous observation programs that detect anomalous behaviour. Genuine practices based on data analysis, along with practical experience, help organizations to adopt preventive measures to ensure that the occurrence of ransomware attacks, as well as the potential damage that follows it, is reduced. The best practices in cybersecurity consist of many different things: these include the least privilege access rules that are mentioned above, system security, and strong backup protocols and MFA authentication systems. Network segmentation is a best practice for preventing ransomware from spreading across business networks. Frequent examination of backups accompanied by confirmation of their integrity is an indispensable practice because offline or cloud-based backup solutions provide the fastest recovery of encrypted data as they bypass the need to pay the ransom. The incident response plan is what organizations can use to battle an attack from beginning to end. The team should keep training for real incidents and conduct planned exercises using revised identity response plans. Prior ransomware attacks tell us that organizations require employees who are prepared to understand their part in defending the organization. As for employees, safety against ransomware will be determined by their training, which will help them detect both phishing messages and malicious email attachments, because social engineering remains a primary vector of ransomware infection. Regularly functioning security awareness training and phishing simulations for organizations considerably reduce the successful cyber events. When teams have to investigate an attack to find where the attackers are and decrypt data locked via ransomware, external cybersecurity firms and law enforcement agencies become invaluable. Continuous quality improvement looms through daily business operations by merging practice-based lessons with industry-leading standards. Monitoring closed incidents allows the organization to explore its weaknesses, allowing for remedial action to be taken, thus enhancing its systems. This approach is necessary for organizations to sustain their operational edge in the face of security threats that are constantly evolving in cyberspace. Those organizations that have ongoing threat intelligence monitoring and vulnerability testing are better prepared to fend off the next round of ransomware. So the damage is less severe when new strains do emerge.

13.2 The Evolving Landscape of Cyber-Threat

Data-driven insight coupled with real-world experience empowers organizations to take proactive measures to reduce the occurrence and impact of ransomware attacks, and authentic practices offer the most effective way to do this. For example, system security merged with least privilege access rules along with strict backup protocols and MFA authentication systems represent best practices in cybersecurity. Best practices solution #9 – Network segmentation to stop ransomware from traversing the entire business network. Regular inspection of backups together with their integrity validation remains an indispensable condition, as offline or cloud backups provide the fastest means to recover encrypted data without paying a ransom. Having an incident response plan allows organizations to not only defend themselves against an attack but also to combat an attack from start to finish. The team must remain ready for real scenarios and exercise regularly against refreshed identity response plans. When analysing how ransomware operations developed before, focus on getting your personnel prepared to play their assigned roles in safeguarding the organisation against the threat. Therefore, stopping social engineering is more important than ever, and worker training to identify phishing messages and malicious email attachments is critical to preventing ransomware attacks. Organizations that conduct practical security awareness training and regularly simulate phishing attacks will limit the successful cyber incidents. Working with external cyber firms and law enforcement agencies is critical in investigating these attacks, identifying threats, and decrypting data that has been seized.

Combining practice with best practice facilitates a daily business practice environment for continuous quality improvement. Organizations always focus on settled incidents to identify their loopholes that enable them to conduct corrective actions that enhance the systems. This process is essential for organizations so that they can keep focusing on the real threats and hold the tactical for ever-changing security threats. When a new strain of ransomware hits, organizations that continuously monitor for threat intelligence and run regular vulnerability tests will come out on top, as they will have mitigated the risk of major damage. One more reason for the increase in cyber threats is the global nature of cyber criminal activities. Cybercriminals use anonymity tools, including VPNs and Tor networks, and cryptocurrencies to create a borderless cyberspace where they can conceal themselves and evade criminal investigation. New technological methods that criminals use themselves make it complicated for law enforcement agencies to find the criminals. A successful digital systems attack on one organisation will create network effects as damage flows to many interconnected organizations. At the top of the list of cybercriminal capabilities is supply chain attacks since they specifically target third-party vendors, as hackers exploited SolarWinds with access to organizational systems. Such events reveal the security vulnerabilities that lie between enterprises when they rely on third-party vendors. This increasing reliance on digital across a variety of fields has acted as a key catalyst in the evolution of cyber threats. COVID-19 accelerated remote work to take advantage of them all, opening attack paths hackers could use to fight the cure-all organizations were devoting their resources to combat. Cloud computing and Internet of Things (IoT), in fact, are crucial for business operations today and are generating new security challenges. Artificial intelligence and machine learning have also synchronized the pace of cybercriminals, who are now capable of automating their cyberattack systems, analyzing security weaknesses through attack propagation techniques, and examining these systems for wide area attacks. These technologies allow cybercriminals to better optimize their operational efficiency by tailoring their attacks to specific user systems and users. Such malware reforms its behaviours post-intrusion into new environments powered by AI, leading to increased difficulty in detection. As a result, advanced cyber threats require equally advanced strategies for defence. The establishment of incident response and recovery plans acts as a prerequisite to help organizations pinpoint, tackle, and recover from cyberattacks successfully. Business plans should include steps to identify attacks and to isolate the infected systems, as well as measures to protect evidence and recover after the attack. This enables traceability of attacks and forensic investigation of the perpetrator and malware through digital forensics investigations. Forensics capabilities have a number of standard procedures, including analyzing network traffic and tracking IP addresses used in attacks to help investigate the incident and protect against future attacks. This list includes malware reverse engineering. The bulk of this defense will be on active data exchange between institutions that are essential, like authorities, the police force, and all other community activities in the security environment. Sharing threat intelligence makes international cybercriminals relatively simple to deal with. By detecting risks early, both organizations are better prepared for not just assessing the risk but also defending themselves. Digital forensic teams always need to work hand in hand with law enforcement authorities at the Federal Bureau of Investigation and INTERPOL levels to capture and prosecute cybercriminals. The challenge arises when cyber-attacks are state-sponsored, as the geopolitical implications make threat response much more difficult, and therefore establishing collaboration amongst law enforcement agencies is of utmost importance. This next generation of cyberattacks will likely evolve based on three major factors: technological advances, artificial intelligence applications in attacks and defenses, and cybercriminal ability to adapt. As business entities and even governments are becoming more digitally connected, the scope and reach available to cybercriminals to wreak havoc is expanding. In order to protect sensitive data from the most prominent cyber threats, organizations will continue to deploy pre-emptive cybersecurity measures, and holders will also invest in cutting-edge security platforms and post-continuous upgrades to their defences. The development of recent methods of decryption tools along with recovery systems is one of the most important elements that can lead to a minimization of the effects when resolving ransomware attacks. Such regulations concerning cybercrime by the government are bound to bring about incident reporting and punitive measures against organizations failing to secure the sensitive information of organizations. Ransomware, APTs, supply chain attacks, and continued changes in the cyber threat environment are only some of the many challenges organizations face today. As cybercriminals become sophisticated and their techniques become harder, businesses have to make more investments in digital forensics and collaborate with other organizations in the war against cybercrime. However, through continued innovation and vigilance, the threats to critical infrastructure, sensitive data, and public safety can be effectively managed.

REFERENCES

3-2-1 backup strategy explained: Is it effective?| Definition from TechTarget. (n.d.). Retrieved March 26, 2025, from https://www.techtarget.com/searchdatabackup/definition/3-2-1-Backup-Strategy

Albshaier, L., Almarri, S., & Rahman, M. M. H. (2024). Earlier Decision on Detection of Ransomware Identification: A Comprehensive Systematic Literature Review. *Information 2024, Vol. 15, Page 484, 15*(8), 484. DOI: 10.3390/info15080484

Aquilina, J. M. (2008). Memory Forensics. *Malware Forensics*, 121–192. DOI: 10.1016/B978-1-59749-268-3.00003-7

Aslan, Ö., Aktuğ, S. S., Ozkan-Okay, M., Yilmaz, A. A., & Akin, E. (2023). A Comprehensive Review of Cyber Security Vulnerabilities, Threats, Attacks, and Solutions. *Electronics 2023, Vol. 12, Page 1333, 12*(6), 1333. DOI: 10.3390/electronics12061333

Azure backup and restore plan to protect against ransomware | Microsoft Learn. (n.d.). Retrieved March 26, 2025, from https://learn.microsoft.com/en-us/azure/security/fundamentals/backup-plan-to-protect-against-ransomware

Cartwright, E., Hernandez Castro, J., & Cartwright, A. (2019). To pay or not: Game theoretic models of ransomware. *Journal of Cybersecurity, 5*(1), tyz009. Advance online publication. DOI: 10.1093/cybsec/tyz009

Crypto Currency Regulation and Law Enforcement Perspectives. (n.d.). Retrieved March 26, 2025, from https://www.researchgate.net/publication/354328712_Crypto_Currency_Regulation_and_Law_Enforcement_Perspectives

Enomoto, S., Kuzuno, H., Yamada, H., Shiraishi, Y., & Morii, M. (2024). Early mitigation of CPU-optimized ransomware using monitoring encryption instructions. *International Journal of Information Security, 23*(5), 3393–3413. DOI: 10.1007/s10207-024-00892-2

Ermoshina, K., & Musiani, F. (2019). "Standardising by running code": The Signal protocol and de facto standardisation in end-to-end encrypted messaging. *Internet Histories, 3*(3–4), 343–363. DOI: 10.1080/24701475.2019.1654697

File carving | Infosec. (n.d.). Retrieved March 26, 2025, from https://www.infosecinstitute.com/resources/digital-forensics/file-carving/

File Carving vs. Metadata Recovery: What is the Difference? (n.d.). Retrieved March 26, 2025, from https://www.salvationdata.com/knowledge/file-carving/

Gallegos-Segovia, P. L., Vintimilla-Tapia, P. E., Bravo-Torres, J. F., Yuquilima-Albarado, I. F., Larios-Rosillo, V. M., & Jara-Saltos, J. D. (2017). Social engineering as an attack vector for ransomware. *2017 CHILEAN Conference on Electrical, Electronics Engineering, Information and Communication Technologies, CHILECON 2017 - Proceedings, 2017-January*, 1–6. DOI: 10.1109/CHILECON.2017.8229528

GRIT Ransomware Report: July 2024 | GuidePoint Security. (n.d.). Retrieved March 26, 2025, from https://www.guidepointsecurity.com/blog/grit-ransomware-report-july-2024/

How to Prevent Ransomware Attacks: Top 10 Best Practices | UpGuard. (n.d.). Retrieved March 26, 2025, from https://www.upguard.com/blog/best-practices-to-prevent-ransomware-attacks

Jun, M. A. Y., Jinu, B. A., Seng, L. K., Maharaiq, M. H. F. B. Z., Khongsuwan, W., Junn, B. T. K., Hao, A. A. W., & Sindiramutty, S. R. (2024). *Exploring the Impact of Crypto-Ransomware on Critical Industries: Case Studies and Solutions*. DOI: 10.20944/preprints202409.1325.v1

Kogias, G., Karkazis, P. A., Xevgenis, M. G., Atlam, H. F., Ekuri, N., Azad, M. A., & Lallie, H. S. (2024). Blockchain Forensics: A Systematic Literature Review of Techniques, Applications, Challenges, and Future Directions. *Electronics 2024, Vol. 13, Page 3568, 13*(17), 3568. DOI: 10.3390/electronics13173568

Liu, D. (2009). Digital Forensics and Analyzing Data. *Cisco Router and Switch Forensics*, 15–38. DOI: 10.1016/B978-1-59749-418-2.00001-6

Maccoll, J., Hüsch, P., Mott, G., Sullivan, J., Nurse, J. R. C., Turner, S., & Pattnaik, N. (n.d.). *The Scourge of Ransomware: Victim Insights on Harms to Individuals, Organisations and Society*. Retrieved March 26, 2025, from www.rusi.org

Master Network Traffic Analysis with Wireshark | LevelBlue. (n.d.). Retrieved March 26, 2025, from https://levelblue.com/blogs/security-essentials/network-traffic-analysis-using-wireshark

McIntyre, D. L., & Frank, R. (2021). *No Gambles with Information Security: The Victim Psychology of a Ransomware Attack*. 43–60. DOI: 10.1007/978-3-030-60527-8_4

3. *Methods to Preserve Digital Evidence for Computer Forensics*. (n.d.). Retrieved March 26, 2025, from https://www.criticalinsight.com/blog/3-methods-to-preserve-digital-evidence-for-computer-forensics

Miramirkhani, N., Appini, M. P., Nikiforakis, N., & Polychronakis, M. (2017). Spotless Sandboxes: Evading Malware Analysis Systems Using Wear-and-Tear Artifacts. *Proceedings - IEEE Symposium on Security and Privacy*, 1009–1024. DOI: 10.1109/SP.2017.42

Navigating the Cybersecurity Landscape: A Comprehensive Review of Cyber-Attacks, Emerging Trends, and Recent Developments. (n.d.). Retrieved March 26, 2025, from https://www.researchgate.net/publication/378343830_Navigating_the_Cyber_security_Landscape_A_Comprehensive_Review_of_Cyber-Attacks_Emerging_Trends_and_Recent_Developments

Network Segmentation and How it Can Prevent Ransomware. (n.d.). Retrieved March 26, 2025, from https://www.threatintelligence.com/blog/network-segmentation

Ransomware Attack - What is it and How Does it Work? - Check Point Software. (n.d.-a). Retrieved March 26, 2025, from https://www.checkpoint.com/cyber-hub/threat-prevention/ransomware/

Ransomware Attack - What is it and How Does it Work? - Check Point Software. (n.d.-b). Retrieved March 26, 2025, from https://www.checkpoint.com/cyber-hub/threat-prevention/ransomware/

Ransomware Attacks and Types | How do Locky, Petya, and other ransomware differ? (n.d.-a). Retrieved March 26, 2025, from https://www.kaspersky.com/resource-center/threats/ransomware-attacks-and-types

Ransomware Attacks and Types | How do Locky, Petya, and other ransomware differ? (n.d.-b). Retrieved March 26, 2025, from https://www.kaspersky.com/resource-center/threats/ransomware-attacks-and-types

Ransomware Data Recovery: How to Save Your Data. (n.d.). Retrieved March 26, 2025, from https://cloudian.com/guides/ransomware-backup/ransomware-data-recovery-5-ways-to-save-your-data/

26. *Ransomware Examples Explained in 2025*. (n.d.). Retrieved March 26, 2025, from https://www.sentinelone.com/cybersecurity-101/cybersecurity/ransomware-examples/

Ransomware: Paying Cyber Extortion Demands in Cryptocurrency | Marsh. (n.d.). Retrieved March 26, 2025, from https://www.marsh.com/en/services/cyber-risk/insights/ransomware-paying-cyber-extortion-demands-in-cryptocurrency.html

The Power of Cyber Forensics in Solving Crimes. (n.d.). Retrieved March 26, 2025, from https://www.salvationdata.com/knowledge/cyber-forensics/

The Psychology of Ransomware: Tactics of Manipulation Used by Cybercriminals – Best Recipes Ever. (n.d.). Retrieved March 26, 2025, from https://ransomdecrypt.com/the-psychology-of-ransomware-tactics-of-manipulation-used-by-cybercriminals/

The role of cryptocurrency in ransomware attacks. (n.d.). Retrieved March 26, 2025, from https://www.manageengine.com/log-management/cyber-security/cryptocurrency-role-in-ransomware.html

What Are Air-Gapped Backups? - How Air-Gapped Backups Work. (n.d.). Retrieved March 26, 2025, from https://stonefly.com/resources/what-are-air-gapped-backups/

What Are the Most Common Attack Vectors for Ransomware? (n.d.). Retrieved March 26, 2025, from https://www.cybereason.com/blog/what-are-the-most-common-attack-vectors-for-ransomware

What is a Cyber Crime Investigation? (n.d.). Retrieved March 26, 2025, from https://www.recordedfuture.com/threat-intelligence-101/incident-response-management/cyber-crime-investigation

What is a Lateral Movement? Prevention and Detection Methods | Fortinet. (n.d.). Retrieved March 26, 2025, from https://www.fortinet.com/resources/cyberglossary/lateral-movement

What is a Memory Dump? - GeeksforGeeks. (n.d.). Retrieved March 26, 2025, from https://www.geeksforgeeks.org/what-is-a-memory-dump/

What Is Ransomware-as-a-Service (RaaS)? | IBM. (n.d.). Retrieved March 26, 2025, from https://www.ibm.com/think/topics/ransomware-as-a-service

What is Social Engineering | Attack Techniques & Prevention Methods | Imperva. (n.d.). Retrieved March 26, 2025, from https://www.imperva.com/learn/application-security/social-engineering-attack/

Wireshark: An Effective Tool for Network Analysis. (n.d.). Retrieved March 26, 2025, from https://www.researchgate.net/publication/374675769_Wireshark_An_Effective_Tool_for_Network_Analysis

Xia, T., Sun, Y., Zhu, S., Rasheed, Z., & Shafique, K. (2018). Toward A Network-Assisted Approach for Effective Ransomware Detection. *ICST Transactions on Security and Safety*, *168506*, 168506. Advance online publication. DOI: 10.4108/eai.28-1-2021.168506

Zakaria, W. Z. A., Alta, N. M. K. M., Abdollah, M. F., Abdollah, O., & Yassin, S. M. W. M. S. M. M. (2024). Early Detection of Windows Cryptographic Ransomware Based on Pre-Attack API Calls Features and Machine Learning. *Journal of Advanced Research in Applied Sciences and Engineering Technology*, *39*(2), 110–131. DOI: 10.37934/araset.39.2.110131

Chapter 9
Supply Chain and Third Party Risk Transfer:
Designing Coverage for Vendor Ecosystems

Mohammad Al Khaldy
https://orcid.org/0009-0009-7502-4668
Department of Business Intelligence and Data Analytics, University of Petra, Jordan

Ahmad Al-Qerem
https://orcid.org/0000-0003-2187-6194
Computer Science Department, Faculty of Information Technology, Zarqa University, Jordan

Ala Hamarsheh
https://orcid.org/0000-0002-4736-7331
Computer Science, Faculty of Information Technology, Arab American University, Jenin, Palestine

Amjad Aldweesh
https://orcid.org/0000-0001-9358-1323
College of Computing and Information Technology, Shaqra University, Saudi Arabia

ABSTRACT

Organizations face expanding attack surfaces due to digital supply chain integration and third-party dependencies. Current insurance frameworks fail to address cascading cyber vulnerabilities that propagate through interconnected vendor networks. This chapter examines structural elements required for effective risk transfer mechanisms

DOI: 10.4018/979-8-3373-5545-0.ch009

specifically designed for multi-tiered supply chain ecosystems. Research integrates theoretical risk transfer models with practical policy construction parameters across various industry verticals. Findings demonstrate that parametric triggers, continuous monitoring integration, and differential premium models create more effective coverage structures for complex vendor networks. Implementation requires standardized assessment protocols, quantification methodologies, and mechanisms to address information asymmetry and aggregation risk. This work contributes an operational framework for implementing cyber risk transfer across interconnected vendor relationships that enhances organizational resilience against propagating attacks.

1. INTRODUCTION

1.1 Context and Evolution of Supply Chain Risk

Modern organizations operate in complex webs of vendors, suppliers and service providers. Risk has evolved in the wake of the gradual transition between linear supply chains and networks of ecosystems, with formerly separated malfunctions becoming mutually dependent and cascading (Gordon et al., 2023). The classical approaches to risk management focused mainly on physical disruption, product quality and logistics; with the digital transformation of the world, the emphasis has shifted and now focuses on data integrity, system availability and information security.

This shift to digitally connected supply chains has even produced new vectors of attack. According to a 2023 study by the Ponemon Institute, 67 percent of organizations have either been a victim of cyber-incidents that have started at third-party entry points (Tyas Tunggal, 2025). Such incursions bypass security controls at the boundary level to go to the integration points outside the organizational perimeter.

These dynamics were reflected by the 2020 SolarWinds hack. The attackers have proven that reliance on widely used software may be used to leverage the attack by targeting the development environments, inserting malicious code into software updates distributed to thousands of customers, and creating long-term access points across government agencies and enterprises (CISA, 2021). The two similar incidents with Kaseya in 2021 and Log4j in 2022 highlight the strategic goal of threat actors: to access thousands of clients via trusted distribution chains by infecting vulnerable nodes of vendor ecosystems.

1.2 Problem Statement

Organizations face challenges transferring supply chain cyber risks due to complexities in:

1. Risk visibility across multi-tier vendor relationships
2. Attribution of breach origins within interconnected systems
3. Quantification of cascading impacts from third-party failures
4. Allocation of liability among supply chain participants

Existing insurance models inadequately address these challenges. Current policies contain exclusions targeting third-party originated incidents, creating coverage gaps for supply chain risks. Standard policies focus on first-party losses rather than cascading impacts that propagate through vendor networks (Woods & Simpson, 2022).

The insurance market lacks standardized approaches for:

- Assessing concentration risk across shared service providers
- Quantifying downstream impacts from upstream failures
- Defining coverage triggers for supply chain incidents
- Structuring premiums that reflect ecosystem dependencies

1.3 Research Objectives

This chapter addresses these gaps through research focused on:

1. Developing integrated frameworks for transferring supply chain cyber risks
2. Analyzing coverage structures for multi-tier vendor ecosystems
3. Examining parametric trigger designs for supply chain disruptions
4. Evaluating differential premium approaches based on ecosystem risk profiles
5. Assessing implementation challenges for supply chain cyber insurance programs

1.4 Significance and Contribution

This research contributes both theoretical models and practical applications for transferring supply chain cyber risks. Organizations increasingly depend on third-party services, yet insurance instruments lag behind operational realities. The developed frameworks provide:

1. Risk transfer mechanisms aligned with complex ecosystem dependencies
2. Coverage structures that address cascading impacts

3. Premium models that incorporate vendor risk profiles
4. Implementation pathways that overcome market limitations

This work bridges risk management theory and insurance practice, establishing parameters for effective transfer of risks that cross organizational boundaries.

1.5 Chapter Organization

The chapter proceeds with a review of literature on supply chain risk management and cyber insurance evolution. Section 3 presents theoretical frameworks for risk transfer in vendor ecosystems. Sections 4 and 5 examine risk assessment methodologies and management strategies. Section 6 analyzes insurance design parameters for supply chain coverage. Section 7 compares risk transfer mechanisms. Section 8 addresses implementation challenges. Section 9 explores emerging trends. The chapter concludes with recommendations for practitioners and researchers.

2. LITERATURE REVIEW

2.1 Supply Chain Risk Management Evolution

Supply chain risk management practices evolved significantly over the past two decades. Early frameworks focused primarily on physical disruptions, financial stability, and product quality (Christopher & Peck, 2004). Digital transformation shifted research toward cyber vulnerabilities within interconnected networks.

Peltier (2013) identified the expansion of organizational attack surfaces through digital supplier integration. This work established foundational concepts for understanding how risk propagates across connected entities. Johnson et al. (2020) expanded this model by documenting propagation patterns across multi-tier relationships, finding that impacts cascade nonlinearly through network connections.

Research by Nazir et al. (2021) established that organizations with mature supply chain risk management practices experienced 45% fewer third-party incidents. Their study identified critical practices including:

- Multi-tier visibility beyond immediate suppliers
- Common assessment frameworks across vendor categories
- Continuous monitoring rather than point-in-time assessments
- Integration of risk data across procurement functions

Recent studies focus on quantitative approaches to supply chain cyber risk. Zhang and Li (2022) developed network modeling techniques that trace impact propagation through connected systems. Their work demonstrated that traditional risk modeling fails to capture cascading effects in interconnected environments.

2.2 Third-Party Risk in Digital Ecosystems

Research on third-party risk establishes clear connections between ecosystem complexity and organizational vulnerability. Friedberg and Skopik (2018) analyzed data from 450 organizations, finding that every additional critical vendor increased breach probability by approximately 3.5%. Their research established that risk accumulates nonlinearly as vendor dependencies increase.

Woods and Böhme (2021) examined information asymmetry problems that prevent effective third-party risk management. Their work identified:

1. Limited visibility into vendor security practices
2. Misaligned incentives between service providers and customers
3. Challenges in verifying security claims
4. Inability to monitor changes in vendor security posture

Recent studies focus on concentration risk within digital supply chains. Khan and Estay (2022) analyzed cloud service provider dependencies, finding that 67% of Fortune 500 companies share critical dependencies on five major providers. This creates systemic risk through common points of failure that impact multiple organizations simultaneously.

Research increasingly focuses on fourth-party risk - the dependencies of third-party vendors. Work by Müller et al. (2023) demonstrated that organizations typically identify only 15% of their fourth-party connections, creating blind spots in risk assessments. Their network analysis revealed average path lengths of 3.7 connections between organizations and their most distant dependencies.

2.3 Cybersecurity Insurance Evolution

Cybersecurity insurance emerged as a market segment in the early 2000s but gained significant traction only in the past decade. Early policies covered limited perils with substantial exclusions (Bolot & Lelarge, 2009). Market growth accelerated as breach costs increased and regulatory requirements expanded.

Research by Woods et al. (2019) traced the development of cyber insurance products, identifying key evolutionary stages:

1. Initial coverage as endorsements to existing policies (2000-2005)
2. Standalone products with limited scope (2005-2010)
3. Comprehensive first-party coverage (2010-2015)
4. Expansion to third-party liability (2015-2020)
5. Emerging focus on supply chain coverage (2020-present)

This evolution reflects increasing organizational dependency on digital systems and recognition of third-party risk sources.

Studies of insurance market development reveal challenges specific to cyber risks. Gordon et al. (2022) analyzed policy data from 2015-2021, finding:

1. Premium increases averaging 27% annually
2. Coverage restrictions expanding particularly for systemic risks
3. Exclusions increasingly targeting incidents originating from third parties
4. Limited capacity for large-scale cyber events

Recent research examines the coverage gap for supply chain cyber incidents. Franke (2023) analyzed 265 cyber claims, finding that 43% involved third-party origins but only 17% received coverage. The study identified exclusions and attribution challenges as primary reasons for coverage denials.

2.4 Risk Transfer Mechanisms

Research on risk transfer mechanisms establishes theoretical foundations for insurance structures. Böhme and Schwartz (2010) established economic models for cyber risk transfer, identifying information asymmetry and moral hazard as key challenges. Their work questioned the insurability of cyber risks without appropriate mechanisms to address these market imperfections.

Studies by Romanosky et al. (2019) examined alternative risk transfer mechanisms including captive insurance structures, risk pools, and parametric insurance. Their analysis identified strengths and limitations of each approach for cyber risk transfer.

Eling and Schnell (2022) evaluated parametric insurance designs for cyber incidents, finding that objective triggers reduce information asymmetry problems but introduce basis risk. Their work proposed triggers based on:

1. Technical measures like network outage duration
2. Verified incident declarations by trusted third parties
3. Severity indices for specific incident categories
4. Market-based indicators of cyber event impacts

Recent research explores contractual risk transfer mechanisms as complements to insurance. Work by Fleming et al. (2023) analyzed vendor contract structures, finding wide variation in risk allocation clauses. Their study revealed that only 34% of contracts clearly defined security responsibilities and liability bounds for third-party incidents.

Table 1. Summary of key literature on supply chain cyber risk transfer

Author(s)	Year	Focus Area	Key Findings	Methodological Approach
Christopher & Peck	2004	Supply chain resilience	Established framework for understanding supply chain vulnerability	Conceptual framework development
Bolot & Lelarge	2009	Cyber insurance economics	Identified market issues in early cyber insurance products	Economic modeling
Böhme & Schwartz	2010	Insurability of cyber risks	Established economic foundations for cyber risk transfer	Theoretical analysis
Peltier	2013	Third-party security	Documented expansion of attack surface through vendor connections	Case study analysis
Woods et al.	2019	Cyber insurance evolution	Traced development stages of cyber insurance market	Longitudinal market analysis
Johnson et al.	2020	Risk propagation	Demonstrated nonlinear cascading of impacts through supply chains	Network analysis
Woods & Böhme	2021	Information asymmetry	Identified barriers to effective third-party risk assessment	Game theory modeling
Nazir et al.	2021	Vendor risk management	Linked mature practices to reduced incident rates	Survey research (n=235)
Gordon et al.	2022	Insurance market trends	Documented coverage restrictions for third-party incidents	Policy content analysis
Zhang & Li	2022	Quantitative risk modeling	Developed network techniques for modeling cascading failures	Mathematical modeling
Khan & Estay	2022	Concentration risk	Identified systemic risk through shared service providers	Dependency mapping
Woods & Simpson	2022	Coverage gaps	Analyzed policy exclusions targeting third-party incidents	Legal analysis
Franke	2023	Claims analysis	Documented coverage denials for third-party originated incidents	Claims data analysis
Fleming et al.	2023	Contractual risk transfer	Identified variation in vendor contract risk allocation	Contract analysis
Müller et al.	2023	Fourth-party risk	Measured visibility gaps in extended supplier networks	Network analysis
Lawrence et al.	2023	Parametric insurance	Evaluated objective triggers for cyber coverage	Design science research

3. THEORETICAL FRAMEWORK FOR RISK TRANSFER

3.1 Risk Transfer Theory in Vendor Ecosystems

Risk transfer theory provides foundations for understanding how cyber risks move across organizational boundaries. Traditional risk transfer relies on clear causality, quantifiable impacts, and definable triggers (Dionne, 2013). Cyber risk in vendor ecosystems challenges these fundamentals through complex interdependencies and attribution difficulties.

Theoretical models rely on network theory to explain risk propagation. Park et al. (2021) established that cyber risk transfers through vendor relationships follow power law distributions rather than normal distributions. Their model demonstrated that a small number of highly connected nodes create disproportionate risk transfer points within ecosystems.

The theoretical basis for transferring cyber risks across supply chains requires examining:

1. **Interdependence Structures**: How organizations connect through data and system interactions
2. **Information Flows**: How risk-relevant information moves between parties
3. **Decision Rights**: How control over risk factors distributes across entities
4. **Incentive Alignment**: How economic factors influence risk management behavior

Liu and Johnson (2023) developed an integrated model connecting these elements, establishing that effective risk transfer requires:

- Clear visibility across interdependence structures
- Balanced information sharing between parties
- Aligned incentives for risk management
- Defined responsibility boundaries

This theoretical framework explains why traditional insurance structures struggle with cyber risks in supply chains, as these conditions rarely exist in practice.

3.2 Vendor Ecosystem Risk Models

Models for vendor ecosystem risk build on network theory, applying specific characteristics of digital supply chains. Huang and Madnick (2021) developed a propagation model demonstrating how impacts cascade through:

1. **Vertical propagation**: From supplier to customer through product/service dependencies
2. **Horizontal propagation**: Between organizations sharing common third parties
3. **Indirect propagation**: Through unanticipated connections between seemingly unrelated parties

These propagation patterns explain why traditional risk management approaches focused on immediate vendors fail to capture ecosystem risk dynamics.

Recent theoretical work by Züst et al. (2022) established a mathematical framework for quantifying risk transfer across vendor tiers. Their model incorporates:

- Dependency strength between organizations
- Security maturity differentials between connected entities
- Redundancy factors within supply networks
- Time-based decay functions for propagating impacts

This work creates theoretical foundations for quantifying transferred risk, establishing parameters necessary for insurance instruments that address supply chain exposures.

3.3 Insurance Economics for Cyber Ecosystems

Economic theories explain challenges in insuring cyber risks across organizational boundaries. Work by Woods and Böhme (2021) applied information economics to third-party cyber risk, demonstrating how information asymmetries create adverse selection problems within insurance markets.

Their model identified three critical information barriers:

1. Vendors possess more information about their security than customers
2. Customers lack visibility into fourth-party relationships
3. Risk characteristics change rapidly while contracts remain static

These asymmetries explain premium inefficiencies and coverage limitations in current market offerings.

Theories of moral hazard further explain challenges in cyber risk transfer. Romanosky et al. (2019) demonstrated that insurance coverage may reduce incentives for upstream security investments, creating externalized risks. Their model suggests that coverage structures must incorporate mechanisms to maintain security incentives across the supply chain.

Recent theoretical work focuses on ecosystem-level risk pooling. Models by Eling and Schnell (2022) demonstrate potential efficiency gains through collective coverage structures that address:

1. Correlated losses across supply chain participants
2. Limited capacity in traditional insurance markets
3. Information sharing barriers between organizations
4. Free-rider problems in security investments

These models establish theoretical foundations for designing insurance products that address the unique characteristics of cyber risk in vendor ecosystems.

Figure 1. Theoretical framework for cyber risk transfer in supply chains

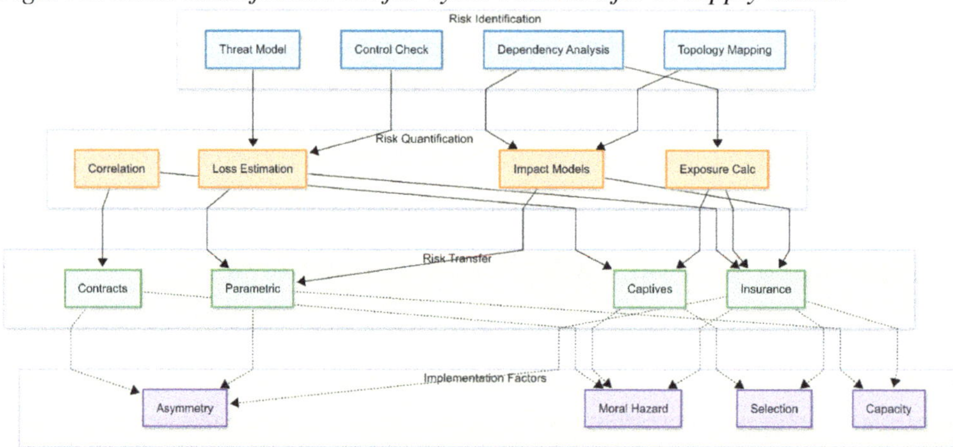

4. SUPPLY CHAIN RISK ASSESSMENT

4.1 Identification of Supply Chain Vulnerabilities

Effective risk transfer requires systematic identification of vulnerabilities across vendor ecosystems. Traditional assessment approaches focus on immediate vendors, missing extended supply chain risks. Research by Johnson et al. (2020) found that organizations typically identify 75% of first-tier risks but only 25% of second-tier risks and 10% of third-tier risks.

Comprehensive vulnerability identification requires mapping:

1. **System dependencies**: Technical connections between organization and vendor systems
2. **Data flows**: Information exchanges across organizational boundaries
3. **Business process integration**: Operational dependencies on vendor functions
4. **Shared infrastructure**: Common platforms creating concentration risk

Organizations struggle with visibility beyond immediate suppliers. Müller et al. (2023) documented that 62% of organizations lack processes to identify fourth-party connections. Their research demonstrated that effective identification requires:

- Supply chain mapping methodologies that traverse multiple tiers
- Vendor attestation mechanisms that reveal dependencies
- Centralized risk registers that capture connection points
- Technology solutions that automatically discover connections

Recent approaches leverage data sharing across organizations. Collective approaches improve visibility through shared intelligence about vendor relationships. Research by Khan and Estay (2022) found that consortium models increased fourth-party visibility by 47% compared to individual assessment approaches.

4.2 Risk Quantification Methodologies

Quantifying cyber risk across supply chains creates distinct challenges compared to internal risk assessment. Traditional quantification methods use historical loss data, which remains limited for supply chain cyber events. Alternative approaches use estimation techniques based on dependency mapping and scenario modeling.

Research by Zhang and Li (2022) established methodologies for quantifying propagating impacts. Their approach uses:

1. Dependency strength weights between organizations
2. Critical function mapping across suppliers
3. Recovery time objectives for connected services
4. Monte Carlo simulation for probability distribution

This methodology allows organizations to quantify potential losses from cascading failures, creating foundations for insurance valuation.

Empirical studies demonstrate correlation between supply chain complexity and breach impacts. Friedberg and Skopik (2018) found that organizations with high supplier concentration experienced 35% higher breach costs on average. Their research established quantitative relationships between ecosystem characteristics and risk exposure.

Industry frameworks increasingly incorporate supply chain dependencies into risk quantification. Factor-based models adjust inherent risk scores based on:

- Number of critical vendors
- Concentration within specific service categories
- Access privileges granted to third parties
- Data sensitivity shared with suppliers

These approaches create structured methodologies for quantifying risk exposure through vendor relationships, establishing foundations for differential premium models.

4.3 Cascading Effects in Vendor Networks

Understanding cascading effects requires network analysis techniques applied to vendor ecosystems. Research by Huang and Madnick (2021) developed propagation models that trace impact pathways through interconnected organizations. Their work demonstrates that impacts follow non-intuitive paths due to hidden dependencies.

Empirical studies of major supply chain incidents reveal propagation patterns. Analysis of the SolarWinds incident by CISA (2021) documented how impacts cascaded through:

1. Initial compromise of development environment
2. Distribution of malicious updates to customers
3. Lateral movement within customer environments
4. Exfiltration of sensitive data
5. Further propagation through connected systems

This cascade demonstrates why traditional security boundaries fail to contain supply chain attacks.

Recent research focuses on time factors in cascading impacts. Züst et al. (2022) developed temporal models showing that propagation velocity varies based on:

- Integration depth between connected systems
- Monitoring capabilities across boundaries
- Detection mechanisms for anomalous behavior
- Isolation capabilities within environments

These factors determine how quickly impacts spread through vendor networks, creating critical parameters for designing response coverage.

Table 2. Supply chain cyber risk assessment methodologies comparison

Methodology	Primary Focus	Strengths	Limitations	Key Metrics	Reference
Vendor Security Assessment Questionnaires	Security controls implementation	Standardized approach across vendors; Comparable results	Self-reported data; Point-in-time assessment; Limited validation	Control maturity scores; Compliance status	Nazir et al. (2021)
Network Dependency Mapping	Technical connections	Identifies propagation paths; Reveals hidden dependencies	Resource intensive; Requires technical access; Rapidly becomes outdated	Connection counts; Critical path identification; Redundancy measures	Johnson et al. (2020)
Business Impact Analysis	Operational dependencies	Links technical failures to business outcomes; Prioritizes critical vendors	Subjective estimates; Difficult to validate assumptions	Recovery time objectives; Maximum tolerable downtime; Criticality ratings	Zhang & Li (2022)
Monte Carlo Simulation	Probabilistic risk quantification	Produces distributions rather than point estimates; Incorporates uncertainty	Requires extensive assumptions; Sensitive to input parameters	Probable maximum loss; Expected annual loss; Loss exceedance curves	Züst et al. (2022)
Supply Chain Attack Trees	Attack vector analysis	Models attacker perspective; Identifies vulnerable paths	Resource intensive; Requires threat intelligence; Limited to known attack patterns	Path complexity; Control coverage; Exploitation probability	Huang & Madnick (2021)
Concentration Risk Analysis	Shared dependencies	Identifies common failure points; Reveals systemic risks	Limited by visibility into fourth parties; Data collection challenges	Vendor concentration ratios; Service provider overlap; Geographic distribution	Khan & Estay (2022)

continued on following page

Table 2. Continued

Methodology	Primary Focus	Strengths	Limitations	Key Metrics	Reference
Continuous Monitoring	Real-time risk indicators	Provides current security posture; Detects changes in risk profile	High implementation cost; Technical integration challenges; Data interpretation issues	Security posture scores; Anomaly detection rates; Trend analysis	Franke (2023)
Ecosystem Risk Modeling	Holistic network risk	Captures interdependencies; Models cascading failures	Complexity limits accuracy; Data requirements extensive; Requires specialized expertise	Network centrality measures; Propagation coefficients; Systemic impact factors	Müller et al. (2023)

5. THIRD-PARTY RISK MANAGEMENT STRATEGIES

5.1 Vendor Due Diligence Frameworks

Vendor due diligence is the foundation of risk transfer as it sets the minimum required amount of security expectations. In the case of standardized assessment frameworks, empirical literature shows the increased efficiency and effectiveness. According to Nazir et al. (2021), companies with standardized frameworks performed assessments 43 percent quicker and revealed 27 percent more control gaps than the ones that utilized custom frameworks.

A good regime of vendor assessment presents the following features:

1. Tiered assessment models: varying the level of evaluation to the level of vendor importance.
2. Control validation: validation of attestations by collecting evidence.
3. Contextual risk factors: modifying the requirements in line with the characteristics of the services.
4. On-going updates: updating evaluations due to changing risk profiles.

The industry standards provide procedural approaches. Security requirements are defined by frameworks like the NIST Cybersecurity Framework, ISO 27001, and CMMC and have a common language. Fleming et al. (2023) noticed that organizations that implemented known standards obtained 37 percent higher rates of vendor compliance compared to those using in-house standards.

The focus has been diverted to the mechanisms of validation other than self assessment. The reliability of the assessments is improved by third party attestation, security rating, and technical validation. According to Woods and Boehme (2021), the information asymmetry was decreased by 42 percent when using validated assessments in comparison with the self-attestation models.

Continuous monitoring serves to overcome the reduced visibility achieved by point-in-time assessment. The study by Franke (2023) revealed that the organizations that continuously monitor security identify security degradation an average of 58 days earlier than the organizations that use annual cycle assessments.

Some of the good continuous monitoring modalities are:

1. External security scoring: Internet facing security indicators monitoring.
2. Threat intelligence incorporation: Monitoring vendor references in threat intelligence.
3. Access activity monitoring: Studying the actions of vendors in systems.
4. Monitoring of supply chain threats: Monitoring attacks against other providers.

Issues of implementation include data integration, controlling false positives and resource limitations. According to Johnson et al. (2020), successful programs started with highly rated vendors on the critical rating and progressively increased coverage and selected resources on the highest-risk relationships.

New studies explore the relations between monitoring indicators and real incidents. Zhang and Li (2022) showed that some external security indicators have a correlation of 64% with the probability of breach; the main predictors are the practices of managing certificates, patch management in time, email security settings, and implementations of domain security. These results justify the use of monitoring data to adjust insurance premia in relation to the changing risk profiles.

5.2 Contractual Risk Transfer

Contracts establish legal foundations for risk allocation between organizations and vendors. Research by Fleming et al. (2023) found wide variation in how organizations structure risk transfer clauses. Their analysis identified common contractual mechanisms including:

1. **Indemnification clauses**: Shifting financial responsibility for incidents
2. **Limitation of liability provisions**: Capping potential damages
3. **Security requirements**: Establishing baseline control expectations

4. **Right to audit clauses**: Enabling verification of control implementation
5. **Insurance requirements**: Mandating specific coverage types and limits

Effectiveness varies significantly across these mechanisms. Studies by Romanosky et al. (2019) found that 76% of organizations included security requirements in contracts, but only 34% verified compliance. Their research demonstrated that contractual risk transfer without verification creates illusory protection.

Recent research examines the interplay between contractual and insurance risk transfer. Woods and Simpson (2022) found that misalignment between contract provisions and insurance coverage creates protection gaps. Their study documented that 58% of organizations experienced denials for third-party claims due to contractual exclusions in policies.

Emerging practices integrate contractual and insurance mechanisms through:

- Aligning contract language with insurance policy terms
- Implementing coverage verification processes
- Coordinating claims processes across organizations
- Developing shared incident response protocols

These practices create more effective risk transfer by ensuring consistency between legal and financial protection mechanisms.

Figure 2. Third-party risk management process flow

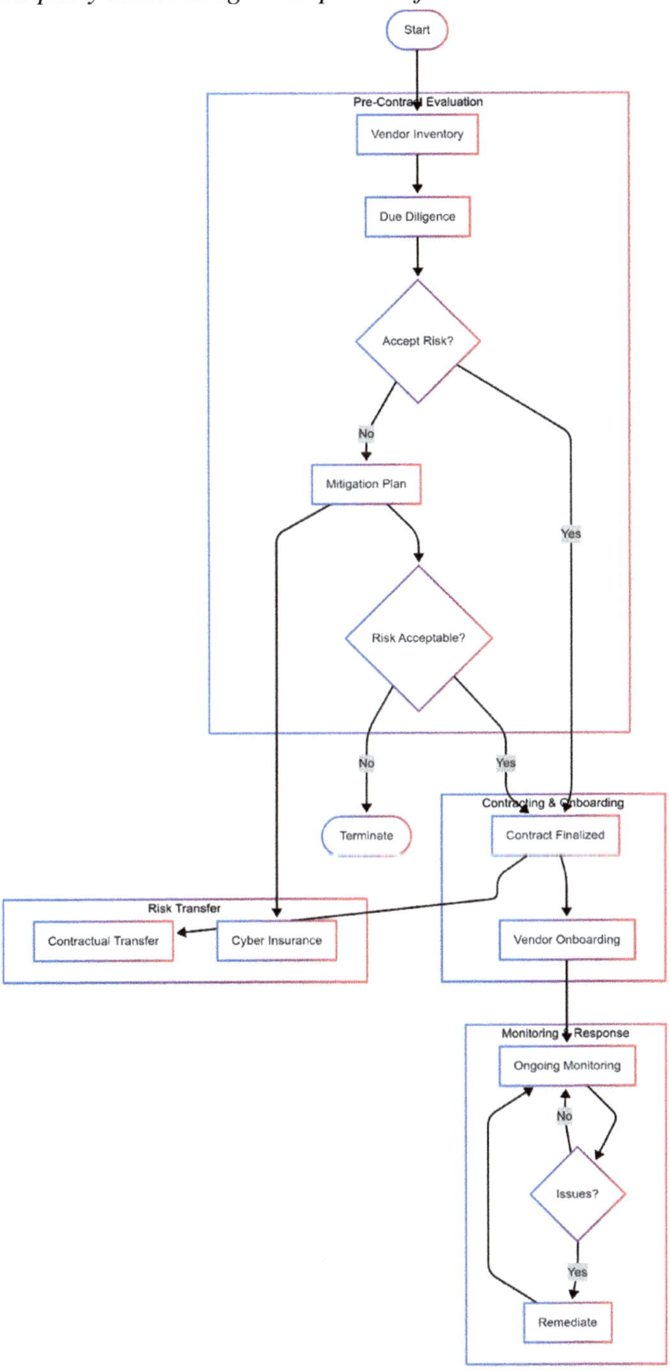

6. CYBERSECURITY INSURANCE DESIGN FOR VENDOR ECOSYSTEMS

6.1 Coverage Parameters for Supply Chain Risks

The relevance of the existing practice of insurers in terms of dealing with the cyber risks affecting the chain of supplies is restricted by the lack of specific coverage parameters. Traditional cyber policies tend to cover direct financial losses only and offer little coverage on damages caused by events beyond the immediate network of the policyholder. The analyses performed by Gordon et al. (2022) suggest that merely 23% of standard cyber policies provide unambiguous coverage due to supply-chain events, and 67% of them include exclusions that exclude the third-party-generated losses to be reimbursed.

The supply-chain vulnerabilities-specific coverage mechanisms are:

1. Contingent Business Interruption: Coverage against losses incurred due to breakdown of supplier-systems
2. Dependent Systems: Coverage: Mitigation of damage occasioned by interference to critical service providers
3. Supply-Chain Extortion Coverage: The payment of ransom payments imposed on suppliers
4. Vicarious Liability Protection: Protection against claims due to vendor security failure
5. Vendor Subrogation Waivers: Exclusions of recovery action seeking defective vendors

Development toward standardized, supply-chain oriented coverage is imbalanced. Woods et al. (2019) record an unfinished harmonization of the market: the analysts indicate a coefficient of variation of 0.78 regarding the main terms of coverage, which indicates a strong disparity in terms of what insurers offer.

The new policy innovations are likely to concentrate on networkwide provisions instead of organization-specific coverage. According to Eling and Schnell (2022), some of the emergent structures aimed at insurance of the whole supply chains include:

- Master both primary insureds and key vendors policies
- Mutual schemes whereby the supply chain participants cross-insure
- Structured coverage arrangements in terms of matched term structures
- Common constraints, which cross boundaries in an organization, at the same time

These advancements curb the disintegration that is characteristic of the conventional policies whereby every company secures individual coverage of its activities.

6.2 Policy Structure and Exclusions

The performance of supply-chain risk mitigation strategies relies on interactions between policies design and incident response capabilities. In order to evaluate these dynamics, Woods and Simpson (2022) reviewed modern policy language and identified a number of limitations that limit the broad coverage of supply-chains:

- System Control Exclusions: the insurance protection is denied when the insured system is not under his/her direct control and the system faces complications.
- Known Vulnerability Exclusions: insurance cover is barred when a vendor has not addressed the known vulnerabilities.
- Insufficient Diligence Exclusions: claims are denied in cases where the insured diligence procedures with the suppliers can be termed as being inadequate.
- Multiple-Trigger Exclusions: multiple triggers are necessary to trigger a supply-chain coverage.
- Territorial Exclusions: coverage restrictions are provided on the basis of geographical locations of vendors.

The analysis revealed that 62% of the policies sampled had at least three of these restrictive provisions and hence they reduced the overall effectiveness of the policies in case of supply-chain incidents.

At the same time as this analysis, parametric supply-chain insurance triggers are becoming subjects of research in the scholarly community. The conventional indemnity policies require evidence of causation and quantification of damage, which to the complex incidents crossing organisational boundaries, makes them difficult to resolve. Parametric designs use objective triggers that cause coverage to occur to specified events as opposed to demonstrated losses.

In the paper by Eling and Schnell (2022), parametric cyber-insurance designs, applied to supply-chain settings, were considered, and the following were noted as the benefits:

- Reduced information needs on claims
- Expedited payments in case of business-interruption
- Streamlined causation findings
- Removal of complex requirements of damage quantification

Such features overcome fundamental shortcomings of conventional coverage schemes of complex events transcending organisational boundaries.

6.3 Premium Calculation Models

High-end supply-chain cyber coverages remain underdeveloped. Traditional methodologies are based on organizational factors instead of being able to capture ecosystemic interdependencies adequately. Boehme and Schwartz (2010) defined a theoretical basis of premium calculation, but in practice, it has not followed the theory.

New models incorporate aspects of supply-chain including:

- Vendor Security Ratings: Rating vendors on the security posture and pricing premiums accordingly
- Concentration Risk Factors: Incorporation of the shared-dependency measures
- Complexity Measures of the Ecosystem: Consideration of relationship depth and breadth
- Supply-Chain Maturity Factors: Correcting the management-program effectiveness

Liu and Johnson (2023) show that when such factors are included in modeling, the correlation with the actual loss experience is 46% higher in comparison with traditional rating methods.

The issues affecting implementation are data availability, standardization and the dynamicity of risk profiles. Woods and B Bohme (2021) demonstrate that adverse-selection dynamics are caused by information asymmetry, and hence the efficiency of premiums is impacted. In their work, they suggest four information-sharing mechanisms, which are standardized vendor assessment frameworks, independent security certifications, shared intelligence on vendor security posture, and continuous-monitoring data integration, as possible ways to overcome informational barriers to accurate calculation of premiums that can arise with supply-chain risks.

Table 3. Comparison of insurance coverage types for supply chain cyber risks

Coverage Type	Description	Triggers	Typical Limits	Key Exclusions	Best Application
Traditional First-Party Cyber	Covers direct losses to insured organization	Defined security incidents affecting insured systems	$1-50M depending on organization size	Third-party originated incidents; Systems not under direct control	Organizations with limited vendor dependencies
Contingent Business Interruption	Covers business interruption losses from vendor outages	Service provider outages impacting insured operations	Sub-limited to 25-50% of policy limit	Gradual degradation; Performance issues; Scheduled maintenance	Organizations with critical SaaS dependencies
Dependent Systems Coverage	Broader protection for incidents affecting service providers	Cyber incidents impacting named service providers	Sub-limited to 25-50% of policy limit	Unnamed providers; Fourth-party dependencies; Insured-caused incidents	Organizations with identified critical vendors
Supply Chain Extortion Coverage	Covers ransom demands affecting vendors in insured's supply chain	Extortion demands against vendors that impact insured	Sub-limited to 10-25% of policy limit	Incidents not impacting insured; Unreported incidents; Non-critical vendors	Organizations in industries targeted by extortion actors
Network Security Liability	Covers third-party claims arising from security failures	Claims alleging security failures harmed others	Full policy limits typically apply	Claims between insureds; Known control failures; Contractual liability	Organizations with substantial downstream customers
Vicarious Liability Protection	Covers claims arising from vendor security failures	Claims alleging responsibility for vendor incidents	Sub-limited in many policies	Inadequate vendor oversight; Failure to enforce security requirements	Organizations with regulatory vendor requirements
Parametric Supply Chain Coverage	Provides fixed payments based on defined trigger events	Objective triggers (e.g., named vendor outage exceeding 12 hours)	Fixed payment amounts based on trigger events	Events not meeting precise trigger definitions; Partial disruptions	Organizations requiring rapid liquidity after incidents
System Failure Coverage	Covers technical failures without security breach	System failures causing business interruption	Sub-limited in most policies	Gradual deterioration; Regular maintenance; Design defects	Technology-dependent operations

continued on following page

Table 3. Continued

Coverage Type	Description	Triggers	Typical Limits	Key Exclusions	Best Application
Media Liability Extension	Covers content-related liabilities	Claims regarding content distributed through supply chain	Varies widely between insurers	Intentional publication; IP infringement; Known inaccuracies	Content distribution networks
Cyber Physical Damage	Covers physical damage from cyber incidents	Physical damage resulting from cyber attacks	Typically sub-limited	Wear and tear; Gradual damage; Design defects	Manufacturing and critical infrastructure

Figure 3. Insurance policy design process for vendor ecosystems

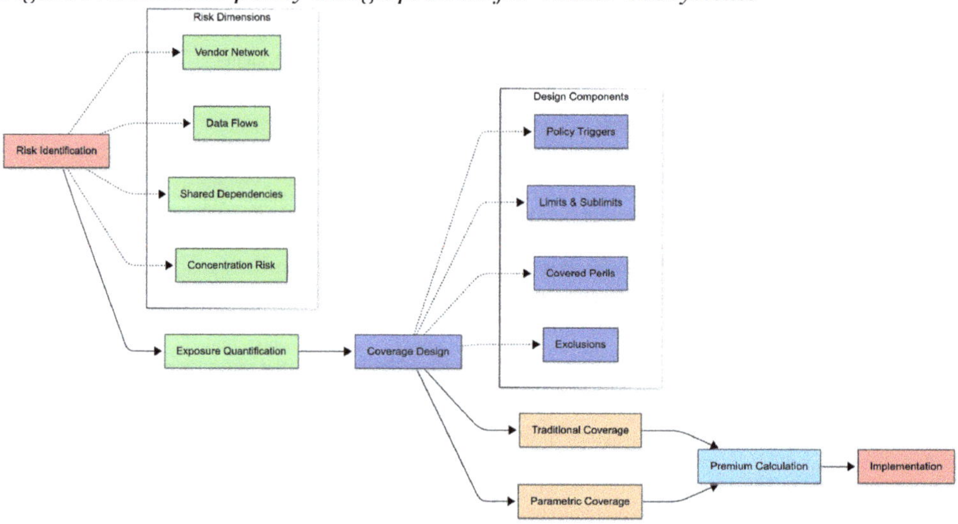

7. RISK TRANSFER MECHANISMS

7.1 Insurance vs. Other Transfer Instruments

Organizations employ multiple mechanisms to transfer supply chain cyber risks. Research by Romanosky et al. (2019) compared effectiveness across transfer instruments, finding complementary strengths and limitations. Their study evaluated transfer mechanisms against specific risk scenarios, establishing applicability patterns for different ecosystem characteristics.

Traditional insurance provides primary financial protection but faces challenges with supply chain risks. Studies by Gordon et al. (2022) identified limitations including:

1. Exclusions targeting third-party dependencies
2. Coverage triggers requiring direct causation
3. Claims complexity for cascading incidents
4. Limited capacity for systemic events

Alternative transfer mechanisms address specific limitations of traditional insurance. Contractual risk transfer through vendor agreements provides direct recourse against suppliers but depends on vendor financial viability and jurisdictional factors. Research by Fleming et al. (2023) found that 73% of organizations incorporated security requirements in contracts, but only 28% included financially meaningful liability provisions.

Financial instruments beyond insurance include:

- Letters of credit securing vendor performance
- Performance bonds guaranteeing security obligations
- Risk retention groups sharing vendor-related exposures
- Self-insurance through dedicated reserves

Each mechanism addresses specific aspects of supply chain risk transfer. Effective programs typically combine multiple approaches to create comprehensive protection.

7.2 Captive Insurance Structures

Captive insurance provides alternative risk transfer for organizations facing market limitations. Research by Friedberg and Skopik (2018) found increasing adoption of captives for cyber risks, with 32% of Fortune 500 companies using captives for at least partial cyber coverage by 2021.

Captives offer advantages for supply chain risks including:

1. **Coverage Customization**: Designing protection specific to ecosystem risks
2. **Data Collection**: Gathering detailed information across relationship networks
3. **Premium Stability**: Reducing volatility through long-term risk retention
4. **Risk Pool Formation**: Creating shared protection across supply chain participants

Studies by Eling and Schnell (2022) found that captives achieved 34% better alignment between premiums and actual loss experience compared to commercial insurance for cyber risks. This efficiency derives from reduced information asymmetry and administrative costs.

Implementation models include:

- Single-parent captives for organizations with sufficient scale
- Group captives shared across industry participants
- Association captives serving specific industry segments
- Rent-a-captive structures for organizations seeking partial benefits

Research increasingly focuses on supply chain captives that include both organizations and critical vendors. These structures create shared incentives for security investments while distributing costs proportionally to risk contributions.

7.3 Parametric Insurance Solutions

Cyber insurance is a multi-faceted exposure and one of the aspects is the concept called supply chain incidents. Conventional indemnity coverage necessitates evidence of causation and exact measurement of the losses, which is especially cumbersome in the case of supply chains. Parametric insurance, in its turn, is rooted in objective triggers, which are related to pre-defined payouts and make the claims process easier. Such designs in relation to cyber incidents were discussed by Eling and Schnell (2022), who pointed at the format to be more beneficial in the instance of supply chains. The authors have singled out four categories of triggers:

1. Service Provider Outage Duration: Compensations activated by durations of outage in specified providers.
2. Security Event Declarations: Event triggers over confirmed incidences on predetermined vendors.
3. Aggregate Impact Indices: Industry-wide measures of the severity of a cyber event.
4. Technical Indicators: Disruption or availability at the network level.

Since such triggers do not depend on issues of causation or quantum, they are able to allow fast payments after an event of supply chain disruption.

However, the application of parametric policies comes with the problem of basis risk which is the difference between real losses and parametric payments. As Liu and Johnson (2023) found out, effective coordination of the indicators can correlate with the business-specific metrics, and the correlation coefficient can vary between 0.65

and 0.82. In their study, they come up with a few design principles that minimize basis risk without sacrificing the benefit of objectivity and simplicity:

- The multi-factor triggers that entail the conglomeration of various indicators
- Fixed payment systems based on level of severity
- Triggers that are customized according to the characteristics of dependency
- Independent third party technical verification

Overall, these tenets help to minimize basis risk without diluting the pace, impartiality, and transparency that characterize parametric cyber insurance.

Table 4. Risk transfer instrument comparison matrix

Risk Transfer Mechanism	Financial Protection	Implementation Complexity	Coverage Customization	Claim Process Efficiency	Cost Efficiency	Market Availability	Regulatory Considerations
Traditional Cyber Insurance	High for first-party risks; Limited for supply chain	Moderate	Limited - standardized policies with endorsements	Moderate - complex for supply chain events	Moderate - rising premiums	High - numerous carriers	Limited - standard insurance regulations
Supply Chain Coverage Endorsements	Moderate - subject to sublimits	Moderate	Moderate - some customization within carrier guidelines	Low - complex causation determination	Moderate - premium surcharges	Moderate - limited market	Limited - standard insurance regulations
Parametric Cyber Insurance	Moderate - fixed payments may not match actual loss	High - requires trigger design	High - custom triggers possible	High - objective trigger verification	Moderate - higher premiums offset by simplified claims	Low - emerging market	Moderate - regulatory classification questions
Captive Insurance	High - fully customizable	Very High - requires substantial setup	Very High - fully customizable	Moderate - internal process design	High for large organizations; Low for small	Limited - requires scale	High - domicile selection, capital requirements
Risk Retention Groups	Moderate - shared capacity	High - requires group formation	High - designed by members	Moderate - group governed	High - shared administrative costs	Low - industry-specific	High - state regulations vary
Contractual Risk Transfer	Limited - depends on vendor resources	Low - standard contract provisions	High - negotiable terms	Low - often involves litigation	High - included in vendor costs	High - standard approach	Moderate - enforceability varies by jurisdiction
Vendor Performance Bonds	Moderate - limited to specific obligations	Moderate - specialized instrument	Moderate - tailored to specific performance	Moderate - formal claim process	Moderate - bond premium costs	Low - limited market	Low - standard financial instrument
Letters of Credit	Limited - specific financial guarantees	Low - standard banking instrument	Low - standardized instrument	High - direct drawing mechanism	High - minimal costs for creditworthy parties	High - standard banking service	Low - standard banking regulations
Self-Insurance/ Reserves	Limited by allocated capital	Low - internal process	Very High - fully customizable	Very High - internal decision	High - no risk transfer costs	High - always available	Moderate - may affect financial reporting
Supply Chain Captives	High - tailored to ecosystem risks	Very High - requires multi-party agreement	Very High - designed for specific ecosystem	High - aligned incentives	High - shared infrastructure costs	Very Low - emerging concept	Very High - cross-jurisdictional complexities

8. PRACTICAL IMPLEMENTATION CHALLENGES

8.1 Information Asymmetry Issues

Information asymmetry creates fundamental challenges for insurance markets. Research by Woods and Böhme (2021) demonstrated that information imbalances between insurers, insureds, and vendors inhibit efficient coverage design. Their work identified specific asymmetry problems in supply chain contexts:

1. **Insurers lack visibility** into vendor security practices and fourth-party connections
2. **Organizations possess incomplete information** about vendor security implementations
3. **Vendors maintain informational advantages** regarding their actual security posture
4. **All parties face uncertainty** about attacker capabilities and emerging threats

These asymmetries create adverse selection problems where higher-risk entities obtain coverage while lower-risk entities find premiums unattractive. Insurance markets respond through coverage restrictions and broad exclusions that limit effectiveness.

Research proposes mechanisms to address information barriers. Standardized assessment frameworks create common languages for security evaluation. Independent verification services provide objective validation. Continuous monitoring tools deliver current information about changing risk profiles.

Liu and Johnson (2023) found that organizations implementing these mechanisms reduced adverse selection problems by 37% compared to traditional approaches. Their research demonstrated correlation between information sharing practices and coverage availability, with organizations engaging in transparent information exchange receiving 42% broader coverage terms.

Implementation approaches include:

- Consortium models for shared vendor assessments
- Third-party certification programs
- Technical validation services
- Integrated monitoring platforms

These mechanisms create information equilibrium between parties, enabling more efficient coverage design for supply chain risks.

8.2 Aggregation Risk Management

Aggregation risk presents critical challenges for supply chain coverage. Traditional insurance relies on risk independence, where incidents affect limited numbers of policyholders simultaneously. Supply chain interconnections create correlated risk profiles that challenge this fundamental assumption.

Research by Khan and Estay (2022) documented concentration risk within digital supply chains, finding that 67% of Fortune 500 companies share critical dependencies on five major cloud providers. This concentration creates systemic risk that exceeds traditional insurance capacity.

Studies by Gordon et al. (2022) found that insurers increasingly implement aggregation management strategies including:

1. **Vendor-Based Sublimits**: Restricting coverage for specific service providers
2. **Aggregation Exclusions**: Limiting coverage for widespread events
3. **Systemic Risk Exclusions**: Carving out major platform failures
4. **Reinsurance Restructuring**: Transferring concentrated exposures

These approaches protect insurer solvency but create coverage gaps for insureds, particularly for systemic events that typically represent highest-impact scenarios.

Alternative approaches include:

- Parametric structures for systemic events
- Risk pools that distribute concentrated exposures
- Government backstops for catastrophic scenarios
- Capital market instruments that distribute peak risks

Research by Romanosky et al. (2019) found that combined public-private approaches created most effective structures for managing aggregation risk while maintaining meaningful coverage for insureds.

8.3 Claims Process Complexities

Claims processes for supply chain incidents face distinct challenges compared to traditional first-party claims. Attribution difficulties, cascading impacts, and loss quantification complexities create friction in claims settlement. Research by Franke (2023) analyzed 265 cyber claims, finding that third-party originated incidents experienced:

1. 64% longer claim resolution timeframes

2. 37% higher claim denial rates
3. 58% more frequent coverage disputes
4. 73% higher legal expenses during resolution

These findings demonstrate practical implementation challenges for supply chain coverage.

Research identifies specific claim complexities including:

- **Attribution Challenges**: Identifying origins within connected systems
- **Evidence Preservation Issues**: Accessing data across organizational boundaries
- **Multiple-Party Coordination**: Aligning incident response across entities
- **Cascading Impact Quantification**: Measuring propagating effects

Emerging practices address these challenges through:

- Pre-incident coordination protocols
- Joint investigation agreements
- Shared forensic service providers
- Standardized business impact measurement

Studies by Woods and Simpson (2022) found that organizations with formalized incident coordination procedures across supply chains resolved claims 47% faster and achieved 36% higher claim approval rates compared to those without established protocols.

Table 5. Implementation challenges and potential solutions

Challenge Category	Specific Challenges	Impact on Risk Transfer	Potential Solutions	Implementation Considerations	Reference
Information Asymmetry	Limited visibility into vendor security practices	Adverse selection; Coverage restrictions; Premium inefficiencies	Standardized assessment frameworks; Independent verification services; Shared assessment repositories	Requires industry collaboration; Data privacy considerations; Resource investment	Woods & Böhme (2021)
Information Asymmetry	Incomplete fourth-party visibility	Coverage gaps for unknown dependencies; Exclusions for undisclosed vendors	Supply chain mapping tools; Dependency analysis requirements; Vendor attestation frameworks	Technical implementation challenges; Continuous updates required; Scalability issues	Müller et al. (2023)
Information Asymmetry	Rapidly changing risk profiles	Static assessments quickly outdated; Premium adjustments lag risk changes	Continuous monitoring services; Dynamic rating models; Real-time data integration	Technical integration complexities; Signal interpretation challenges; Alert management	Franke (2023)
Aggregation Risk	Concentration in critical service providers	Systemic risk exceeding market capacity; Coverage restrictions for major providers	Diversification requirements; Sublimits for concentrated providers; Alternative risk transfer instruments	Operational impacts of diversification; Limited provider options; Cost implications	Khan & Estay (2022)
Aggregation Risk	Correlated failure modes across vendors	Simultaneous claims exceeding capacity; Coverage restrictions for widespread events	Scenario-based limits; Industry catastrophe models; Government backstop programs	Regulatory approval requirements; Actuarial modeling limitations; Political feasibility	Gordon et al. (2022)
Aggregation Risk	Limited reinsurance capacity	Market hardening during periods of loss; Coverage availability constraints	Capital market instruments; Risk pools; Multi-year capacity commitments	Investor education requirements; Structural complexity; Implementation timeframes	Romanosky et al. (2019)

continued on following page

Table 5. Continued

Challenge Category	Specific Challenges	Impact on Risk Transfer	Potential Solutions	Implementation Considerations	Reference
Claims Process	Attribution challenges for incidents	Claim disputes; Extended resolution timeframes; Increased litigation	Forensic readiness planning; Pre-established investigation protocols; Coordinated incident response	Multi-party agreement requirements; Legal complexities; Resource allocation	Franke (2023)
Claims Process	Business impact quantification	Disagreements over loss valuation; Evidence challenges	Standardized impact measurement; Pre-incident business modeling; Documented dependencies	Historical data limitations; Business model variations; Scenario complexity	Woods & Simpson (2022)
Claims Process	Multiple policy coordination	Coverage gaps between policies; Overlapping coverage disputes	Coordinated policy wording; Primary/excess coordination; Claims cooperation provisions	Carrier willingness to coordinate; Legal review requirements; Renewal alignment	Liu & Johnson (2023)
Regulatory Compliance	Cross-jurisdictional requirements	Conflicting obligations; Coverage validity questions	Regulatory mapping; Compliance attestation requirements; Aligned disclosure practices	Jurisdictional expertise requirements; Evolving regulatory landscape; Interpretation challenges	Züst et al. (2022)
Regulatory Compliance	Evolving disclosure mandates	Coverage uncertainty for new requirements; Regulatory coverage gaps	Affirmative regulatory coverage; Compliance assistance services; Regulatory monitoring	Coverage scope limitations; Premium implications; Carrier expertise	Fleming et al. (2023)
Economic Viability	Premium affordability	Limited adoption; Insufficient protection; Self-insurance defaults	Risk-based pricing models; Premium incentives for controls; Multi-year rate commitments	Actuarial data limitations; Market competition factors; Risk differentiation	Eling & Schnell (2022)

Figure 4. Challenge mitigation framework

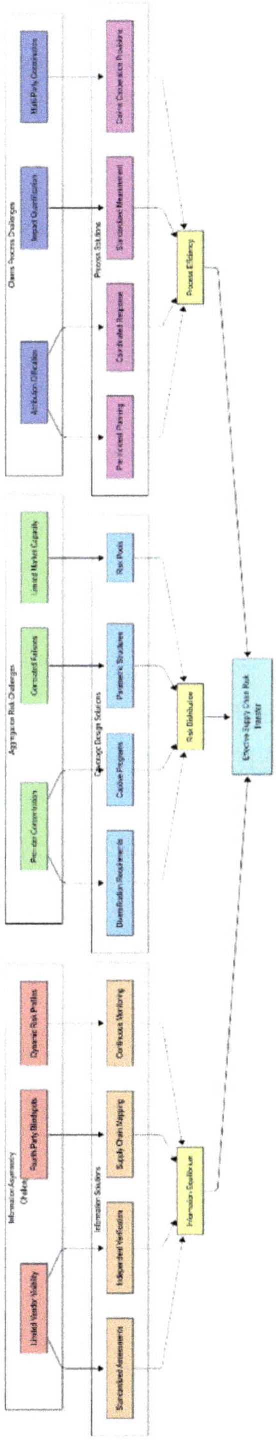

REFERENCES

Böhme, R., & Schwartz, G. (2010). Modeling cyber-insurance: Towards a unifying framework. Workshop on the Economics of Information Security (WEIS). Retrieved from https://www.econinfosec.org/archive/weis2010/papers/session5/weis2010_boehme.pdf

Bolot, J., & Lelarge, M. (2009). Cyber insurance as an incentive for internet security. In Johnson, M. E. (Ed.), *Managing information risk and the economics of security* (pp. 269–290). Springer., DOI: 10.1007/978-0-387-09762-6_13

Christopher, M., & Peck, H. (2004). Building the resilient supply chain. *International Journal of Logistics Management, 15*(2), 1–14. DOI: 10.1108/09574090410700275

CISA. (2021). Remediating networks affected by the SolarWinds and Active Directory/M365 compromise. Cybersecurity and Infrastructure Security Agency. Retrieved from https://www.cisa.gov/sites/default/files/publications/Remediating-Networks-Affected-by-the-SolarWinds-and-Active-Directory-M365-Compromise.pdf

Dionne, G. (2013). Risk management: History, definition, and critique. *Risk Management & Insurance Review, 16*(2), 147–166. DOI: 10.1111/rmir.12016

Fleming, P., Edwards, S. G., Bayliss, A. P., & Seger, C. R. Vendor risk management practices: Analysis of contractual risk allocation in digital supply chains. *Journal of Cybersecurity, 9*(1), 1–18. DOI: 10.1093/cybsec/tyad005

Franke, U. (2023). Cyber insurance claims analysis: Third-party origins and coverage gaps. *Journal of Cybersecurity, 9*(1), 1–16. DOI: 10.1093/cybsec/tyad006

Friedberg, I., & Skopik, F. (2018). Measuring the impact of vendor security on cyber risk exposure. *IEEE Security and Privacy, 16*(5), 54–63. DOI: 10.1109/MSP.2018.3761723

Gordon, L. A., Loeb, M. P., & Zhou, L. (2022). Cyber insurance market trends: Evidence from policy data 2015-2021. *Journal of Cybersecurity, 8*(1), 1–15. DOI: 10.1093/cybsec/tyac003

Gordon, S., Ford, R., & Mathieson, K. (2023). The expanding attack surface: Digital supply chain risk in interconnected economies. *Journal of Information Security and Applications, 72*, 103419. DOI: 10.1016/j.jisa.2023.103419

Huang, K., & Madnick, S. (2021). Systematically understanding supply chain cyber attack patterns. *IEEE Security and Privacy, 19*(1), 66–75. DOI: 10.1109/MSEC.2020.3018177

Johnson, B., Laszka, A., & Grossklags, J. (2020). The complexity of estimating systemic risk in networks. In 2020 IEEE 31st International Conference on Software Engineering (pp. 89-100). IEEE. https://doi.org/DOI: 10.1109/ICSE-COMPANION.2020.00045

Khan, R., & Estay, D. A. S. (2022). Concentration risk in cloud service provision: Implications for cyber security. *Journal of Network and Systems Management*, *30*(1), 1–25. DOI: 10.1007/s10922-021-09642-4

Lawrence, W., Tarr, J.-A., Brook, N., Chaperon, M., & Sorel, A. (2023). Parametric insurance. In A. A. Tarr, J.-A. Tarr, M. Thompson, & D. Wilkinson (Eds.), The global insurance market and change (1st ed., pp. 127–156). Informa Law from Routledge. https://doi.org/10.4324/9781003319054-6

Liu, W., & Johnson, R. (2023). An integrated framework for supply chain cyber risk transfer. *The Geneva Papers on Risk and Insurance. Issues and Practice*, *48*(1), 151–186. DOI: 10.1057/s41288-022-00268-4

Müller, C., Nagaraj, S., & Patterson, B. (2023). Measuring fourth-party risk: Analysis of extended supply chain vulnerabilities. *Information and Computer Security*, *31*(2), 257–276. DOI: 10.1108/ICS-08-2022-0126

Nazir, S., Patel, S., & Patel, D. (2021). Assessing and augmenting SCADA cybersecurity: A survey of techniques. *Computers & Security*, *112*, 102513. DOI: 10.1016/j.cose.2021.102513

Park, K., Tran, H., & Kim, H. K. (2021). Network analysis of cyber security risk propagation in vendor ecosystems. *IEEE Transactions on Information Forensics and Security*, *16*, 3415–3429. DOI: 10.1109/TIFS.2021.3082307

Peltier, T. R. (2013). *Information security fundamentals*. CRC Press., DOI: 10.1201/b15573

Romanosky, S., Ablon, L., Kuehn, A., & Jones, T. (2019). Content analysis of cyber insurance policies: How do carriers price cyber risk? *Journal of Cybersecurity*, *5*(1), 1–19. DOI: 10.1093/cybsec/tyz002

Tyas Tunggal, A. (2025, July 2). What is the cost of a data breach in 2023? UpGuard. https://www.upguard.com/blog/cost-of-data-breach

Woods, D. W., Agrafiotis, I., & Nurse, J. R. C. (2019). Mapping the coverage of security controls in cyber insurance proposal forms. *Journal of Internet Services and Applications*, *10*(1), 1–20. DOI: 10.1186/s13174-019-0104-0

Woods, D. W., & Böhme, R. (2021). SolarWinds and the challenges of patching: Can backup create new problems? *IEEE Security and Privacy*, *19*(4), 88–92. DOI: 10.1109/MSEC.2021.3070059

Woods, D. W., & Simpson, A. C. (2022). Policy limits, exclusions, and the interpretation of cyber insurance. *Journal of Cybersecurity*, *8*(1), 1–16. DOI: 10.1093/cybsec/tyac004

Zhang, L., & Li, H. (2022). Network approaches to modeling cascading impacts in supply chain cyber incidents. *Computers & Security*, *115*, 102630. DOI: 10.1016/j.cose.2022.102630

Züst, S., Huonder, M., West, S., & Stoll, O. (2022). Life-cycle oriented risk assessment using a Monte Carlo simulation. Applied Sciences, 12(1), 8. https://doi.org/10.3390/app12010008

Chapter 10
The Role of AI in Developing a Corporate Governance Index

Hamza Naim
https://orcid.org/0000-0002-8260-8735
KR Mangalam University, India

Lata Rani
https://orcid.org/0000-0002-8882-2548
Delhi Skill and Entrepreneurship University, India

Indira Bharadwaj
KR Mangalam University, India

Takrar Ahmad Yattoo
KR Mangalam University, India

Mohd Anas
https://orcid.org/0009-0005-1395-940X
KR Mangalam University, India

Mohammed Nizamuddin
KR Mangalam University, India

Gouher Ahmed
https://orcid.org/0000-0001-7686-7581
Skyline University College, UAE

Jitin Kumar Gambhir
KR Mangalam University, India

ABSTRACT

The present study deals in developing a Corporate Governance Index model with the help of Artificial Intelligence (AI) with respect to different regions and markets. As the different markets are accumulated in different regions and the characteristics of the existing markets differ, hence one type of corporate governance measures doesn't fits all. This strategy could be included as an approach in policy customization using Generative AI. As per according to the different characteristics involved in different markets, the AI could segregate these characteristics for different markets and as per the significance of the results, a comprehensive Corporate Governance Index (CGI) could be developed which would further applicable for different markets in various regions. However, qualitative data, emerging technologies and application

DOI: 10.4018/979-8-3373-5545-0.ch010

of policies at the ground level are some of the constraints in developing a Corporate Governance Index with the help of AI.

1.0 INTRODUCTION

Corporate governance measures clearly defines the policies and practices by which the companies operating in respective countries could be directed and controlled. A number of studies have been published earlier in view of developing a corporate governance index for respective countries. For instance, (Akbar et. al., 2016) examines the relationship between corporate governance compliance and the firm performance in UK by developing a corporate governance index using Generalised Methods of Moments (GMM), a more robust technique which controls for potential endogeneity in a sample of 435 non-financially public over the period 1999-2009. Moreover, another study, in addition to developing a corporate governance index also developed a Reporting Quality Index (RQI) for the public firms in Indonesia thus measuring the firms' quality of reporting and disclosures (Siagian et. al., 2013). On a similar note for India, a non-parametric index of corporate governance have been constructed for 40 Indian banks by aggregating six different dimensional sub-indices including board effectiveness, audit function, risk management, remunerations, shareholder rights and information and disclosure as well as transparency (Gulati et. al., 2020).

Moreover, a similar study on the Slovak financial market measured the level of corporate governance by the construction of a first corporate governance index which contained the information about the disclosure of annual reports, corporate governance information in the annual reports, board of companies, remuneration of board members, risk management, audit, remuneration, and nomination committee measures (Musa et. al., 2015). Many studies have reported the construction of a corporate governance index for different countries, but the earlier studies lacks in using Artificial Intelligence (AI) for the development of corporate governance index. Moreover, the role of Generative AI in developing a corporate governance index with the application of corporate governance measures and formulation as well as restructuring of policies could be beneficial for the respective countries in the present as well as in the future.

The present study deals the application of Generative AI such as ChatGPT and many more in the construction of a corporate governance index for different countries. For the application of Generative AI, the researchers have taken India as a sample by which it could be further applicable to different countries with different policies and context. As far as the researchers acknowledge, this is the very first study in using Generative AI for the development of a corporate governance index.

Moreover, further examining of the corporate governance index impact on firm performance could also be achieved with the use of Generative AI which generally suggests that whether the corporate governance developed is beneficial or not for the companies in different countries context. The rest of the chapter follows with the section 2 describing regarding the construction of corporate governance index, section 3 illustrates the application of Generative AI techniques in the development of the corporate governance index and section 4 provides the discussion and conclusion as well as the last section Appendix (A) describes the corporate governance measures.

2.0 CONSTRUCTION OF CORPORATE GOVERNANCE INDEX

A number of similar studies have constructed a corporate governance index examining the firm performance and stating that whether a corporate governance index could be valuable for the specific country. For, instance, in the case of US, Dow Jones (Khanchel, 2007; Tarchouna et. al., 2017; Gompers et. al., 2003; Litov, 2005; Martynova & Renneboog, 2010; Hirst & Kastiel, 2019; Kelton & Yang, 2008; Bebchuk et. al., 2009; Brown & Caylor, 2006; Bhagat & Bolton, 2008; Li et. al., 2013), in the case of Thailand (Hodgson et. al., 2011), for (Gulf Corporation Council) GCC countries (including UAE, Saudi Arabia, Oman, Qatar and Kuwait) (Al-Malkawi et. al., 2014), in Brazil (Black et. al., 2014; Silva & Leal, 2005), for Russia (Black et. al., 2006), for Syria (Mardnly et. al., 2018), for Poland (Kowalewski et. al., 2007), for Japan (Bauer et. al., 2008), for Vietnam (Tu et. al., 2014), for Pakistan (Javaid & Saboor, 2015), for India (Srivastava et. al., 2019; Gulati et. al., 2020; Balasubramanian et. al., 2010) and many more studies have developed a corporate governance index for different countries in different contexts of economy.

In the present study, country India has been chosen as a sample for the construction of corporate governance index based on convenience sampling as the researchers are Indian and are familiar with the corporate governance policies in the Indian context. India being a mixed economy country has different sets of policies for the public and private sector units (Haldar & Rao, 2013). Moreover, in the respect of corporate governance numerous measures have been identified and are provided in section 5 Appendix. The corporate governance index so formed have been divided into sub-indices representing the different dimensions of corporate governance measures. Moreover, the different indices so formed could be examined in having an impact on the firm performance measures. The corporate governance measures have been taken in reference to the earlier studies, policies formed as per the Companies Act, 2013, and different corporate governance committees that have evolved over the years in the country with respect to corporate governance measures adopted subsequently.

3.0 APPLICATION OF GENERATIVE AI TECHNIQUES

As per the earlier studies the Generative AI techniques such as ChatGPT and many more have incorporated numerous applications in the business sector, education, health care and content creation (Nah et. al., 2023). However, with the application of AI there are some challenges that have to be faced based on different perspectives such as ethics, technology, regulations and policies and economy. Moreover, the issues with the application of AI also states that the quantitative data could be very well taken care off while the qualitative data could not be harnessed as appropriately as taken from the primary data studies in the context of the companies. Moreover, with the application of AI, the ethical considerations such as plagiarism detection and conceptual challenges are more profound nowadays (Zohny et. al., 2023). Studies suggest that Large Language Models (LLMs) including ChatGPT, BLOOM and many more raise widespread concerns, as there propensities to return falsehoods and unethical information (Walker & Noorden, 2023). Moreover, with the publication of GPTZero, two major problems of perplexity-a problem of how familiar the text seems to LLM and burstiness-a measure by which the AI generated text tends to be more consistent in tone, cadence and perplexity than done by humans could be resolved further.

In the present study as the corporate governance indices seems to be of multivariate analysis, hence the use AI should also belong to multivariate time variant features. This could be further harnessed with AI unimodal and multimodal analysis with the application of different Generative AI techniques (Brizuela & Merchan, 2023). The study has also acknowledged more than 350 Generative AI techniques which could be further applied in the development of a corporate governance index and its impact on the firm performance. This has also been in view with the earlier studies which states that despite the limitations Generative AI techniques could better resolve the problems of social sciences (Bail, 2024). Moreover, the use of Conversational AI has been applicable nowadays in various services. These services act as chatbots and are capable of a variety of tasks converting text prompts into text outputs. As they are powered by LLMs, these refers to Transformer language models that contain hundreds of billions (or more) of parameters which are further treated on massive text data such as GPT-3, PaLM, Galactica and LLaM (Brizuela & Merchan, 2023). These services offers solution to text generation, common-sense reasoning, spatial reasoning, mathematical reasoning, or programming assistance. Moreover, in the case of business solutions, these applications also provides services for demand forecasting, inventory optimization and risk management.

The present study proposes a unique way of idealizing corporate governance measures using chatbots through which the measures those having a positive significant impact on the firm performance could be framed in developing a corporate governance index. Hence, the first step aims in identifying the corporate governance measures through the Generative AI which could be further verified with the existing corporate governance measures adopted by Securities & Exchange Board of India (SEBI) and Ministry of Corporate Affairs (MCA) in the Indian context. Though, since privatization, liberalization and globalization, 1991, there have been many corporate governance committees, policies have emerged and amendments have taken place, still the road is ahead for development and we can't ignore the role of Generative AI techniques and technological development.

In addition to this there are many multilingual code generation applications through just text-inputs. These are capable of generating code through text prompts. For instance, Alphacode, Amazon Codewhisperer, Blackbox AI, CodeComplete and many more applications are there which are used to complete, explain, transform and generate code. The function of these applications are to generate new lines based on context and syntax (Brizuela & Merchan, 2023). Moreover, there are multimodal language models such as Kosmos-1, Prismer, PALM-E, and GATO which are multitasking applications and could be assigned to a wide range of economically useful tasks as well as are capable of providing assistance to scientific research. Hence, the Generative AI could be used as a tool in developing a corporate governance index for different countries in different contexts as it will help in the policy formulation with its own creativity and policy implications (Epstein et. al., 2023). However, there is a need to regulate the ChatGPT and Large Generative AI models so that these could work for the society in a more profound and beneficial way (Hacker et. al., 2023; Lv, 2023; Saetra, 2023).

4.0 DISCUSSIONS AND CONCLUSIONS

The present study identifies the ways by which the Generative AI could be used in developing a corporate governance index for different countries with different contexts. For this purpose, India has been chosen as a sample in the identification of the corporate governance measures by which the parameters obtained through the Generative AI could be verified and improved further upon. The need of corporate governance index clearly states that there should be some parameters and policies by which the companies operating in a specific country should adhere to and hence could be regulated and controlled in a more profound way. Moreover, with the addition of Generative AI, it could also enhance the process of developing a corporate governance index as the AI reflects its own creativity and intellect.

In the present study the researchers have discussed certain Generative AI techniques with their applications and implications. However, this is the limitation of the present study as to which Generative AI model suits best in constructing a corporate governance index and hence could be obtained through simulation techniques for different countries with different contexts. This is in view of the fact that one size doesn't fits all which clearly states that corporate governance index developed for a particular country may not be applicable for another country (Haldar & Rao, 2013). However, with the advent of technologies such as Generative AI and Large Language Models (LLMs) there is much scope of development in many sectors especially in the development of corporate governance indices. One more application of these technologies could be with respect to different geographical regions as there is market connectedness within different regions and there are volatility spillover effects too.

REFERENCES

Akbar, S., Poletti-Hughes, J., El-Faitouri, R., & Shah, S. Z. A. (2016). More on the relationship between corporate governance and firm performance in the UK: Evidence from the application of generalized method of moments estimation. *Research in International Business and Finance, 38*, 417–429. DOI: 10.1016/j.ribaf.2016.03.009

Al-Malkawi, H. A. N., Pillai, R., & Bhatti, M. I. (2014). Corporate governance practices in emerging markets: The case of GCC countries. *Economic Modelling, 38*, 133–141. DOI: 10.1016/j.econmod.2013.12.019

Bail, C. A. (2024). Can Generative AI improve social science? *Proceedings of the National Academy of Sciences of the United States of America, 121*(21), e2314021121. DOI: 10.1073/pnas.2314021121 PMID: 38722813

Balasubramanian, N., Black, B. S., & Khanna, V. (2010). The relation between firm-level corporate governance and market value: A case study of India. *Emerging Markets Review, 11*(4), 319–340. DOI: 10.1016/j.ememar.2010.05.001

Bauer, R., Frijns, B., Otten, R., & Tourani-Rad, A. (2008). The impact of corporate governance on corporate performance: Evidence from Japan. *Pacific-Basin Finance Journal, 16*(3), 236–251. DOI: 10.1016/j.pacfin.2007.05.001

Bebchuk, L., Cohen, A., & Ferrell, A. (2009). What matters in corporate governance? *Review of Financial Studies, 22*(2), 783–827. DOI: 10.1093/rfs/hhn099

Bebchuk, L., Cohen, A., & Ferrell, A. (2009). What matters in corporate governance? *Review of Financial Studies, 22*(2), 783–827. DOI: 10.1093/rfs/hhn099

Bhagat, S., Bolton, B., & Romano, R. (2008). The promise and peril of corporate governance indices. *Colum. L. Rev., 108*, 1803.

Black, B. S., De Carvalho, A. G., & Sampaio, J. O. (2014). The evolution of corporate governance in Brazil. *Emerging Markets Review, 20*, 176–195. DOI: 10.1016/j.ememar.2014.04.004

Black, B. S., Love, I., & Rachinsky, A. (2006). Corporate governance indices and firms' market values: Time series evidence from Russia. *Emerging Markets Review, 7*(4), 361–379. DOI: 10.1016/j.ememar.2006.09.004

Brown, L. D., & Caylor, M. L. (2006). Corporate governance and firm valuation. *Journal of Accounting and Public Policy, 25*(4), 409–434. DOI: 10.1016/j.jaccpubpol.2006.05.005

da Silva, A. L. C., & Leal, R. P. C. (2005). Corporate governance index, firm valuation and performance in Brazil. *Revista Brasileira de Finanças, 3*(1), 1–18.

Eng, L. L., & Mak, Y. T. (2003). Corporate governance and voluntary disclosure. *Journal of Accounting and Public Policy, 22*(4), 325–345. DOI: 10.1016/S0278-4254(03)00037-1

Epstein, Z., Hertzmann, A., Akten, M., Farid, H., Fjeld, J., Frank, M. R., Groh, M., Herman, L., Leach, N., Mahari, R., Pentland, A. S., Russakovsky, O., Schroeder, H., & Smith, A. (2023). Art and the science of generative AI. *Science, 380*(6650), 1110–1111. DOI: 10.1126/science.adh4451 PMID: 37319193

Fui-Hoon Nah, F., Zheng, R., Cai, J., Siau, K., & Chen, L. (2023). Generative AI and ChatGPT: Applications, challenges, and AI-human collaboration. *Journal of information technology case and application research, 25*(3), 277-304.

Gompers, P., Ishii, J., & Metrick, A. (2003). Corporate governance and equity prices. *The Quarterly Journal of Economics, 118*(1), 107–156. DOI: 10.1162/00335530360535162

Gozalo-Brizuela, R., & Garrido-Merchán, E. C. (2023). A survey of Generative AI Applications. *arXiv preprint arXiv:2306.02781.*

Gulati, R., Kattumuri, R., & Kumar, S. (2020). A non-parametric index of corporate governance in the banking industry: An application to Indian data. *Socio-Economic Planning Sciences, 70*, 100702. DOI: 10.1016/j.seps.2019.03.008

Hacker, P., Engel, A., & Mauer, M. (2023, June). Regulating ChatGPT and other large generative AI models. In *Proceedings of the 2023 ACM conference on fairness, accountability, and transparency* (pp. 1112-1123). DOI: 10.1145/3593013.3594067

Haldar, A., & Rao, S. N. (2013). Corporate Governance Index for Indian Companies. In *Conference Paper.*

Hirst, S., & Kastiel, K. (2019). Corporate governance by index exclusion. *BUL Rev., 99*, 1229.

Hodgson, A., Lhaopadchan, S., & Buakes, S. (2011). How informative is the Thai corporate governance index? A financial approach. *International Journal of Accounting & Information Management, 19*(1), 53–79. DOI: 10.1108/18347641111105935

Javaid, F., & Saboor, A. (2015). Impact of Corporate Governance index on Firm Performance: Evidence from Pakistani manufacturing sector. *Journal of Public Administration and Governance, 5*(2), 1–21. DOI: 10.5296/jpag.v5i2.7498

Kelton, A. S., & Yang, Y. W. (2008). The impact of corporate governance on Internet financial reporting. *Journal of Accounting and Public Policy*, *27*(1), 62–87. DOI: 10.1016/j.jaccpubpol.2007.11.001

Khanchel, I. (2007). Corporate governance: Measurement and determinant analysis. *Managerial Auditing Journal*, *22*(8), 740–760. DOI: 10.1108/02686900710819625

Kowalewski, O., Stetsyuk, I., & Talavera, O. (2007). Corporate governance and dividend policy in Poland.

La Porta, R., Lopez-de-Silanes, F., Shleifer, A., & Vishny, R. (2000). Investor protection and corporate governance. *Journal of Financial Economics*, *58*(1-2), 3–27. DOI: 10.1016/S0304-405X(00)00065-9

Leal, R. P., & Carvalhal-da-Silva, A. L. (2007). Corporate governance and value in Brazil (and in Chile). *Investor protection and corporate governance: Firm-level evidence across. Latinskaia Amerika = América Latina*, •••, 213–287.

Li, H., Jahera, J. S.Jr, & Yost, K. (2013). Corporate risk and corporate governance: Another view. *Managerial Finance*, *39*(3), 204–227. DOI: 10.1108/03074351311302773

Litov, L. P. (2005). Corporate governance and financing policy: New evidence. *Unpublished working paper*.

Lv, Z. (2023). Generative artificial intelligence in the metaverse era. *Cognitive Robotics*, *3*, 208–217. DOI: 10.1016/j.cogr.2023.06.001

Mardnly, Z., Mouselli, S., & Abdulraouf, R. (2018). Corporate governance and firm performance: An empirical evidence from Syria. *International Journal of Islamic and Middle Eastern Finance and Management*, *11*(4), 591–607. DOI: 10.1108/IMEFM-05-2017-0107

Martynova, M., & Renneboog, L. D. R. (2010). A corporate governance index: convergence and diversity of national corporate governance regulations.

Mohanty, P. (2003). Institutional investors and corporate governance in India. *National Stock Exchange of India Research Initiative Paper*, (15).

Musa, H., Musová, Z., & Debnárová, L. (2015). Responsibility in the corporate governance framework and financial decision making process. *Procedia Economics and Finance*, *23*, 1023–1029. DOI: 10.1016/S2212-5671(15)00371-8

Sætra, H. S. (2023). Generative AI: Here to stay, but for good? *Technology in Society*, *75*, 102372. DOI: 10.1016/j.techsoc.2023.102372

Sarkar, J., Sarkar, S., & Sen, K. (2012). A corporate governance index for large listed companies in India. *Pace University Accounting Research Paper*, (2012/08).

Siagian, F., Siregar, S. V., & Rahadian, Y. (2013). Corporate governance, reporting quality, and firm value: Evidence from Indonesia. *Journal of Accounting in Emerging Economies*, *3*(1), 4–20. DOI: 10.1108/20440831311287673

Srivastava, V., Das, N., & Pattanayak, J. K. (2019). Impact of corporate governance attributes on cost of equity: Evidence from an emerging economy. *Managerial Auditing Journal*, *34*(2), 142–161. DOI: 10.1108/MAJ-01-2018-1770

Stokel-Walker, C., & Van Noorden, R. (2023). What ChatGPT and generative AI mean for science. *Nature*, *614*(7947), 214–216. DOI: 10.1038/d41586-023-00340-6 PMID: 36747115

Tarchouna, A., Jarraya, B., & Bouri, A. (2017). How to explain non-performing loans by many corporate governance variables simultaneously? A corporate governance index is built to US commercial banks. *Research in International Business and Finance*, *42*, 645–657. DOI: 10.1016/j.ribaf.2017.07.008

Tu, T. T. T., Khanh, P. B., & Quyen, P. D. (2014). Developing corporate governance index for Vietnamese banking system. *International Journal of Financial Research*, *5*(2), 175–188.

Zohny, H., McMillan, J., & King, M. (2023). Ethics of generative AI. *Journal of Medical Ethics*, *49*(2), 79–80. DOI: 10.1136/jme-2023-108909 PMID: 36693706

APPENDIX (A)

A-1: Corporate Governance Variables Adopted in India and Worldwide Clubbed Together in Different Sub-Indices

1. Board of directors:
   a. Presence of non-executive or promoter chairman (Haldar & Rao, 2013).
   b. Percentage of independent directors (Haldar & Rao, 2013).
   c. Total no. of directorships held by directors (Haldar & Rao, 2013).
   d. Total number of committee membership held by directors (Haldar & Rao, 2013).
   e. CEO duality (Haldar & Rao, 2013).
   f. Tenure of independent director (Haldar & Rao, 2013).
   g. Percentage of directors who attend Annual General Meetings (AGM) (Haldar & Rao, 2013).
   h. Board composition (type of director): Inside, Non-executive, Independent, Separate CEO and chairman (for firms in range for independent directors) (Balasubramanian et al., 2010).
   i. Non-executive director has staggered terms (Balasubramanian et al., 2010).
   j. Executive directors have multiyear term (Balasubramanian et al., 2010).
   k. Regular system for evaluating CEO (Balasubramanian et al., 2010).
   l. Regular system for evaluating other executives (Balasubramanian et al., 2010).
   m. Succession plan for CEO (Balasubramanian et al., 2010).
   n. Annual separate meeting for non-executive directors (Balasubramanian et al., 2010).
   o. Board replaced CEO in 5 years (Balasubramanian et al., 2010).
   p. Regular system for evaluating non-executive directors (recommended) (Balasubramanian et al., 2010).
   q. Retirement age for non-executive directors (Balasubramanian et al., 2010).
   r. Director not renominated or resigned due to performance or policy dispute during last 5 years (Balasubramanian et. al., 2010).
   s. Board size (Sarkar et al., 2012).
   t. Percentage of outside directors (Sarkar et al., 2012).
   u. Presence of nominee directors (Sarkar et al., 2012).
   v. Presence of promoter on board (Sarkar et al., 2012).
   w. Classified Board (Gompers et al., 2003).
   x. Providing valuable and timely information to shareholders (Mohanty, 2003).
   y. Exceeding projections made at the time of issue of shares (Mohanty, 2003).

z. Asymmetric treatment of shareholders (Mohanty, 2003).
aa. Consistent difference between cash flow to equity and dividends (Mohanty, 2003).
bb. Quality of shareholder earnings (Mohanty, 2003).
cc. Investor grievances (Mohanty, 2003).
dd. Credit rating of bondholders (Mohanty, 2003).
ee. Transfer of wealth form bondholders to shareholders (Mohanty, 2003).
ff. Bondholder grievances (Mohanty, 2003).
gg. Default in payment of interest and repayment of capital (Mohanty, 2003).
hh. Total number of points awarded for voluntary disclosure of strategic, non-financial and financial information independent variables (Eng & Mak, 2003).
ii. The proportion of ordinary shares held by CEO and executive directors and shares in which they are deemed to have interest (Eng & Mak, 2003).
jj. The proportion of ordinary shares owned by substantial shareholders (with equity of 5% or more) (Eng & Mak, 2003).
kk. Managers respond to shareholders proposals within 12 months of shareholder meetings (Brown & Caylor, 2006).
ll. CEO serves on no more than two additional boards of other public sector companies (Brown & Caylor, 2006).
mm. All directors attended at least 75% of board meetings or have a valid excuse for non-attendance (Brown & Caylor, 2006).
nn. Size of board of directors is at least 6 but not more than 15 members (Brown & Caylor, 2006).
oo. No former CEO serves on board (Brown & Caylor, 2006).
pp. CEO is not listed as having a "related party transaction" in proxy statement (Brown & Caylor, 2006).
qq. Board is controlled by more than 50% independent outside directors (Brown & Caylor, 2006).
rr. Compensation committee is comprised solely of independent outside directors (Brown & Caylor, 2006).
ss. The CEO and chairman duties are separated or a lead director is specified (Brown & Caylor, 2006).
tt. Shareholders vote on directors selected to fill vacancies (Brown & Caylor, 2006).
uu. Board members are elected annually (no staggered board) (Brown & Caylor, 2006).
vv. Shareholder approval is required to change board size (Brown & Caylor, 2006).

ww. Nominating committee is comprised solely of independent outside directors (Brown & Caylor, 2006).
xx. Governance committee meets at least once during the year (Brown & Caylor, 2006).
yy. Shareholders have cumulative voting rights to elect directors (Brown & Caylor, 2006).
zz. Board guidelines are in each proxy statement (Brown & Caylor, 2006).
aaa. Policy exists requiring outside directors on no more than five additional boards (Brown & Caylor, 2006).

2. Board practices and processes:
   a. Board meeting frequency (Haldar & Rao, 2013).
   b. Percentage of board meetings attended by the directors (Haldar & Rao, 2013).
   c. Gap between board meetings (Haldar & Rao, 2013).
   d. Minimum of four physical meetings (Balasubramanian et al., 2010).
   e. Number of physical meetings (Balasubramanian et al., 2010).
   f. Minutes prepared (Balasubramanian et al., 2010).
   g. Dissents recorded in minutes (Balasubramanian et al., 2010).
   h. Code of conduct (Balasubramanian et al., 2010).
   i. Policy restricting insider trading (Balasubramanian et al., 2010).
   j. Board members typically receive materials at least (Balasubramanian et al., 2010).
   k. One day in advance of meeting (Balasubramanian et al., 2010).
   l. Regular director training (recommended) (Balasubramanian et al., 2010).
   m. Percentage of board meetings attended by independent directors (Sarkar et al., 2012).
   n. Employee turnover (Mohanty, 2003).
   o. Issue of ESOPs to employees (Mohanty, 2003).
   p. Strikes and lock outs (Mohanty, 2003).
   q. Limits to amend by laws (Bebchuk et al., 2009).
   r. Limits to amend charter (Bebchuk et al., 2009).
   s. Supermajority (Bebchuk et al., 2009).
   t. Golden parachutes (Bebchuk et al., 2009).
   u. Poison pills (Bebchuk et al., 2009).
   v. Country allows shareholders to mail their proxy vote to the firm (La Porta et al., 2000).
   w. Shareholders are not required to deposit their shares prior to the General Shareholder's Meeting (La Porta et al., 2000).

x. Cumulative voting or proportional representation of minorities in the board of directors is allowed (La Porta et al., 2000).
y. An oppressed minority mechanism is in place (La Porta et al., 2000).
z. The minimum percentage of share capital that entitles a shareholder to call for an extraordinary shareholder meeting is less than or equal to 10% (sample median) (La Porta et al., 2000).
aa. Shareholders have pre-emptive rights that can only be waived by a shareholder's vote (La Porta et al., 2000).
bb. Country imposes restrictions such as creditor's consent or minimum dividends to file for organizations (La Porta et al., 2000).
cc. Secured creditors are able to gain possession of their security once the reorganization petition has approved (no automatic stay) (La Porta et al., 2000).
dd. Secured creditors are ranked first in the distribution of the proceeds that result from the disposition of the assets of a bankrupt firm (La Porta et al., 2000).
ee. Debtor does not retain the administration of its property pending the resolution of its organization (La Porta et al., 2000).
ff. Are the chairman of the board and the CEO not the same person (Leal et al., 2007)?
gg. Is the board clearly not made up of corporate insiders and controlling shareholders (Leal et al., 2007)?
hh. Do members serve continuous one year term (Leal et al., 2007)?
ii. Is there a permanent fiscal board (Leal et al., 2007)?

3. Audit Committee:
    a. Qualified auditor report (Haldar & Rao, 2013).
    b. Percentage of independent directors (Haldar & Rao, 2013).
    c. Audit committee chaired by independent director (Haldar & Rao, 2013).
    d. Presence of the chairman in the AGM (Haldar & Rao, 2013).
    e. No. of audit committee meetings (Haldar & Rao, 2013).
    f. Quorum at the audit committee meeting (Haldar & Rao, 2013).
    g. Size of audit committee (Sarkar et al., 2012).
    h. No. of meetings held (Sarkar et al., 2012).
    i. Percentage of non-audit fees to total payment to auditors (Sarkar et al., 2012).
    j. Top auditor in terms of audit fees (Sarkar et al., 2012).
    k. Top auditor in terms of audit clients (Sarkar et al., 2012).
    l. Change in auditor from last year (Sarkar et al., 2012).

m. Audit committee consists solely of independent outside directors (Brown & Caylor, 2006).
n. Auditors were ratified at the most recent annual meeting (Brown & Caylor, 2006).
o. Consulting fees paid to auditors are less than audit fees paid to auditors (Brown & Caylor, 2006).
p. Company has a formal policy on auditor rotation (Brown & Caylor, 2006).
q. Shareholders can vote by postal ballot (Balasubramanian et al., 2010).
r. Percent of shares voted at most recent AGM (Balasubramanian et al., 2010).
s. Company had shareholder resolution in last 5 years (Balasubramanian et al., 2010).
t. Disputes with shareholder resolved by arbitration (Balasubramanian et al., 2010).
u. Shareholders requested extraordinary meetings in last 5 years (Balasubramanian et al., 2010).
v. Shareholders asked SEBI or Tribunal to investigate oppression within last 5 years (Balasubramanian et al., 2010).

4. Shareholder grievance committee:
   a. Number of investor grievance received and redressed (Haldar & Rao, 2013).
   b. Number of investor grievance committee meetings held and attended (Haldar & Rao, 2013).
   c. Independence of members (Haldar & Rao, 2013).
5. Nomination and Remuneration committee:
   a. Presence of Committee (Haldar & Rao, 2013).
   b. Percentage of independent directors (Haldar & Rao, 2013).
   c. Remuneration Commensurate with Government Policies (Haldar & Rao, 2013).
   d. Committee chaired by Independent Director (Haldar & Rao, 2013).
   e. Presence of the Chairman in the AGM (Haldar & Rao, 2013).
   f. Quorum at the Remuneration Committee Meeting (Haldar & Rao, 2013).
   g. Compensation (Balasubramanian et al., 2010).
      1. CEO cash compensation
      2. Compensation of all other executives
      3. Executives receive stock option
   h. Disclosure and shareholder approval (Balasubramanian et al., 2010).
   i. CEO total pay (Brown & Caylor, 2006).
   j. Total pay of non-executive directors (Brown & Caylor, 2006).
   k. Total pay of all directors (Brown & Caylor, 2006).
   l. No interlocks exist among directors on the compensation committee (Brown & Caylor, 2006).

m. Non-employees do not participate in company pension plans (Brown & Caylor, 2006).
n. Option re-pricing did not occur within last three years (Brown & Caylor, 2006).
o. Stock incentive plans were adopted with shareholder approval (Brown & Caylor, 2006).
p. Directors receive all or a portion of their fees in stock (Brown & Caylor, 2006).
q. Company does not provide any loans to executives for exercising options (Brown & Caylor, 2006).
r. The last time shareholders voted on a pay plan; ISS did not deem its cost to be excessive (Brown & Caylor, 2006).
s. The average options granted in the past three years as a percentage of basic shares outstanding did not exceed 3% (option burn rate is not excessive) (Brown & Caylor, 2006).
t. Option re-pricing is prohibited (Brown & Caylor, 2006).
u. Company expenses stock options (Brown & Caylor, 2006).

6. Ownership and control structure:
   a. Percentage of promoter ownership (Sarkar et al., 2012).
   b. Percentage of foreign institutional ownership (Sarkar et al., 2012).
   c. Percentage of domestic financial institution ownership (Sarkar et al., 2012).
   d. Percentage of dispersed ownership (Sarkar et al., 2012).
   e. The proportion of ordinary shares held by CEO and executive directors and shares in which they are deemed to have interest (Eng & Mak, 2003).
   f. The proportion of ordinary shares owned by substantial shareholders (with equity of 5% or more) (Eng & Mak, 2003).
   g. Existence of government ownership, coded as 1 if a company is government-linked (where government is a significant shareholder with 20% ownership or more) and 0 if company is not government-linked (Eng & Mak, 2003).
   h. The proportion of ordinary shares owned by the government (Eng & Mak, 2003).
   i. Do controlling shareholders own less than 50% of the voting shares? (Leal et al., 2007)
   j. Is the percentage of voting shares in total capital more than 80%? (Leal et al., 2007)?
   k. Is the controlling shareholders' ratio of cash-flow rights to voting rights greater or equal to 1? (Leal et al., 2007).
   l. All directors with more than one year of service own stock (Brown & Caylor, 2006).

m. Officers' and directors' stock ownership is at least 1% but not over 30% of total shares outstanding (Brown & Caylor, 2006).
n. Executives are subject to stock ownership guidelines (Brown & Caylor, 2006).
o. Directors are subject to stock ownership guidelines (Brown & Caylor, 2006).

7. Related party transaction:
   a. No specific requirement (Balasubramanian et al., 2010).
   b. Approval by Audit committee (Balasubramanian et al., 2010).
   c. Approval by board of directors (Balasubramanian et al., 2010).
   d. Approval by shareholders (Balasubramanian et al., 2010).
   e. Approval by non-conflicted directors (Balasubramanian et al., 2010).
   f. Approval by non-conflicted shareholders (Balasubramanian et al., 2010).
   g. RPTs must be on arm's length terms (Balasubramanian et al., 2010).
   h. Material RPTs are disclosed to shareholders (Balasubramanian et al., 2010).
8. Disclosure practices:
   a) Corporate Governance Philosophy (Haldar & Rao, 2013).
   b) Contingent Liabilities (Haldar & Rao, 2013).
   c) Related Party Transactions (RPT) (Haldar & Rao, 2013).
   d) Remuneration to Directors (Haldar & Rao, 2013).
   e) Non-compliance, Penalty or Stricture (Haldar & Rao, 2013).
   f) Accounting treatment (Haldar & Rao, 2013).
   g) Code of conduct (Haldar & Rao, 2013).
   h) Whistle Blower Policy (Haldar & Rao, 2013).
   i) Management Discussion and Analysis Report (MDAR) (Haldar & Rao, 2013).
   j) CEO/CFO Certification (Haldar & Rao, 2013).
   k) Compliance Report on Corporate Governance (Haldar & Rao, 2013).
   l) Training of the Non-Executive Directors (Haldar & Rao, 2013).
   m) Postal Ballot Facility (Haldar & Rao, 2013).
   n) Company Website timely updated with Governance Report and Annual Report (Haldar & Rao, 2013).
   o) Compliance Officer (Haldar & Rao, 2013).
   p) Non-mandatory Requirement (Haldar & Rao, 2013).
   q) Company has cross listed shares in another country (Balasubramanian et al., 2010).
   r) Annual financial statements (Balasubramanian et al., 2010).
   s) Annual report to shareholders (Balasubramanian et al., 2010).
   t) Share price information (Balasubramanian et al., 2010).
   u) Press releases (Balasubramanian et al., 2010).
   v) Notice of upcoming shareholder meetings (Balasubramanian et al., 2010).

w) Results of shareholder meetings (Balasubramanian et al., 2010).
x) Does the company produce its legally required financial reports by the required date? (Leal et al., 2007).
y) Does the company use an international accounting standard (IASB or US GAAP)? (Leal et al., 2007).
z) Does the company use one of the leading global auditing firms? (Leal et al., 2007).
aa) Mandatory retirement age for directors exists (Brown & Caylor, 2006).
bb) Performance of the board is reviewed regularly (Brown & Caylor, 2006).
cc) A board-approved CEO succession plan is in place (Brown & Caylor, 2006).
dd) Board has outside advisors (Brown & Caylor, 2006).
ee) Directors are required to submit their resignation upon a change in job status (Brown & Caylor, 2006).
ff) Outside directors meet without the CEO and disclose the number of times they met (Brown & Caylor, 2006).
gg) Director term limits exist (Brown & Caylor, 2006).

9. Stakeholders index:
   a. Customer satisfaction (Mohanty, 2003).
   b. Losing to customer in court cases (Mohanty, 2003).
   c. Customer dissatisfaction (Mohanty, 2003).
   d. Customers view neither in the positive nor in the negative form (Mohanty, 2003).
   e. Deferring payments to the supplier (Mohanty, 2003).
   f. Losing court cases against supplier (Mohanty, 2003).
   g. Non negative form (Mohanty, 2003).
   h. Evasion of duties and taxes (Mohanty, 2003).
   i. Violating other legal provisions (Mohanty, 2003).
   j. Building social infrastructure (Mohanty, 2003).
   k. Producing socially useful products (Mohanty, 2003).
   l. Adopting street children (Mohanty, 2003).
   m. Polluting environment (Mohanty, 2003).
   n. Producing socially harmful products (Mohanty, 2003).
   o. Reneging on commitments made to the society (Mohanty, 2003).
   p. Does the company charter establish arbitration to resolve corporate conflicts? (Leal et al., 2007).
   q. Does the company charter grant additional voting rights beyond what is legally required? (Leal et al., 2007).

r. Does the company grant tag along rights beyond what is legally required? (Leal et al., 2007).
s. Total amount incurred to be spent as per Companies Act, 2013 on Corporate Social Responsibility.
t. Total amount spent actually on Corporate Social Responsibility.

10. Rest of the Committees:
    a. Presence of Corporate Social Responsibility Committee.
    b. Number of Corporate Social Responsibility Committee meetings held per annum.
    c. Presence of Chairperson in the Corporate Social Responsibility Committee meetings.
    d. Presence of Nomination and Remuneration Committee.
    e. Number of Nomination and Remuneration Committee meetings held per annum.
    f. Presence of Chairperson in the Nomination and Remuneration Committee meetings.
    g. Presence of Risk Management Committee.
    h. Number of Risk Management Committee meetings held per annum.
    i. Presence of Chairperson in the Risk Management Committee meetings.
    j. Presence of Shareholder Grievance Committee.
    k. Number of Shareholder Grievance Committee meetings held per annum.
    l. Presence of Chairperson in the Shareholder Grievance Committee meetings.
    m. Presence of Stakeholder Relationship Committee.
    n. Number of Stakeholder Relationship Committee meetings held per annum.
    o. Presence of Chairperson in the Stakeholder Relationship Committee meetings.
    p. Presence of Compensation Committee.
    q. Number of Compensation Committee meetings held per annum.
    r. Presence of Chairperson in the Compensation Committee meetings.
11. Insider Trading Transactions:
    a. Number of Insider Trading Transactions held per annum.
    b. Number of Insider Trading Shares Transacted per annum.
    c. Type of Insider Trading Transaction per annum (Buy-Sell/ None).
12. **Dependent Variable:** Tobin's Q (Haldar & Rao, 2013) and Stock Returns (Gompers et. al., 2003).

Compilation of References

Achuthan, K., Ramanathan, S., Srinivas, S., & Raman, R. (2024). Advancing cybersecurity and privacy with artificial intelligence: Current trends and future research directions. *Frontiers in Big Data*, *7*, 1497535. DOI: 10.3389/fdata.2024.1497535 PMID: 39703783

Adeyeye, O. J., Akanbi, I., Emeteveke, I., & Emehin, O. (2024). Leveraging secured AI-driven data analytics for cybersecurity: Safeguarding information and enhancing threat detection. *International Journal of Research and Publication and Reviews*, *5*(10), 3208–3223. DOI: 10.55248/gengpi.5.1024.2911

Adhikari, P., Hamal, P., & Jnr, F. B. (2024). Artificial intelligence in fraud detection: Revolutionizing financial security. *International Journal of Science and Research Archive*, *13*(01), 1457–1472. DOI: 10.30574/ijsra.2024.13.1.1860

Adriko, R., & Nurse, J. R. (2024). Cybersecurity, cyber insurance and small-to-medium-sized enterprises: A systematic Review. *Information and Computer Security*, *32*(5), 691–710. DOI: 10.1108/ICS-01-2024-0025

Agboola, D. (2025). The Evolving Landscape of Data Privacy: How Regulations are Shaping the Digital World. *Available at SSRN* 5187183. DOI: 10.2139/ssrn.5187183

Ahmad, A. S. (2023). Application of big data and artificial intelligence in strengthening fraud analytics and cybersecurity resilience in global financial markets. *International Journal of Advanced Cybersecurity Systems, Technologies, and Applications*, *7*(12), 11–23.

Ahmad, A. Y. A. B. (2024, April). Fraud prevention in insurance: Biometric identity verification and AI-based risk assessment. In *2024 International Conference on Knowledge Engineering and Communication Systems (ICKECS)* (Vol. 1, pp. 1–6). IEEE. DOI: 10.1109/ICKECS61492.2024.10616613

Akbar, S., Poletti-Hughes, J., El-Faitouri, R., & Shah, S. Z. A. (2016). More on the relationship between corporate governance and firm performance in the UK: Evidence from the application of generalized method of moments estimation. *Research in International Business and Finance, 38*, 417–429. DOI: 10.1016/j.ribaf.2016.03.009

Akhai, S., & Kumar, V. (2024). Quantum resilience and distributed trust: The promise of blockchain and quantum computing in defense. In *Sustainable Security Practices Using Blockchain, Quantum and Post-Quantum Technologies for Real Time Applications* (pp. 125–153). Springer Nature Singapore. DOI: 10.1007/978-981-97-0088-2_7

Akkor, D. G., & Ozyukse, S. (2020). The effects of new technologies on the insurance sector: A proposition for underwriting qualifications for the future. *Eurasian Journal of Business and Management, 8*(1), 36–50. DOI: 10.15604/ejbm.2020.08.01.004

Al Mansoori, M. (2024). *AI-driven anomaly detection in cybersecurity* (Master's thesis, Rochester Institute of Technology).

Al Maqousi, A. (2025). Cybersecurity in Smart. Examining Cybersecurity Risks Produced by Generative AI, 357.

Al Siam, A., Alazab, M., Awajan, A., & Faruqui, N. (2025). A comprehensive review of AI's current impact and future prospects in cybersecurity. *IEEE Access : Practical Innovations, Open Solutions, 13*, 14029–14050. DOI: 10.1109/ACCESS.2025.3528114

Alagic, G., Alagic, G., Apon, D., Cooper, D., Dang, Q., Dang, T., ... & Smith-Tone, D. (2022). Status report on the third round of the NIST post-quantum cryptography standardization process.

Alagic, G., Bros, M., Ciadoux, P., Cooper, D., Dang, Q., Dang, T., & Waller, N. (2025). *Status report on the fourth round of the nist post-quantum cryptography standardization process*. National Institute of Standards and Technology. DOI: 10.6028/NIST.IR.8545

Alauthman, M., Aldweesh, A., Al-Qerem, A., Al Maqousi, A. Y., & Almomani, A. (2024). Cryptographic protocols for Internet of Things (IoT) security: Lightweight schemes and practical deployment. In Innovations in Modern Cryptography (pp. 431–448). DOI: 10.4018/979-8-3693-5330-1.ch018

Alauthman, M., Aldweesh, A., Al-Qerem, A., Aburub, F., Al-Smadi, Y., Abaker, A. M., Alzubi, O. R., & Alzubi, B. (2023). Tabular data generation to improve classification of liver-disease diagnosis. *Applied Sciences (Basel, Switzerland), 13*(4), 2678. DOI: 10.3390/app13042678

Alauthman, M., Al-Qerem, A., Sowan, B., Alsarhan, A., Eshtay, M., Aldweesh, A., & Aslam, N. (2023). Enhancing small medical-dataset classification performance using GAN. *Informatics (MDPI), 10*(1), 28. DOI: 10.3390/informatics10010028

Alauthman, M., Aslam, N., Al-Kasassbeh, M., Khan, S., Al-Qerem, A., & Raymond Choo, K.-K. (2020). An efficient reinforcement-learning-based botnet detection approach. *Journal of Network and Computer Applications, 150*, 102479. DOI: 10.1016/j.jnca.2019.102479

Albshaier, L., Almarri, S., & Rahman, M. M. H. (2024). Earlier Decision on Detection of Ransomware Identification: A Comprehensive Systematic Literature Review. *Information 2024, Vol. 15, Page 484, 15*(8), 484. DOI: 10.3390/info15080484

Alhawari, S., Al Jarrah, M. A., & Hadi, W. (2017). Implementing risk-management processes into a cloud-computing environment. *International Journal of Web Portals, 9*(1), 1–12. DOI: 10.4018/IJWP.2017010101

Alkhelb, A. A., & Alshagrawi, S. (2025). Role of artificial intelligence in healthcare insurance: Systematic literature review. Exploration of Digital Health Technologies, 3, Article 101145. https://doi.org/10.37349/edht.2025.101145

AllahRakha, N. (2024). Cybersecurity Regulations for Protection and Safeguarding Digital Assets (Data) in Today's Worlds. *Lex Scientia Law Review, 8*(1).

Al-Malkawi, H. A. N., Pillai, R., & Bhatti, M. I. (2014). Corporate governance practices in emerging markets: The case of GCC countries. *Economic Modelling, 38*, 133–141. DOI: 10.1016/j.econmod.2013.12.019

Alnahawi, N., Schmitt, N., Wiesmaier, A., Heinemann, A., & Grasmeyer, T. (2023). On the state of crypto-agility. *Cryptology ePrint Archive*.

Alqahtani, H., & Kumar, G. (2024). Cybersecurity in electric and flying vehicles: Threats, challenges, AI solutions & future directions. *ACM Computing Surveys, 57*(4), 1–34. DOI: 10.1145/3697830

Alquwayzani, A., Aldossri, R., & Frikha, M. (2024). Prominent Security Vulnerabilities in Cloud Computing. *International Journal of Advanced Computer Science and Applications, 15*(2). Advance online publication. DOI: 10.14569/IJACSA.2024.0150281

Alsalman, A. I. S. (2023). Accelerating Quantum Computing Readiness: Risk Management and Strategies for Sectors. *Journal of Quantum Information Science, 13*(2), 33–44. DOI: 10.4236/jqis.2023.132003

Alsmadi, D., Maqousi, A., & Abuhussein, T. (2024). Engaging in cybersecurity proactive behavior: Awareness in COVID-19 age. *Kybernetes, 53*(1), 451–466. DOI: 10.1108/K-08-2022-1104

Al-Smadi, Y., Eshtay, M., Al-Qerem, A., Nashwan, S., Ouda, O., & Abd El-Aziz, A. A. (2023). Reliable prediction of software defects using Shapley interpretable machine-learning models. *Egyptian Informatics Journal, 24*(3), 100386. DOI: 10.1016/j.eij.2023.05.011

Amirineni, S. (2024). Leveraging Machine Learning, Cloud Computing, and Artificial Intelligence for Fraud Detection and Prevention in Insurance: A Scalable Approach to Data-Driven Insights. *International Journal of Automation. Artificial Intelligence and Machine Learning, 4*(2), 155–172. DOI: 10.61797/ijaaiml.v4i2.371

Apergis, A. (2024). The role of cognitive assistants in medical insurance underwriting.

Aquilina, J. M. (2008). Memory Forensics. *Malware Forensics*, 121–192. DOI: 10.1016/B978-1-59749-268-3.00003-7

Arbore, A. (2025). *Market strategies in a hyper-connected world.* EGEA spa.

Arefin, S., & Simcox, M. (2024). AI-Driven Solutions for Safeguarding Healthcare Data: Innovations in Cybersecurity. *International Business Research, 17*(6), 1–74. DOI: 10.5539/ibr.v17n6p74

Argetsinger, C. R. (2024). The Promise and Peril of Quantum Computing and Its Implications for Cyber Insurance. *Journal of Emerging Issues in Litigation/Winter, 4*(1), 65-73.

Ashfin, P. (2024). AI-driven threat detection and response in cybersecurity. *Bulletin of Engineering Science and Technology, 1*(2), 125–143.

Aslam, A. (2025). *Quantum Computing Threats to Cryptography: A Comprehensive Analysis of Vulnerabilities.* Countermeasures, and Future-Proofing Strategies.

Aslan, Ö., Aktuğ, S. S., Ozkan-Okay, M., Yilmaz, A. A., & Akin, E. (2023). A Comprehensive Review of Cyber Security Vulnerabilities, Threats, Attacks, and Solutions. *Electronics 2023, Vol. 12, Page 1333, 12*(6), 1333. DOI: 10.3390/electronics12061333

Awotidebe, M. (2025). The Race to Quantum-Resilient Infrastructure: National and Global Strategies for Cybersecurity Readiness.

Aydeger, A., Zeydan, E., Yadav, A. K., Hemachandra, K. T., & Liyanage, M. (2024). Towards a quantum-resilient future: Strategies for transitioning to post-quantum cryptography. In *2024 15th International Conference on Network of the Future (NoF)* (pp. 195-203). IEEE.

Azure backup and restore plan to protect against ransomware | Microsoft Learn. (n.d.). Retrieved March 26, 2025, from https://learn.microsoft.com/en-us/azure/security/fundamentals/backup-plan-to-protect-against-ransomware

Baanstra, C. A. (2024). Scenarios and Interventions for the Dutch Energy Market: Preparing to be Quantum-Safe.

Babu, B. S., Umakanth, M., & Bhanumathi, P. (2025). Generative Artificial. *Organizational Sociology in the Digital Age*, 413.

Bahuguna, A., Bisht, R. K., & Pande, J. (2020). Country-level cybersecurity posture assessment: Study and analysis of practices. *Information Security Journal: A Global Perspective, 29*(5), 250–266.

Bail, C. A. (2024). Can Generative AI improve social science? *Proceedings of the National Academy of Sciences of the United States of America, 121*(21), e2314021121. DOI: 10.1073/pnas.2314021121 PMID: 38722813

Balan, M. (2022). *AI-powered IAM and threat intelligence: Safeguarding patient data in the age of cybersecurity breaches.*

Balarabe, K. (2025). Quantum Computing and the Law: Navigating the Legal Implications of a Quantum Leap. *European Journal of Risk Regulation, 16*(2), 1–20. DOI: 10.1017/err.2025.8

Balasubramanian, N., Black, B. S., & Khanna, V. (2010). The relation between firm-level corporate governance and market value: A case study of India. *Emerging Markets Review, 11*(4), 319–340. DOI: 10.1016/j.ememar.2010.05.001

Balcıoğlu, Y. S. (2024). Revolutionizing risk management: AI and ML innovations in financial stability and fraud detection. In *Navigating the Future of Finance in the Age of AI* (pp. 109–138). IGI Global. DOI: 10.4018/979-8-3693-4382-1.ch006

Bansal, U., Bharatwal, S., Bagiyam, D. S., & Kismawadi, E. R. (2024). Fraud detection in the era of AI: Harnessing technology for a safer digital economy. In *AI-Driven Decentralized Finance and the Future of Finance* (pp. 139–160). IGI Global. DOI: 10.4018/979-8-3693-6321-8.ch006

Bardhan, I., Oh, J., & Zheng, Z. (2020). Predictive analytics for reducing hospital readmissions of high-risk patients. *Information Systems Research, 31*(3), 855–875.

Baseri, Y., Chouhan, V., & Hafid, A. (2024). Navigating quantum security risks in networked environments: A comprehensive study of quantum-safe network protocols. *Computers & Security, 142*, 103883. DOI: 10.1016/j.cose.2024.103883

Bauer, R., Frijns, B., Otten, R., & Tourani-Rad, A. (2008). The impact of corporate governance on corporate performance: Evidence from Japan. *Pacific-Basin Finance Journal, 16*(3), 236–251. DOI: 10.1016/j.pacfin.2007.05.001

Bebchuk, L., Cohen, A., & Ferrell, A. (2009). What matters in corporate governance? *Review of Financial Studies, 22*(2), 783–827. DOI: 10.1093/rfs/hhn099

Beckley, J. (2025). Advanced risk assessment techniques: Merging data-driven analytics with expert insights to navigate uncertain decision-making processes. *Int J Res Publ Rev, 6*(3), 1454–1471. DOI: 10.55248/gengpi.6.0325.1148

Bello, O. A., Folorunso, A., Onwuchekwa, J., & Ejiofor, O. E. (2023). A comprehensive framework for strengthening USA financial cybersecurity: Integrating machine learning and AI in fraud detection systems. *European Journal of Computer Science and Information Technology, 11*(6), 62–83.

Bello, O. A., & Olufemi, K. (2024). Artificial intelligence in fraud prevention: Exploring techniques and applications, challenges, and opportunities. *Computer Science & IT Research Journal, 5*(6), 1505–1520. DOI: 10.51594/csitrj.v5i6.1252

Benzaid, C., & Taleb, T. (2020). AI-driven zero-touch network and service management in 5G and beyond: Challenges and research directions. *IEEE Network, 34*(2), 186–194. DOI: 10.1109/MNET.001.1900252

Bergese, F. (2021). *Bond Risk Assessment from Fundamental Analysis to Portfolio Optimization* (Doctoral dissertation, Politecnico di Torino).

Beuchelt, G. (2025). Information Technology Security Management. In *Computer and Information Security Handbook* (pp. 475–508). Morgan Kaufmann. DOI: 10.1016/B978-0-443-13223-0.00027-8

Bhagat, S., Bolton, B., & Romano, R. (2008). The promise and peril of corporate governance indices. *Colum. L. Rev., 108*, 1803.

Bi, M. (2023). *Distributed decision-making in disrupted industrial environments using a multi-agent framework* (Doctoral dissertation).

Bibri, S. E., Huang, J., & Krogstie, J. (2024). Artificial intelligence of things for synergizing smarter eco-city brain, metabolism, and platform: Pioneering data-driven environmental governance. *Sustainable Cities and Society, 108*, 105516. DOI: 10.1016/j.scs.2024.105516

Black, B. S., De Carvalho, A. G., & Sampaio, J. O. (2014). The evolution of corporate governance in Brazil. *Emerging Markets Review*, *20*, 176–195. DOI: 10.1016/j.ememar.2014.04.004

Black, B. S., Love, I., & Rachinsky, A. (2006). Corporate governance indices and firms' market values: Time series evidence from Russia. *Emerging Markets Review*, *7*(4), 361–379. DOI: 10.1016/j.ememar.2006.09.004

Böhme, R., & Schwartz, G. (2010). Modeling cyber-insurance: Towards a unifying framework. Workshop on the Economics of Information Security (WEIS). Retrieved from https://www.econinfosec.org/archive/weis2010/papers/session5/weis2010_boehme.pdf

Bokka, V. V. R. M. (2025). Crafting a comprehensive strategy to prevent fraud and enable recovery in mobile insurance in the USA.

Bolot, J., & Lelarge, M. (2009). Cyber insurance as an incentive for internet security. In Johnson, M. E. (Ed.), *Managing information risk and the economics of security* (pp. 269–290). Springer., DOI: 10.1007/978-0-387-09762-6_13

Bompos, K. (2020). *Development time of Zero-Day cyber exploits in support of offensive cyber operations* (Doctoral dissertation, Monterey, CA; Naval Postgraduate School).

Bonta, R. (2022). California consumer privacy act (CCPA). *Retrieved from State of California Department of Justice: https://oag. ca. gov/privacy/ccpa.*

Boretti, A. (2024). Technical, economic, and societal risks in the progress of artificial intelligence driven quantum technologies. *Discover Artificial Intelligence*, *4*(1), 67. DOI: 10.1007/s44163-024-00171-y

Boto, K., Amos, G., Moran, J., Robbins, J., & Welden-Iley, J. (2023). The Rise of Fintech: Liability and Insurance. In *The Global Insurance Market and Change* (pp. 246–285). Informa Law from Routledge. DOI: 10.4324/9781003319054-10

Brokešová, Z., & Ondruška, T. (2025). Internal controls and insurance in Industry 5.0. In *Business Challenges and Opportunities in the Era of Industry 5.0* (pp. 195–213). Emerald Publishing Limited. DOI: 10.1108/978-1-83549-676-320251011

Brown, L. D., & Caylor, M. L. (2006). Corporate governance and firm valuation. *Journal of Accounting and Public Policy*, *25*(4), 409–434. DOI: 10.1016/j.jaccpubpol.2006.05.005

Canetti, R., Kalai, Y. T., Lysyanskaya, A., Rivest, R. L., Shamir, A., Shen, E., ... & Weitzner, D. J. (2020). Privacy-preserving automated exposure notification. *IACR Cryptol. ePrint Arch.*

Cartwright, E., Hernandez Castro, J., & Cartwright, A. (2019). To pay or not: Game theoretic models of ransomware. *Journal of Cybersecurity*, *5*(1), tyz009. Advance online publication. DOI: 10.1093/cybsec/tyz009

Challa, K. (2024). Artificial Intelligence and Generative Neural Systems: Creating Smarter Customer Support Models for Digital Financial Services. *Journal of Computational Analysis and Applications*, *33*(8).

Challoumis, C. (2023). Risk on the tax system of the EU from 2016 to 2022. *ECONOMICS-INNOVATIVE AND ECONOMICS RESEARCH JOURNAL, 11*(Sp. issue), 55-72.

Chowdhary, M. A. M. (2025). *Financial Network Infrastructure: Scalability.* Security and Optimization.

Christopher, M., & Peck, H. (2004). Building the resilient supply chain. *International Journal of Logistics Management*, *15*(2), 1–14. DOI: 10.1108/09574090410700275

CISA. (2021). Remediating networks affected by the SolarWinds and Active Directory/M365 compromise. Cybersecurity and Infrastructure Security Agency. Retrieved from https://www.cisa.gov/sites/default/files/publications/Remediating-Networks-Affected-by-the-SolarWinds-and-Active-Directory-M365-Compromise.pdf

Cornell, B., & Damodaran, A. (2020). *Valuing ESG: Doing good or sounding good?* NYU Stern School of Business.

Correia, H. C. (2023). *Investment policy statement for individual investors: medium-low risk aversion client multi-asset balanced portfolio* (Master's thesis, Universidade de Lisboa (Portugal)).

Crypto Currency Regulation and Law Enforcement Perspectives. (n.d.). Retrieved March 26, 2025, from https://www.researchgate.net/publication/354328712_Crypto_Currency_Regulation_and_Law_Enforcement_Perspectives

da Silva, A. L. C., & Leal, R. P. C. (2005). Corporate governance index, firm valuation and performance in Brazil. *Revista Brasileira de Finanças*, *3*(1), 1–18.

Dalal, Y. M., Supreeth, S., Amuthabala, K., Satheesha, T. Y., Asha, P. N., & Somanath, S. (2024, September). Optimizing Security: A Comparative Analysis of RSA, ECC, and DH Algorithms. In *2024 IEEE North Karnataka Subsection Flagship International Conference (NKCon)* (pp. 1-6). IEEE. DOI: 10.1109/NKCon62728.2024.10775183

Dambra, S., Bilge, L., & Balzarotti, D. (2020, May). SoK: Cyber insurance–technical challenges and a system security roadmap. In *2020 IEEE Symposium on Security and Privacy (SP)* (pp. 1367-1383). IEEE. DOI: 10.1109/SP40000.2020.00019

Dash, B., Sharma, P., & Ali, A. (2022). Federated learning for privacy-preserving: A review of PII data analysis in Fintech. [IJSEA]. *International Journal of Software Engineering and Its Applications*, *13*(4).

Deep, S., Kumar, S., & Kalra, P. (2024). AI-driven data security in healthcare: Safeguarding data and financial transactions. *International Journal of Novel Research and Development.*

Deshpande, A. (2024). *Cybersecurity in Financial Services: Addressing AI-Related Threats and Vulnerabilities.* Paper presented at the 2024 International Conference on Knowledge Engineering and Communication Systems (ICKECS). DOI: 10.1109/ICKECS61492.2024.10616498

Devaraj, S. M. (2023). Ai And Cloud For Claims Processing Automation In Property And Casualty Insurance. *International Journal Of Engineering And Technology Research (Ijetr)*, *8*(1), 38–46.

Dhieb, N., Ghazzai, H., Besbes, H., & Massoud, Y. (2020). A secure ai-driven architecture for automated insurance systems: Fraud detection and risk measurement. *IEEE Access : Practical Innovations, Open Solutions*, *8*, 58546–58558. DOI: 10.1109/ACCESS.2020.2983300

Dickerson, P., & Worthen, J. (2024, May). Optimizing Pipeline Systems for Greater Precision, Efficiency & Safety Using Emerging Technologies. In *PSIG Annual Meeting* (pp. PSIG-2426). PSIG.

Dionne, G. (2013). Risk management: History, definition, and critique. *Risk Management & Insurance Review*, *16*(2), 147–166. DOI: 10.1111/rmir.12016

Dixon, D., Sattar, H., Moros, N., Kesireddy, S. R., Ahsan, H., Lakkimsetti, M., & Hassan, M. J. (2024). Unveiling the influence of AI predictive analytics on patient outcomes: A comprehensive narrative review. *Cureus*, *16*(5), e59954. DOI: 10.7759/cureus.59954 PMID: 38854327

Dorri, A., Kanhere, S. S., & Jurdak, R. (2018). Multi-agent systems: A survey. *IEEE Access : Practical Innovations, Open Solutions*, *6*, 28573–28593. DOI: 10.1109/ACCESS.2018.2831228

Egho-Promise, E., Lyada, E., & Aina, F. (2024). Towards improved vulnerability management in digital environments: A comprehensive framework for cybersecurity enhancement. *International Research Journal of Computer Science*, *11*(5), 441–449. DOI: 10.26562/irjcs.2024.v1105.01

Ejjami, R. (2024). Enhancing cybersecurity through artificial intelligence: Techniques, applications, and future perspectives. *Journal of Next-Generation Research, 5.0.*

Eng, L. L., & Mak, Y. T. (2003). Corporate governance and voluntary disclosure. *Journal of Accounting and Public Policy*, *22*(4), 325–345. DOI: 10.1016/S0278-4254(03)00037-1

Enomoto, S., Kuzuno, H., Yamada, H., Shiraishi, Y., & Morii, M. (2024). Early mitigation of CPU-optimized ransomware using monitoring encryption instructions. *International Journal of Information Security*, *23*(5), 3393–3413. DOI: 10.1007/s10207-024-00892-2

Epstein, Z., Hertzmann, A., Akten, M., Farid, H., Fjeld, J., Frank, M. R., Groh, M., Herman, L., Leach, N., Mahari, R., Pentland, A. S., Russakovsky, O., Schroeder, H., & Smith, A. (2023). Art and the science of generative AI. *Science*, *380*(6650), 1110–1111. DOI: 10.1126/science.adh4451 PMID: 37319193

Ermoshina, K., & Musiani, F. (2019). "Standardising by running code": The Signal protocol and de facto standardisation in end-to-end encrypted messaging. *Internet Histories*, *3*(3–4), 343–363. DOI: 10.1080/24701475.2019.1654697

Faheem, M. A. (2021). AI-Driven Risk Assessment Models: Revolutionizing Credit Scoring and Default Prediction. *Iconic Research and Engineering Journals*, *5*(3), 177–186.

Faisal, N. A., Nahar, J., Sultana, N., & Mintoo, A. A. (2024). Fraud detection in banking: Leveraging AI to identify and prevent fraudulent activities in real time. *Journal of Machine Learning. Data Engineering and Data Science*, *1*(01), 181–197.

Falco, G. J., & Rosenbach, E. (2022). *Confronting cyber risk: An embedded endurance strategy for cybersecurity*. Oxford University Press. DOI: 10.1093/oso/9780197526545.001.0001

File carving | Infosec. (n.d.). Retrieved March 26, 2025, from https://www.infosecinstitute.com/resources/digital-forensics/file-carving/

File Carving vs. Metadata Recovery: What is the Difference? (n.d.). Retrieved March 26, 2025, from https://www.salvationdata.com/knowledge/file-carving/

Fleming, P., Edwards, S. G., Bayliss, A. P., & Seger, C. R. Vendor risk management practices: Analysis of contractual risk allocation in digital supply chains. *Journal of Cybersecurity*, *9*(1), 1–18. DOI: 10.1093/cybsec/tyad005

Franke, U. (2023). Cyber insurance claims analysis: Third-party origins and coverage gaps. *Journal of Cybersecurity*, *9*(1), 1–16. DOI: 10.1093/cybsec/tyad006

Freitas, S., Kalajdjieski, J., Gharib, A., & McCann, R. (2024). AI-driven guided response for security operation centers with Microsoft Copilot for security. *arXiv preprint arXiv:2407.09017.*

Friedberg, I., & Skopik, F. (2018). Measuring the impact of vendor security on cyber risk exposure. *IEEE Security and Privacy*, *16*(5), 54–63. DOI: 10.1109/MSP.2018.3761723

Fui-Hoon Nah, F., Zheng, R., Cai, J., Siau, K., & Chen, L. (2023). Generative AI and ChatGPT: Applications, challenges, and AI-human collaboration. *Journal of information technology case and application research, 25*(3), 277-304.

Gallegos-Segovia, P. L., Vintimilla-Tapia, P. E., Bravo-Torres, J. F., Yuquilima-Albarado, I. F., Larios-Rosillo, V. M., & Jara-Saltos, J. D. (2017). Social engineering as an attack vector for ransomware. *2017 CHILEAN Conference on Electrical, Electronics Engineering, Information and Communication Technologies, CHILECON 2017 - Proceedings, 2017-January*, 1–6. DOI: 10.1109/CHILECON.2017.8229528

Gautam, A. (2023). Evaluating the impact of artificial intelligence on risk management and fraud detection in the banking sector. *AI. IoT and the Fourth Industrial Revolution Review*, *13*(11), 9–18.

Gawankar, S., Nair, S., Pawar, V., Vhatkar, A., & Chavan, P. (2024, August). Patient privacy and data security in the era of AI-driven healthcare. In *2024 8th International Conference on Computing, Communication, Control and Automation (ICCUBEA)* (pp. 1–6). IEEE. DOI: 10.1109/ICCUBEA61740.2024.10775004

George, A. S. (2024). Emerging trends in AI-driven cybersecurity: An in-depth analysis. *Partners Universal Innovative Research Publication*, *2*(4), 15–28.

George, A. S. (2024). Emerging Trends in AI-Driven Cybersecurity: An In-Depth Analysis. *Partners Universal Innovative Research Publication*, *2*(4), 15–28.

George, A. S. (2025). The Critical Role of Cybersecurity Insurance in an Era of Exponential Threats: A Review of Emerging Risk Realities and Policy Safeguards for Enterprise Resilience. *Partners Universal International Research Journal*, *4*(1), 1–23.

Georgiadou, A., Mouzakitis, S., & Askounis, D. (2021). Assessing mitre att&ck risk using a cyber-security culture framework. *Sensors (Basel)*, *21*(9), 3267. DOI: 10.3390/s21093267 PMID: 34065086

Geremew, A., & Mohammad, A. (2024). Preparing critical infrastructure for post-quantum cryptography: Strategies for transitioning ahead of cryptanalytically relevant quantum computing. *International Journal of Engineering Science and Technology*, *6*(4), 338–365. DOI: 10.46328/ijonest.240

Gheysari, M., & Tehrani, M. S. S. (2022). The Role of Multi-Agent Systems in IoT. In *Multi Agent Systems: Technologies and Applications towards Human-Centered* (pp. 87–114). Springer Nature Singapore. DOI: 10.1007/978-981-19-0493-6_5

Glintschert, M. (2020). AI-driven IT and its potentials–a state-of-the-art approach. *Available at SSRN* 3576417. DOI: 10.2139/ssrn.3576417

Gompers, P., Ishii, J., & Metrick, A. (2003). Corporate governance and equity prices. *The Quarterly Journal of Economics*, *118*(1), 107–156. DOI: 10.1162/00335530360535162

Gopal, M. K., Shetty, J., Yenduri, G., Maddikunta, P. K. R., Murugan, R., & Gadekallu, T. R. (2024). Experts Opinion on Generative AI: Adoption and Challenges in Actuarial Science. In *Artificial Intelligence and Actuarial Science* (pp. 21-36). Chapman and Hall/CRC.

Gordon, L. A., Loeb, M. P., & Zhou, L. (2022). Cyber insurance market trends: Evidence from policy data 2015-2021. *Journal of Cybersecurity*, *8*(1), 1–15. DOI: 10.1093/cybsec/tyac003

Gordon, S., Ford, R., & Mathieson, K. (2023). The expanding attack surface: Digital supply chain risk in interconnected economies. *Journal of Information Security and Applications*, *72*, 103419. DOI: 10.1016/j.jisa.2023.103419

Gorine, A., & Suhaib, M. (2024). Exploring AES Encryption Implementation Through Quantum. *Computing Techniques*.

Goyal, A., Friesen, A., Banino, A., Weber, T., Ke, N. R., Badia, A. P., & Guez, A.. "Retrieval-augmented reinforcement learning." In *International Conference on Machine Learning*, pp. 7740-7765. PMLR, 2022.

Gozalo-Brizuela, R., & Garrido-Merchán, E. C. (2023). A survey of Generative AI Applications. *arXiv preprint arXiv:2306.02781.*

Grabowska, M. (2022). Legal, Political and Organizational Aspects of Cybersecurity in the European Union. *Online Journal Modelling the New Europe*, (38), 106–132. DOI: 10.24193/OJMNE.2022.38.05

GRIT Ransomware Report: July 2024 | GuidePoint Security. (n.d.). Retrieved March 26, 2025, from https://www.guidepointsecurity.com/blog/grit-ransomware-report-july-2024/

Gulati, R., Kattumuri, R., & Kumar, S. (2020). A non-parametric index of corporate governance in the banking industry: An application to Indian data. *Socio-Economic Planning Sciences, 70*, 100702. DOI: 10.1016/j.seps.2019.03.008

Hacker, P., Engel, A., & Mauer, M. (2023, June). Regulating ChatGPT and other large generative AI models. In *Proceedings of the 2023 ACM conference on fairness, accountability, and transparency* (pp. 1112-1123). DOI: 10.1145/3593013.3594067

Hadi, W. M., Salam, M., & Al-Widian, J. A. (2010, June). Performance of NB and SVM classifiers in Islamic Arabic data. In Proceedings of the 1st International Conference on Intelligent Semantic Web-Services and Applications (ISWSA) (pp. 14:1–14:6). ACM. https://doi.org/10.1145/1874590.1874604

Hadijah, A. S., & Karmila, K. (2024). Evaluating the Role, Costs, and Benefits of Insurance and Hedging in Financing Decisions. *Advances in Economics & Financial Studies*, *2*(2), 88–101. DOI: 10.60079/aefs.v2i2.313

Haldar, A., & Rao, S. N. (2013). Corporate Governance Index for Indian Companies. In *Conference Paper.*

Hammad, A., Saleh, H., & Alomari, M. (2024). Advancements in Cybersecurity: Novel Approaches to Protecting Against Emerging Threats and Vulnerabilities. *CyberSystem Journal, 1*(1), 9–23. DOI: 10.57238/r15e5074

Hasan, I., & Rizvi, S. (2022). *AI-driven fraud detection and mitigation in e-commerce transactions.* Paper presented at the Proceedings of Data Analytics and Management: ICDAM 2021, Volume 1. DOI: 10.1007/978-981-16-6289-8_34

Hasan, K. F., Simpson, L., Baee, M. A. R., Islam, C., Rahman, Z., Armstrong, W., Gauravaram, P., & McKague, M. (2024). A framework for migrating to post-quantum cryptography: Security dependency analysis and case studies. *IEEE Access : Practical Innovations, Open Solutions, 12*, 23427–23450. DOI: 10.1109/ACCESS.2024.3360412

Hassan, M. M., Abrar, M. F., & Hasan, M. (2023). An explainable AI-driven machine learning framework for cybersecurity anomaly detection. In *Cyber Security and Business Intelligence* (pp. 197–219). Routledge. DOI: 10.4324/9781003285854-13

Hassan, M., Aziz, L. A. R., & Andriansyah, Y. (2023). The role of artificial intelligence in modern banking: An exploration of AI-driven approaches for enhanced fraud prevention, risk management, and regulatory compliance. *Reviews of Contemporary Business Analytics*, *6*(1), 110–132.

Heinl, P., Patapovas, A., & Pilgermann, M. (2024). Towards AI-enabled cyber threat assessment in the health sector. *arXiv preprint arXiv:2409.12765.*

Hirst, S., & Kastiel, K. (2019). Corporate governance by index exclusion. *BUL Rev.*, *99*, 1229.

Hodgson, A., Lhaopadchan, S., & Buakes, S. (2011). How informative is the Thai corporate governance index? A financial approach. *International Journal of Accounting & Information Management*, *19*(1), 53–79. DOI: 10.1108/18347641111105935

Holland, H. (2024). Quantum Computing and US Cybersecurity: A Case Study of the Breaking of RSA and Plan for Cryptographic Algorithm Transition.

Hossain, S., Ahmed, A., Khadka, U., Sarkar, S., & Khan, N. (2024). AI-driven predictive analytics, healthcare outcomes, cost reduction, machine learning, patient monitoring. *Advanced International Journal of Multidisciplinary Research*, *2*(5), 1–20.

How to Prevent Ransomware Attacks: Top 10 Best Practices | UpGuard. (n.d.). Retrieved March 26, 2025, from https://www.upguard.com/blog/best-practices-to-prevent-ransomware-attacks

Huang, K., & Madnick, S. (2021). Systematically understanding supply chain cyber attack patterns. *IEEE Security and Privacy*, *19*(1), 66–75. DOI: 10.1109/MSEC.2020.3018177

Hubbard, D. W. (2020). *The failure of risk management: Why it's broken and how to fix it.* John Wiley & Sons. DOI: 10.1002/9781119521914

Hudson, J. (2024). *Artificial intelligence and cybersecurity integration: Modern database techniques for securing AI models.*

Hu, H., Wen, Y., Chua, T. S., & Li, X. (2014). Toward scalable systems for big data analytics: A technology tutorial. *IEEE Access : Practical Innovations, Open Solutions*, *2*, 652–687. DOI: 10.1109/ACCESS.2014.2332453

Insua, D. R., Baylon, C., & Vila, J. (Eds.). (2020). *Security Risk Models for Cyber Insurance*. CRC Press. DOI: 10.1201/9780429329487

Intaratat, K., Lomchavakarn, P., Boonsawad, P., Boonsiri, K., Kantaboon, K., Intaratat, D., & Kumar, R. Innovations in Smart Healthcare: Integrating Generative Artificial Intelligence with Federated Learning. In *Generative Artificial Intelligence in Healthcare* (pp. 224-246). CRC Press.

Isreal, S., Joseph, O., & Joseph, S. (2025). *AI in financial services: Using big data for risk assessment and fraud detection*.

Jansen, M., Nguyen, H. Q., & Shams, A. (2025). Rise of the machines: The impact of automated underwriting. *Management Science*, *71*(2), 955–975. DOI: 10.1287/mnsc.2024.4986

Javaid, F., & Saboor, A. (2015). Impact of Corporate Governance index on Firm Performance: Evidence from Pakistani manufacturing sector. *Journal of Public Administration and Governance*, *5*(2), 1–21. DOI: 10.5296/jpag.v5i2.7498

Jawhar, S., Kimble, C. E., Miller, J. R., & Bitar, Z. (2024). *Enhancing cyber resilience with ai-powered cyber insurance risk assessment.* Paper presented at the 2024 IEEE 14th Annual Computing and Communication Workshop and Conference (CCWC). DOI: 10.1109/CCWC60891.2024.10427965

Johnson, B., Laszka, A., & Grossklags, J. (2020). The complexity of estimating systemic risk in networks. In 2020 IEEE 31st International Conference on Software Engineering (pp. 89-100). IEEE. https://doi.org/DOI: 10.1109/ICSE-COMPANION.2020.00045

Jun, M. A. Y., Jinu, B. A., Seng, L. K., Maharaiq, M. H. F. B. Z., Khongsuwan, W., Junn, B. T. K., Hao, A. A. W., & Sindiramutty, S. R. (2024). *Exploring the Impact of Crypto-Ransomware on Critical Industries: Case Studies and Solutions*. DOI: 10.20944/preprints202409.1325.v1

Kamuangu, P. (2024). A Review on Cybersecurity in Fintech: Threats, Solutions, and Future Trends. *Journal of Economics. Finance and Accounting Studies*, *6*(1), 47–53.

Kanavas, A. (2023). *Cyberinsurance as a risk management tool* (Master's thesis, Πανεπιστήμιο Πειραιώς).

Kapadiya, K., Patel, U., Gupta, R., Alshehri, M. D., Tanwar, S., Sharma, G., & Bokoro, P. N. (2022). Blockchain and AI-empowered healthcare insurance fraud detection: An analysis, architecture, and prospects. *IEEE Access : Practical Innovations, Open Solutions*, *10*, 79606–79627. DOI: 10.1109/ACCESS.2022.3194569

Kaul, D. (2021). AI-Driven Dynamic Upsell in Hotel Reservation Systems Based on Cybersecurity Risk Scores. [IJCET]. *International Journal of Computer Engineering and Technology, 12*(3), 114–125.

Kelton, A. S., & Yang, Y. W. (2008). The impact of corporate governance on Internet financial reporting. *Journal of Accounting and Public Policy, 27*(1), 62–87. DOI: 10.1016/j.jaccpubpol.2007.11.001

Keskin, O. F., Caramancion, K. M., Tatar, I., Raza, O., & Tatar, U. (2021). Cyber third-party risk management: A comparison of non-intrusive risk scoring reports. *Electronics (Basel), 10*(10), 1168. DOI: 10.3390/electronics10101168

Khan, A., Jhanjhi, N., Hamid, D. H. H., Omar, H. A. H. B. H., Amsaad, F., & Wassan, S. (2025). Future Trends and Challenges in Cybersecurity and Generative AI. *Reshaping CyberSecurity With Generative AI Techniques*, 491-522.

Khanchel, I. (2007). Corporate governance: Measurement and determinant analysis. *Managerial Auditing Journal, 22*(8), 740–760. DOI: 10.1108/02686900710819625

Khan, R., & Estay, D. A. S. (2022). Concentration risk in cloud service provision: Implications for cyber security. *Journal of Network and Systems Management, 30*(1), 1–25. DOI: 10.1007/s10922-021-09642-4

Khatam, D. (2022). *Regulating Data Privacy in the Age of Surveillance Capitalism: The Making of the European General Data Protection Regulation and the California Consumer Privacy Act.* Stanford University.

Kiranbabu, M. N. V., Viji, A. J., Chandanan, A. K., Birchha, V., Pandey, T. K., & Sar, S. K. (2025). The challenge of adversarial attacks on AI-driven cybersecurity systems. *Journal of Cybersecurity & Information Management, 15*(1).

Kogias, G., Karkazis, P. A., Xevgenis, M. G., Atlam, H. F., Ekuri, N., Azad, M. A., & Lallie, H. S. (2024). Blockchain Forensics: A Systematic Literature Review of Techniques, Applications, Challenges, and Future Directions. *Electronics 2024, Vol. 13, Page 3568, 13*(17), 3568. DOI: 10.3390/electronics13173568

Kolhar, A. (2025). Future Trends and Innovation in Machine Intelligence for Cyber Risk Management. In *Machine Intelligence Applications in Cyber-Risk Management* (pp. 415–438). IGI Global Scientific Publishing.

Kolluru, V., John, R., Chen, J., Konkathi, P., Kolluru, S., Saraf, S., Henebry, G. M., Xiao, J., Jain, K., & Kussainova, M. (2024). Dominant role of grazing and snow cover variability on vegetation shifts in the drylands of Kazakhstan. *Communications Earth & Environment, 5*(1), 424. DOI: 10.1038/s43247-024-01587-1

Kowalewski, O., Stetsyuk, I., & Talavera, O. (2007). Corporate governance and dividend policy in Poland.

Koza, E. (2022). Semantic analysis of ISO/IEC 27000 standard series and NIST cybersecurity framework to outline differences and consistencies in the context of operational and strategic information security. *Med. Eng. Themes*, *2*, 26–39.

Kubecka, C. (2024). Secrets From the Future: Hacking in a Post-Quantum Cryptography World: Implications for Cyber Security and National Defense.

Kulkarni, P., Pathak, P., Pillai, S., & Tigga, V. (2025). Role of Generative AI for Fraud Detection and Prevention. *Generative Artificial Intelligence in Finance: Large Language Models, Interfaces, and Industry Use Cases to Transform Accounting and Finance Processes*, 175-198.

Kwame, A., & Petrucka, P. M. (2021). A literature-based study of patient-centered care and communication in nurse-patient interactions: Barriers, facilitators, and the way forward. *BMC Nursing*, *20*(1), 158. DOI: 10.1186/s12912-021-00684-2 PMID: 34479560

La Porta, R., Lopez-de-Silanes, F., Shleifer, A., & Vishny, R. (2000). Investor protection and corporate governance. *Journal of Financial Economics*, *58*(1-2), 3–27. DOI: 10.1016/S0304-405X(00)00065-9

Landoll, D. (2021). *The security risk assessment handbook: A complete guide for performing security risk assessments.* CRC press. DOI: 10.1201/9781003090441

Lawrence, W., Tarr, J.-A., Brook, N., Chaperon, M., & Sorel, A. (2023). Parametric insurance. In A. A. Tarr, J.-A. Tarr, M. Thompson, & D. Wilkinson (Eds.), The global insurance market and change (1st ed., pp. 127–156). Informa Law from Routledge. https://doi.org/10.4324/9781003319054-6

Leal, R. P., & Carvalhal-da-Silva, A. L. (2007). Corporate governance and value in Brazil (and in Chile). *Investor protection and corporate governance: Firm-level evidence across. Latinskaia Amerika = América Latina*, •••, 213–287.

Lehto, M. (2022). Cyber-attacks against critical infrastructure. In *Cyber security: Critical infrastructure protection* (pp. 3–42). Springer International Publishing. DOI: 10.1007/978-3-030-91293-2_1

Li, H., Jahera, J. S.Jr, & Yost, K. (2013). Corporate risk and corporate governance: Another view. *Managerial Finance*, *39*(3), 204–227. DOI: 10.1108/03074351311302773

Lindsay, J. R. (2020). Surviving the quantum cryptocalypse. *Strategic Studies Quarterly*, *14*(2), 49–73.

Litov, L. P. (2005). Corporate governance and financing policy: New evidence. *Unpublished working paper.*

Liu, D. (2009). Digital Forensics and Analyzing Data. *Cisco Router and Switch Forensics*, 15–38. DOI: 10.1016/B978-1-59749-418-2.00001-6

Liu, W., & Johnson, R. (2023). An integrated framework for supply chain cyber risk transfer. *The Geneva Papers on Risk and Insurance. Issues and Practice*, *48*(1), 151–186. DOI: 10.1057/s41288-022-00268-4

Lv, Z. (2023). Generative artificial intelligence in the metaverse era. *Cognitive Robotics*, *3*, 208–217. DOI: 10.1016/j.cogr.2023.06.001

Maccoll, J., Hüsch, P., Mott, G., Sullivan, J., Nurse, J. R. C., Turner, S., & Pattnaik, N. (n.d.). *The Scourge of Ransomware: Victim Insights on Harms to Individuals, Organisations and Society*. Retrieved March 26, 2025, from www.rusi.org

Madhavan, K., Yazdinejad, A., Zarrinkalam, F., & Dehghantanha, A. (2025). Quantifying security vulnerabilities: A metric-driven security analysis of gaps in current AI standards. *arXiv preprint arXiv:2502.08610.*

Maldonado, D., Cruz, E., Torres, J. A., Cruz, P. J., & Benitez, S. D. P. G. (2024). Multi-agent Systems: A survey about its components, framework and workflow. *IEEE Access : Practical Innovations, Open Solutions*, *12*, 80950–80975. DOI: 10.1109/ACCESS.2024.3409051

Malempati, M., Pandiri, L., Paleti, S., & Singireddy, J. (2023). Transforming Financial And Insurance Ecosystems Through Intelligent Automation, Secure Digital Infrastructure, And Advanced Risk Management Strategies. *Jeevani, Transforming Financial And Insurance Ecosystems Through Intelligent Automation, Secure Digital Infrastructure, And Advanced Risk Management Strategies* (2023).

Mangharamani, R., & Agarwal, R. (2025). AI-driven predictive risk modeling in health insurance: Optimizing coverage and cost efficiency with self-learning systems. *International Journal of Progressive Research in Engineering Management and Science, 5*(3), 1 420–1 430.

Mardnly, Z., Mouselli, S., & Abdulraouf, R. (2018). Corporate governance and firm performance: An empirical evidence from Syria. *International Journal of Islamic and Middle Eastern Finance and Management, 11*(4), 591–607. DOI: 10.1108/IMEFM-05-2017-0107

Marrow, A. A. (2025). *Quantum Computing: Evaluating the Threat Landscape and Risk Management Strategies* (Doctoral dissertation, Capitol Technology University).

Martynova, M., & Renneboog, L. D. R. (2010). A corporate governance index: convergence and diversity of national corporate governance regulations.

Master Network Traffic Analysis with Wireshark | LevelBlue. (n.d.). Retrieved March 26, 2025, from https://levelblue.com/blogs/security-essentials/network-traffic-analysis-using-wireshark

Mathauer, I., & Oranje, M. (2024). Machine learning in health financing: Benefits, risks and regulatory needs. *Bulletin of the World Health Organization, 102*(3), 216–224. DOI: 10.2471/BLT.23.290333 PMID: 38420574

Mbah, G. O., & Evelyn, A. N. (2024). AI-powered cybersecurity: Strategic approaches to mitigate risk and safeguard data privacy.

McIntosh, T. R., Susnjak, T., Liu, T., Watters, P., Xu, D., Liu, D., Nowrozy, R., & Halgamuge, M. N. (2024). From COBIT to ISO 42001: Evaluating cybersecurity frameworks for opportunities, risks, and regulatory compliance in commercializing large language models. *Computers & Security, 144*, 103964. DOI: 10.1016/j.cose.2024.103964

McIntyre, D. L., & Frank, R. (2021). *No Gambles with Information Security: The Victim Psychology of a Ransomware Attack*. 43–60. DOI: 10.1007/978-3-030-60527-8_4

Mehrizi, M. H. R., Nicolini, D., & Modol, J. R. (2022). How do organizations learn from information system incidents? A synthesis of the past, present, and future. *Management Information Systems Quarterly, 46*(1), 531–590. DOI: 10.25300/MISQ/2022/14305

Mehta, N., & Pandit, A. (2018). Concurrence of big data analytics and healthcare: A systematic review. *International Journal of Medical Informatics, 114*, 57–65. DOI: 10.1016/j.ijmedinf.2018.03.013 PMID: 29673604

Miramirkhani, N., Appini, M. P., Nikiforakis, N., & Polychronakis, M. (2017). Spotless Sandboxes: Evading Malware Analysis Systems Using Wear-and-Tear Artifacts. *Proceedings - IEEE Symposium on Security and Privacy*, 1009–1024. DOI: 10.1109/SP.2017.42

Mohammed, A. F. A., & Rahman, H. M. A. A. (2024). The role of artificial intelligence (AI) in fraud detection in the private sector in Saudi Arabia. *Risk Management, 100*, 472–506.

Mohanty, P. (2003). Institutional investors and corporate governance in India. *National Stock Exchange of India Research Initiative Paper*, (15).

Mohapatra, H., & Mishra, S. R. (2024). Analysis of Sector-Specific Responses of AI Generative. In Generative, A. I. (Ed.), *Current Trends and Applications* (pp. 167–184). Springer Nature Singapore. DOI: 10.1007/978-981-97-8460-8_9

Moolchandani, S. (2025). AI-driven risk platform automating data aggregation and risk insight generation. *International Journal of Science Engineering and Technology*, *13*(1), 12.

Morales, E. F., & Escalante, H. J. (2022). A brief introduction to supervised, unsupervised, and reinforcement learning. In *Biosignal processing and classification using computational learning and intelligence* (pp. 111–129). Academic Press. DOI: 10.1016/B978-0-12-820125-1.00017-8

Mucskova, M. (2024). Transforming Banking with Artificial Intelligence: Applications, Challenges, and Implications. *Trends Economics and Management*, *18*(42), 21–37. DOI: 10.13164/trends.2024.42.21

Müller, C., Nagaraj, S., & Patterson, B. (2023). Measuring fourth-party risk: Analysis of extended supply chain vulnerabilities. *Information and Computer Security*, *31*(2), 257–276. DOI: 10.1108/ICS-08-2022-0126

Musa, H., Musová, Z., & Debnárová, L. (2015). Responsibility in the corporate governance framework and financial decision making process. *Procedia Economics and Finance*, *23*, 1023–1029. DOI: 10.1016/S2212-5671(15)00371-8

Narayan, M., Shukla, P., Dileep Kumar, M., & Mani, N. (2025). Generative AI in FinTech: Revolutionizing Fraud Detection, Personalized Advising, and Predictive Analytics. In *Generative AI in FinTech: Revolutionizing Finance Through Intelligent Algorithms* (pp. 137–154). Springer Nature Switzerland. DOI: 10.1007/978-3-031-76957-3_7

Näther, C., Herzinger, D., Gazdag, S. L., Steghöfer, J. P., Daum, S., & Loebenberger, D. (2024). Migrating Software Systems Towards Post-Quantum Cryptography–A Systematic Literature Review. *IEEE Access : Practical Innovations, Open Solutions*, *12*, 132107–132126. DOI: 10.1109/ACCESS.2024.3450306

Navigating the Cybersecurity Landscape: A Comprehensive Review of Cyber-Attacks, Emerging Trends, and Recent Developments. (n.d.). Retrieved March 26, 2025, from https://www.researchgate.net/publication/378343830_Navigating_the_Cyber_security_Landscape_A_Comprehensive_Review_of_Cyber-Attacks_Emerging_Trends_and_Recent_Developments

Nazir, S., Patel, S., & Patel, D. (2021). Assessing and augmenting SCADA cybersecurity: A survey of techniques. *Computers & Security*, *112*, 102513. DOI: 10.1016/j.cose.2021.102513

Neethirajan, S. R. (2023). AI-driven climate neutrality in dairy farming: Benchmarking emissions for sustainable transformation: *Preprints*.

Neftci, E. O., & Averbeck, B. B. (2019). Reinforcement learning in artificial and biological systems. *Nature Machine Intelligence*, *1*(3), 133–143. DOI: 10.1038/s42256-019-0025-4

Network Segmentation and How it Can Prevent Ransomware. (n.d.). Retrieved March 26, 2025, from https://www.threatintelligence.com/blog/network-segmentation

Nguyen, P. N. (2025). Quantum technology: A financial risk assessment. *Digital Finance*, ●●●, 1–40.

Nuhiu, A., & Aliu, F. (2025). The Transformative Role of Big Data Analytics and Generative AI in Redefining FinTech for New Business Models. In *Generative Artificial Intelligence (AI) Approaches for Industrial Applications* (pp. 281–304). Springer Nature Switzerland. DOI: 10.1007/978-3-031-76710-4_14

Obermeyer, Z., Powers, B., Vogeli, C., & Mullainathan, S. (2019). Dissecting racial bias in an algorithm used to manage the health of populations. *Science*, *366*(6464), 447–453. DOI: 10.1126/science.aax2342 PMID: 31649194

Odeh, A., Aboshgifa, A., & Belhaj, N. (2023). *Mitigating DDoS Attacks in Cloud Computing Environments: Challenges and Strategies*. Paper presented at the 2023 International Conference on Electrical, Computer and Energy Technologies (ICECET). DOI: 10.1109/ICECET58911.2023.10389269

Odeh, A., Keshta, I., & Abdelfattah, E. (2021). *Machine learningtechniquesfor detection of website phishing: A review for promises and challenges*. Paper presented at the 2021 IEEE 11th Annual Computing and Communication Workshop and Conference (CCWC). DOI: 10.1109/CCWC51732.2021.9375997

Odeh, A., Abdelfattah, E., & Salameh, W. (2024). Privacy-Preserving Data Sharing in Telehealth Services. *Applied Sciences (Basel, Switzerland)*, *14*(23), 10808. DOI: 10.3390/app142310808

Odeh, A., & Abu Taleb, A. (2023). Ensemble-Based Deep Learning Models for Enhancing IoT Intrusion Detection. *Applied Sciences (Basel, Switzerland)*, *13*(21), 11985. DOI: 10.3390/app132111985

Odeh, A., Al-Haija, Q. A., Aref, A., & Taleb, A. A. (2023). Comparative study of catboost, xgboost, and lightgbm for enhanced URL phishing detection: A performance assessment. *Journal of Internet Services and Information Security, 13*(4), 1–11. DOI: 10.58346/JISIS.2023.I4.001

Odeh, A., & Taleb, A. A. (2023). A Multi-Faceted Encryption Strategy for Securing Patient Information in Medical Imaging. *Journal of Wireless Mobile Networks, Ubiquitous Computing and Dependable Applications, 14*(4), 164–176. DOI: 10.58346/JOWUA.2023.I4.012

Odeh, A., & Taleb, A. A. (2024). Utilizing linear regression and random forest models for money laundering identification. *Telkomnika, 22*(6), 1573–1580. DOI: 10.12928/telkomnika.v22i6.26163

Odeh, A., Taleb, A. A., Alhajahjeh, T., Aparicio, F., Hamed, S., Al Daradkeh, N., & Al-Jarallah, N. A. (2024). *Data Privacy and Compliance in IoT Smart and Agile Cybersecurity for IoT and IIoT Environments*. IGI Global.

Odeh, A., Taleb, A. A., Alhajahjeh, T., & Aparicio-Navarro, F. (2024). *Cryptographic Solutions Smart and Agile Cybersecurity for IoT and IIoT Environments*. IGI Global.

Ofoegbu, W. C., & LAGUO, L. G. (2023). Simulation: A tool for system design and analysis. *GPH-International Journal of Social Science and Humanities Research, 6*(11), 98-111.

Okenwa, C. D., David, O. D., Orelaja, A., & Akinwande, O. T. (2024). Exploring the role of explainable AI in compliance models for fraud prevention. *International Journal of Research and Scientific Innovation, 13*(5), 232–239.

Oliver Wyman Health. (2020). AI will enable personalized, proactive, and smarter care [). Oliver Wyman.]. *The Innovation Journal, 4*, •••.

Orji, U., & Ukwandu, E. (2024). Machine learning for an explainable cost prediction of medical insurance. *Machine Learning with Applications, 15*, 100516. DOI: 10.1016/j.mlwa.2023.100516

Pallaria, A. (2023). Risk-mitigation techniques: from (re-) insurance to alternative risk transfer.

Pandey, P., & Katsikas, S. (2023). The future of cyber risk management: AI and DLT for automated cyber risk modelling, decision making, and risk transfer. In *Handbook of Research on Artificial Intelligence, Innovation and Entrepreneurship* (pp. 272–290). Edward Elgar Publishing.

Pandey, P., & Kapoor, A. (2025). CYBERCRIME IN THE DIGITAL ERA: IMPACTS, AWARENESS, AND STRATEGIC SOLUTIONS FOR A SECURE FUTURE. *Sachetas, 4*(1), 32–37. DOI: 10.55955/410004

Pant, P. (2025). Revolutionizing Insurance Data Modernization: Enhancing Property and Casualty Insurance with Cloud Solutions, Data Lakes, and Real-Time Reporting to Propel Advanced Analytics, Ensure Unified Governance and Compliance, and Foster Innovation and Experimentation. *Journal of Computational Analysis and Applications, 34*(5).

Pareek, C. S. (2023). From detection to prevention: The evolution of fraud testing frameworks in insurance through AI. *Journal of Artificial Intelligence. Machine Learning & Data Science, 1*(2), 1805–1812.

Park, J. Y., Moon, Y. H., Lee, W., Kim, S. H., & Sakurai, K. (2021). A survey of polynomial multiplication with RSA-ECC coprocessors and implementations of NIST PQC Round3 KEM algorithms in Exynos2100. *IEEE Access : Practical Innovations, Open Solutions, 10*, 2546–2563. DOI: 10.1109/ACCESS.2021.3138807

Park, K., Tran, H., & Kim, H. K. (2021). Network analysis of cyber security risk propagation in vendor ecosystems. *IEEE Transactions on Information Forensics and Security, 16*, 3415–3429. DOI: 10.1109/TIFS.2021.3082307

Park, S., & Han, J. (2018). Using predictive analytics to identify high-risk patients for cost-effective care management. *Journal of Medical Systems, 42*(12), 233.

Parveen, N. (2024). *Law and AI-Powered Actuarial Revolution: Navigating the Future of Insurance Risk Assessment Artificial Intelligence and Actuarial Science.* Chapman and Hall/CRC. DOI: 10.1201/9781003472551-19

Pasek, A., Lin, C. K., Cooper, Z. G. T., & Kinder, J. B. (2023). *Digital Energetics.* U of Minnesota Press.

Patil, D. (2024). Artificial Intelligence In Financial Services: Advancements In Fraud Detection, Risk Management, And Algorithmic Trading Optimization. *Risk Management, And Algorithmic Trading Optimization (November 20, 2024).*

Patil, D. (2024). Artificial intelligence in financial services: Advancements in fraud detection, risk management, and algorithmic trading optimization. *Risk Management.*

Patterson, L. A., & Doyle, M. W. (2021). Measuring water affordability and the financial capability of utilities. *AWWA Water Science, 3*(6), e1260. DOI: 10.1002/aws2.1260

Peltier, T. R. (2013). *Information security fundamentals*. CRC Press., DOI: 10.1201/b15573

Porwal, P. D. (2025). Ethics and Laws: Governing Generative AI's Role in Financial Systems. Generative Artificial Intelligence in Finance: Large Language Models, Interfaces, and Industry Use Cases to Transform Accounting and Finance Processes, 283-298.

Prakash, V., & Deokar, R. (2025). Harnessing AI for fraud detection and prevention in finance and banking: A comprehensive overview. In *Real-World Applications of AI Innovation* (pp. 389–406).

Radanliev, P. (2024). Cyber diplomacy: Defining the opportunities for cybersecurity and risks from artificial intelligence, IoT, blockchains, and quantum computing. *Journal of Cyber Security Technology*, *1*, 1–51.

Radanliev, P., De Roure, D., Maple, C., Nurse, J. R., Nicolescu, R., & Ani, U. (2024). AI security and cyber risk in IoT systems. *Frontiers in Big Data*, *7*, 1402745. DOI: 10.3389/fdata.2024.1402745 PMID: 39449740

Rah, A. (2023). *Device Management in the Security of "Bring Your Own Device" (BYOD) for the Post-pandemic, Remote Workplace*. University of Fairfax.

Rahman, M. M., Pokharel, B. P., Sayeed, S. A., Bhowmik, S. K., Kshetri, N., & Eashrak, N. (2024). riskAIchain: AI-driven IT infrastructure—blockchain-backed approach for enhanced risk management. *Risks*, *12*(12), 206. DOI: 10.3390/risks12120206

Ramachandran, M. S., Sajithabanu, S., Ponmalar, A., Sithik, M. M., & Anand, A. J. (2024). Fraud detection and risk management using AI in business intelligence. In *Intersection of AI and Business Intelligence in Data-Driven Decision-Making* (pp. 117–150). IGI Global. DOI: 10.4018/979-8-3693-5288-5.ch005

Ramakrishna, D., & Shaik, M. A. (2024). A Comprehensive analysis of Cryptographic Algorithms: Evaluating Security, Efficiency, and Future Challenges. *IEEE Access : Practical Innovations, Open Solutions*.

Randhawa, R. H., Aslam, N., Alauthman, M., Khalid, M., & Rafiq, H. (2024). Deep reinforcement learning-based Evasion Generative Adversarial Network for botnet detection. *Future Generation Computer Systems*, *150*, 294–302. DOI: 10.1016/j.future.2023.09.011

Rangaraju, S. (2023). Secure by intelligence: Enhancing products with AI-driven security measures. *EPH-International Journal of Science And Engineering*, *9*(3), 36–41.

Ransomware Attack - What is it and How Does it Work? - Check Point Software. (n.d.-a). Retrieved March 26, 2025, from https://www.checkpoint.com/cyber-hub/threat-prevention/ransomware/

Ransomware Attack - What is it and How Does it Work? - Check Point Software. (n.d.-b). Retrieved March 26, 2025, from https://www.checkpoint.com/cyber-hub/threat-prevention/ransomware/

Ransomware Attacks and Types | How do Locky, Petya, and other ransomware differ? (n.d.-a). Retrieved March 26, 2025, from https://www.kaspersky.com/resource-center/threats/ransomware-attacks-and-types

Ransomware Attacks and Types | How do Locky, Petya, and other ransomware differ? (n.d.-b). Retrieved March 26, 2025, from https://www.kaspersky.com/resource-center/threats/ransomware-attacks-and-types

Ransomware Data Recovery: How to Save Your Data. (n.d.). Retrieved March 26, 2025, from https://cloudian.com/guides/ransomware-backup/ransomware-data-recovery-5-ways-to-save-your-data/

Ransomware: Paying Cyber Extortion Demands in Cryptocurrency | Marsh. (n.d.). Retrieved March 26, 2025, from https://www.marsh.com/en/services/cyber-risk/insights/ransomware-paying-cyber-extortion-demands-in-cryptocurrency.html

Rao, B., Harrison, A. J., & Mulloth, B. (2020). Defense technological innovation: Issues and challenges in an era of converging technologies.

Rao, A. R., Jain, R., Singh, M., & Garg, R. (2024). Predictive interpretable analytics models for forecasting healthcare costs using open healthcare data. *Healthcare Analytics*, *6*, 100351. DOI: 10.1016/j.health.2024.100351

Rao, A. S., Radanovic, M., Liu, Y., Hu, S., Fang, Y., Khoshelham, K., Palaniswami, M., & Ngo, T. (2022). Real-time monitoring of construction sites: Sensors, methods, and applications. *Automation in Construction*, *136*, 104099. DOI: 10.1016/j.autcon.2021.104099

Reddy, A. S. (2023). *Future Proofing Insurance Operations: A Guidewire-Centric Approach to Cloud.* Cybersecurity, and Generative AI.

Redman, J. C. A. (2014). *The diwaniyya: guestroom sociability and bureaucratic brokerage in Kuwait.* The University of Utah.

Rehan, H. (2024). AI-driven cloud security: The future of safeguarding sensitive data in the digital age. [JAIGS]. *Journal of Artificial Intelligence General Science*, *1*(1), 132–151.

Romanosky, S., Ablon, L., Kuehn, A., & Jones, T. (2019). Content analysis of cyber insurance policies: How do carriers price cyber risk? *Journal of Cybersecurity*, *5*(1), 1–19. DOI: 10.1093/cybsec/tyz002

Sætra, H. S. (2023). Generative AI: Here to stay, but for good? *Technology in Society*, *75*, 102372. DOI: 10.1016/j.techsoc.2023.102372

Sahni, N., Stein, G., Zemmel, R., & Cutler, D. M. (2023). The potential impact of artificial intelligence on healthcare spending (NBER Working Paper No. 30866). National Bureau of Economic Research.

Salem, A. H., Azzam, S. M., Emam, O. E., & Abohany, A. A. (2024). Advancing cybersecurity: A comprehensive review of AI-driven detection techniques. *Journal of Big Data*, *11*(1), 105. DOI: 10.1186/s40537-024-00957-y

Sarin, S., Singh, S. K., Kumar, S., Goyal, S., Gupta, B. B., Alhalabi, W., & Arya, V. (2024). Unleashing the Power of Multi-Agent Reinforcement Learning for Algorithmic Trading in the Digital Financial Frontier and Enterprise Information Systems. *Computers, Materials & Continua*, *80*(2), 3123–3138. DOI: 10.32604/cmc.2024.051599

Sarkar, J., Sarkar, S., & Sen, K. (2012). A corporate governance index for large listed companies in India. *Pace University Accounting Research Paper*, (2012/08).

Saxena, A., Verma, S., & Mahajan, J. (2024). The Evolution of Insurance in the Digital Age. In *Generative AI in Banking Financial Services and Insurance: A Guide to Use Cases, Approaches, and Insights* (pp. 201–237). Apress. DOI: 10.1007/979-8-8688-0559-2_7

Seethala, S. C. (2025). Revolutionizing Insurance with AI, Cloud, and Cybersecurity: A Strategic Guidewire Approach. *Cloud, and Cybersecurity: A Strategic Guidewire Approach (April 01, 2025)*. in enhancing organizational resilience against cyber threats. *Cybersecurity Education Journal*, *5*(1), 35–50.

Segate, R. V., & Daly, A. (2024). Encoding the enforcement of safety standards into smart robots to harness their computing sophistication and collaborative potential: A legal risk assessment for European Union policymakers. *European Journal of Risk Regulation*, *15*(3), 665–704. DOI: 10.1017/err.2023.72

Shahidi, S., Darmel, F. A., Jalalzai, S., & Amiri, G. A. (2024). Opportunities and Challenges in AI-Driven Cybersecurity: A Systematic Literature. *Journal of Social Science Utilizing Technology*, *2*(4), 516–530.

Shamo, S. A. (2024). Bridging the Quantum Divide: A Comprehensive Analysis of NIST and ISO Standards for Post-Quantum Cryptography and Strategies for Global Harmonization. *Available at SSRN* 4864519. DOI: 10.2139/ssrn.4864519

Sharma, R., Mehta, K., & Sharma, P. (2024). Role of artificial intelligence and machine learning in fraud detection and prevention. In *Risks and Challenges of AI-Driven Finance: Bias, Ethics, and Security* (pp. 90–120). IGI Global. DOI: 10.4018/979-8-3693-2185-0.ch005

Shen, Y. (2025). Risk Quantification-based Underwriting Assessment Model. *Highlights in Business. Economics and Management*, *48*, 123–133.

Shreedevi, K. S., Chayadevi, M. L., & Geetha, S. (2024). Advancing security in the modern digital era–A comprehensive exploration of elliptic curve cryptography. In *Computer Science Engineering* (pp. 252–261). CRC Press. DOI: 10.1201/9781003565024-28

Siagian, F., Siregar, S. V., & Rahadian, Y. (2013). Corporate governance, reporting quality, and firm value: Evidence from Indonesia. *Journal of Accounting in Emerging Economies*, *3*(1), 4–20. DOI: 10.1108/20440831311287673

Sindiramutty, S. R. (2023). Autonomous threat hunting: A future paradigm for AI-driven threat intelligence. *arXiv preprint arXiv:2401.00286.*

Sindiramutty, S. R., Prabagaran, K. R. V., Jhanjhi, N. Z., Murugesan, R. K., Brohi, S. N., & Masud, M. (2025). Generative AI in Network Security and Intrusion Detection. In *Reshaping CyberSecurity With Generative AI Techniques* (pp. 77–124). IGI Global.

Singhal, N., Goyal, S., & Singhal, T. (2024). Emerging Trends in Regulatory and Legal Frameworks for Decentralized Insurance. *Potential, Risks, and Ethical Implications of Decentralized Insurance*, 211-260.

Singh, S., & Sakk, E. (2024). Implementation and Analysis of Shor's Algorithm to Break RSA Cryptosystem Security. *Authorea Preprints*. DOI: 10.36227/techrxiv.170259160.05374043/v2

Singireddy, S., Adusupalli, B., Pamisetty, A., Mashetty, S., & Kaulwar, P. K. (2024). Redefining Financial Risk Strategies: The Integration of Smart Automation, Secure Access Systems, and Predictive Intelligence in Insurance, Lending, and Asset Management. *Journal of Artificial Intelligence and Big Data Disciplines*, *1*(1), 109–124. DOI: 10.70179/k86dcv60

Sivamayil, K., Rajasekar, E., Aljafari, B., Nikolovski, S., Vairavasundaram, S., & Vairavasundaram, I. (2023). A systematic study on reinforcement learning based applications. *Energies, 16*(3), 1512. DOI: 10.3390/en16031512

Sodiya, E. O., Umoga, U. J., Amoo, O. O., & Atadoga, A. (2024). Quantum computing and its potential impact on US cybersecurity: A review: Scrutinizing the challenges and opportunities presented by quantum technologies in safeguarding digital assets. *Global Journal of Engineering and Technology Advances, 18*(02), 049-064.

Sorensen, G., Dennerlein, J. T., Peters, S. E., Sabbath, E. L., Kelly, E. L., & Wagner, G. R. (2021). The future of research on work, safety, health and wellbeing: A guiding conceptual framework. *Social Science & Medicine, 269*, 113593. DOI: 10.1016/j.socscimed.2020.113593 PMID: 33341740

Srinivasagopalan, L. N. (2024). Reinforcement Learning For Optimizing Healthcare Insurance Premium Pricing.

Srivastava, V., Das, N., & Pattanayak, J. K. (2019). Impact of corporate governance attributes on cost of equity: Evidence from an emerging economy. *Managerial Auditing Journal, 34*(2), 142–161. DOI: 10.1108/MAJ-01-2018-1770

Stettinger, G., Weissensteiner, P., & Khastgir, S. (2024). Trustworthiness assurance assessment for high-risk AI-based systems. *IEEE Access : Practical Innovations, Open Solutions, 12*, 22718–22745. DOI: 10.1109/ACCESS.2024.3364387

Stoddart, K. (2022). Non and sub-state actors: cybercrime, terrorism, and hackers. In *Cyberwarfare: threats to critical infrastructure* (pp. 351–399). Springer International Publishing. DOI: 10.1007/978-3-030-97299-8_6

Stokel-Walker, C., & Van Noorden, R. (2023). What ChatGPT and generative AI mean for science. *Nature, 614*(7947), 214–216. DOI: 10.1038/d41586-023-00340-6 PMID: 36747115

Strich, F., Mayer, A.-S., & Fiedler, M. (2021). What do I do in a world of artificial intelligence? Investigating the impact of substitutive decision-making AI systems on employees' professional role identity. *Journal of the Association for Information Systems, 22*(2), 9. DOI: 10.17705/1jais.00663

Sun, M. M. (2024). Comprehensive statistical modeling of cyber risks and analysis of data breaches with applications in cyber insurance.

Sutradhar, M. S., Mondal, M. S., Bose, R., Dey, M. R. K., & Golder, M. S. S. (2025). *Securing the Future with Cyber Intelligence Innovations*. Authors Click Publishing.

Takamoto, M., Praditia, T., Leiteritz, R., MacKinlay, D., Alesiani, F., Pflüger, D., & Niepert, M. (2022). Pdebench: An extensive benchmark for scientific machine learning. *Advances in Neural Information Processing Systems*, *35*, 1596–1611.

Tarchouna, A., Jarraya, B., & Bouri, A. (2017). How to explain non-performing loans by many corporate governance variables simultaneously? A corporate governance index is built to US commercial banks. *Research in International Business and Finance*, *42*, 645–657. DOI: 10.1016/j.ribaf.2017.07.008

Tariq, M. U. (2024). Leading Smart Technologies and Innovations for E-Business 5.0: Applications and Management Frameworks. In Popkova, E. (Ed.), *Smart Technologies and Innovations in E-Business* (pp. 25–46). IGI Global., DOI: 10.4018/978-1-6684-7840-0.ch002

Tariq, M. U. (2024). Leveraging AI for Entrepreneurial Innovation in Healthcare. In Özsungur, F. (Ed.), *Generating Entrepreneurial Ideas With AI* (pp. 192–216). IGI Global., DOI: 10.4018/979-8-3693-3498-0.ch009

Tariq, M. U. (2024). The role of AI ethics in cost and complexity reduction. In Tennin, K., Ray, S., & Sorg, J. (Eds.), *Cases on AI ethics in business* (pp. 59–78). IGI Global., DOI: 10.4018/979-8-3693-2643-5.ch004

Tariq, M. U. (2024). The role of AI in skilling, upskilling, and reskilling the workforce. In Doshi, R., Dadhich, M., Poddar, S., & Hiran, K. (Eds.), *Integrating generative AI in education to achieve sustainable development goals* (pp. 421–433). IGI Global., DOI: 10.4018/979-8-3693-2440-0.ch023

Tariq, M. U. (2025). AI-Driven Research Methodologies: Revolutionizing Data-Driven Discoveries in Engineering and Physical Sciences. In Basha, J., Alade, T., Al Khazimi, M., Vasudevan, R., & Khan, J. (Eds.), *Optimizing Research Techniques and Learning Strategies With Digital Technologies* (pp. 97–122). IGI Global Scientific Publishing., DOI: 10.4018/979-8-3693-7863-2.ch004

Tariq, M. U. (2025). Leveraging Artificial Intelligence to Enhance Diversity and Drive Business Innovation. In Margaretha van der Poll, H., Andrew van der Poll, J., & Ngwakwe, C. (Eds.), *Diversity, AI, and Sustainability for Financial Growth* (pp. 79–96). IGI Global Scientific Publishing., DOI: 10.4018/979-8-3693-6011-8.ch004

Tariq, M. U. (2025). Navigating the Convergence of IoMT and Generative AI in Global Healthcare: Opportunities, Challenges, and Ethical Considerations. In Kumar, V., Katina, P., & Zhao, J. (Eds.), *Convergence of Internet of Medical Things (IoMT) and Generative AI* (pp. 513–534). IGI Global Scientific Publishing., DOI: 10.4018/979-8-3693-6180-1.ch022

Tariq, M. U. (2025). Quantum Algorithms and Predictive Analytics: Revolutionizing Consumer Insight. In Gajbhiye, P., Kannan, H., Rodriguez, R., & Rojas-Méndez, J. (Eds.), *The Quantum AI Era of Neuromarketing* (pp. 173–202). IGI Global Scientific Publishing., DOI: 10.4018/979-8-3693-7673-7.ch008

Thapaliya, S. (2024). Examining the influence of AI-driven cybersecurity in financial sector management. *The Batuk*, *10*(2), 129–144. DOI: 10.3126/batuk.v10i2.68147

The Power of Cyber Forensics in Solving Crimes. (n.d.). Retrieved March 26, 2025, from https://www.salvationdata.com/knowledge/cyber-forensics/

The Psychology of Ransomware: Tactics of Manipulation Used by Cybercriminals – Best Recipes Ever. (n.d.). Retrieved March 26, 2025, from https://ransomdecrypt.com/the-psychology-of-ransomware-tactics-of-manipulation-used-by-cybercriminals/

The role of cryptocurrency in ransomware attacks. (n.d.). Retrieved March 26, 2025, from https://www.manageengine.com/log-management/cyber-security/cryptocurrency-role-in-ransomware.html

Thilagavathi, M., Saranyadevi, R., Vijayakumar, N., Selvi, K., Anitha, L., & Sudharson, K. (2024). *AI-driven fraud detection in financial transactions with graph neural networks and anomaly detection*. Paper presented at the 2024 International Conference on Science Technology Engineering and Management (ICSTEM). DOI: 10.1109/ICSTEM61137.2024.10560838

Tiwari, S., Sresth, V., & Srivastava, A. (2020). The role of explainable AI in cybersecurity: Addressing transparency challenges in autonomous defense systems. *International Journal of Innovative Research in Science, Engineering and Technology*, *9*(3), 718–733. DOI: 10.15680/IJIRSET.2020.0903165

Tiwo, O. J., Adesokan-Imran, T. O., Babarinde, D. C., Oyekunle, S. M., Olutimehin, A. T., & Olaniyi, O. O. (2025). Advancing Security in Cloud-based Patient Information Systems with Quantum-resistant Encryption for Healthcare Data. *Asian Journal of Research in Computer Science*, *18*(4), 187–208. DOI: 10.9734/ajrcos/2025/v18i4615

Tom, J. J., Anebo, N. P., Onyekwelu, B. A., Wilfred, A., & Eyo, R. E. (2023). Quantum computers and algorithms: A threat to classical cryptographic systems. *International Journal of Engineering and Advanced Technology*, *12*(5), 25–38. DOI: 10.35940/ijeat.E4153.0612523

Topol, E. J. (2019). High-performance medicine: The convergence of human and artificial intelligence. *Nature Medicine*, *25*(1), 44–56. DOI: 10.1038/s41591-018-0300-7 PMID: 30617339

Tsohou, A., Diamantopoulou, V., Gritzalis, S., & Lambrinoudakis, C. (2023). Cyber insurance: State of the art, trends and future directions. *International Journal of Information Security, 22*(3), 737–748. DOI: 10.1007/s10207-023-00660-8 PMID: 36684688

Tu, T. T. T., Khanh, P. B., & Quyen, P. D. (2014). Developing corporate governance index for Vietnamese banking system. *International Journal of Financial Research, 5*(2), 175–188.

Tyas Tunggal, A. (2025, July 2). What is the cost of a data breach in 2023? UpGuard. https://www.upguard.com/blog/cost-of-data-breach

Vajjhala, N. R., Roy, S. S., Taşcı, B., & Chowdhury, M. E. H. (2025). Foundations and Emerging Trends in Generative Artificial Intelligence (AI) for Industrial Applications. *Generative Artificial Intelligence (AI) Approaches for Industrial Applications*, 1-18.

Voolstra, C. R., Suggett, D. J., Peixoto, R. S., Parkinson, J. E., Quigley, K. M., Silveira, C. B., & Bourne, D. G. (2021). Extending the natural adaptive capacity of coral holobionts. *Nature Reviews. Earth & Environment, 2*(11), 747–762. DOI: 10.1038/s43017-021-00214-3

Vose, R., Huang, B., Yin, X., Arndt, D., Easterling, D., Lawrimore, J., . . . Zhang, H. (2021). Implementing full spatial coverage in NOAA's global temperature analysis. *Geophysical Research Letters, 48*(4), e2020GL090873.

Wall, A. M. (2021). *Guidelines for artificial intelligence-driven enterprise compliance management systems* (Doctoral dissertation).

What Are Air-Gapped Backups? - How Air-Gapped Backups Work. (n.d.). Retrieved March 26, 2025, from https://stonefly.com/resources/what-are-air-gapped-backups/

What Are the Most Common Attack Vectors for Ransomware? (n.d.). Retrieved March 26, 2025, from https://www.cybereason.com/blog/what-are-the-most-common-attack-vectors-for-ransomware

What is a Cyber Crime Investigation? (n.d.). Retrieved March 26, 2025, from https://www.recordedfuture.com/threat-intelligence-101/incident-response-management/cyber-crime-investigation

What is a Lateral Movement? Prevention and Detection Methods | Fortinet. (n.d.). Retrieved March 26, 2025, from https://www.fortinet.com/resources/cyberglossary/lateral-movement

What is a Memory Dump? - GeeksforGeeks. (n.d.). Retrieved March 26, 2025, from https://www.geeksforgeeks.org/what-is-a-memory-dump/

What Is Ransomware-as-a-Service (RaaS)? | IBM. (n.d.). Retrieved March 26, 2025, from https://www.ibm.com/think/topics/ransomware-as-a-service

What is Social Engineering | Attack Techniques & Prevention Methods | Imperva. (n.d.). Retrieved March 26, 2025, from https://www.imperva.com/learn/application-security/social-engineering-attack/

Wilkens, S., & Moorhouse, J. (2023). Quantum computing for financial risk measurement. *Quantum Information Processing*, *22*(1), 51. DOI: 10.1007/s11128-022-03777-2

Wireshark: An Effective Tool for Network Analysis. (n.d.). Retrieved March 26, 2025, from https://www.researchgate.net/publication/374675769_Wireshark_An_Effective_Tool_for_Network_Analysis

Woods, D. W., & Böhme, R. (2021). *SoK: Quantifying cyber risk.* Paper presented at the 2021 IEEE Symposium on Security and Privacy (SP). DOI: 10.1109/SP40001.2021.00053

Woods, D. W., Agrafiotis, I., & Nurse, J. R. C. (2019). Mapping the coverage of security controls in cyber insurance proposal forms. *Journal of Internet Services and Applications*, *10*(1), 1–20. DOI: 10.1186/s13174-019-0104-0

Woods, D. W., & Böhme, R. (2021). SolarWinds and the challenges of patching: Can backup create new problems? *IEEE Security and Privacy*, *19*(4), 88–92. DOI: 10.1109/MSEC.2021.3070059

Woods, D. W., & Simpson, A. C. (2022). Policy limits, exclusions, and the interpretation of cyber insurance. *Journal of Cybersecurity*, *8*(1), 1–16. DOI: 10.1093/cybsec/tyac004

Xia, T., Sun, Y., Zhu, S., Rasheed, Z., & Shafique, K. (2018). Toward A Network-Assisted Approach for Effective Ransomware Detection. *ICST Transactions on Security and Safety*, *168506*, 168506. Advance online publication. DOI: 10.4108/eai.28-1-2021.168506

Yanamala, A. K. Y., Suryadevara, S., & Kalli, V. D. R. (2024). Balancing innovation and privacy: The intersection of data protection and artificial intelligence. *International Journal of Machine Learning Research in Cybersecurity and Artificial Intelligence*, *15*(1), 1–43.

Zakaria, W. Z. A., Alta, N. M. K. M., Abdollah, M. F., Abdollah, O., & Yassin, S. M. W. M. S. M. M. (2024). Early Detection of Windows Cryptographic Ransomware Based on Pre-Attack API Calls Features and Machine Learning. *Journal of Advanced Research in Applied Sciences and Engineering Technology, 39*(2), 110–131. DOI: 10.37934/araset.39.2.110131

Zhang, L., & Li, H. (2022). Network approaches to modeling cascading impacts in supply chain cyber incidents. *Computers & Security, 115*, 102630. DOI: 10.1016/j.cose.2022.102630

Zirar, A., Ali, S. I., & Islam, N. (2023). Worker and workplace Artificial Intelligence (AI) coexistence: Emerging themes and research agenda. *Technovation, 124*, 102747. DOI: 10.1016/j.technovation.2023.102747

Zohny, H., McMillan, J., & King, M. (2023). Ethics of generative AI. *Journal of Medical Ethics, 49*(2), 79–80. DOI: 10.1136/jme-2023-108909 PMID: 36693706

Zornetta, A. (2024). Quantum-safe global encryption policy. *International Journal of Law and Information Technology, 32*(1), eaae020. DOI: 10.1093/ijlit/eaae020

Züst, S., Huonder, M., West, S., & Stoll, O. (2022). Life-cycle oriented risk assessment using a Monte Carlo simulation. Applied Sciences, 12(1), 8. https://doi.org/10.3390/app12010008

About the Contributors

Moatsum Alawida is an Assistant Professor of Cybersecurity at Abu Dhabi University. He earned his PhD in Computer Science with a specialization in Cybersecurity (Cryptography) from the School of Computer Sciences, Universiti Sains Malaysia, in 2020. He has published over 55 articles in high-impact factor journals. From 2021 to 2024, he was ranked among the top 2% of scientists worldwide. His research interests include cybersecurity, chaotic systems, chaos-based cryptography, multimedia security, blockchain, quantum-based cryptography, and traditional cryptography. Dr. Alawida has served as a referee for esteemed journals such as IEEE, Springer, Elsevier and others. He has also contributed to numerous conferences as a committee member, presenter, and organizer. Additionally, he has received multiple internal and external research grants.

Ammar Almomani is an academic staff member in the School of Computing at Higher Colleges of Technology (HCT) in Sharjah, UAE, specializing in cybersecurity with a focus on artificial intelligence. He also served as the Head of the Research and Innovation Department before. and is a professor at Al-Balqa Applied University in Jordan. Academic and Professional Background: Prof. Almomani holds a Ph.D. in advanced internet security and monitoring from Universiti Sains Malaysia (USM), ranked #142 in the QS World University Rankings 2021. He also possesses a Master's degree in Computer Information Systems focusing on e-commerce security and a Bachelor's degree in Computer Science. With over 20 years of combined teaching and industry experience, he has worked at four leading academic institutions since 2006, teaching more than 47 topics across cybersecurity, computer science, and engineering disciplines. His expertise spans network security, wireless security, cryptography, cloud computing, ethical hacking, artificial intelligence, and big data analytics. Prof. Almomani also brings three years of industrial experience from the National Information Technology Center in Jordan. Research and Publications: A globally recognized researcher, Prof. Almomani was ranked among the Top 2% of influential researchers worldwide by Stanford University and the Scopus Index (2023-2024). With a prolific publication record of over 150 peer-reviewed articles, including 100 in Scopus-indexed journals (Scopus citations: 2000; H-index: 22), he also holds 10 patents granted in Germany and India. His works have earned 4080 citations on Google Scholar (H-index: 331; I-index: 66). He is a consultant and expert member of the UAE Research Map (R&D), frequently chairs international journals and conferences, and has a strong online following with over 108,000 readers on ResearchGate. Research Interests: Prof. Almomani's research interests focus on cybersecurity topics, including internet and network security, wireless security, cryptography, intrusion detection systems (IDS), IoT security, and cloud computing. His work often leverages intelligent techniques for threat detection, especially in combating botnets, worms, and other cyber threats. With over 100 publications in cybersecurity, AI, and data science, he remains at the forefront of innovation in these fields.

Mohammad Alauthman is an associate professor and chair of the Information Security Department at the Faculty of Information Technology, University of Petra inAmman, Jordan. His research interests lie in network security, intrusion detection systems,and the application of artificial intelligence techniques like machine learning and deep learning for botnet detection, DDoS detection, spam email filtering, IoT security, and network traffic classification. He obtained his Ph.D. in computer science with a focus on network security from Northumbria University in the UK in 2016. Alauthman has been awarded several research grants in the field of network security, supporting his work on advanced intrusion detection systems and the development of AI-driven security solutions. These grants have enabled him to conduct extensive research and collaborate with international experts. His funded projects have focused on enhancing the resilience of network infrastructures against emerging threats and improving the accuracy of threat detection mechanisms.

***

Abobakr Aboshgifa is a dedicated researcher at the Libyan Higher Technical Center for Training and Production in Tripoli, Libya. His work primarily focuses on cybersecurity, cloud computing, and the application of artificial intelligence in securing digital infrastructures. Over the years, he has contributed to several international publications that address key challenges in modern computing environments.

Gouher Ahmed has over 25 years of experience in various academic leadership, social and business settings, and consulting through North America, South Asia, and the Middle East. He is a Certified PMP Project Manager from USA. Prof. Gouher Ahmed is the Vice President of the Academy of Global Business Research & Practice, NJ, USA. He is an Advisor to the Government of Dubai, EIAC, Dubai and also a Congress Ambassador to Dubai Economy and Tourism, Government of Dubai, UAE. He has organized global conferences in different continents.

Mohammad Al-Khaldy is an Assistant professor of Business Intelligence and Data Analytics at University of Petra, Jordan. He completed his PhD in Atrificial Intelligence and Data Science for the University of Hull -United Kingdom - 20017. Alkhaldy's research interests include data analytics, machine learning, predictive analytics, NLP, and decision support systems. His research has been published extensively in academic journals and conferences. Alkhaldy taught a variety of courses in Artificial intelligence and business intelligence, including Data Mining, Business Analytics, Computer Programming, Intelligent business systems, Data Visualization, and machine learning. Alkhaldy is a member of Jordan Computers Society, and Arab Robotics & AI Association. He also a reviewer for several other academic conferences and journals.

Nabeel Alassaf Received his bachelor's degree in computer science from university of Jordan in Jordan, in 2002. And received his master's degree in computer science from university of Jordan in Jordan, in 2005, Currently, he is doing PHD in network resource management at in Cybersecurity Research Centre, Universiti Sains Malaysia (USM). He is currently a lecturer with computer science department at university of Jordan with master's degree. His research interest includes Computer Networks, Internet Communication Protocols (IPv6), Network Security, mobile agents, cybersecurity, AI and Internet of Thing (IoT).

Amjad Aldweesh is a computer associate professor interested in the Blockchain and Smart contracts technology as well as cyber security. Amjad has a Bachelor degree in computer science. He has a MSc degree in advanced computer science and security from the University of Manchester with distinction. Amjad is the second in the UK and the first in the middle east to have a PhD in the Blockchain and Smart contracts technology from Newcastle University.

Salam Al-E'mari earned her Ph.D. in Cybersecurity from Universiti Sains Malaysia (USM) in 2022. She is the Chair of the Information Security Department and an Assistant Professor at the University of Petra (UoP). With expertise in Blockchain, Deep Learning, and Network Security, she has contributed significantly to cybersecurity research. She previously earned her Bachelor's and Master's in Computer Science from Yarmouk University, Jordan, shaping her strong foundation in security and technology.

Mohd. Anas is an eminent academician whose journey in academia has been marked by a relentless pursuit of knowledge and a commitment to excellence. He pursued his Ph.D. in Commerce from Aligarh Muslim University with a solid foundation in commerce established through a Master's degree from Jamia Millia Islamia and a Bachelor's degree from the University of Delhi. He currently serves as an Assistant Professor at KR Mangalam University in Gurugram.

Manmeet Kaur Arora is a Research Scholar at the School of Law, Sharda University, Greater Noida. She is a graduate of Law and has completed her Master's in Law from Amity University, Noida. Manmeet Kaur is a qualified Company Secretary Executive Programme. She has over 8+ years of Industry Experience and 1 year of experience as an Associate at a reputed IPR Law Firm. Manmeet Kaur has attended 20+ National & International Conferences, Webinars, Seminars, Symposiums, and Paper Presentations and participated in 5+ Faculty Development programs. She has over 50+ publications in various esteemed Journals and Books. She is active at the Family Dispute Resolution Clinic, Meditation Centre, Greater Noida. Manmeet Kaur has a keen interest in the areas of Corporate Law, Intellectual Property Rights, Insolvency, Artificial Intelligence, Machine Learning, and Blockchain Technology.

Nabil Belhaj is a researcher at the Libyan Higher Technical Center for Training and Production in Tripoli, Libya. His research interests lie at the intersection of cloud computing, cybersecurity, and intelligent data analysis. Through his academic and professional contributions, he actively supports the advancement of secure and efficient computing solutions within the Libyan technical and educational sectors.

Indira Bhardwaj is an academician with more than 26 years of teaching and corporate experience across institutions in India. She has done her FDP from IIM Indore and has also worked at IIM Indore as Academic and Research Associate. Her PhD is from AMU, Aligarh in Understanding Corporate Value Using Intellectual Capital Assets and Reporting. Her research interests include Corporate Valuation, Corporate Finance and Banking. Her other areas of interest include Sustainability Management and Sustainability Reporting.

Saurabh Chandra is an accomplished legal scholar and currently serves as an Associate Professor & Assistant Dean at the School of Law, Bennett University, India. With a robust academic foundation, he earned his Bachelor of Arts and Bachelor of Laws (B.A. LL.B.) from the prestigious Aligarh Muslim University (A.M.U.). He further specialized in Business Laws, completing his Master of Laws (LL.M.) at the renowned National Law School of India University (NLSIU), Bangalore. Dr. Chandra's academic journey culminated in a Doctorate in Law (Ph.D.) from the esteemed National Law University (NLU) Delhi. In addition to his impressive legal education from some of India's most prestigious institutions, Dr. Saurabh Chandra also holds a master’s degree in Management with specialization in Human Resources in Management and another in Journalism and Mass Communication. With 16 years of teaching experience, he has established himself as an expert in Business and Corporate Laws, with numerous publications to his credit. Dr. Saurabh Chandra is a distinguished expert in Business and Corporate Laws, with a profound understanding of the intricate legal frameworks that govern the business world. His expertise is complemented by a robust portfolio of scholarly publications, which underscores his commitment to advancing knowledge in his field. Throughout his career, Dr. Chandra has consistently produced high-impact research that addresses critical issues in Business and Corporate Law. His publications are widely recognized for their depth of analysis, innovative perspectives, and practical relevance. He has contributed extensively to leading journals, where his work has often set new standards for legal scholarship. His publications not only reflect his scholarly rigor but also his dedication to addressing contemporary challenges faced by businesses and policymakers. By bridging the gap between theoretical insights and real-world applications, Dr. Chandra's work serves as a valuable resource for academics, legal practitioners, and industry professionals alike. Dr. Chandra brings a wealth of experience in Academic Administration, having successfully held various key administrative positions. His diverse qualifications and extensive experience make him a distinguished figure in the academic and legal communities.

Kiranbhai Ramabhai Dodiya is an experienced Cyber Forensic Expert and Assistant Professor specializing in cyber security and digital forensics. He has taught at prestigious institutions and is currently pursuing a PhD in Biochemistry and Forensic Science. With a strong background in ethical hacking and malware analysis, Kiranbhai is passionate about educating students and contributing to the field of cyber forensics. His expertise includes malware forensic, computer forensics, and data recovery software. Kiranbhai's commitment to professional growth is evident through his participation in workshops, seminars, and research publications. He is dedicated to shaping the next generation of professionals in the field and combatting cybercrimes.

Mohammed F.R. Anbar Received the bachelor’s degree in computer system engineering from Al-Azhar University, Palestine, the M.Sc. degree in information technology from Universiti Utara Malaysia (UUM), Malaysia, and the Ph.D. degree in advanced internet security and monitoring from the University Sains Malaysia (USM). His research interests include malware detection, web security, intrusion detection systems (IDS), intrusion prevention systems (IPS), network monitoring, the Internet of Things (IoT), and IPv6 security.

Jitin Gambhir Known for his engaging teaching style, dedication to student mentorship and administration with over 16 years of experience in reputed universities and institutes. A professional with a strong academic background, contributed to develop academic concepts and ethical standards among students to help them grow professionally in the competitive environment. An administrator with a versatile experience on various positions.

Wael M. Hadi is a distinguished computer scientist and academic leader who currently serves as Dean of the Faculty of Information Technology at the University of Petra in Jordan. He also holds the rank of Professor of Data Science. Over the course of his career, he has advanced through various roles, including Head of the Computer Information Systems Department, Chair of the Information Security program, and Director of the E-Learning Center. He earned his Ph.D. in Computer Information Systems, which laid a strong foundation for his extensive research in Artificial Intelligence, Machine Learning, Data Mining, and Big Data analytics. His work covers a wide spectrum of areas, from renewable energy and groundwater resource management to medical diagnostics and Arabic text mining. Notably, Professor Hadi has made significant contributions in associative classification, introducing novel algorithms that enhance both the speed and accuracy of data-driven solutions. In addition to his research and leadership duties, he has contributed to numerous Erasmus projects, fostering international academic collaborations and expanding IT education opportunities.

Ala Hamarsheh is an associate professor at the Faculty of Engineering and Information Technology of the Arab American University of Jenin. Dr. Hamarsheh has obtained a PhD in engineering sciences from Vrije Universiteit Brussel (VUB)/ Brussels-Belgium in 2012. He graduated in computer science at the Faculty of Science, Birzeit University, Palestine, in 2000. He obtained an MSc degree in computer science at the Kind Abdullah II School for IT, The University of Jordan, Jordan, in 2003. Dr. Hamarsheh has published numerous papers in international refereed journals and conferences.

Shams ul arfeen Laghari is a seasoned computer scientist with over 24 years of experience, is passionate about advancing cybersecurity and network security. Currently serving as an Assistant Professor at the School of ICT, Bahrain Polytechnic, Dr. Laghari is committed to nurturing the next generation of cybersecurity experts. Dr. Laghari earned his PhD. in Cybersecurity from Universiti Sains Malaysia (USM), where he delved into the intricacies of safeguarding digital systems. His academic journey was further enriched by a postdoctoral research position at the Cybersecurity Research Centre within USM, where he contributed to cutting-edge research in network security. Beyond academia, Dr.Laghari has honed his skills through collaborations with leading technology companies, gaining invaluable insights into the practical challenges and opportunities in the field. His industry experience has equipped him with a deep understanding of real-world cybersecurity threats and mitigation strategies. Dr. Laghari's research interests span a wide range of topics, including cybersecurity, the Internet of Things (IoT), Industry 4.0, distributed systems, cloud computing, and mobile cloud computing. His contributions to the field are evident in his numerous publications in top-tier international journals.

Selvakumar Manickam He is the Director of the Cybersecurity Research Centre and a Professor specializing in cybersecurity, the Internet of Things, industry 4.0, cloud computing, big data, and machine learning. He has authored and co-authored more than 220 articles in journals, conference proceedings, and book reviews. He has graduated 18 Ph.D. Students in addition to master's and bachelor's students. He has given several keynote speeches and dozens of invited lectures and workshops at conferences, international universities, and industry. He has given talks and training on Internet security, the Internet of Things, industry 4.0, IPv6, machine learning, software development, and embedded and OS kernel technologies at various organizations and seminars. He also lectures in various computer science and IT courses, including developing new courseware in tandem with current technology trends. He is involved in various organizations and forums locally and globally. Previously, he was with Intel Corporation and a few start-ups working in related areas before moving to academia. While building his profile academically, he is still very involved in industrial projects.

Hamza Naim is an Assistant Professor at K. R. Mangalam University, Gurugram, Haryana. He earned a PhD in Finance, MBA, and a Bachelor's degree in Engineering (Electrical) from Aligarh Muslim University. He is NET as well as MANF qualified. His research interests lie in corporate finance and corporate governance.

Mohammed Nizamuddin is an academician with more than 12 years of experience. He has expertise in financial modeling, financial derivatives and risk management. He has contributed his expertise and experience through his publications in national and international journals indexed in Scopus, Web of sciences and ABDC. He also contributed to the workshops as a resource person as well as keynote speaker in various conferences.

Ammar Odeh is an Associate Professor and the Director of the Training and Consultation Center at Princess Sumaya University for Technology. He has extensive experience in teaching, scientific research, and cybersecurity technology, specializing in systems development and student training programs. His work focuses on progressive systems, diverse software applications, and industry-aligned education. Dr. Odeh earned his PhD in Computer Science and Engineering from the University of Bridgeport in 2015, where he received the Phi Kappa Phi Award for academic excellence.

Lata Rani is an academician having 15 years of experience in teaching, research, administration, training and consultancy. She has also done a Course on Financial Accounting from Harvard Business School (Online). She is a permanent member of All India Commerce Association. She has been reviewer and technical member for Technical Program Committee for “2021 The 9th ICBMG-2021”, organized by The University of Western Australia.

Bhupinder Singh working as Professor at Sharda University, India. Also, Honorary Professor in University of South Wales UK and Santo Tomas University Tunja, Colombia. His areas of publications as Smart Healthcare, Medicines, fuzzy logics, artificial intelligence, robotics, machine learning, deep learning, federated learning, IoT, PV Glasses, metaverse and many more. He has 3 books, 139 paper publications, 163 paper presentations in international/national conferences and seminars, participated in more than 40 workshops/FDP's/QIP's, 25 courses from international universities of repute, organized more than 59 events with international and national academicians and industry people’s, editor-in-chief and co-editor in journals, developed new courses. He has given talks at international universities, resource person in international conferences such as in Nanyang Technological University Singapore, Tashkent State University of Law Uzbekistan; KIMEP University Kazakhstan, All’ah meh Tabatabi University Iran, the Iranian Association of International Criminal law, Iran and Hague Center for International Law and Investment, The Netherlands, Northumbria University Newcastle UK,

Muhammad Usman Tariq has more than 16+ year’s experience in industry and academia. He has authored more than 200+ research articles, 110+ case studies, 130+ book chapters and several books other than 4 patents. He is founder and CEO of The Case HQ, a unique repository for courses, narrative and video case studies. He has been working as a consultant and trainer for industries representing six sigma, quality, health and safety, environmental systems, project management, and information security standards. His work has encompassed sectors in aviation, manufacturing, food, hospitality, education, finance, research, software and transportation. He has diverse and significant experience working with accreditation agencies of ABET, ACBSP, AACSB, WASC, CAA, EFQM and NCEAC. Additionally, Dr. Tariq has operational experience in incubators, research labs, government research projects, private sector startups, program creation and management at various industrial and academic levels. He is Certified Higher Education Teacher from Harvard University, USA, Certified Online Educator from HMBSU, Certified Six Sigma Master Black Belt and has been awarded PFHEA, SFSEDA, SMIEEE, and CMBE.

Takrar Ahmad Yattoo who is currently working as an Assistant Professor at KR Mangalam University India is an academician with extensive experience working alongside Nobel Laureate Professor Muhammad Yunus on Sustainable Development Goals (SDGs), particularly focusing on Social Business. His primary research interests include Social Business, Entrepreneurship, and International Business.

Index

A

B

C

Q

R

S

U

V

www.ingramcontent.com/pod-product-compliance
Ingram Content Group UK Ltd.
Pitfield, Milton Keynes, MK11 3LW, UK
UKHW052003051026
15624UKWH00003B/530

9 798337 355450